D1381217

THE SCENERY AND ANTIQUITIES
of
IRELAND

This edition published 2003 by Mercury Books (London)
an imprint of The Caxton Publishing Group

ISBN: 1-904668-41-0

THE SCENERY AND ANTIQUITIES
of
IRELAND

J. Stirling Coyne

Drawings by W. H. Bartlett

MERCURY BOOKS
LONDON

THE SCENERY AND ANTIQUITIES OF IRELAND

I

THE prominent association with the name of Ireland, to one who does not draw his ideas of the country from the English newspapers, is that of a prolific mother of orators, warriors, patriots, and poets. Out of sight of the froth that is thrown up from the angry cauldron of political strife, and out of hearing of the bitter contentions of party spirit, the inhabitant of another country looks upon the small space occupied by Ireland on the map of the world, with feelings of mingled wonder and admiration. The veil that obscures her past glory is with drawn, the cloud that lowers over her social horizon melts away, and the distant observer opening the volume of her mournful history, counts the long roll of her illustrious names, and reads in those pages of shame and sorrow,—blotted by the best blood of her children,—the true character of an enthusiastic people. An undying love of liberty, and an untamed and restless genius, make them turbulent, excitable, and vindictive under real or imaginary wrongs; while the natural warmth and kindness of their disposition make us willing to forget the faults which under more favourable circumstances would never have had existence. In a work like this. however, of a pictorial character, and intended for circulation among all parties, the great question at issue in Ireland can only be thus far adverted to; and in recording my own observations while travelling in the country, I feel convinced that by avoiding the irritating topics of political and religious discussion, my readers will journey along with me more pleasantly through the wild and beautiful scenery of this Western Eden. Nor do I fear that we shall tire on the way for lack of objects worthy the attention of the antiquary and the poet, where every valley boasts the remains of some old abbey or monastery the fast-decaying relics of the faded grandeur of the ancient Irish church; and where the romantic legends of an imaginative peasantry have peopled every hill-side with the fantastic and graceful creations of Fairy-land. Let me then, in the language of Ireland's favourite bard, invite those who love nature in her wild and simple attire, to follow me in my pilgrimage through those lovely scenes; for

"Never did Ariel's plume,
At golden sunset, hover
O'er Bach scenes of bloom
As I will waft them over."

After enjoying the chivalric festivities at Eglintoun Castle, I turned my face westward, and, following the example of St. Patrick, embarked on the 1st of September, at the narrowest point of the Channel, for Ireland. Port Patrick was named, they say, after the saint who introduced Christianity into the island, and banished every venomous creature from its soil. The miraculous ejectment of the 'varmin' was accomplished, according to the old song, in a manner no less singular than it was expeditious :—

"Ten hundred thousand vipers blue,
He charmed with sweet discoorses,
And dined on them at Killaloe,
In soups and second coorses.

"The frogs went hop—the toads went flop,
Slap dash into the water,
And the snakes committed shooicide
To save themselves from slaughter."

Though I cannot coincide with the saint's taste in cookery, and would decidedly prefer an eel-pie at Battersea to his miraculous viper-broth at Killaloe, I confess that the absence of noxious reptiles is not one of the least blessings which this country possesses. Our passage was a very quick one, being little more than two hours from land to land, but in that short time I experienced all the horrors of seasickness; and it was with feelings of inexpressible delight that I found myself approaching the Irish shore, which I fancied spread forth her green arms to receive the stranger with the national "*Cead milk failthe,*" a hundred thousand welcomes.

We ran into the little harbour of Donaghadee, and was rather surprised to find it a very neat Scotch-looking town: the streets clean, the inn tidy, and not a beggar to welcome us to Ireland. The piers are of white granite, (the harbour was the design I believe of Sir John Rennie,) and with a couple of towers crowning an abrupt mound—the port has a picturesque and flourishing air. On the opposite side of the lough stands Carrickfergus, so celebrated in Irish history. Its castle is strongly situated on a rock, and commands the best harbour on the north-east coast of Ireland. It was built on the site of an ancient fort, by John de Courcey, who received from Henry II. a grant of all the land he might conquer in Ulster. In 1315, Lord Edward Bruce, with an army of six thousand men, landed from Scotland for the purpose of conquering Ireland, and forced the garrison of Carrickfergus to surrender, after an obstinate defence. But being shortly after defeated and slain near Dublin, this place fell again

Carrickfergus Castle

into the hands of the English, and continued for many years to be their stronghold. During the wars of 1641 the castle became an object of interest to the contending parties, being alternately in the possession of the Scotch, English, and Irish. The year 1760 is memorable as being the year in which the French, under Commodore Thourot, attacked this town the garrison, though few in number, made a gallant defence, but were at length forced to surrender to a superior force. After keeping possession of the place for some time, the enemy re-embarked on board their vessels, and putting to sea, were two days afterwards attacked by an English squadron, when Commodore Thourot was killed, and the French fleet captured and destroyed. The importance which Carrickfergus once enjoyed as a trading port has been transferred to Belfast; but it still possesses the honour of being the county-town where the assizes are held.

The distance from Donaghadee to Belfast is about twenty miles by the shortest route; but having heard that the coast-road was the most interesting in point of scenery, I determined to go by that way; and for which purpose I was obliged to hire a jaunting-car, a vehicle peculiar I believe to this country. The landlady, a stout, smiling personage, came out of doors, and with a good natured energy that amused me, arranged the *quo modo* of our conveyance, with a strange-looking, squinting fellow, whose age might be taken at any figure between twenty and forty. By the careless air he wore his battered hat on the side of his head, and the indicative accompaniment of a short whip, with which he continued to lash an unoffending paving-stone until the negotiation was concluded, I set him down rightly for the driver of the vehicle by which I was to be transported to Belfast.

As this was to be my novitiate in car-travelling, I took a critical survey of the singular machine as it was drawn up to the door, and I must confess that its appearance was the reverse of tempting. Those who have never had the pleasure of recreating on an Irish jaunting-car must fancy two low-backed garden-chairs, with cushioned seats placed *dos-à-dos;* with a space of about eighteen inches between them, forming a receptacle called a well, in which loose coats, cloaks, or a small trunk may be deposited. A board or step on which the traveller's feet rest is attached to either seat. The entire machine is fixed on springs and wheels, and a pair of shafts project from one end, between which is harnessed a lean, ill-groomed, ill-conditioned horse; and above his crupper, in a small seat, sits the horse's counterpart, a ragged, lounging, unpromising-looking driver. But horse and man are both deceptions; the one generally turns out to be a hardy, wiry creature, with a pace that would soon blow the *élite* of Newman's stables—and the other a shrewd intelligent fellow that by his drollery could create laughter for a long summer's day.

In a few minutes my portmanteau was thrust by Barney, along with a remnant of hay snatched from his horse's head, into the above-mentioned well. My new charioteer then giving a preliminary crack of his whip and a jerk of his loose greatcoat upon his shoulder, mounted his perch. Following his example, I took my seat on one side of the vehicle, and away we dashed with a wild whoop from Barney, and an encouraging cheer from half-a-dozen of his companions, accompanied by the barking of an equal number of curs of low degree, which gave us what Barney called a "chivvey" for some hundred yards on our journey. The scenery of the lough is not bold, it is rather soft and pleasing: its breadth may be about five miles, and the shores on both sides are thickly studded with the most interesting objects. Here a noble mansion, with its thick woods behind and spacious lawn in front, sloping to the water; there a cluster of neat cottages, frequented in the summer by bathers from Belfast and other adjoining towns. The cottages in Ireland being generally white, it is impossible not to admire their picturesque appearance, embosomed as they are amidst trees of delicious verdure. Indeed the singular freshness of the foliage and the sward always strikes the eye of a stranger, and fully justifies the epithet of "The Emerald Isle" being bestowed upon this favoured country. The day was delightfully serene; the quiet beauty of the scenery, and the quaint humour of my companion, who was highly pleased to have an opportunity of displaying his descriptive and anecdotal talents, made me not regret the mode of conveyance I had chosen. A specimen or two, which just now occur to me, of the readiness of the Irish peasantry in jest and repartee, may entertain my readers. A young fellow, driving an ass before him, was coming towards us, when Barney, who never let a chance for a joke escape him, gave me one of those glances of sly humour over his shoulder, which it would be impossible to describe, and hitching up his coat, thus accosted the ass-driver, with the utmost gravity.

"Good morrow, neighbour!—Is that ass your own?"

"No," replied the boy, "he's my father's."

"In troth—I knew he was one of the family, for he's the very picther of the ould man," retorted Barney, with a loud guffaw; at the same time applying the whip vigorously to his horse to escape the vengeance of the irritated lad, who was searching on the road for a "lump of a two-year old," i.e. a stone not larger than a bullock's kidney, with which he meant to return Bamey's witticism. His next essay was upon a good-looking country girl, who, with bare feet and well-gathered-up petticoats, was daintily picking her steps along a plashy part of the road." Mind your steps, *ma cailleen dhas,* or you'll dirty your birthday stockings," cried he.

"Never fear *abouchal.* But if I do, where's the harm? Sure they're warranted to wash, and hould the colour always," replied the girl, smartly.

"I wonder then how they'd look turned?" inquired Barney, with a grin.

"About as purty as your own eyes," answered she, glancing knowingly at the questioner.

The girl's allusion to the obliquity of Barney's optics disconcerted him a little; he

Belfast Lough

flourished his whip, began to whistle vehemently, and looked out for a fitter object to crack his next joke upon. In this manner we proceeded; Barney maintaining a running fire of raillery upon every person that came within hail; sometimes gaining an easy victory, but oftener provoking a biting retort upon the appearance of himself, his horse, and not unfrequently of his passenger. At the foot of a sharp hill, where a convenient roadside public-house offered "ENTERTAINMENT FOR MAN AND HORSE," Barney threw the reins over his steed's neck, and telling him to stand quiet while he was lighting his pipe, he darted into the whiskey-shop, from whence in less than a minute he returned with a black *dhudeen* stuck in the corner of his mouth, and a thick cloud of tobacco-smoke curling round his nose. This practice of smoking, which is so prevalent amongst the lower classes of Ireland, is, I find, of much greater antiquity than the introduction of tobacco into Europe. Bronze pipes are found in the most ancient *tumuli* or sepulchral mounds; and "a curious instance of the bathos in sculpture," says a writer on the subject, "but which also illustrates the antiquity of the custom, occurs on the monument of Donogh O'Brien, King of Thomond, who was killed in 1267, and interred in the Abbey of Corcumroe, in the county of Clare, of which his family were the founders. He is represented in the usual recumbent posture, with the short pipe or *dhudeen* of the Irish in his mouth." Certain herbs are still smoked by the peasantry in some of the remote districts where tobacco cannot be procured.

The finest view of the lough on this road is to be had between Bangor and Hollywood. The latter place is a pretty bathing village about four miles from Belfast. Leaving Hollywood behind us, I got the first view of the great emporium of Ulster, with its numerous tall chimneys and dingy factories, reminding me of a busy manu-facturing English town. The inland scenery on every side of the town corresponds in character with that of the shores of the bay. It is varied and picturesque, but never rises into the sublime or magnificent. The surface of the adjacent country is mountainous to the north and north-west, where Divis mountain, about two miles distant, rises to the height of one thousand five hundred and sixty-seven feet above the sea level. On the south and west the land runs into lofty hills, the most remarkable of which is the Cave Hill, that takes its name from some curious caves near its summit. It is topped with a large *rath,* or ancient earthen fortification, named M'Art's Fort, one side of which rests on the precipice that overlooks the bay, and the others still show traces of a rampart and broad ditch. This spot is a favourite place of recreation for the town's-people, particularly during the Easter holidays. A railway is carried from it for the purpose of conveying stone to the town.

Our entrance into Belfast, over a long, narrow, dilapidated bridge, was ill calculated to give me a favourable opinion of the place; but I determined not to allow myself to be prejudiced by first impressions; and I confess I was afterwards agreeably surprised to find in my rambles through the town, fine broad streets and handsome squares, stretching in all directions from the centre of the town. Having now fairly got upon the paving-stones, Barney determined to show off the superior capabilities of his steed to the gazers, and regardless of my repeated injunctions to him to go slowly, he drove at full gallop through the streets, which were thronged with people, it being fair-day in Belfast. At last, after endangering the lives of sundry of her Majesty's lieges, and very nearly amputating the legs of a young lady who sat on an outside car near the side-walk, Barney, exulting in his dexterity, suddenly pulled up at the door of "The Donegal Arms." It is situated in a handsome broad street; and in its internal arrangements, its comfort and cleanliness, need not shrink from a comparison with some of the best hotels in England. After an early dinner, the landlord, a courteous and gentlemanly person, presented me with a ticket signed by himself, as a subscriber, to visit the Botanical Gardens, and offered to procure me a "walking dictionary" to the objects of curiosity in the town. I accepted his admission, but declining the services of a guide, started off in the direction he pointed out, and strolled through a succession of clean and spacious streets to the other suburb of Belfast.

Before proceeding further, I shall take a rapid glance at the history of this town, which has sprung into such considerable importance within the last half century. No authentic record of its foundation has been preserved, and the first mention of it in history relates to its destruction by Edward Bruce, whom I have already alluded to in speaking of Carrickfergus. After being sacked and wasted it fell into the hands of the Irish, who for a long time continued to hold possession of Ulster, the attention of England being engrossed by the civil wars of York and Lancaster. In the reign of Henry VIII., the Earl of Kildare, then Lord Deputy of Ireland, took the castle of Belfast; but being unable to maintain his ground there against the O'Neills, he dismantled the fortress, and returned to Dublin. It is, however, a remarkable proof of the slight importance of Belfast in 1586, that in Holingshed's Chronicle, printed in that year, we find no mention made of it in the enumeration of the chief towns and havens of Down and Antrim. James I. granted it a corporation, and from this period may Belfast date its political and commercial advancement. The monopoly which Carrickfergus enjoyed of receiving one-third of the duties of all goods imported into Belfast, was purchased by the Crown, and the result was, that the trade of the former place was rapidly transferred to Belfast. The rebellion of 1641 greatly retarded the improvement of the town, which was successively occupied by the Royalist and Parliamentary forces, having sustained four sieges, and as many times changed masters in the lapse of not more than six years. The tranquillity which succeeded the Revolution and the establishment of William III. on the throne of these kingdoms, soon began to manifest its beneficial influence in the increasing prosperity of Belfast; but it was not until the commencement of the present century that it began to advance with rapid strides to the place it now holds amongst the commercial towns of the empire. The evidences of enterprise and capital are everywhere abundant. Inglis, in his excellent Tour through Ireland in 1834, says, "On all sides are seen, near and far, manufactories, or mills, as they are called, of immense extent, evidently newly erected, and vying, nay, I think, surpassing in size and in all other respects the mills and factories of our great manufacturing towns . . . . No mud-cabins, no poor cottages form a suburb or disfigure it; and neither in the streets nor in the suburbs is the eye arrested by objects of compassion."

No town that I have since visited is so un-Irish in its appearance, or in the character of its inhabitants. Industry, temperance, and frugality seem to be the guiding principle amongst every class. "Business is life here, and life is business: we find none of the deep-drinking and careless merriment of the south, which leave tomorrow to do for itself. A shrewd calculating spirit pervades the whole mass of the community, proving incontestably their genuine Scotch descent.

Yet, with all their money—getting habits, the people of Belfast are not so engrossed by business but that they can afford a large portion of their time and money to the advancement of literature and the fine arts. Their numerous scientific and literary institutions attest this sufficiently, arid so celebrated has this town become for its patronage and love of learning, that it has acquired—I will not venture to use the word assumed—the proud title of "the Modern Athens," and disputes the palm of literary fame with its southern rival, Cork; which boasts of having fostered a greater amount of native talent than any other town or city in Ireland: I shall not attempt to decide in favour of either. Amongst the most important of the societies intended for intellectual culture in Belfast, is the "Academical Institution," which comprehends a school and a collegiate department, affording education on a liberal and enlightened system. The Natural History Society, to which a museum is attached, the first ever erected in Ireland by voluntary subscription; the Literary Society, the Historic Society, a Mechanics' Institute, and a Botanical Garden, to which latter place I was directing my steps when I began this, I fear, tedious digression.

Just at the edge of the town I was compelled to charge through a phalanx of car-drivers, whose obliging distress at seeing me on foot was expressed with a variety of eloquence that was worthy of a better theme. I persisted in thinking that the dirt was good enough for "the likes of me," and walked them off their beat, after receiving a solemn assurance, that the Botanical Garden, which they knew I was in quest of, was three good Irish miles off, that is to say, four English miles, which I walked in the incredibly small space of five minutes. Not content with this enterprising investment of eloquence and imagination, one of the drivers gave me, what I took to be a purely ostentatious display of the paces of his horse, driving backwards, and in every description of gait that could be got up by cries, whipping, chirruping, coaxing, and other persuasives. The man never looked at me for applause between his flourishes, till within forty yards of our destination, when he suddenly drove up, and with a smile of the most winning sincerity, recommended us to take his car to the Botanical Garden. "Where is the Botanical Garden?" I asked of a little girl who was standing near: she pointed to the gate a few steps further on. "Then, sir," said the driver, by no means disconcerted at the failure of his impudent attempt, "perhaps your honor 'ud like me to wait for you going back?" My resentment at the imposition was entirely absorbed in admiration of the boldness, fertility of invention, readiness, and perseverance displayed by this character. What would not such qualities achieve, (and I believe they are natural to the whole nation,) well-regulated and directed into proper channels! With the same outlay of thought, ingenuity, and assurance as was expended in this fruitless endeavour to procure a sixpenny fare, what return would an American expect? Certainly enough to buy the car and horse, with a long lease of the driver.

The Botanical Gardens are laid out with great taste and beautifully kept. I enjoyed my stroll through the long alleys extremely; and in spite of a cautionary placard, and the keeper standing under time porch looking on, I plucked a *heart'sease* as an expressive remembrance of my visit.

Strolling back leisurely to the hotel, my ear was attracted by the merry sounds of a fiddle issuing from a small public-house in the suburbs. On inquiry I learned that some young people of both sexes were assembled there for the purpose of recreating themselves with a dance. This fondness for dancing and music is not the least remarkable trait in the national picture. Ireland has been happily called the land of song. Here the love of music is not an artificial or acquired taste; it is the genius of the people, that by an irresistible impulse prompts them to give vent to their feelings of mirth or sadness in the expressive language of the soul. Song seems to be a portion of an Irishman's nature: if he be merry he sings, as he says, "because he can't help it; "if sorrowful, "because it lightens the trouble at his heart." The peculiar character of the Irish music must strike even an indifferent observer, alternately joyous and pathetic, soothing and abrupt; mingling bursts of exhilarating liveliness, with strains and cadences of the most touching melancholy. The spirit of sorrow seems to hang upon the chords of Ireland's harp, and though it still gives forth "the light notes of gladness," we feel the painful truth of her poet's passionate address to it, when he exclaims—

> "So oft hast thou echoed the deep sigh of sadness,
> That ev'n in thy mirth it will steal from thee still."

This mingling of the wild and beautiful,—of gloom and sunshine,—of tears and smiles,—which marks the scenery, the climate and the history of Ireland, has impressed its character upon her music, and thrilling in her exquisite melodies, awakens emotions in the heart of the listener, which none but those who have experienced them can comprehend.

While I am upon the subject of Irish music, I may remark that an association called "The Irish Harp Society" was established by private subscription in Belfast, at the beginning of the present century, by some lovers of ancient Irish music, who with praiseworthy patriotism, endeavoured to revive the declining taste for the national instrument. The Marquis of Hastings and the Irish in the East Indies subscribed liberally for the purpose. Mr. Bunting, who in his valuable collection of "The Ancient Music of Ireland" has rescued some of the most beautiful airs of the country from oblivion, was also one of the founders of this interesting society, which I regret to say has lately been suffered to fall to the ground.

But the Irish harp and the Irish harper have passed away; the first is now only to be found in the cabinets of the curious, and the other in the memories of those who can look back distinctly forty years; when a poor travelling harper, bending beneath the load of his loved instrument, might be met wandering on foot from house to house,—one of the last mournful relics of the ancient bards,—of those honoured minstrels, whose place was at the board of princes, and whose songs perpetuated the valiant deeds of heroes, or the romantic lays of love and legendary lore. The personal appearance of an old harper, who once used to travel the western counties, is thus described by a living writer who had seen him in his youth : "Freney could not then have been less than ninety years old. He was about the middle height, but much bent by age; with a head of the Homeric cast, and venerably crowned with the whitest hair. His harp was a dark-framed, antique-looking instrument, closely strung with thin brass wires, which produced that wild music, that might be compared to the ringing of a fairy-chime. The effect of this was heightened by the old man's peculiar expression of intense, and sometimes placid attention to his own music as he stooped forward, holding his head close to the wires, while he swept them with a feeble, uncertain, and trembling hand, the too obvious effects of extreme age. His appearance thus bowed beside the instrument, which towered far above his head, was of the most picturesque character, and might well have served to illustrate Scott's description of his more poetic brother in 'The Lay.' "

Before quitting Belfast, I was shown the site of a very curious piece of antiquity,— the coronation-chair of the O'Neills of Castlereagh. It originally stood on the hill of that name, within two miles of Belfast; but after the downfall of the family, it was thrown down and neglected, until the year 1750, when it was removed to Belfast, and built into the wall of the market-house. On the taking down of the market-house a few years ago, it again changed its quarters, and is now in the possession of a gentleman named Walker, of Rathcarrick, in the county Sligo, where it is preserved with the care due to so interesting a relic. The chair, I have been told, is very rudely constructed, and made of common whin or grit-stone; the seat is lower than that of an ordinary chair, and the back higher and narrower. These inaugural chairs were sometimes merely large stones, in which the impression of two feet was sculptured, and were anciently placed in some elevated spot in every principality or lordship. The curious mode of electing the chiefs or *tanists* is mentioned in Spenser's "View of the State of Ireland." The history of this ancient seat, associated with it in my mind the coronation-stone in Westminster Abbey, called "the Stone of Fate," which it is said was brought by the Milesians into Ireland; and to which much superstitious veneration was paid, not only by the Irish but by the Scotch : the tradition being, that in whatever country this stone was preserved, a sovereign of the Scythian race should govern.

Departing from Belfast, I took the coach for Drogheda; it was well horsed, and driven at ten miles an hour. There was something very graceful, I thought, in the shape of the hills and the general outline of the country, though to my eye, the scantiness of wood was a great drawback to its beauty; scarcely a tree was to be seen except in the vicinity of gentlemen's seats : this remark, however, is not so applicable to the southern as the northern counties; in the former, the very great number and extent of the new plantations show an awakened attention on the subject, that promises soon to remedy the deficiency.

We entered Drogheda through a row of mud-cabins, which extend nearly a mile from the town. The interior of it contains several good streets and excellent houses; but in the more ancient parts, the buildings are all huddled together, so as to be under the protection of the walls, without much regard to regularity or convenience. In Drogheda, I could perceive a marked difference between the population of Ulster and the southern provinces: the air of comfort which distinguishes the appearance of the northern peasant, had been gradually diminishing since we left Newry behind; but I fancied that I could observe an increasing careless gaiety in the countenances of the people as we receded from the "black north." In the neighbourhood of this town I first visited a genuine Irish cabin. Overtaken in one of my rambles by a shower of rain,—none of your gentle poetic sprinklings, but a downright unmistakable Irish shower, that at once let you perceive it meant wetting you to the skin,—I was glad to seek the nearest shelter that offered, which happened to be a poor-looking hovel. Its inmates were a young woman, apparently under thirty years of age; yet she was the mother of six fine, rosy-cheeked, curly-headed, potato-fed children, five of whom were shouting and scrambling about the earthen floor, unencumbered by much needless apparel. An inhospitable puff of smoke and a shaggy wire-haired cur, rushing from the "dim profound," assailed me on the threshold, and seemed determined to oppose the invasion of the stranger. I, however, forced my way through these obstacles. The woman rose to receive me on my entrance, and though her clothing was mean and scanty, there was a gentleness and modesty in her deportment that gave an indescribable interest to her appearance. A turf fire was smouldering on the hearth, and a few stones placed in front prevented it encroaching too far upon the floor. Suspended from an iron crane, a pot of potatoes hung over the fire, boiling for her husband's dinner, who was abroad engaged in some field-work. A deal table, a couple of chairs, and a dresser, on which a few plates and simple culinary

20

utensils were displayed, comprised the entire of the furniture of the apartment, with the exception of a wicker cradle, in which a chubby little fellow lay sleeping soundly, covered by his mother's cloak. In an inner apartment, I got a glimpse of a strawbed, with a rug coverlet; and beside it stood a large deal chest, which I fear was kept rather for ornament than use. Everything around me betokened penury and privation; yet the whole family, including the pig, who had sagaciously returned from a country ramble during my visit, seemed perfectly contented and happy; and if these poor people possess few of the comforts of life, they at least enjoy those that have fallen to their share with a keen relish and grateful hearts. Nor has the Irish cabin, uninviting as it may appear, been uncelebrated in song. One of the most beautiful women J met in the country sang for me, with an expression of humour perfectly delightful, the following amusing caricature description, which I have taken down *verbatim;* and though it is of modern date, and rather Scoto-Irish in its dialect, it is still clever enough to merit being preserved.

Oh weep for the day we were forced from our cot,
From our praties and milk and our stirabout pot
When Judy kept everything piping and hot,
So snug with the cat in the corner.
The pigs and the dogs and childre, *agrah!*
Lay down on the floor, so dacent in straw,
While the cocks and the hens they were perch'd up ava,
Just over the cat in the corner.

Our house was so tidily covered with thatch,
It looked like a harlequin's coat, patch for patch;
And the door opened nately by rising the latch
With a fong that hung down in the corner.

A scythe was stuck here, and a raping-hook there;
And Paddy's shilelagh, the pride of the fair,
Was placed in the chimney to sayson with care,
Just over the cat in the corner.

Our window so clane, by an unlucky stroke,
Had three of the purtiest panes in it broke :
We fastened up two with the tail of a cloak,
And the smoke went through one in the corner.

Our dresser was decked out in elegant style,
The trenchers and noggins your heart would beguile;
And the goose she was hatching her eggs all the while,
Right under them all in the corner.

Och! Paddy's the boy, with a stick in his fist,
With a spur in his head, and a bone in his wrist,
And a straw round his hat—you must call it gold twist,
Or he'll murdher you all in the corner.

21

Drogheda fills an important page in history, and there is probably no town in Ireland more worthy the notice of the antiquary or historian. It was at or near this place that Milesius and his followers are said to have first landed in Ireland, after a hard struggle, in which his son was killed. In 911 it was fortified by Turgesius, the Dane, who made it his stronghold. At Duleek, in this vicinity, the first stone church in Ireland was erected; and it was there, in 1395, that the sovereignty of Ireland was surrendered to Richard II. by four Irish princes doing homage and fealty in the church of St. Magdalene. Here many of the English viceroys kept their courts and held their parliaments. In 1641, the progress of the northern Irish, under Owen Roe O'Neill, was stopped by the bravery of the garrison of Drogheda; and in 1649, Cromwell committed a most inhuman barbarity, by the slaughter of the inhabitants for their loyalty to the cause of the unfortunate Charles I. Last, and not least, Drogheda resisted the attack of a division of King William's army; and within two miles of its walls was fought the famous battle which decided the possession of the British crown. The scene of the contest between the two monarchs, James and William, at the Boyne Water, is too interesting for the traveller to pass without refreshing his memory with the story. William landed at Carrickfergus, attended by Prince George of Denmark, the young Duke of Ormond, the Earls of Oxford, Scarborough, and Manchester, and other persons of distinction; was met by Duke Schomberg, the Prince of Wirtemberg, Kirk, and other officers; received an address from the northern clergy, presented by Walker, and published his proclamation for the suppression of rapine, violence, and injustice. His military genius prompted him, and the present distracted state of England, together with the formidable preparations of France obliged him to a vigorous prosecution of the war. From Belfast he advanced to Lisburne and Hillsborough. Here he commenced the exercise of his civil authority, by an act highly acceptable to the inhabitants of the northern province. The teachers of dissenting congregations, which abounded in this province, had acted with zeal against the cause of popery and the late king. One of this order had the merit of first encouraging the populace to shut the gates of Derry. Several had patiently endured the hardships of the siege; and in every part of Ulster these ministers had shared deeply in the distresses of war. William now issued his warrant, granting them an annual pension of twelve hundred pounds, to be paid by the collector of customs in the port of Belfast; a pension afterwards inserted in the civil list, and made payable from the exchequer. His forces were ordered to take the field; and when some cautious counsels were suggested by his officers, he rejected them with indignation. "I came not to Ireland," said he, "to let grass grow under my feet." At Loughbrickland, his whole army assembled from their different quarters, and were joined by the king and his train. William ordered them to change their encampment, that he might review the regiments on their march to the new ground. The officers imagined, that on a tempestuous and dusty day, he would content himself with a general view from some convenient station; but they saw him dart quickly into the throng, riding eagerly from place to place, examining every regiment distinctly and critically. His soldiers were thus pleased and animated; every man considering himself as under the immediate inspection of his royal leader, who took his quarters in the camp, was the whole day on horseback, at the head of an advanced party, viewing the adjacent country; reconnoitering, or directing the accommodations necessary for his soldiers. When an order was presented to him to be signed for wine for his own table, he passionately exclaimed, that his men should be first provided. "Let them not want," said he, "I shall drink water." An army of thirty-six thousand men, thus animated, and excellently appointed, advanced southward, to decide the fate of Ireland; while the fleet coasted slowly in view, to supply them with every necessary, and thus to increase their confidence.

Six days had elapsed from the time of William's landing, when James received the first intelligence that a prince, who, he confidently believed must be detained in England by faction and discontent, was already on his march to meet him. He committed the guard of Dublin to a militia, under the command of Lutterel, the governor, and marched with six thousand French infantry to join the main body of his army, which, at the approach of the enemy, had retired from Dundalk and Ardee, and now lay near Drogheda, on the banks of the river Boyne. His numbers were about thirty-three thousand. His council of officers reminded him, that the naval armament of France was completed, and the fleet, perhaps, already on the English coast; that Louis had promised, as soon as the squadron attending on William should return, he would send a fleet of frigates into the Irish seas to destroy his transports, that he would be thus fatally detained in Ireland, while Britain was threatened by foreign invasion, and the domestic enemies of the reigning prince concerting an insurrection. In such circumstances, they advised him to wait the event of those designs formed in his favour, not to hazard an engagement against superior numbers; to strengthen his garrisons, to march to the Shannon with his . cavalry and a small body of foot, and thus to maintain a defensive war against an enemy, which, in a strange and unfriendly climate, without provisions or succours, must gradually perish by disease and famine. James, on the contrary, contended that to abandon the capital were to confess himself subdued; that his reputation must be irreparably ruined : that the Irish, who judged by appearances, would desert; and what was still of more moment, his friends in England and Scotland must be dispirited, and deterred from their attempts to restore him. He expressed satisfaction, that he had at last the opportunity of one fair battle for the crown. He insisted on maintaining his present post; and from such animated language, his officers concluded that he meant to take a desperate part in the engagement; yet, with an ominous precaution, he dispatched Sir Patrick Prout, one of his commissioners of revenue, to Waterford, to prepare a ship for conveying him to France in case of any misfortune.

William was no stranger to the motions of the French, and the machinations of his enemies. Whatever was the proper conduct for James, it was evidently his interest to bring their contest to an immediate decision. On the last day of June, at the first dawn of morning, his army moved towards the river in three columns. He marched at the head of his advanced guard, which by nine o'clock appeared within two miles of Drogheda. William, observing a hill west of the town, rode to the summit with his principal officers, to take a view of the enemy. On their right was Drogheda, filled with Irish soldiers. Eastward of the town, on the farther banks of the river, their camp extended in two lines, with a morass on the left, difficult to be passed. In their front were the fords of the Boyne, deep and dangerous, with rugged banks, defended by some breast-works, with huts and hedges, convenient to be lined with infantry. On their rear, at some distance, lay the church and village of Donore; three miles further was the pass of Duleek, on which they depended for a retreat. The view of their encampment was intercepted by some hills to the south-west; so that Sgravenmore, one of William's generals, who counted but forty-six regiments, spoke with contempt of the enemy's numbers. The king observed, that more might be concealed behind these hills, and many be stationed in the town; "But it is my purpose," said he, "to be speedily acquainted with their whole strength."

His army was now marching into camp; when William, anxious to gain a nearer and more distinct view of the enemy, advanced, with some officers, within musket-shot of a ford opposite to a village, called Old-bridge : here he conferred for some time on the methods of passing, and planting his batteries; when riding on still westward, he alighted and sat down to refresh himself on a rising ground. Neither the motions of William nor of his army were unnoticed. Berwick, Tyrconnel, Sarsefield, and some other generals, rode slowly on the opposite banks, viewing the army in their march, and soon discovered the present situation of the king. A party of about forty horse immediately appeared in a ploughed field opposite to the place on which he sat. In their centre they carefully concealed two field-pieces, which they planted unnoticed under cover of a hedge, and retired. William mounted his horse; at that moment the first discharge killed a man and two horses on a line, (at some distance,) with the king; another ball instantly succeeded, grazed on the banks of the river, rose, and slanted on his right shoulder, tearing his coat and flesh. His attendants crowded round him, and appeared in confusion. An universal shout of joy rung through the Irish camp at the news that Orange was no more. It was conveyed rapidly to Dublin; it was wafted to Paris : Louis received it with ecstacy; and the guns of the Bastile proclaimed the meanness of his triumph.

While some squadrons of the enemy's horse drew down to the river, as if to pursue a flying enemy, William rode through his camp to prevent all alarms or false reports of his danger. On the arrival of his artillery, the batteries were mounted, and the cannonading continued on each side, not without some execution, till the close of evening. Some deserters were received, and gave various accounts of the strength and disposition of the enemy. One, who appeared of some note, spoke so plausibly, and, at the same time, so magnificently of their numbers, that William seemed disconcerted. To Sir Robert Southwell, his secretary of state, who had given him different intelligence, he expressed his suspicion that the enemy was really stronger than he imagined. Southwell communicated the king's doubts to Cox, his under-secretary, through whose channel the intelligence had been conveyed. Cox, with an acuteness which seems to have laid the foundation of his future fortune, led the deserter through the English camp; and when he had surveyed it, asked to what he computed the amount of William's forces. The man confidently rated them at more than double their number. The king was thus satisfied that his reports arose from ignorance and presumption. Other deserters made reports more unfavourable to the enemy; and the king was assured, that James, in expectation of a defeat, had already conveyed part of his baggage to Dublin.

About nine at night William called a council of war, not to deliberate, but to receive his orders; and here he declared his resolution of passing the river in front of the enemy. Duke Schomberg, with the caution natural to his years, endeavoured to dissuade him from this hazardous enterprise; and when he could not prevail, insisted that part of the army should be immediately detached to secure the bridge of Slane, about three miles westward of their camp, so as to flank the enemy, and to cut them off from Duleek, the pass through which they might retreat. It is generally imputed to the indifference with which his counsel was received, that this general retired in disgust, and received the order of battle in his tent, declaring that "it was the first ever sent to him." Nor did James discover more attention to this important pass of Slane. In his council of war, Hamilton recommended that eight regiments might be sent immediately to secure the bridge. James proposed to employ fifty dragoons in this service; the general, in astonishment, bowed, and was silent.

William directed that the river should be passed in three different places; by his right wing, commanded by Count Schomberg, son of the duke; and General Douglas on the west, at some fords discovered near the bridge of Slane; by the centre, commanded by Duke Schomberg, in front of the Irish camp; and by the left wing, led by the king himself, at a ford between the army and the town of Drogheda. At midnight William once more rode through his camp with torches, inspecting every post, and issuing his final orders.

Early on the succeeding morning, Count Schomberg with the cavalry, and Douglas with the infantry, which composed the right wing, marched towards Slane with greater alacrity than the troops sent from the other side to oppose them. They crossed the river without any opposition, except from a regiment of dragoons stationed over night at the ford, of which they killed seventy, before their retreat could be secured. They advanced and found their antagonists drawn up in two lines.

They formed, ranging their horse and foot, squadron with battalion, till on the arrival of more infantry they changed their position, drawing the horse to the right, by which they considerably out-flanked the enemy. But they were to force their way through fields, enclosed by deep ditches, difficult to be surmounted, especially by the horse; who, in the face of an enemy, were obliged to advance in order; beyond these lay the morass, still more embarrassing. The infantry were ordered to plunge in, and while the horse found a firm passage to the right, forced their way with fatigue and difficulty. The enemy, astonished at their intrepidity, fled instantly towards Duleek, and were pursued with slaughter.

By the time when it was supposed that the right wing had made good their passage, the infantry in the centre was set in motion. The Dutch guards first entered the river on the right, opposite to Old-bridge. The French Protestants and Enniskilleners, Brandenburghers, and English, at their several passes to the left, plunged in with alacrity, checking the current, and swelling the water, so that it rose in some places to their middle, in others to their breasts, and obliged the infantry to support their arms above their heads. The Dutch had marched unmolested to the middle of the river, when a violent discharge was made from the houses, breast-works, and hedges, but without execution; they moved on, gained the opposite banks, formed gradually, and drove the Irish from their posts. As they still advanced, the squadrons and battalions of the enemy suddenly appeared in view behind the eminences which had concealed them. Five of these battalions bore down upon those Dutch who had already passed, but were received firmly, and repulsed. The efforts of the Irish horse were equally unsuccessful. Two attacks were bravely repelled, when the French and Enniskilleners arrived to the support of the Dutch, and drove back a third body of horse, with considerable execution.

In the meantime General Hamilton led the Irish infantry to the very margin of the river, to oppose the passage of the French and English. But his men, although stationed in the post of honour at the requisition of their officers, shrunk from the danger. Their cavalry proved more spirited. A squadron of Danes was attacked with such fury and success, that they fled back through the river. The Irish horse pursued, and, on their return, fell furiously on the French Huguenots, who had no pikes to sustain their shock, and were instantly broken. Caillemote, their brave commander, received his mortal wound, and when borne to the English camp, with his last breath animated his countrymen who were passing the river. As lie lay bleeding in the arms of four soldiers, he collected strength to exclaim repeatedly, in his own language, "A la gloire, mes enfans! à la gloire!" "To glory, ray boys! to glory!" The rapidity of the Irish horse, the flight of the Danes, and the disorder of the French, spread a general alarm; and the want of cavalry struck the minds even of the peasants, who were but spectators of the battle, so forcibly, that a general cry of "Horse! horse!" suddenly raised, was mistaken for an order to Halt,

26

surprised and confounded the centre, was conveyed to the right wing, and, for a while, retarded their pursuit.

In this moment of disorder, Duke Schomberg, who had waited to support his friends on any dangerous emergency, rushed through the river, and placing himself at the head of the Huguenot forces,who were now deprived of their leader, pointed to some French regiments in their front, and cried, "Allons, messieurs; voila vos persecuteurs." "Come on, gentlemen, these are your persecutors." These were his last words. The Irish horse, who had broken the French Protestants, wheeled through Old-bridge, in order to join their main body, but were here cut down by the Dutch and Enniskilleners. About sixteen of their squadron escaped, and returning furiously from the slaughter of their companions, were mistaken by the Huguenots for some of their own friends, and suffered to pass. They wounded Schomberg in the head, and were hurrying him forward, when his own men fired and slew him. About the same time, Walker, of Londonderry, whose passion for military glory had hurried him unnecessarily into this engagement, received a wound in his belly, and instantly expired.

After an uninterrupted firing of an hour, the disorder on both sides occasioned some respite. The centre of the English army began to recover from their confusion. The Irish retreated towards Donore, where James stood during the engagement, surrounded by his guards; and here, drawing up in good order, once more advanced. William had now crossed the river at the head of Dutch, Danish, and English cavalry, through a dangerous and difficult pass, where his horse floundering in the mud, obliged him to dismount, and accept the assistance of his attendants. And now, when the enemy had advanced almost within musket-shot of his infantry, he was seen with his sword drawn, animating his squadrons, and preparing to fall on their flank. They halted, and again retreated to Donore. But here, facing about vigorously, they charged with such success, that the English cavalry, though led on by their king were forced from their ground. William, with a collection of thought which accompanies true courage, rode up to the Enniskilleners, and asked, "What they would do for him?" Their officer informed them who he was : they advanced with him, and received the enemy's fire. But, as he wheeled to the left, they followed by mistake; yet, while William led up some Dutch troops, they perceived their error, and returned bravely to the charge. The battle was now maintained on each side with equal ardour, and with variety of fortune. The king who mingled in the hottest part of the engagement, was constantly exposed to danger. One of his own troopers mistaking him for an enemy, presented a pistol to his head; William calmly put it by. "What!" said he, "do you not know your friends?" The presence of such a prince gave double vigour to his soldiers. The Irish infantry were finally repulsed. Hamilton made one desperate effort to turn the fortune of the day, at the head of his horse. Their shock was furious, but neither orderly nor steady. They were routed, and their general conveyed a prisoner to William. The king asked him, whether the Irish would fight more, "Upon my honour," said Hamilton, "I believe they will; for they have yet a good body of horse." William surveyed the man who had betrayed him in his transactions with Tyrconnel, and in a sullen and contemptuous tone exclaimed, "Honour! YOUR honour!"

Nor was this asseveration of Hamilton well-grounded. The right wing of William's army had by this time forced their way through difficult grounds, and pursued the enemy close to Dunleek. Langan rode up to James, who still continued at Donore, advising him to retreat immediately, as he was in danger of being surrounded. He marched to Dunleek at the head of Sarsefield's regiment; his army followed, and poured through the pass, not without some annoyance from a party of English dragoons, which they might easily have cut to pieces, had they not been solely intent on flying. When they reached the open ground, they drew up and cannonaded their pursuers. Their officers ordered all things for a retreat, which they made in such order, as was commended by their enemies. Their loss in this engagement was computed at fifteen hundred; that of William's army scarcely amounted to one-third of this number.

Here was the final period of James's Irish loyalty. He arrived at Dublin in great disorder, and damped the joy of his friends, who, at the intelligence of William's death, every moment expected to receive him in triumph. He assembled the popish magistrates and council of the city; he told them that in England his army had deserted him; in Ireland they had fled in the hour of danger, nor could be persuaded to rally, though their loss was inconsiderable; both he and they must therefore shift for themselves. It had been deliberated, whether, in case of such a misfortune, Dublin should not be set on fire; but on their allegiance he charged them to commit no such barbarous outrage, which must reflect dishonour on him, and irritate the conqueror. He was obliged, he said, to yield to force, but would never cease to labour for their deliverance; too much blood had been already shed; and Providence seemed to declare against him; he therefore advised them to set their prisoners at liberty, and submit to the Prince of Orange, who was merciful. The reflection on the courage of his Irish troops was ungracious, and provoked their officers to retort it on the king. They contended, that in the whole of the engagement their men, though not animated by a princely leader, had taken no inglorious part. They observed, that while William shared the danger of his army, encouraging them by his presence, by his voice, by his example, James stood at a secure distance, a quiet spectator of the contest for his crown and dignity. "Exchange kings," said they, "and we will once more fight the battle." Their indignation was increased, when they saw the prince, who inveighed against Irish cowardice, fly precipitately to Waterford, breaking down the bridges to prevent a pursuit, and instantly embark for France. They, who did not impute this conduct to a defect of spirit, at least, complained, that his Irish adherents were shamefully sacrificed to his interests and designs in England. Nor did the officers of William express entire satisfaction at his conduct. They complained, that the enemy were not pursued with sufficient vigour, without weighing the disadvantage sustained by the loss of Duke Schomberg, or the danger of pursuit through a difficult pass, and an unknown country. They contended, that at the very moment of victory, ten thousand men should have been detached to Athlone and Limerick, to seize these important places, and prevent the Irish from re-assembling. But they were strangers to those anxieties which oppressed the king's mind. He every moment looked for an invasion in England, and expecting to be recalled, deemed it imprudent to divide his army, or to remove to any distance from the coast. Drogheda was summoned; the Irish governor hesitated; but being assured, that if the cannon were brought up no quarter was to be expected, he surrendered on condition that the garrison should be conveyed, unarmed, to Athlone; and William now advanced slowly towards the capital.

II.

WHILE the reader has been refreshing his memory with this warm page of history, we have been refreshing ourselves with a warm dinner at Drogheda—a better dinner, it may as well be recorded, than one usually gets at English inns, and twice the time to eat it. I smiled while at table, at another instance of the national talent for persuasion, and reminded my companions that no service had been rendered us since our landing in the country, unaccompanied with a bit of advice, or an attempt in some way to change our mode of arriving at the object in question. The waiter at Belfast had interfered with my selection of a mutton-chop from the dish, and had run after us from the hotel to change the direction of our walk ; and I have already given, (a little out of place, for they occurred after dinner,) instances of the suggestive and persuasive talent of Irish beggars. "No, sir," said the waiter at Drogheda, when I asked for a bit of a very promising beefsteak, "take the fish, sir, and *be* that time there'll be a hot one!" I followed his advice, and after doing excellent trencher-service on the second steak, asked for a glass of brandy-and-water. "The whiskey's bett*h*er, sir," was the reply, and it was poured out before I had time to give an opinion upon it. So whiskey was my fate, though taste and rheumatism (the latter by advice) were both of contrary mind. You might pass a life in English inns without finding a waiter with an opinion, and two lives without getting advice, or, indeed, anything else not charged in the bill.

We left the rain behind us at Drogheda, and got a fair view of the country, till the night closed in about us, a few miles from Dublin. The cultivation improved, and the seats of the gentry occurred oftener as we approached the capital, though still there was the same dearth of human beings which I had remarked all the way—scarce a soul to be seen out of the streets of the towns for the entire distance. I think two groups of men and women, digging and weighing potatoes in the field, (in both cases, the men weighing and the women digging,) were all the people I observed off the road in a hundred miles' travel. I remarked the same indolence of attitude everywhere that had struck me in Belfast—the hands uniformly thrust into the pockets or breast, and the shoulder against the wall or the post; the pocket, if by chance the hand were out, gaping with a most expressive fixedness, and the hand dropping into it, when the action was achieved, with the ease of a foot into a slipper. If this national love of ease does not extend to Irish horses it is not for want of temptation. I saw several standing up to their bellies in the bogs, grazing, in great apparent comfort, from the sward just at their breasts, without drawing up a leg oftener than once in fifteen minutes. Grazing in a bog must be very delicate work, however, and from several leaps over mud-fences and stonewalls, which I observed during the day, by very indifferent looking steeds, I should think the Irish horse an animal of rather uncommon judgment and tractableness.

Who ever entered a great city without paying tribute in his heart to the truth of that part of natural history, which asserts, that "man is a gregarious animal?" * What delight, after long travel through the lonely fields and over the bleak hills of the country, to be driven suddenly into the streets of a crowded metropolis, to see the gay shops, the whirling past of splendid equipages, the press of vehicles, the thronging of gay and busy multitudes, and to hear once more, with unaccustomed ears, the stir and murmur of these seas of human life! What heart's blood does not quicken with sympathy at the spectacle? What heart's grief is not unseated or charmed to sleep by the grand monotone of human stir and utterance? The entrance to any great city, *for the first time,* more especially, is to me a thing looked forward to and looked back upon as an era. I am free to confess that I have numbered the Capitals of the world, and those I have not seen are as unopened chambers in my soul—cardinal sensations unfelt—great pleasures still possible while life exists, and so to be hoped and struggled for. Oh! to see Rome again with new eyes Athens Constantinople! There is a flood in the feeling with which such events come to pass, which carries the soul off its feet. We forget everything, in the magnitude of the

* I remember to have met but one person who excepted himself from this attribute of the human family. Dining one day with Mr. Charles Kemble, the eccentric author of "The Adventures of a Younger Son," chanced to be of the party. He had just returned from America, and a gentleman at the table broke the silence of the soup, by enquiring of him, in what packet he had sailed. "*I'm not gregarious, sir,*" was the singular reply: "I took the cabin of a merchantman to myself."

novelty even, (as the story has it,) the skeleton under our cloaks. But I am getting into an essay.

At another time, I made a visit, of more leisure, to Dublin, and I shall defer all description of it till I come to that portion of my journal. Retracing, subsequently, my route from Belfast to Dublin, I followed the artist of this work to MALAHIDE; whose village and castle are much visited, from their vicinity to the capital. Malahide stands in a very secluded spot, upon a creek of the Irish sea, scarce twelve miles from Dublin, and promised at one time, from the commodiousness of its bay, to become the principal sea-port of Ireland. The inlet, on whose margin it is placed, possesses sufficient depth to admit vessels of considerable tonnage, and the islands of Lambay and Ireland's Eye, check the violence of the storm, and break the fury of a raging sea, thereby affording a safe asylum in waters at all periods but little agitated. "These advantages," says Wright, "were fully appreciated by our ancestors, and the preference given to the little cove of Malahide excited the keen envy of the corporation of Dublin, who caused a fine to be imposed upon Sir Peter Talbot, of Malahide Castle, for suffering vessels to break hulk at this port, contrary to the king's grants made to the city of Dublin. No commercial advantage is now derived from the security of the harbour, nor any benefit from its marine position, except that it has encouraged the settlement of a little colony of hardy sailors, engaged in the perilous life of deep-sea fishing: and others who follow the more secure, but less profitable employment, of oyster-dredging. For all their produce they find a convenient market, and an expeditious sale in Dublin.

The lordship of Malahide was granted by Henry II. to an ancestor of the present proprietor, the eldest representative of Sir Geoffrey Talbot, who held Hereford Castle against King Stephen for the Empress Maud. He was contemporary with Sir Armoricus, of Howth, and other bold adventurers, who sought acquisitions by the sword, at a time when disorganisation amongst the inhabitants appears to have left their country an easy prey. Of all the successful chieftains, whose grants were confirmed, and enjoyed by their descendants, the Talbots and St. Lawrences alone continue in possession. Attainder dispossessed some, improvidence impoverished others. The piety of the first Talbot, who settled here, induced him to grant away a portion of his estate, called Mallagh-hide-beg, to the Abbey of St. Mary's, in Dublin. It may be mentioned, in continuation of the family history, that Thomas Talbot was summoned to parliament in 1372, by the style and title of Lord Talbot de Mallagh-hide, and that in the year 1475, by a grant of Edward IV., in addition to the different manorial rights, and privileges of holding courts leet and baron within his lordship, the Lord of Malahide was created high admiral of the seas, with power to hear and determine upon all offences committed upon the high-seas or elsewhere, by the tenants, vassals, or residents of the manor of Malahide.

In the dark records of 1641, Thomas Talbot is written down an outlaw, for having

31

Interior of a Room at Malahide Castle

been a participator in the Irish rebellion: and, in 1653, a lease was granted of the hall of his forefathers, together with five hundred acres of land, for a period of seven years, to Myles Corbet, the regicide, who sustained the weight of his guilt within its walls for several years. The exterior of the castle is venerable, and the principal front displays much grandeur. The date of its foundation is probably coeval with that of the acquisition of the manor: but uniformity is preserved in the front alone, which this brief description professes to illustrate. There a centre of strong masonry, and jealousy pierced with windows, is flanked by two lofty, handsome round towers, finished with a graduated parapet. The entrance is through a low pointed doorway, in the northern front, giving access, by a spiral staircase, to the oak-parlour. This ancient apartment is the most interesting in this spacious and comfortable residence: it is wainscotted with dark oak, highly polished, and divided into small compartments, ornamented with rich carvings of figures, in small life, chiefly scriptural subjects.

During the desecration of this venerable apartment, by the presence of a regicide we are told the little effigy of the Blessed Virgin, which occupied the panel immediately above the chimney-piece, miraculously disappeared, and in a manner equally unaccountable, returned to its position upon Corbet's flight from Malahide. A window, whose light is derived through the medium of the stained glass that adorns it, augments the gloomy effects produced by the solemn character of the architectural decorations, and reminds the spectator of the proud spirits of these halls, that have passed away from their earthly grandeur. Other ages find here their illustration in coats-of-mail, vizors, gauntlets, and greaves of ponderous cast, exhibited to the curious. The other state-apartments are spacious, yet comfortable, but have lost much of their interest, by being deprived of all their original furniture and decorations.

The paintings, which adorn the different apartments, are of the highest merit: and the manner of their acquisition confers upon them a deep degree of interest. The portraits of Charles I. and his queen, are by Vandyke: of James II. and his queen, by Sir P. Lely: a fascinating portrait of the Duchess of Portsmouth, together with one of her son, the first Duke of Richmond, were the gifts of that celebrated lady to Mrs. Wogan , from whom they have passed, as heirlooms, to the present owner. There is also a half-length of King James's faithful adherent, Talbot, Duke of Tyrconnel, and portraits of his daughters: all by Sir P. Lely. But the *chef-d'œvre* of this collection is an exquisite painting by Albert Durer, intended for an altar-piece, and representing the Nativity, Adoration, and Circumcision, divided, as was his manner, into compartments. Many other works of conspicuous merit are here omitted, not from inclination, but necessity.

Adjoining the castle, and embowered in a thick grove of chestnuts, that, in their leafy honours, cast a melancholy gloom upon the picture, are the roofless ruins of a

33

by the Trades Union, and received ten pounds for killing him, is equal in atrocity to almost any Irish murder."

I would fain hope, (though one or two highly educated and intelligent Irishmen have assured me that Mr. Lewis's view is an incorrect one,) that in this statement lies some apology for Irish murders.

Ross-trevor is the united surnames of two respectable families, whose properties were here united by a marriage of their representatives. On the beach stands a slender and graceful obelisk, erected to the memory of one of the former name, who fell at the attack on Baltimore, the brave GENERAL ROSS.

On the road from Newry to Ross-trevor stands the pretty CASTLE OF NARROW-WATER, situated most picturesquely among the graceful mountains of Ulster, on the river Newry. The broad surface of the river is here contracted by a protruding rock, on whose surface stands the castle, in a position that enables it to command, in the most entire manner, the only pass to the town of Newry. The date of its foundation is not precisely known, but it was subsequent to the Restoration, and its erection is ascribed to the Duke of Ormonde. When its defensive properties were no longer necessary, it was abandoned to a commercial speculator, who established salt-works within it, and upon their removal, it was occupied for some time as a dog kennel. This interior desecration has not detracted from the permanent beauty that accompanies its position, nor impaired the majesty of its exterior form. The contraction of the channel rendered this an advantageous place for the establishment of a castle, for the defence of a pass or exaction of toll: and it is supposed, that the founder constructed a causeway of large stones, with an opening for vessels in the centre, directly across the river here. The rocks used in its construction continued to interrupt the navigation for many years hack, and engineers were consulted upon the practicability and expense of their removal: but, considering it to be a natural formation, they represented the task as difficult, and returned an estimate in proportion. Accident discovered the true character of the rocky bar, which, in the year 1831, was removed at a trifling expense, and the navigation opened from the sea to Newry.

Narrow Water Castle

III.

I LEFT Belfast for Larne, in company with my kinsman, Dr. Wall, of Dublin, on a rainy morning at daylight. Cowering under an umbrella, on an outside car, we felt that the promise for the day's enjoyment was a poor one ; but we .had scarce reached the base of Cave Hill, before the clouds broke away, and the chequered light thrown over the landscape through the flying clouds, was more favourable even than clear sunshine to the scenery. The view of BELFAST LOUGH from CAVE HILL is exceedingly fine, commanding, besides the whole of the Lough, the greater part of the Down county, and in clear weather, the coast of Scotland. The fine sheet of water lying below the eye, (the Vinderius of Ptolemy,) is called, indiscriminately, the Bay of Carrickfergus and Belfast Lough. It is (says Curry's Guide to the County of Antrim, to which I am indebted for much information) measuring about twelve miles long and five broad, from Groomsport, in Down, to Whitehead, on the Antrim side. The breadth gradually diminishes from the entrance to the embouchure of the river Logan, and the channel, formerly very shallow near that place, has been so deepened by skilful management, as to admit vessels which draw thirteen feet of water, close to the wharfs. There is a deep pool, called Carmoyl or Garmoyle, about one mile from the south shore, opposite Hollywood, where vessels ride at low water, when the bank within twenty yards is completely dry. There are scarcely any rocks in this bay, except one reef on the north side, (which is covered at high water,) called by the Irish the Briggs, *i.e.* the tombs; but by the Scotch the Clachan, from its resemblance to a village when uncovered at low water. There is a shoal a little south-west of Carrickfergus, over which lies three fathom of water at ebb-tide. The Speedwell, a Scotch ship, in King William's reign, was the only ship ever known to suffer on it. The Down coast is distinctly seen during the drive to Carrickfergus, and is beautifully diversified with seats and villages; of these the most important are Hollywood and Bangor, whose sites appear peculiarly well chosen. Near the latter town, at a little inlet called Groomsport Bay, the Duke Schomberg first cast anchor. At the entrance are seen the Copeland Isles, so called from a family of that name settled on the coast of Down in the twelfth century *;* and passing a few miles onward, by a range of fine villas, the town and castle of Carrickfergus are presented in the front field of the view. The latter is a hold and magnificent object, standing upon a reef of rocks projecting into the bay, by which means in this approach its outline is most clearly and strongly defined to the eye of the spectator. The shore near

40

Carrickfergus is said to be particularly adapted to bathing, from its freedom from mud and ooze, and the cottages erected along the shore, are let at high rents during the bathing-season. It was in the Bay of Carrickfergus that Paul Jones appeared in 1778, and, after a bloody engagement, captured the British sloop-of-war, DRAKE.

The CASTLE OF CARRICKFERGUS forms a most noble projection on the bay, and in every view of the town is a most conspicuous and picturesque object. At common tides three sides of the building are enclosed by water. The greatest height of the rock is at its further extremity, where it is about thirty feet, shelving considerably towards the land; the walls of the castle following exactly its different windings.* Towards the town are two towers, called, from their shape, half—moons, and between these is the only entrance, which is defended by a strait passage, with embrasures for fire-arms. About the centre of this passage was formerly a draw-bridge; a part of the barbican that protected the bridge can still be seem. A dam, west of the castle, is believed to have been originally made to supply the ditch at this entrance with water. Between the half-moons is a strong gate, above which is a machicolation, or aperture for letting fall stones, melted lead or the like, on the assailants. Inside this gate is a portecullis, and an aperture for the like purpose as that just mentioned; the arches and each side of this aperture are of the Gothic kind, and the only ones observed about the building. In the gun—room of these towers are a few pieces of light ordnance. A window in the east tower, inside, is ornamented with round pillars; the columns are five feet high, including base and capital, and five inches and a half in diameter. The centre column seems to be a rude attempt at the Ionic; the flank columns have the leaves of the Corinthian; their bases consist of two toruses. Within the gates is the lower yard, or balium; on the right are the guard-room and a barrack; the latter was built in 1802. Opposite these are large vaults, said to be bomb-proof, over which are a few neat apartments occupied by the officers of the garrison, ordnance—storekeeper, and master-gunner. A little southward are the armourer's forge, and a furnace for heating shot; near which, on the outer wall of the castle, is a small projecting tower, called the lion's den.

The tower is divided into five stories; the largest room was formerly in the third story, with semicircular windows. It was called Fergus's dining-room, and was twenty-five feet ten inches high, forty feet long, and thirty-eight broad. Within tine keep was formerly a draw-well, thirty-seven feet deep, the water of which was anciently celebrated for medicinal purposes. This well is now nearly filled up with rubbish.

The following notice of this castle is given in a survey by George Clarkson, in 1367. "The building of the said castle on the south part is three towers, viz., the gate-house tower in the middle thereof, which is the entry at a draw-bridge, over a dry moat; and

* M'Skimmin's History of Carrickfergus.

41

Larne

42

in said tower is a prison and porter-lodge, and over the same a fair lodging, called the constable's lodging; and in the contain between the gate-house and west tower in the corner, being of divers squares, called Cradyfergus, is a fair arid comely building, a chapel, and divers houses of office, on the ground, and above the great chamber and the lords' lodging, all which is now in great decaie as well as the couverture being lead, also in timber and glass, and without help and reparation, it will soon come to utter ruin."

We enjoyed the delightful view of Carrickfergus Bay, by snatches, during almost the whole of the road from Cave Hill to Larne. It was the first week in February, a time of the year when in America we have almost forgotten the colour of the snow-covered ground, and here were fields of the brightest and tenderest green, cattle grazing, birds singing, every sign of an October morning, indeed, except the leaves on the trees. The wintriest picture of the scene was an occasional bleaching-field, where, in long stripes upon the grass, lay the white linen, resembling the vanishing snow-wreaths in an American thaw. There seemed to me very little difference between summer and winter in Ireland, for in my first visit to the country, in August I was travelling with the same degree of clothing, and I am sure tIne winds were as chilly then as now, and the fields no greener.

We came very suddenly upon LARNE, and at the same moment that we turned over the edge of the deep glen on which it lies, tine sun broke out upon the lovely bay and village below, illuminating the whole scene with a light such as a painter would have chosen. It was, indeed, a delicious picture, and there was something Italian, no less in the soft vapoury light in which it was bathed, than in the position and aspect of the town. Island Magee lay in fine outline across time bay, and on a narrow tongue of land, called the Curraàn, stood the ruins of an old castle, giving a romantic and foreign look to the entire scene. Our car-driver descended too fast for us , though our breakfast was at the foot of the hill, and entering a narrow and old-fashioned street, be deposited us at a small and tidy inn, so like the same thing in Italy, (the street and inn of a small village between Rome and Florence,) that the illusion was difficult to shake off. We ordered our breakfast, and started out for a stroll along the crescent of the little bay, and, hungry as we were, the impression made on us by its spiring-like softness and beauty, is among the most agreeable of my Irish recollections. Larne, (says the Guide Book to the Giant's Causeway,) was anciently called Inver, (which signifies *lowly situated.*) Its trade was once of some importance, and even yet it is not contemptible. The duties in the year 1810, amounted to £14,000, and there is still occasion to make it time residence of a collector. The chief articles of commerce here are rock-salt and limestone, both of which are exported in very considerable quantities. There is a good deal of cotton-weaving, and a manufacture of sail-cloth, with some other traffic connected with nautical affairs, Larne being the best harbour on this coast, from Belfast Lough to Derry.

The town consists of two divisions, usually called the old and new towns; the old one is built on rather an irregular plan, the latter consists of one long avenue, in which there are several excellent houses. The population amounts to about three thousand souls. There are, besides the parish church, one Methodist meeting-house, three Presbyterian, and one Roman Catholic chapel.

The most interesting historical record, in the vicinity of Larne, is the castle of Olderfleet, before mentioned, standing on the extremity of the peninsula, called the Curraàn,* a sort of natural pier, forming the northern side of the Larne harbour; and completely commanding the strait by which it is entered. In the road from the town to the castle, the ruins of a little chapel, called Clondumales, are passed. The castle is now an insignificant ruin, but the advantage and dignity of its situation can never fail of attracting the visitor. It is supposed to have been erected by one of the Bissetts, a powerful Scotch family, upon whom Henry III. bestowed large possessions in the barony of Glenarm, some of which were forfeited by Hugh Bissett ma the reign of Edward II. for rebellion. James M'Donnell, Lord of Kantyre, asserted his claim to this land in right of the Bissetts, but his son was content to accept of them on conditions approved of by Elizabeth, viz., that he would not carry arms under any but the kings of England, and would pay an annual tribute of hawks and cattle.

It was on the peninsula of the Curraàn that Edward Bruce effected his landing, in 1315, with the expectation of making himself king of Ireland, which vain and foolish ambition caused so much bloodshed through the east of Ireland, and was productive of such dreadful calamities, to the English settlers particularly.

The castle of Olderfleet became important as a defensive fortress against the predatory bands of Scots, who infested the north-eastern coasts, and was generally under the direction of a governor. In 1569, we find Sir Moyses Hill held this office, but in 1598, being thought no longer useful, it was abolished. After changing proprietors several times, the castle was finally granted to Sir Arthur Chichester, in 1610, by James I. At Olderfleet will be found a ferry-boat, which plies regularly between that point and Island Magee, for which passage one penny is demanded; and, having landed, the pedestrian will find two roads, one towards Brown's Bay, another along the Larne side : let him take the former. Of this island a curious and brief account is to be met with in a private MS. in this county, which mentions, that in the reign of Elizbeth it was a complete waste, without any wood; although a fertile soil; and that the queen had granted a lease of it to Savage, a follower of the Earl of Essex. At this time, says the MS., it was inhabited by the Magees, from whom it derives its name.

Not far from the landing-place stands a druidical cromlech. The covering stone,

* Curraàn is a corruption of the Irish word *carrian,* a hoop, which the curved form of the peninsula suggested originally.

which rests on three supporters, is six feet in length, and of a triangular shape; its inclination is to the rising sun. On the east of Brown's Bay is a rocking-stone, or giant's cradle, which was said to acquire a rocking, tremulous motion at the approach of sinners or malefactors : there were many of these over the face of the kingdom, but they are now dislodged in most places, so that the few which remain are most interesting curiosities. They were so ingeniously poised, that the slightest impulse was capable of rocking a mass which the greatest strength was unable to dislodge; nor does there appear to be any contrivance adopted but the circumstance of placing the stone upon its rude pedestal. Until a very late period, Island Magee was time residence of witches, and the theatre of sorcery : in 1711, eight females were tried upon this extraordinary charge in Carrickfergus, and the memory of Fairy Brown is still a cause of terror among the neighbouring peasantry.

IV.

THE inn parlour at Larne was very clean, and the breakfast excellent. Two books graced the old-fashioned sideboard, of which one was a volume I scarce thought to stumble upon so far from home, a Biography of the Heroes of the American Revolution, printed in Cincinnati, Ohio. I had no time to refresh my memory with it, however, for the day shone bright through the little inn-windows, and our expeditious landlord, who was to drive us himself to Glenarm, had his tandem-car at the door, by the time we had polished our first egg-shell. The car and team were the worst we met with on our excursion, but all deficiencies were made up by the enthusiasm with which we were driven. I never saw a much more damaged grey mare than the wheeler, but she was "persuaded" in a style that would have worked speed into a tortoise. Our Jehu was a merry, pleasure-loving looking boy, with a very big arm, and a most formidable whip, and spite of the dreadful dislocation of the car's movement, I was in a constant laugh at the tender terms with which he accompanied blows that threatened to break in the poor creature's ribs at every repetition. Imagine the contrast between tune and accompaniment in a performance like this: "Come up, woman!" (thwack) "Go along, pet!" (thwack! thwack!) "Whew, sweetheart!" (thwack!) "Hip, old mare!" (thwack! thwack! thwack!) And *da capo* for twelve Irish miles.

The coast from Larne to Glenarm reminded me of the road along the Mediterranean in the south of France. The hills are not so high, nor the road carried so loftily as that over the maritime Alps, but the profiles of the coast of Antrim are bolder and finer, and, indeed, nothing can surpass the beauty of the successive views got at every turn of the road. We rounded a noble promontory into Glenarm, the church spire first breaking on the view, and the towers of the castle immediately after—the whole apparition of the town and its fine points of picturesque resembling the moving tableaux of theatrical scenery. We lost no time in making for the castle, and, turning out of the street, came directly upon the bridge connected with its lofty and superb barbican. A small mountain river brawls between the town and the lofty structure which, in feudal days, lodged its master the M'Donnell, and from the deep water rises directly the stern old wall, with its embrasures and towers, in as high preservation as on the day it was completed. A great part of the walls and ornamental architecture of Glenarm are modern, but all the additions are executed in the finest spirit of antiquity. A more beautiful gem than the castellated structure, nestled between the overhanging sides of this ravine, I never have seen. It has all the charms, beside, of high care and cultivation, the deer park stretching away up the valley, and the green swards and walks within the grounds kept with the nice care which distinguishes the noble demesnes of England. The excellent Guide to Antrim, (which is graced with drawings by the distinguished scholar Petrie,) gives the following information relative to Glenarm and its dependencies.

"The village of Glenarm consists of about two hundred cottages, and appears originally to have been built for the clansmen of the noble family, whose castle stands beyond the river The castle is a stately, ancient pile, in a commanding position; from one front there is a view of the bay and its enclosing promontories, and from the other a prospect up the wooded glen towards the deer park. The castle is large, and contains some excellent apartments; its exterior presents something of the character of a baronial castle of the fifteenth century. The approach to the castle is by a lofty barbican standing on the northern extremity of the bridge. Passing through this, a long terrace, overhanging the river, and confined on the opposite side by a lofty, embattled curtain-wall, leads through an avenue of ancient lime trees, to the principal front of the castle, the appearance of which from this approach is very impressive. Lofty towers, terminated with cupolas and gilded vanes occupy the angles of the building; the parapets are crowded with gables, decorated with carved pinnacles, and exhibiting various heraldic ornaments.

The hall is a noble apartment, forty-four feet in length by twenty in breadth, and thirty-feet high; in the centre of which stands a handsome billiard table. Across one end passes a gallery, communicating with the bed-chambers, and supported by richly ornamented columns, from the grotesque ornaments of which springs a beautiful grained ceiling.

On the principal floor are several noble apartments; the dining-parlour, forty feet by twenty-four, and the drawing-room, forty-four by twenty-two, are the most spacious : the small drawing-room, library, &c., though of considerably less dimensions, are most commodious apartments. The demesne of Glenarm is very

Glenarm

extensive, and beautifully wooded: it has latterly been much improved, and many obstructions to the view removed. There is also an enclosure in the glen, called the Great Deer Park, which is generally supposed to be the most comprehensive park in the kingdom , and the venison fed here the choicest.

The parish church stands near one of the entrances to the demesne, upon the beach, with a small enclosed cemetery around. There are no monuments in the interior.

In the burying ground, around the church, stand time remains of a cruciformed building, formerly a monastery for Franciscan friars of the third order.

This monastery was founded in 1465, by Robert Bissett, a Scotchman, who was banished his country for aiding in the murder of the Duke of Athol, and was established here by Henry III. The estates were subsequently forfeited by the rebellion of Hugh Bisett, in the reign of Edward II. About this time, John More M'Donnell, son of John, Lord of the Isles, landed here, and marrying Mary, daughter of Sir John Bissett, claimed the lands called Glenshiesk, that is, the baronies of Carey and Glenarm; and thus it was that the Antrim family became entitled to the Bissett's property. The barony of Dunluce became the property of the M'Donnell's in right of M'Quillan's daughter, who married a M'Donnell, and so the claim of the M'Donnells to three baronies of the county became perfectly plain. This family was ennobled by the title of Viscount Dunluce, in the person of Sir Randal M'Sorley M'Donnell, of Dunluce, June 25th, 1618. The same distinguished personage was two years after raised to the Earldom of Antrim. His son Randal, afterwards Marquis of Antrim was equally remarkable for his abilities and misfortunes. He was treacherously arrested on one occasion by Munro, while entertaining him with hospitality at his castle of Dunluce, and confined in the castle of Carrickfergus, whence be escaped to York, and complained to the queen. Returning to Ireland again with instructions, he was seized once more by the avaricious and, treacherous general, and committed to the same castle, from which he a second time effected his escape, and flying into England, by the assistance of the Marquis of Montrose, was commissioned to raise a force in Ireland for his majesty, and transport it into Scotland to oppose the Covenanters. The marquis married, first, the widow of George Villiers, Duke of Buckingham, and, secondly, Rose, daughter of Sir Henry O'Neill, of Shane's Castle, but dying without issue, the title of marquis became extinct, and the earldom devolved on his brother Alexander.

The monastery of Glenarm, though founded by the Bissetts, appears to have been retained by the crown from the time of Edward II., and granted to Alexander M'Donnell in 1557, in the reign of Queen Mary, at which time he was presented by the lord deputy, the Earl of Sussex, with a gold sword and silver gilt spurs for his services against the Scots.

The remains of the monastery are very insignificant. Near the eastern end stands a monument, dated 1720, bearing the crest of a hand and dagger, but the inscription is not legible. The tombstones all round are ornamented by the arms of each family carved thereon; and from the ages on the slabs, it would appear, that longevity is a gift bestowed upon the innocent inhabitants of Glenarm. The ages on the tombs, some exceeding one hundred years, may, perhaps, prove this to be that blessed portion of "this sainted isle," where the inhabitants live so long, that they sometimes find a continuance of existence burdensome, in which case their friends are said to convey them to an adjacent country, where the spirit will sooner relax its tenacious hold.

There are some members of the Antrim family buried at Glenarm; but the Abbey of Bona Margery, near Ballycastle, is their place of rest. In the fifteenth century, O'Neill the Great was killed in the camp of Sorley Boy, and his body, being removed to Glenarm, was interred in the Franciscan monastery of that place. Not long after, a friar from Armagh appeared at the monastery, and was admitted to its shelter and hospitality; and when near about to take his leave, he thus addressed the abbot : "Father, I am come from our brothers of Armagh , to beg that you would grant me leave to remove the body of the great O'Neill, who lies buried here, to the grave of his ancestors at Armagh."

The abbot paused awhile, then answered, "Have you brought hither the corpse of my Lord James, of Cantyre, which was interred amongst the strangers at Armagh? "To which the friar replying, that he had not; "Then," said the abbot, "while you walk over the grave of my Lord James, of Cantyre, at Armagh, I will trample upon the great O'Neill at Glenarm;" and so, at midnight, dismissed his guest.

The Bay of Glenarm is formed by a deep circular winding of the shore, and is protected on each side by lofty headlands. There is, deep water here, and a quay might readily be formed by building upon a natural basaltic pier on the north side of the bay This would be not only of great advantage here, but of very universal benefit to the shipping in the northern part of the Irish Sea; for, from the tremendous swell, and precipitous shore, the land is unapproachable when the wind blows from the north-east, nor is there a sheltering harbour on this coast from Lough Foyle to Larne. Further, the fishing along the coast is at present so exceedingly precarious, that it does not yield a sufficient return to the poor seaman, who has the hardihood to prosecute it. This would be remedied, to a certain extent, by the erection of a pier in this harbour, where the little skiff might fly for protection when the sea assumed one of those angry perturbations which are so sudden and so frequent on the Antrim coast. At present, for seven months and upwards, the fisherman's boat is drawn up on the beach, and the inverted hulk secured by a quantity of large stones until the return of the milder season; for as he has no place of retreat in the hurricane, and he dares not approach the shore while it continues, he is obliged to abandon this vocation altogether, and seek another and less perilous mode of subsistence.

49

Glenariff

We were very glad to be rid of our two miserable jades and the Larne post-car, and, with many a lingering look behind at the romantic castle of Glenarm and its green valley and bright river, we took the new road to Cushendall. If the engineer of the new and capital coast road of Antrim had worked with a poet and painter at his back, he could not have laid out its course more agreeably to the eye and the imagination. It is constructed with equal skill, taste, and enterprise, cliffs cut through, chasms crossed, water courses walled and bridged a roughly ribbed and jagged coast, in short, traversed by a road as smooth and almost as level as a tennis-court. I have been surprised by the excellence of the roads all over Ireland, but by none so agreeably as this.

With an easy car, a smart little Shetland mare, a silent, but good-natured driver, and a bright sun , we should have been difficult not to have enjoyed our drive from Glenarm to Cushendall. We crossed the outlets of several deep and romantic glens, and observed that there was not one without its waterfall. Over one or two, at the brow of the precipice from which the white torrent took its first leap, we noticed light bridges, and plantations in their neighbourhood, indicating park-scenery on the table-land above. We soon entered upon the curve of the Red Bay, and crossed the entrance of the wild VALE of GLENARIFF," called sometimes Glen-aireamp, the valley of numbers, and Glen-aireachaib, the valley of chiefs."Up this glen is the waterfall with the musical name of Isnaleara, which sends its waters to the sea near the caves of Red Bay. The prospect to the west is terminated by the lofty conical summit of Cruach-a-crue, while that to the north is limited by the extraordinary mountain of Lurgeidan, not unlike the frustum of an enormous cone of considerable altitude, but whose base is disproportionately narrow. Passing the neglected hamlet of Waterford, at the mouth of the Glenariff river, the caves of Red Bay are reached: they are excavations probably formed at some remote period by the inroads of the tide, which is now excluded by the embankment in front, in a species of soft red sandstone. There are three of tolerable magnitude, one of which is very appropriately converted into a smith's forge, and affords a very Cyclopean appearance. A second is reported to be the residence of a female, (Nancy Murray, the driver called her,) whose trade is the sale of illicit spirits. The ruined castle of Red Bay towered above us as we passed from a lofty arch cut through the southern extremity of one of the red cliffs, and beneath this is a cave, said once to have been used as a school. The castle was built, it is said, by the Bissetts, from whom the Antrim family derive this barony.

A fine conical mound rose up before us as we approached Cushendall, and a few minutes brought us in sight of this most picturesque little village. I was immediately reminded of Amalfi, in looking down upon it; and, indeed, this whole coast has the peculiar character of that of the Bay of Salerno. The softness of the atmosphere added something no doubt to the resemblance—for I descended Scaracatoja, on my way to Salerno in the same month, and with very much such weather.

Fairhead

We entered the small inn of Cushendall, and found the hostess, a remarkably handsome young woman, reading the Bible. Religion and neatness are inseparable, as every traveller knows; and after a look into the cheerful kitchen and tidy little parlour, I regretted that night had not overtaken us at Cushendall. While our next Jehu was getting ready his car, however, we sat down by the kitchen—fire and lunched upon most exemplary bread and butter, our modest and neatly-dressed landlady attending upon us with a kindness and ease that would have graced the castle of Glenarm. If I were ever in want of romantic scenery and a pleasant retreat from the world, Cusliendall would be among the first spots that would occur to my memory. Our horse and car from this inn were the best we saw on our tour to the north, and, with a fine lad for a driver, we whirled away towards the wild mountain road that lies between Cushendall and Ballycastle. We left the coast for some time, and on reaching it again, came in sight of the magnificent headland of FAIR HEAD, one of the noblest points of this remarkable coast. "The promontory of Fair Head rises perpendicularly to the height of six hundred and thirty-one feet above the level of the sea. On approaching its summit, the tourist will perceive two small lakes, Lough Dhu and Lough-na-Cranagh, and near to its highest point, a curious cave, said to have been a Pict's house" The view from this headland is of a most enchanting description—to the west, the whole line of finely variegated limestone and basaltic coast, as far as Bangore Head; the beautiful promontory of Renbaan or Whitehead, majestically presenting its snow-white front to the foaming ocean—the swinging bridge and bay of Carric-a-rede—beyond this, Sheep Island—and directly in front, the island of Raghery; and to the east, the Scottish coast, &c. as already described.

The promontory of Fairhead is formed of a number of basaltic colossal pillars, many of them of a much larger size than any to be seen at the Causeway; in some instances exceeding two hundred feet in length, and five in breadth; one of them forming a quadrangular prism, thirty-three feet by thirty-six on the sides, and of the gigantic altitude we have just mentioned. It is said to be the largest basaltic pillar yet discovered upon the face of our globe, exceeding in diameter the pedestal that supports the statue of Peter the Great, at Petersburgh, and considerably surpassing in length the shaft of Pompey's Pillar, at Alexandria. At the foot of this magnificent colonnade is seen an immense mass of rock, similarly formed, like a wide waste of natural ruins, which are by some supposed to have been, in the course of successive ages, tumbled down from their original foundation, by storms or some violent operation of nature. These massive bodies have sometimes withstood the shock of their fall, and often lie in groups and clumps of pillars, resembling many of the varieties of artificial ruins, and forming a very novel and striking landscape—the deep waters of the sea rolling at their base with a full and heavy swell.

V.

NEAR FAIR HEAD is a singular fissure in the face of the precipice, called Fhir Leith, or the GRAY MAN'S PATH. The entrance to the pass at the top is extremely narrow; and a joint of green-stone, which has fallen across it, forms a sort of natural gate, through which the bold inquirer must descend, and which conducts to a gradually expanding passage leading to the base. There are said to be one or two similar chasms along the summit, which have frequently proved fatal to cattle pasturing upon the headland. These cliffs suggest the probability of accidents of a more serious kind, and in the Dublin Penny Journal, (the best conducted and most valuable work of its kind in Great Britain,) I find the following anecdotes relative to accidents in this neighbourhood. "From the Aird Snout, a man, named J. Rane, tumbled down while engaged in searching for fossil-coal, during a severe winter; and, strange to say, was taken up alive, although seriously injured by the fall. Another man, named Adam Morning, when descending a giddy path that leads to the foot of Port-na-Spania, with his wife's breakfast, who was at the time employed in making kelp, missed his footing, and tumbling headlong, was dashed to atoms ere he reached the bottom. The poor woman witnessed the misfortune from a distance; but supposing, from the kind of coat he wore, that it had been one of the sheep that had been grazing on the headland, she went to examine it, when she found instead, the mangled corpse of her husband."Another story is told of a poor girl, who, being betrothed to one she loved, in order to furnish herself and her intended husband with some of the little comforts of life, procured employment on the shore, in the manufacture alluded to, with some other persons in the neighbourhood. Port-na-Spania, as will be observed, is completely surrounded by a tremendous precipice from three to four hundred feet high, and is only accessible by a narrow pathway, by far the most difficult and dangerous of any of those nearly perpendicular ascents to be met with along the entire coast. Up this frightful foot way was this poor girl, in common with all who were engaged in the same manufacture, obliged to climb, heavily laden with a burden of the kelp; and, having gained the steepest point of the peak, was just about to place her foot on the summit, when, in consequence of the load on her shoulders shifting a little to one side, she lost her balance, fell backwards, and ere she reached the bottom, was a lifeless and mangled corpse. To behold women and children toiling up this dreadful ascent, bearing heavy loads, either on their heads or fastened from their necks and shoulders, is really painful, even to the least sensitive, unaccustomed to the sight—and yet the natives themselves appear to think nothing whatever of it.

An anecdote is also related of a man who was in the habit of seating himself on the

Kenbane Castle

edge of a cliff which overhung its base, at Poortmoor, to enjoy the beauty of the widely extended scene. One fine summer morning, however, having gained the height, and taken his accustomed seat, while indulging in the thoughts and feelings which we may suppose the scene likely to inspire, "a change came o'er the spirit of his dream"—the rock upon which he was perched gave way, and, in the twinkling of an eye, bore him on "its rapid wing" to the foot of a precipice, where it sunk several feet into the earth—safely depositing its ambitious bestrider on the shore, at a distance of fully four hundred feet from the towering eminence off which he had made his involuntary aërial descent.

The shore in this neighbourhood is beautifully indented with coves, made partly by the action of the sea, and partly by the wear of the mountain torrents. One of these forms a beautiful fall, called THE LEAP, which in rainy seasons is an object of great beauty. Night closed upon us as we entered Ballycastle, and we were happy to find ourselves at another comfortable inn, and within a two hours' drive of the Causeway. This little town possesses a very strong interest for the historian and antiquarian, as well as the geologist and traveller. The collieries of Ballycastle have, at different periods, occupied the attention of speculators; and it is confidently believed they will still prove a source of wealth to Ireland. But .a more than ordinary interest is attached to them from a discovery made about seventy years ago by the miners employed in the works. Mr. Hamilton, in his Letters on the Antrim Coast, says, that about the year 1770, while the miners were pushing forward an *adit* towards the bed of coal in an unexplored part of the Ballycastle cliff, they unexpectedly broke through the rock into a narrow passage, so much contracted and choked up with various drippings and deposits on its side and bottom, as to render it impossible for any of the workmen to force through that they might examine it further. Two lads were therefore made to creep in with candles, for the purpose of exploring this subterraneous avenue, they accordingly proceeded for a considerable time, with much labour and difficulty, and at length entered into an extensive labyrinth, diverging into numerous apartments, in the mazes and windings of which they were completely bewildered and lost. After various vain attempts to return, their lights were extinguished, their voices became hoarse and exhausted with frequent shouting; at length, becoming completely fatigued, they sat down together in utter despair. Meanwhile their friends without, alarmed for their safety, used equal exertions to indicate their presence, hut in vain; at length , it occurred to one of the subterranean wanderers, that the sound of his hammer against a stone would be better heard than the sound of a human voice, which artifice succeeded in directing their friends to the place where the two young adventurers were seated in despondence, and so ultimately restored them to the light of the sun, after an absence of twelve hours.

Thirty-six chambers were discovered here, all trimmed and dressed by excellent hands; also baskets and mining instruments, and other demonstrations of the original miner's knowledge and expertness in the art, equal to that of the present age. No tradition remains in the country of the working of this mine; and the peasantry, who attribute all works of antiquity in this kingdom to the Danes or the giants, in this instance prefer the former. But this conclusion is erroneous, as is very satisfactorily proved by the writer of the above extract. Another argument in favour of the supposition, that these collieries were wrought anciently, is derived from this curious circumstance. Bruce's Castle, on the Island of Raghery, appears to have been built with lime, which had been burned with sea coal, some cinders of which may still be detected in the mortar, and bear a strong resemblance to those of Ballycastle coals. Now these coals, in all probability, were brought from Ballycastle; for the English collieries were not then in general use, and this was more than five centuries ago.

About two miles north-west of the town of Ballycastle, on a narrow peninsula, composed of white limestone, which projects its perpendicular front into the sea, are the ruins of the ancient Castle of Kenbaan, or the White Promontory—a name derived from that of the precipitous cliff on which it stands.

At present little remains of this building except a part of the massy walls of the tower or keep, which, from its bold and romantic situation, adds not a little to the beauty of the scenery of this wonderful coast. During summer, it is often frequented by parties, and the scene of many a festive collation; where instead of the grim warder pacing at its gate, are seen inside the portal the "fairest of the fair."

Tradition states, this building to have been erected by the Irish sept of M'Hendrie; but as its scanty ruins bear a striking resemblance to those castles reared by the first English settlers on the coast from the Boyne to the Bann, we think its erection may, with greater probability, be ascribed to them, or, if it be an Irish castle, it is at least erected on the plan of those of the adventurers.

Be this as it may, about the beginning of the reign of Queen Elizabeth, we find it held by the Scottish clan of M'Alister, who arrived in Ireland with the M'Donnells from Cantyre. In 1568, the M'Alisters entered into a conspiracy against the English quartered in those parts, and in an encounter which took place, two English horsemen were slain; and soon after "Rannel Oge M'Alister Caraghe," chief of the M'Alister, was killed in revenge, by some English soldiers. on this commotion, Captain William Piers, governor of Carrickfergus, and seneschal of the county of Antrim, proceeded with some troops to the Glynns, where he made three of the M'Alisters prisoners, one of whom he hung in chains; and Alexander, chief of that sept, making his submission about this time, the M'Alisters sunk beneath the English power. Many of this name are stilt to be found in the *Glynns*.

We were up with the lark on the morning that we left Ballycastle for the Causeway, but our attentive host had anticipated us, and our breakfast was smoking before

Carrick a Rede

Dunseverick Castle

a brilliant turf fire. Dawn was just creeping into a sky fortunately clear, as we flourished away, Irish fashion, from the inn door, and broad daylight found us near the far-famed CARRICK-A-REDE. The new road runs close to this singular chasm, and we had no difficulties to contend with, but the mud and water with which the wet season had covered the whole country. The "flying-bridge," as it is called, is removed during the winter, but the scenery of the spot, in other respects, is not susceptible of change, as there is not a tree within sight, and the grass on the summit is as bright in winter as in spring. Carrick-a-Rede signifies *the rock in the road,* and it is so called because it interrupts the salmon in their passage along the coast. The rock is an insulated crag of rudely prismatic basalt, connected with the mainland by a bridge of ropes, thrown across a chasm, sixty feet in breadth and eighty-four in depth. This flying-bridge which is not unlike the connecting-bridge between Holyhead Mountain and the South Stack, is thus formed;—two strong cables , parallel to each other, are fastened to rings inserted in the solid rock, on each side of the chasm, and the narrow interval of the ropes is occupied by a boarded pathway. The danger in crossing is attributable to an irregularity in planting the foot upon the board, which, of course, recoils against the impression too soon, and precipitates the unguarded and courageous venturer into the deep chasm below. Persons accustomed to walk along planks may safely venture over, and the women and boys attached to the fishery, carry great loads across with the utmost contempt of danger, and apparent ease. It should be remarked, that the Island of Carrick-a-Rede is of nearly equal elevation with the main land, three hundred and fifty feet. In the cliffs, near the island, is a very beautiful cave, about thirty feet in height , formed entirely of columnar basalt, of which the bases appear to have been removed, so that the unsupported polygonal columns compose the cave.

The chief use of this insulated rock appears to be that of interrupting the salmon, who annually coast along the shore in search of rivers in which to deposit their spawn. Their passage is generally made close to the shore, so that Carrick-a-Rede is very opportunely situated for projecting the interrupting nets. It will he here inquired, why the fishermen do not spare themselves the trouble of throwing across this very dangerous bridge, and approach the island by water; but this is perfectly impracticable, owing to the extreme perpendicularity of the basaltic cliffs on every side, except in one small bay, which is not accessible but at particular periods. This fishery, and, indeed, all those along the northern coast, are very productive. The only residents in the little cottage on the island are the clerk and fishermen, and they remain only during the summer months. The fishermen are paid, and all the expenses of fishing defrayed, by proportionate allowances of salmon.

About three miles east of the Giant's Causeway we came in sight of a detached and lofty rock, elevating its head near the centre of a small bay, and crowned with the ruins of the CASTLE OF DUNSEVERICK. This picturesque spot was once the seat of the family of O'Cahan, or as they were commonly called, O'Kane. Mr. M'Skimmin, the distinguished antiquarian of Carrickfergus, displays great learning in an essay in the Dublin Penny Journal, the object of which is to prove that Dunseverick is the ancient and celebrated Dun Sooarke of Irish history—the seat of successive chieftains and powerful families of the north. It is at present a lonely remnant of a structure, and though traces of the outworks are visible, the "keep" is the only part that is still erect, and this too, from its appearance, will soon be as prostrate as the rest. Immense masses of the rock have been hewn away, evidently for the purpose of rendering the castle as inaccessible as possible. An enormous basaltic rock, south of the entrance, also appears to have been cut of a pyramidal form, and flattened on the top, perhaps as a station for a warder, or for the purpose of placing upon it some engine of defence. That the insulated rock on which the castle is placed, should, from its peculiar strength, have been selected by the early settlers in Ireland as a proper situation for one of their strongholds is not to be wondered at; but of that original fortress, M'Skimmin remarks, there are no remains. The present ruin, though of great strength, the walls being eleven feet in thickness, is evidently of an age not anterior to the English invasion, and most probably erected by the M'Quillans, but the annals of the time are silent as to the period of its reedification.

In all the views between Ballycastle and Dunluce, the Island of Rathlin, (or Rathkerry,) is one of the most conspicuous features, stretching its length along the shore within six miles of the cliffs, and backed by the misty tops of the far-seen Scotch coast. The island is the property of Mr. Gage, who holds it by a lease in perpetuity under the Countess of Antrim. This gentleman is completely lord of the isle, and banishes his subjects to the *continent* of Ireland for misconduct or repeated. offences against his laws. Raghery is about five English miles in length by three and a half in breadth. it contains about two thousand acres, one quarter of which grows corn, &c. There are three town-lands, called Shandra, Aila, and Knockard, upon which the majority of the inhabitants, generally about one thousand, reside. It appears from a late census that its population is not increasing, arid varies very little. There are two places of worship here, a Protestant church and a Roman Catholic chapel.

The extreme western end of the island is called Keuramer, and is three hundred and fifty-two feet above the ocean. Formerly distinctions existed between the in-habitants of each end of the island, and the qualifications of each were looked upon as totally dissimilar. This, however, is not quite done away.

Near Ushet, at a place called Doon Point, the disposition of the basaltic columns is very remark able, some being perpendicular, others horizontal, others carved. The base of this little promontory is a natural pier or mole. Above this is a collection of columns of a curved form, apparently assumed in conformity with the surface on which they rest, and inducing a belief that they were so moulded when in a state of

The Giants Causeway

softness; and above both these arrangements, there is a variety of differently disposed columns, partaking of every position in which basalt has been discovered in other places. The form of Raghery Island is that of a right-angle, whose sides or legs are Kenramer and Ushet Points. on the external vertex of the right-angle stands Bruce's Castle. In the early ages of Irish history, the proximity of Scotland and Ireland invited mutual predatory expeditions, to which it is said the Scotch were more addicted than the Irish. In these occasional partial invasions the island of Raghery was found very useful, both as a depót and place; of retreat. During the civil wars which devastated Scotland, between Robert Bruce and Baliol, the former fled to Raghery for shelter; and fortifying himself. in the castle. which now bears his name, made a bold and successful resistance to his enemies. The short time which Bruce remained upon the island, may be very fairly assigned as a reason for his not having been the founder or builder of the castle; besides, in all probability, it was the existence of this fortified place on Raghery which induced the exiled king to fly thither for shelter.

VI.

AFTER passing Dunseverick Castle, the road turns away from the shore, and makes nearly straight for the Causeway, leaving the promontory of Bangore Head far on the right. We were looking out anxiously for the Causeway; but even when within half-a-mile of it, the other headlands looked more attractive than the low line of the shore pointed out to us by the driver, and after seeing Fair Head, the whole of this shore might be passed by the undirected traveller, without suspicion of the neighbourhood of wonders equal to those he had left behind. We stopped at the door of a low hut at last, and a very well-dressed and intelligent-looking man made his appearance from the smoke, and offered his services as a guide. From the season in which we travelled, as well as from the early hour at which we arrived, we missed the throngs of beggars, guides, and mineral-sellers of which all travellers complain; but as we started on the path to the Causeway, we saw dark figures rising up in all directions, and radiating to us from a mile around, with every appearance of haste and expectation. The guide led us down a slippery and stony road, cut in the side of the hill which concealed the Causeway from our view, and, rounding the shoulder of it, we descended to a small mound, from which we got our first view of THE CAUSEWAY. We were at too great a distance to distinguish any peculiarity in the view, except the lines of the basaltic pillars, indistinctly marking the face of the cliff, and I was naturally disappointed with the first glance—but as we descended to the shore, and approached nearer around the bend of the bay, it seemed to me that the ruins of some templed and gigantic city, that had been hurled from the sky, were heaped up before me in a mountain of confused architecture. The Giant's Causeway, indeed, resembles nothing so much as a mountain of hewn stones of noble columns, remnants of vast porticoes, cast down from a height into the sea. The upright and regular pillars in the face of the cliff, give you an impression that there is a city overwhelmed and buried behind them, and the disinterred Pompeii itself was not so like as this to the idea I had formed of Pompeii before visiting Italy.

Our guide kept on his way to the vast projecting quay which descends from the base of these mountain façades into the sea. To borrow the very correct language of a clever tourist, "The principal or grand Causeway, consists of an irregular arrangement of many hundred thousands of columns, formed of a dark rock nearly as hard as marble. The greater part of them are of a pentagon figure, but so closely compacted together, that, though the pillars are perfectly distinct, the very water which falls upon them will scarcely penetrate between. There are some of the pillars which have seven, and a few which have eight sides; a few also have four,. hut only one has been found with three. Not one will be found to correspond exactly with the other, having sides and angles of the same dimensions; while at the same time the sum of the angles of any one of them are found to be equal to four right-angles—the sides of one corresponding exactly to those of the others which lie next to it, although otherwise differing completely in size and form. Each pillar is formed of several distinct joints, closely articulated into each other, the convex end of the one closely fitting into the concave of the next—sometimes the concavity, sometimes the convexity being uppermost. In the entire Causeway it is computed there are from thirty thousand to forty thousand pillars, the tallest measuring about thirty-three feet. Among other wonders, there is also the Giant's Well, a spring of pure fresh water, forcing its way up between the joints of two of the columns—the Giant's Chain, the Giant's Bagpipes, the Giant's Theatre, and time Giant's Organ, the latter a beautiful colonnade of pillars, one hundred and twenty feet long, so called from its accurate resemblance to the pipes of an organ."

The same tourist from whom I have quoted, gives an amusing account of his stumbling upon a legendary explanation of the building of the Causeway. "In lately travelling, "he says," from Dublin to Belfast, we happened to enjoy as companions, a 'traveller' for a Manchester firm, and a rough, ruddy-faced farmer from the black north. The conversation turned on the Causeway. 'Oh,' exclaimed the rider, 'I was there last spring; I just looked at it on my way from Colerain to Ballycastle—never was so disappointed in my life—terrible cold coast, wind from the north-east enough to cut you in two—dreadful hungry place, I assure you, gentlemen, not a morsel to satisfy the cravings of nature, not even a tree to shelter the poor goats that were glad

Scene on the Giants Causeway

to hide themselves under the precipices. Irishmen should come and see our Giant's Causeway, the railway! that's a stupendous work, gentlemen!'

"The wrath of the man of Antrim was roused. 'You Englishmen,' said he, 'are all for the making of money. Why, man alive, if a dacent place that I know about is paved with gold, some of yees would be after getting a pickaxe to pocket the paving-stones. Didn't ould Fin M'Coul all as one as make that Causeway for the honour and glory of Ireland? and what's the use of talking about your dirty bit of a railway. Sure, arn't they going to have one from Dublin to Dunleary? We'll bate the conceit out of yees by and bye!"

"Mr. Trusselbags adjusted his neckcloth, and, with a knowing wink to me, rejoined; 'And pray, my good fellow, for what purpose did this Fin M'Coul make the Causeway? Perhaps you can tell us.'

"With all my heart. You see, sir, a big Scotch giant, one Benandonner, used to brag that he would lick Fin M'Coul any day. And he used to go over the Highlands, crowing like a cock on its own dunghill, that all he wanted was a fair field and no favour. So, by my souks, Fin M'Coul went to the King of Ireland, ould Cormac, may be ye've heard of him, (there was no grand-jury presentments in them days,) and he says to his majesty, says he, I want to let Benandonner come over to Ireland without wetting the sole of his shoe, and if I don't lather him as well as ever he was lathered in his life, it's not myself that's in it. So Fin M'Coul got leave to build the Causeway, and sure he did, all the road clane and nate, to Scotland. And Benandonner came over wid his broadsword and kilt, and right glad he was to get a dacent excuse for laying his own country. He was bate, of coorse, though he stuck up like a Trojan; and then he settled in the place, and became obedient to King Cormac, and got a purty, dacent girl to his wife, and they say the great Earls of Antrim are descended from them.' "

A writer in one of the numbers of the Christian Examiner, gives an account of a curious phenomenon observed, while rowing in a boat along the Causeway. "We had now," he says, "got into the centre of the bay, and could observe the whole bending of the shore from Bangore promontory to Portrush point, and while, as was natural, our eyes were principally directed towards the CAUSEWAY, to which we were approaching, and asking concerning this place and that, one of the men said, 'Look, gentlemen, there are the merry dancers on Portrush Point!' and on looking in that direction we all observed this most extraordinary phenomenon. Portrush Point, which, a few moments before presented a very unmeaning appearance, and was certainly the least interesting object on the coast, now assumed a most commanding aspect. A lofty mountain arose instead of a long flat—a conical peak like Croagh Patrick, rugged rocks with their serrated points pierced the clouds; and instantly all this vanished, and a beautiful softly-swelling wooded hill presented itself, a lofty embattled castle, a broad belt of full-grown wood, green lawns, and all the decorations of a nobleman's domain. You might conceive yourself at once transported to Plymouth harbour, and that you saw Mount Edgecombe before you. And, again, as by talismanic touch, all this disappeared, and on a plain two embattled armies seemed to oppose one another, and dense masses of troops, horse and foot, stood motionless as if in suspense for the battle signal, and now they rushed together, and the opposing battalions closed on each other, and a loose, shapeless cloud rose up, as if it were the mingled dust and smoke ascending from the conflict; and all at once, the whole vision dissolved away, and nothing was seen but the low, uninteresting peninsula of Portrush. I had never before heard of this phenomenon appearing on the coast of Ireland. I had read something like it as occurring in the Straits of Messina, and, on the present occasion, particularly as taken by surprise, my astonishment and delight cannot be expressed. So vivid was the delusion—so strange, so beautiful, so magnificent was the optical representation, that were I in the remotest part of Ireland, and assured that I would see it again, I should, without hesitation, put my foot in the coach, and, at almost any sacrifice of time or trouble, attend to witness it again. The boatmen assured me, it was by no means of frequent occurrence. Some of them declared they never saw it before, and he who was best acquainted with its appearance said, that it required a concurrence of wind, tide, and weather that did not often coincide to produce it."

Proceeding eastward toward the promontory of Bangore , the traveller comes to the PLEASKIN CLIFF, commonly said to be the most beautiful promontory in the world. The natural basaltic rock here lies immediately under the surface. About twelve feet from the summit, the rock begins to assume a columnar tendency, and is formed into ranges of rudely columnar basalt, in a vertical position, exhibiting the appearance of a grand gallery, whose columns measure sixty feet in height. This basaltic colonnade rests upon a bed of coarse, black, irregular rock, sixty feet thick, abounding in air-holes. Below this coarse stratum is a second range of pillars, forty-five feet high, more accurately columnar, and nearly as accurately formed as the Causeway itself. The cliff appears as though it had been painted, for effect, in various shades of green, vermillion rock, red-ochre, grey lichens, &c.; its general form so beautiful, its storied pillars, tier over tier, so architecturally graceful—its curious and varied stratifications supporting the columnar ranges; here the dark brown amorphous basalt—there the red-ochre, and below that again the slender but distinct lines of wood-coal; all the edges of its different stratifications tastefully varied, by the hand of vegetable nature, with grasses, ferns, and rock plants—in the various strata of which it is composed, sublimity and beauty having been blended together in the most extraordinary manner.

West of the Causeway lie one or two very remarkable caves, one of them accessible both by land and sea, the other, the CAVE OF DUNKERRY, accessible by water alone. The entrance to the latter assumes the appearance of a pointed arch, and is remarkably regular. The boatmen are singularly expert in entering these caves. They

Plaiskin Cliff, near the Giants Causeway

Dunkerry Cave

bring the boat's head right in front, and, watching the roll of the wave, quickly ship their oars, and float in majestically upon the smooth heave of the sea. The depth of Dunkerry Cave has not been ascertained, for the extremity is so constructed, as to render the management of a boat there impracticable and dangerous. Besides, from the greasy character of the sides of the cave, the hand cannot he serviceable in forwarding or retarding the boat. Along the sides is a bordering of marine plants, above the surface of the water, of considerable breadth. The roof and sides are clad over with green conferv, which give a very rich and beautiful effect; and not the least curious circumstance connected with a visit to this subterraneous apartment, is the swelling of the water within. It has been frequently observed, that the swell of the sea upon this coast is at all times heavy, and as each successive wave rolls into the cave, the surface rises so slowly and awfully, that a nervous person would be apprehensive of a ceaseless increase in the elevation of the waters until they reached the summit of the cave. Of this, however, there is not the most distant cause of apprehension, the roof being sixty feet above high-water mark. The roaring of the waves in the interior is distinctly heard but no probable conclusion can be arrived at from this as to the depth. It is said, too, that the inhabitants of some cottages, a mile removed from the shore, have their slumbers frequently interrupted in the winter's nights by the subterranean sounds of Dunkerry Cave. The entrance is very striking and grand, being twenty-six feet in breadth, and enclosed between two natural walls of dark basalt, and the visitor enjoys a ranch more perfect view of the natural architecture at the entrance, by sitting in the prow with his face to the stern, as the boat returns.

Of the other cave, an agreeable writer, whom I have before quoted, says, "When the day is fine, and the sun shining in all its lustre,, it is truly a grand and interest— ing sight. The sublime massiveness of the surrounding rocks—the curious stainings and colours of the sides of the roof—the musical cadence of the echoes—the dark mysteriousness of its retiring recesses, contrasted with the brilliancy of all without, and the slow, solemn heave of the translucent water, bearing idly on its surface the purple sea-star, and revealing, fathoms—deep below, multitudinous vegetations, covering its rocky bottom. I do not wonder that mythology had peopled such caverns with naiads, and goddesses, and tritons, nor did I cease to expect that our communicative guide would be able to annex to such a spot as this some legendary lore. At the same time I confess I did not find him in this instance quite fortunate. To be sure, he told us how two bold sea-captains, by name Willoughby and Middleton, not content with witnessing the manifold echoes of a common musket, must needs bring into this cavern a six-pounder, and how, on discharging it, an immense mass of the roof fell in, whereby their lives were placed in imminent peril. He also told us of a piper, who, one day, when the tide was out, wandered into the furthest recesses, no doubt curious to ascertain, in these secret solitudes, the peculiar sound of his romantic instrument. Engaged in the delights of his sweet craft, he wandered on and on, none could tell whither, for he never came out; nor were there ever any tidings of him, save that while the people were at prayers in the church of Ballintoy, and just as the clerk was about giving out the first Psalm, the sound of bagpipes was heard under—ground and tunes were recognized rising up from beneath, which were rather unsuitable to the solemnity of the place.

VII.

A VISIT to the Causeway is rather a leg-weary business, and admiration is well known to travellers in Italy to be the most effective of tonics. on emerging from the cave and climbing the cliff once more, we were not sorry to find our car-man ready to take us to Bushmills, a mile distant, where we found a most excellent inn, and breakfasted on salmon, very much to the refreshment of our enthusiasm. The day was bright and summery, and in high good spirits we mounted our car towards noon, and took our way to DUNLUCE CASTLE. It was but a mile or two from Bushmills, and before we were well settled in our seats, this finest of ruined castles (I think the most picturesque ruin I ever saw) broke upon us, like an apparition, in the road. Dunluce stands on a perpendicular and insulated rock, the entire surface of which is so completely occupied by the edifice, that the external walls are in continuation with the perpendicular sides of the rock. The walls of the building were never very lofty, but from the great area which they enclosed, contained a considerable number of apartments. One small vaulted room is said to be inhabited by a *Bonshee,* whose chief occupation is sweeping the floor. This story originates in the fact, that the floor is at all times as clean as if it had just then been swept; but this difficulty can be explained without the introduction of Maw Roi, the fairy, by the fact, that the wind gains admittance through an aperture on a level with the floor, and thus preserves the appearance of cleanliness and freedom from dust, just now described. In the north-eastern end is a small room, actually projecting over the sea, the rocky base having fallen away, and from the door of this apartment there is a giddy view of the sea beneath. The rock on which the castle stands is not surrounded by water, but is united at the bottom of the chasm to the main land by a ledge of rock a little higher than the surface of the ocean. The castle was entered by a bridge formed in the following manner:—two parallel walls, about eight feet asunder, thrown across the chasm, connected the rock with the main land. Upon these planks were laid

Dunluce Castle

crosswise for the admission of visitors, and removed immediately after the passage was effected. At present but one of the walls remains, about thirteen inches in thickness, and the only pathway to the castle is along its summit, over the awful rocky chasm. The distance at which the other parallel wall was placed may be perceived by the traces of its adhesion to the opposite rock.

On the main land, close to the castle, a second collection of similar buildings are seen, erected at a later period by one of the Antrimn family, in consequence of the giving way of an apartment on the verge of the rock. Beneath the cliff on which the castle stands, is a cave penetrating completely through from the sea to the rocky basin on the land-side of the castle. It may be entered by a small aperture in the south end, and at low-water there is a good deal of the flooring uncovered, which consists of large round stones; this form is the consequence of the action of the waves. The sides and roof are of basalt, possessing merely the usual characters; here also is a very remarkable echo when the surface of the water is unruffled.

Though all accurate knowledge of the date of erection, and name of the founder of Dunluce Castle are completely lost, yet the history of its proprietors for the last few centuries is extremely interesting, and affords a very characteristic account of the state of society in the feudal periods of the fifteenth and sixteenth centuries. It has been conjectured that De Courcy, Earl of Ulster, originally founded this castle, but the architecture is not of so very ancient a date. In the fifteenth century it was held by the English; at which period it seems to have fallen into the hands of a noble English family, called by Camden, M'Willis, from whose hands it passed into the possession of the M'Donalds of the Isles, and to their descendants it belongs to this day.

About the year 1580, Colonel M'Donald, brother to James, Lord of Cantyre, came into Ireland with a band of men to assist Tyrconnell against the great O'Neill, with whom he was then at war. In passing through the Rout, he was hospitably received and entertained by M'Quillan, the lord and master of the Rout and Kilconery. At that time there was a war between M'Quillan and the men of Killiteragh beyond the Bann. On the day when Colonel M'Donald was taking his departure to proceed on his journey to Tyrconnell, M'Quillan, who was not equal in war to his savage neighbours, called together his militia, or *gallogloghs,* to revenge his affronts over the Bann; and M'Donald, thinking it uncivil not to offer his services that day to M'Quillan, after being so kindly treated, sent one of his gentlemen with an offer of assistance in the field. M'Quillan was well pleased with the offer, and declared it to be a perpetual obligation on him and his posterity. So M'Quillan and the Highlanders went against the enemy; and where there was a cow taken from M'Quillan's people before, there were two taken back; after which M'Quillan and Colonel M'Donald returned with great prey, and without the loss of a man.

Winter then drawing nigh, M'Quillan gave Colonel M'Donald an invitation to stay with him at his castle of Dunluce, advising him to settle there until the spring, and to quarter his men up and down the Rout. This M'Donald gladly accepted; but in the course of the winter seduced M'Quillan's daughter, and privately married her; upon which ground the M'Donalds afterwards founded their claim to the M'Quillan's territories. The men were quartered two and two throughout the Rout; that is to say, one of M'Quillan's gallogloghs and a Highlander in every tenant's house. It so happened that the galloglogh, besides his ordinary mess, was entitled to a noggin of milk as a privilege. This the Highlanders esteemed to be a great affront, and at last one of them asked his landlord, "Why don't you give me milk as you give the other?" The galloglogh immediately made answer, "Would you, a Highland beggar as you are, compare yourself to me or any of M'Quillan's gallogloghs?" The poor tenant, heartily tired of both, said, "Come, gentlemen, I'll open the door, and you may go and fight it out in the field, and he that has tlme victory let him take milk and all to himself." The galloglogh was soon slain in the encounter, after which the Highlander came in and dined heartily. M'Quillan's gallogloghs assembled to demand satisfaction; and, in a council which was held, where the conduct of the Scots was debated, their great power, and the disgrace arising from the seduction of M'Quillan's daughter, it was agreed that each galloglogh should kill his comrade Highlander by night, and their lord and master with them; but M'Donald's wife discovered the plot, and told it to her husband. So the Highlanders fled in the night-time, and in attempting to escape into Scotland, were driven into the Island of Raghery.

In 1642, Dunluce Castle was the scene of a villainous act of treachery. In the month of April of that year, General Munroe made a visit to the Earl of Antrim at this castle, and was received with many expressions of joy, and honoured with splendid entertainments; and further, the earl offered him assistance of men and money to reduce the country to tranquillity. But Munroe, when this was over, seized on the earl's person, and put the other castles of his lordship into the hands of the Marquis of Argyle's men. He conveyed the earl to Carrickfergus, and imprisoned him in the castle, but from this he soon effected his escape, and withdrew to England.

There are, of course, numerous traditions connected with Dunluce, but I had not time to inquire them out among the people, and it has been well done by that fruit-gathering traveller, Cesar Otway, whose description of a visit to Dunluce I subjoin.

"It was as fine a morning as ever fell from heaven when we landed at Dunluce, not a cloud in the sky, not a wave on the water; the brown basaltic rock, with the towers of the ancient fortress that capped and covered it—all its grey bastions and pointed gables lay pictured on the incumbent mirror of the ocean; every thing was reposing—every thing so still, that nothing was heard but the flash of our oars and the song of Alick M'Mullen, to break the silence of the sea. We rowed round this peninsular fortress, and then entered the fine cavern that so curiously perforates the rock, and opens its dark arch to admit our boat. He must, indeed, have a mind cased up in all the commonplace of dull existence, who would not while within this cavern and under this fortress, enter into the associations connected with the scene; who could not hold communings with the 'Genius Soci' Fancy I know called up for *me* the war-boats and the foremen, who, either issued from, or took shelter in this sea-cave. I imagined, as the tide was growling amidst the far recesses, that I heard the moanings of chained captives, and the huge rocks around must be bales of plunder, landed and lodged here, and I took an interest, and supposed myself a sharer in the triumphs of the fortunate, and the helplessness of the captive, while suffering under the misery that bold bad men inflicted in troubled times, when the M'Quihlans of the Rout, and the M'Donnels of the Glyns, either gained or lost this debatable strong-hold. Lauding in this cavern, we passed up through its land side entrance towards the ruin: the day had become exceeding warm, and going forth from the coolness of the cave into the sultry atmosphere, we felt doubly the force of the sun's power—the sea-birds had retreated to their distant rocks—the goats were panting under the shaded ledges of the cliffs—the rooks and chaughs, with open beaks and drooping wings, were scattered over the downs, from whose surface they arose with a quivering undulating motion; we were all glad for a time to retire to where, under the shade of the projected cliff, a cold, clear spring offered its refreshing waters.

"Reader, surely you cannot be at a loss for a drawing or print of Dunluce Castle; take it now I pray you in hand, and observe with me the narrow wall that connects the ruined fortress with the main land; see how this wall is perforated, and without any support from beneath, how it hangs there, bearing time and tempest, and still needing no power of arch, simply by the power of its own cemented material; the art of man could not make such another self-supported thing, it is about eighteen inches broad, just the path of a man, do not fear to cross it, rest assured it wont tumble with you, it has borne many a better man, so come on, who's afraid?—'I really cannot bring myself to venture,' was the reply of both my companions. 'Sit ye down then, ye giddy-headed cockneys, and bask your day in the sun, Alick and I will step across and visit the Baushee.' So, with the greatest ease, we tripped across: Carrick-a-Rede is seventy times more fearful. ' And now, Mr. M'Mullen, as you and I have this old place to ourselves, come show me every thing, and tell me all about it.' ' With the greatest pleasure in life, sir" says Alick, 'for it gave me joy to see a gentleman like you, hopping like a jackdaw over that bit of a wall; and indeed many a good one comes here like yon, gentleman and lady, who I believe have their skulls full of what they call nerve, instead of *sensible* steady brains.' 'Well, Alick, beyond a doubt this is a fine old place.' 'Why then, sir, it's you that may say that, for many a battle and bloody head was about it in good old fighting times, when fighting and fun were all one in merry Ireland.' 'Come then, Alick, tell me some of this fighting fun that the good old happy people you speak of enjoyed here in Dunluce.' 'And does it become me to tell your honour of the wars of Dunluce? why I thought as how with your black coat and spatterdashes, you might be a scholar—besides, as you intend to see the Causeway, and the Cave, and Pleaskin, it may be your honour wont have time to hear all I have to tell you about the M'Quillans and M'Donnells, and Surly Boy and Captain Merriman—but, at any rate, I'll tell you, in short, about the boat-race, whereby this castle was won and lost, when the M'Quillans and M'Donnells contended for it in the presence of the King of Scotland, and agreed to leave their right to the issue of a row from Isla to Dunluce—he who first touched the land was to have the castle as his prize; so they started on just such a day as this, wind and wave agreed to sit still and let the oarmen have fair play—and to be sure it was they who rowed for honour and glory as for life, and the M'Quillans prayed enough for St. Patrick, and the M'Donnells to Columkill of the Isles, and neither, you may be sure, spared the *spirits*—for it's hard to say whether John Highlandman, or Pat of the green hills, is better at that work; but, at any rate, on they came, beautiful and abreast, like two swans cutting, with white bosoms, the green waters; and now it was pull Paddy, and now it was pull Sandy, and none on the shore could tell for their lives which was foremost; but at any rate, the Irish boys shouted enough, and prayed enough for the M'Quillans; and now, sir, they were within stone's throw, and now almost within oar's length , when what do you think my Scotchman did? For never put it past canny Sawney, all the world over, for getting the better of others; and if he fails at fair beating, he'll not pass by cheating: so it was here. The two chiefs were each at their boat's bow, and M'Quillan had his long arm outstretched, and M'Donnell held his lochabar axe in his hand, and all at once laying his left wrist on the gunwale before him, he slashed at it with his hatchet; severed it at a blow, and while it was spinning out blood, he flung it with all his force against the rock; and do you see where that sea-parrot is now perched, on that bird's-nest ledge, there the bleeding hand lay, and the red mark is said to be there, though I have never seen it, unto this very day.

'Huzza *for* M'Donnell, Dunluce is our own,
For spite of M'Quillan, the castle is won.'

Such was the cry of the Scotchmen as they landed, and so it was that even the Irish gave it in favour of the foreigner, who, at the expense of his limb, won the prize, and long and many a day the Scotchmen held it, until lie became a good Irishman, and to this hour you may see a bloody hand painted in the middle of Lord Antrim's coat-of-arms."

Londonderry

VIII.

FROM Dunluce we travelled .southward to Coleraine, a remarkably neat and pretty town, and thence by Limavady to Londonderry, a part of Ireland abounding in rural beauty, and wearing more the look of England than any other that I had seen. From the hill by which we descended to Derry, the view was like one of an illuminated city, several large factories, with a bright light streaming from every window, standing opposite to us, and the hill within the walls showing apparently a light in every house. We entered the city over a bridge, built by a townsman of my own, Lemuel Cox, of Boston, United States, another of whose bridges I had crossed at Wexford. This over the Foyle is a wooden structure, one thousand and sixty-two feet in length, and considered here a great curiosity.

Londonderry occupies the sides and summit of a steep promontory, almost penin-sulated by a noble sweep of the smooth, deep Foyle, whose waters glide majestically on towards a broad estuary, where they are mingled with the ocean. The old town is included within the walls, and entered by the ancient gates, still entire, while the gradual increase of population and commercial prosperity have occasioned an extension of the city avenues to a distance beyond them. The steepness of the ascent from the water's edge to the summit of the hill, particularly up the Ship-Quay Street, is so great, as to be nearly impracticable by carriages, or, at all events, to be highly dangerous; and they tell a tale of the respectable inhabitants of this old-fashioned street, that when they visited each other in the winter-season, their passage was accomplished by self-moving sledges; a form turned upside down having once conveyed a group returning from an evening party, in safety and with expedition, to the foot of the hill. The Diamond, so the central square, or marketplace, is generally called, is the regulating point from which the other streets emanate; and here the town-hall and reading-rooms are erected. Some of the buildings appropriated to the public business are handsome; all are spacious and convenient. The court house, a fine elevation in the Grecian style, is after a design by Bowden; the principal front displays much grandeur and beauty, but the lateral entrances and fronts are in a very inferior manner. The old palace, the grammar school, and lunatic asylum, possess no architectural elegance , but are built after liberal and useful designs. on the apex of the hill of Derry stands the church, which is both parochial and capitular: it is a venerable structure, in the pointed style, with finials and graduated battlements, but, incongruously enough as a cathedral, finished with a tower and spire. Within are preserved standards, and trophies, and other relics of the bravery of their ancestors, and of the memorable defence made by the citizens.

Early in the reign of James I., a considerable part of the province of Ulster was vested in the crown, by the attainder of the Roman Catholic families of distinction, and a colonization of the forfeited estates was then suggested to the king by the lord-treasurer, Salisbury. His majesty, conceiving the city of London to be the best qualified to effect so great an object, on the 28th of January, 1609, permitted an agreement to be entered into, between commissioners for the city, and the lords of the privy council, whereby the towns and liberties of Derry and Coleraine, with the "salmon and eel fisheries of the rivers Bann and Foyle, and all other kind of fishing in the river Foyle, so far as the river floweth, and in the Bann to Lough Neagh, should be in perpetuity to the city;"that the liberties of Londonderry should extend three miles every way; with numerous other privileges and conditions, included in twenty-seven articles of agreement. In 1613, the society of the new plantation of Ulster was incorporated; and from this date Derry has been the property of the city of London.

In the wars of William and James, Derry, from the number of its Protestant inhabitants, was looked on with suspicion by one party, and partiality by the other. Hither the Protestants of the north retreated as to a sanctuary; and the improvident precaution of Lord Tyrconnel, in withdrawing Mountjoy's regiment from the place, produced the unhappy effect of augmenting the breach between the contending parties. The lord-deputy had directed that Lord Antrim's regiment, consisting wholly of Roman Catholics, men "tall and terrible of aspect,"should immediately take up their quarters here, and overcome the Protestants of the north; but dilatoriness in the execution of his measures, and the advance of the ferocious-looking body being communicated to the citizens, by Philips, of Newtown Lima-vady, the gates were closed against the advanced guard that had arrived within three hundred yards of the walls.

In the history of the siege of Derry, the particulars of the closing of the gates are thus given. "A letter was dropt at Cumber, in the county of Down, where the Earl of Mount Alexander resided, dated December 3d, 1688, informing that nobleman, that on Sunday, the 9th of that month, the Irish throughout the whole island, in pursuance of an oath which they had taken, were to rise and massacre the Protestants, men, women, and children, and warning him to take particular care of himself, as a captain's commission would be the reward of the man who would murder him." There was no name subscribed to this letter, and the bad writing and low style of it, seemed to argue that it was penned by one of the lowest of the natives.

A copy of this letter was sent by William Coningham, Esq., from Belfast, enclosed in one of his own, to George Canning, Esq., of Garvagh, in the county of Londonderry. Mr. Canning, whose father had been cruelly murdered at his own house in that place, on the commencement of the massacre of 1641, sent this letter with the utmost expedition to Alderman Tomkins, in Derry, according to the strict injunctions of Mr. Coningham A gentleman meeting with this messenger on the way, was informed of the contents of the despatches, and sent the information to George Philips, of Newtown Limavady, on the 6th of December, on which day a part of the Earl of Antrim's new regiment arrived there on its way to Londonderry. Mr. Philips, then in his ninetieth year, with a promptness to be expected in a veteran highly distinguished through the whole of the preceding civil wars, sent a messenger at midnight to the city, with an account of what had been communicated to him, and to acquaint his friends there what description of guests they were likely to have on the ensuing day. He wrote to them, that instead of six or eight companies of Irish Papists and Scottish Highlanders of the same religion, as had been reported, this regiment consisted of about double the number, attended by a multitude of women and boys.

At an early hour next morning, Mr. Philips sent another messenger to Londonderry, expressing his increased apprehension of the consequences of suffering this regiment to enter the city, and advising the citizens to look to their safety. The messenger, who was charged with the delivery of the letter, told them, that he had left some of the foremost companies within two miles of the town, the rest being on their way.

The Protestant inhabitants were terrified; several of them assembled in groups through the streets. The APPRENTICE BOYS, with a mob of the lower orders along with them, muttered something about shutting the gates; they got some private encouragement to do so at first, but that was soon retracted, and the minds of all the men of weight fluctuated in a miserable doubt of the most prudent course to take. In the meantime two companies of the unwelcome regiment arrived at the waterside, commanded by a lieutenant and an ensign. The officers, leaving their men there, were ferried over, and waited on the deputy-mayor and the sheriffs, with their authority for demanding admission. John Buchannan, the deputy, a man secretly devoted to the interest of James, had no objection to give the regiment the most honourable reception; but Horace Kennedy, one of the sheriffs, had given the APPRENTICE BOYS a secret hint during the preceding night, and they were at hand, prepared to shut the gates against the regiment. While they were in some consultation with each other on the subject, the Irish soldiers, impatient at the delay of their officers, or having, it is thought, some intimation of the nature of the reception intended for them, and a strong desire to frustrate it, crossed the river, and appeared on the landing-place, about three hundred yards from the ferry-gate. The young men of the city observing this, about eight or nine of them, whose names deserve to be preserved in letters of gold, viz., HENRY CAMPSIE, WILLIAM CROOKSHANKS, ROBERT SHERRARD, DANIEL SHERRARD, ALEXANDER IRWIN, JAMES STEWARD, ROBERT MORRISON, ALEXANDER CONINGHAM, SAMUEL HUNT, with JAMES SPIKE, JOHN CONINGHAM, WILLIAM CAIRNS, SAMUEL HARVEY, and Some others who soon joined them, ran to the main-guard, Seized the keys, after a slight opposition, came to the ferry-gate, drew up the bridges and locked the gate; Lord Antrim's soldiers having advanced within sixty yards of it. They ran to Secure the other three gates, and having left guards at each of them, assembled in the market-place.

Eleven days King James continued his assaults with repeated mortifications, and withdrew from the camp with peevishness, observing, that an English army would have brought him the town piecemeal in half that time. The protraction of the siege gave birth to enemies not previously thought of,—famine and disease; these had just begun to aid the besieger, when a fleet hove in sight, with troops and provisions, to assist the reformed cause in Ireland. The enemy, taking advantage of the apparent inactivity of the commander, threw a boom across the Foyle, and interrupted the navigation.

The situation of the besieged from this period, became truly deplorable, but the resolution and bravery of its garrison, proved equal to those of the most devoted men that we read of in the history of any nation. Their determination seemed to acquire strength from the increased misery: and, amidst famine and death, one of their governors, Baker, failing from fatigue, they threatened instant destruction to the man who should first advise a surrender. Rosen, who conducted the siege, gave them until the 1st of July to consider; upon which day, finding the garrison still obstinate, he drove a miserable number of Protestants, of all ages and sexes, gathered from the surrounding districts, beneath the walls, who, with true Roman fortitude, and like so many Reguluses, besought their countrymen, on bended knees, and with outstretched arms, to disregard their cries, their tortures, and their deaths, and persevere to defend themselves against the basest and most cruel of enemies. The townsmen now erected gallowses on the walls, and threatened to execute their prisoners, if their wretched countrymen were not suffered to escape; but Rosen persevered, and famine and massacre pursued their cold and devastating way. The Protestant Bishop of Meath now boldly remonstrated with King James, upon the inhuman massacre of the unoffending victims without the walls; to which his majesty coolly replied, "That such severities were usual in foreign service;" but ordered the sufferers to be released.

Time had now almost effected for the enemy what their military skill and courage were unequal to; the flesh of horses, dogs, and vermin now constituted the only sustenance of the besieged, and it was calculated that of this miserable food a supply of a few days was all that could be obtained. In this extremity, Walker's courage and presence of mind never for an instant deserted him; he harangued his brave companions at the crossways, and in his sacred pastoral character addressed them from the pulpit, imploring them to place a firm reliance upon the Almighty Disposer of events. At this critical moment, Kirk, accompanied by his fleet, reappeared below the town, and manifested a determination to attempt its relief. Two provision-ships convoyed by the Dartmouth frigate, approached the city, within view of the half-famished garrison that manned the walls, and reached the boom, the eventful spot, under a heavy fire of musketry, and discharge of cannon from the enemy. All eyes were now intent; the arm of the soldier was suspended for a moment from its work of destruction, while he hearkened to the heavy sound of the victualling-ship striking against the boom, the final proclamation of death or victory. She dashed with giant strength against the barrier, and broke it in two; but from the violence of the shock, rebounded and ran upon the river's bank. The satisfaction of the enemy was displayed by an instantaneous burst of tumultuous joy: they ran with disorder to the shore, prepared to board her, when the vessel, firing a broadside, was extricated by the shock, and floated out nobly into the deep again. During the short interval of these momentous events, the feelings of the besieged can only be compared to the criminal—tried, condemned, reprieved: they underwent the trial, they prepared for their sentence with firmness, and they bore the reprieve with the humility that might be expected to belong to such bravery and resolution.

Upon this happy relief the enemy raised the siege and marched to the southward. Two thousand three hundred of the garrison perished in battle, or by famine, days.

The walls of Derry are in high preservation, and form a most agreeable promenade of, perhaps, a mile in circumference. We walked around them in twenty minutes. There is no street around the interior of the walls, but the houses are in many places backed against them. The view over the Foyle and the country beyond, from that part on which stands the PILLAR erected to the memory of the heroic clergyman, WALKER, is exceedingly fine. Walker's Pillar is a Doric column, eighty feet in height, and finished with a cupola, surmounted by a statue of the patriot, with his arm outstretched, the base of the column surrounded by the cannon used in the defence of the city. Derry is a clean and handsome town, with a general hook of thrift and order. We saw no beggars in the streets, and no signs of the extreme poverty which disfigures the aspect of most towns in Ireland.

The road from Derry to Enniskillen follows the Foyle for a considerable distance, and a most lovely river it is—the deficiency of wood on its shores alone proving an exception to the variety of its beauties. Coasting the northern side of Lough Erne, the traveller arrives at Enniskillen, the chief town of Fermanagh, and the most important in the north-west district of Ireland. The town stands on an elevated island, formed by the branching of the river Erne, in its progress from the upper to the lower lake. Though it cannot boast of high antiquity, (says Fraser, in his excellent Guide Book to Ireland,) it may fairly claim what is of far more immediate importance—a comparatively well-built, well-arranged, and well-governed town, a steady trade, and many respectable inhabitants.

The environs of Enniskillen are very interesting, as well from the naturally rich and broken character of the country, as from its comparative improvement. Two miles

Walker's Pillar, – Walls of Londonderry

Devenish Island

from the town, in the entrance to the Lower Lough Erne, stands DEVENISH ISLAND, the most important of the "three hundred and sixty-five islands," said to dot the bosom of this lovely hake. Most of the other islets present a green and cheerful picture to the eye, but Devenish, says the author of The Story of a Life, "has a deader, duller, paler look than any other of the islets of the lake." A writer, in the Dublin Penny Journal demurs to this description, and declares the island to be remarkably fertile, and, of course, cheerful in its aspect. The ruins of a supposed monastery, of an ancient abbey, and the cell of a venerable man, stand near the centre of this lonely isle, while the tall shaft of the ancient pillar-tower raises its grey height" like a mountain of some patient and abiding grief."Around this place of silence and of ruin, reminiscences of mortality lie scattered, in a way but little grateful to the living; the rude stones that lie upon the graves around, so stained with weather, and time-decayed, and overgrown with rank-weeds, that they are scarcely approachable, and thus their legends are lost. The crypt of the founder stands roofless amidst this scene of decay, and the stone coffin that once enclosed his breast, is firmly buried in the earth beside it. There is a veneration, a religious feeling, or perhaps a superstition, attached to Devenish and its ruined piles. In no country of Europe is more tenderness expressed for the loss of relatives and kindred, or so much posthumous affection manifested in the respect paid to their remains. Perhaps it is imagined that those who flourished at an age nearer to the foundation of Christianity were necessarily more holy, and that the stream is sullied by the length of its course? Whatever be the cause, the veneration for ancient cemeteries, crosses, and ecclesiastical ruins, is unconfined.

The sadness of a funeral procession is so characteristic of this consecrated isle, which melancholy has marked peculiarly her own, that its introduction in the accompanying view does scarcely draw upon the imagination.

The insular position of the cemetery renders the funeral ceremony sometimes insecure. The sorrowing friends, accompanied by those who deplore, in strains both loud and long, the loss sustained by the surviving relative, proceed to some place of embarkation, and thence set sail, in barks of frail materials, for the holy isle. The antiquity of this custom, not only in Ireland but amongst the Romans, Greeks, and Hebrews, is indisputable. "The mourners go about the streets," has an obvious reference to persons analogous to the professional Keeners in Ireland. The Romans had their "prolificæmulieres," who, "with dishevelled hocks, led on the melancholy parade of death; and Homer frequently alludes to this ceremony in describing the, last rites of his most conspicuous heroes:

"The pious maids their mingled sorrows shed,
And mourn the living Hector as the dead."

and again,

> "Alternately they sing, alternate flow
> The obedient tears, melodious in their woe."

The funeral oration, or song, was anciently composed by the bard, who dwelt in the hall of the chieftains, and contained, in its elegiac numbers, a catalogue of the virtues of the deceased. "O why did he die, who had so many sons and fair daughters? O why did he die, who was lord of the hill and the dale, and the golden valley?" &c.; such wild effusions formerly, and even now, constitute the verbal portion of the elegiac lamentation, called "The Irish Cry."

The boats that navigate the smooth surface of Lough Erne, are seldom capable of conveying more than ten or twelve persons, and those that can be procured for hire are much less secure than others. Some twenty years since, a party, too numerous for a vessel of such dimensions and construction, embarked with the remains of one who, in life, had been dear to all around, to pay the last sad honour to his name. The reverend companion of their voyage advised and exhorted to lighten the bark, before they entered on the treacherously smiling surface of the deep, and finding all remonstrances vain, himself leaped out into the shallows and returned to shore. For a few minutes, and a few only, the incautious crew proceeded towards the island, when fate, enveloped in a gust of wind, struck suddenly against the boat, and hurried thirty poor victims into the depths of the lake.

The places of embarkation are the promontory of Portora, at the foot of the eminence on which the endowed school stands, and Tully Devinish on the southwest side. At this latter point, in an old orchard, is shown a rock of about four tons weight; thrown hither from the island by a famous friar, M'Comhal, the Friar of Devinish, the same who leaped also from his monastery over to Derry Inch.

A curious relic, called Molais's Bed, already mentioned, possesses virtues of an unique description, and is a prophetic touchstone of that one's future fate who has the intrepidity to make the experiment. This is done by reclining in the bed: some are relieved of pains in the back by the merit of the stone; and for those whose figures precisely fit to the dimensions, brighter prospects are reserved. The lid of the saint's coffin, a stone six feet two inches in length, lies at the eastern end of the lower church, and has hitherto been incorrectly noticed as the shaft of a cross.

Of the monastic remains, that called "The Upper Church" is the most perfect and the most modern, or probably has been re-edified at a later period. The basement story of the tower is grained, and in the ceiling are two apertures, coeval with the building, through which bell-ropes were formerly passed. A small pointed doorway leads to a spiral staircase, by which the battlements of the tower are reached. The masonry, sculpture it might almost be called, is very remarkable. The angles of the architraves being delicately fluted, and finished equally at top as at bottom, produce an effect both light and graceful. At the height of five feet from the floor, and adjoining the entrance to the belfry, is a mural tablet, bearing an inscription in ancient characters. There is a second doorway in the south wall, with an ornamental architrave, above which, in a canopied niche, were the arms of the founder, or of some benefactor to the priory. The stone used in the building of the tower is a beautiful gray limestone, susceptible of a high polish; one of the varieties found in the district adjoining the lake. The nunnery, or lower church, according to the local nomenclator, is of a more ancient date than the priory, and much more dilapidated. The eastern window, still perfect, is rudely executed, and divided into three compartments, with hancet heads, and banded on the inside; and in the southern wail are two circular-headed windows, of later construction, illuminating a baptistry just below them. The length of the church is eighty-six feet, a fact that in a few years more must be gathered exclusively from the records of its fate. The cell or crypt of the titular saint is wholly unroofed; the side-walls and gable indicate the strength of the cement used in their erection; and from the remnants of the stone roof yet visible, the ceiling appears to have been coved and separated by a void from an exterior angular roof, also of stone, in the manner of St. Revier's kitchen at Glendalough.

The religious institutions on Devinish were originally founded by Lasreau, also denominated St. Molaisse. Although a man of acknowledged piety, and eminent for learning, his biography is but imperfectly known. He was a native of Carberry, near Sligo, and the son of Natfraich. Educated in the celebrated seminary of Clonard, at an early age he withdrew to this island, where he erected a monastery that continued to be famous through many succeeding ages. He was established there previous to the departure of Columbkill from Ireland, in 567; he drew up a rule for his followers, received the visit of St. Aidus of Kildare and other holy men, and was so much esteemed that ecclesiastical writers have supposed, or pretended, that he sat for some time in the see of Chogher. The year of his death is not precisely ascertained; it is assigned by some authors to 563, by others postponed to 570; but the day of his decease, the 12th of September, being well attested, was for many years observed as a festival upon the island. The upper and lower churches possessed the advantage of a bell suspended in each, for many years, but at the suppression it was directed that they should be carried to the cathedral of Armagh. Boats were procured for the purpose, and the bell of the upper church was conveyed safely to shore, and carried to the place of its destination; but the boat in which was Molaisse's bell sunk, with its consecrated load, to the bottom, and has never since been seen or recovered. If a day can influence a deed, it may have done so in this instance, the 12th of September, St. Molaisse's festival, having been the date of the singular Occurrence. Miolaisse was succeeded by Natalis, the son of Ængusius, King of Munster, and we are informed that the monastery was plundered of its wealth by the Danes in the year 962.

87

The walls of Devenish tower are built of hewn stone; those in the external surface cut into truncated wedges, and some of those used within being neatly hollowed. The mortar has fallen away from the external surface of the walls, but within retains its general tenacity. At a height of twelve feet, above the doorway, there is a window with a pointed head, formed by two flags leaning against each other; and a little higher, but not in the same right line, is a second window exactly square. In the upper story are four windows, (usual in all the others,) corresponding to the cardinal points, and above each a key-stone, ornamented with a human head. A projecting course, resembling a block cornice, is carried along the top, and supports a conical cap, or roof, formed by gradually diminishing courses, terminated by a bell-shaped cap-stone. The inside is smooth, and exactly finished, having projecting rests, either meant to support floors, or occasioned by the gradual decrease in the thickness of the walls as they ascend.

Devinish occupies an area of seventy acres, of rich and productive soil. It sustains black cattle, whose approach is almost facilitated by the intervention of the waters through which they are compelled to swim, and sheep, carried over in flat-bottomed boats. A herdsman and his family constitute the population of this romantic abode, and the little cultivation their necessities require varies the tame character of the surface. Devinish had long been the property of the Rynd family, but by the union of the heiress of their house with the grandfather of Sir Edward Denny, of Kerry, it passed to the present owner, to whom it produces a rent of one hundred and ten pounds per annum.

IX.

THE road from Enniskillen and Devinish island to BALLYSHANON skirts the southern shore of Lough Erne, and by ascending the many hills which rise on the left, the traveller easily commands views of the lake, which more than repay him for his trouble. Ballyshannon is beautifully situated at the outlet of the river Erne into Donegal Bay, the *debouchure* into the tide inlet being accomplished over a ledge of rocks sixteen or eighteen feet above the level of the tide. It forms altogether a very beautiful bit of scenery. There is little to arrest the traveller or the antiquarian between this and Sligo, the road crossing the heads of the various small bays which indent the coast, and showing on one side constant views of the sea, and, on the other, the towering mountains of Benbulben, Benwesky and their brethren.

Sligo lies low, and appears at first to be situated upon a very broad and deep river, the dam across the Garwogue, (which runs through the town from Loch Gill,) preserving its waters from the refiux of the tide. Sligo has a remarkably fine neighbourhood of hills, which though wild are very picturesque; and dirty as the town is on examination, it forms one excellent feature of the romantic views got from the eminences around.

Sligo Abbey is an object well deserving the notice of the antiquary. It was originally erected by Maurice Fitzgerald, lord-justice, about the year 1252. In 1414 it was destroyed by fire, but very shortly afterwards re-erected in the present style of architecture. It is a picturesque ruin of very large dimensions, divided into several apartments. The first has a beautiful window of carved stone, under which is the altar, also of cut stone. Here are two ancient monuments, one bearing date 1616, and the other belonging to one of the O'Connor kings. The latter is in good preservation, the figures and inscriptions being very legible. At the top is represented our Saviour on the cross, and below this, in separate compartments, are the figures of O'Connor and his wife, kneeling, their hands lifted up in the act of supplication. The steeple or dome is still entire, supported upon a carved arch or cupola, the inside of which is also carved. Adjoining these are three sides of a square of beautifully carved little arches, of about four feet in height, which seem to have been anciently separated from each other, and probably formed cells for confession and penance. Almost all the little pillars are differently ornamented, and one in particular is very unlike the rest, having a human head cut on the inside of the arch. There are several vaults throughout the ruins, containing the remains of skulls, bones, and coffins. The abbey and yard are still used as a burying place.

Sligo is a busy little place, with a large retail trade, and an export trade larger than any other town in that part of Ireland. "It is," says Mr. Inglis, "a decidedly improving town. With the exception of two or three months in the year, there is employment for the people; and I did not observe many symptoms in the town of a pauper population. In the general aspect of the population, I perceived an improvement. I saw fewer tatters than I had been accustomed to; and fewer bare feet on market day, when all wear shoes and stockings who can. I observed also, that a large portion of the men wore clean linen shirts. The poor in Sligo are not increased in numbers by ejectments in the country. This is not the practice of the landlords here. They do not drive for rent or eject; they excuse the arrear, and allow the tenant to quit. This has the appearance, at first sight, of generosity, but it is, in fact, matter of necessity. Exorbitant rents are irrecoverable by driving, or by any other means. How much more rational it would he to lower rents and actually to receive the amount of one's rent-roll.

"I found at Sligo, a considerable change in the dress and manners of the people. Here, I could not discover any traces of Spanish origin. The women were no longer

Abbey of Sligo

seen with the hoods of their cloaks thrown over their heads; nor were the men seen with huge top-coats, as in the more south-western parts. The women wore caps and bonnets; and the girls nothing on their heads. There appeared to be much love of dress among all ranks; and among the lower classes, singular discrepancies. A well-dressed woman might be seen carrying in her arms a baby, decked out in muslin, lace, and ribbon, and by her side, a boy running with bare feet and ragged clothes; or a girl with a tattered gown, and without shoes and stockings, might display a fine shawl or a handsome frill."

We must quote also Mr. Inglis's account of his visit to LOCH GILL, (or Gilly.) "The chief object of attraction in the neighbourhood of Sligo, is Loch Gilly; a lake which is not sufficiently known to enjoy the reputation it deserves. I hired a boat at Sligo, and ascended the river, through a succession of beautiful scenery, to the domain of Hazlewood, the property of Mr. Wynn. This is a very lovely spot; the views of the lake, from a hundred points, are enchanting; and, in the disposition of lawn, wood, and shrubbery, taste and art have taken ample advantage of the gifts of nature. Finer evergreens I never saw in the most southern countries. The laurels and bays—grown into great trees—rivalled, if they did not surpass, those of Woodstock or Curraghmore; and here I again found the arbutus, not, indeed, quite equal in its perfections to the arbutus of Killarney, but not greatly its inferior; and giving to the scenery all that advantage of colouring, which is the boast of Killarney. The timber too, on this domain, is equal to almost any I have seen; and I often found myself pausing before some magnificent ash, oak, elm, or lime, throwing its deep shade across the green amphitheatre, which it seemed to have made for itself.

"But I must not forget Loch Gilly, which indeed it would be difficult to do. The domain of Hazlewood extends over that part of the banks of the river where it widens into the lake, and forms the first promontory. I embarked on the lake on the other side. Loch Gilly is about eight miles long, and from one to two broad, and in the character of beauty, will bear a comparison with any lake in Ireland. Its scenery is not stupendous—scarcely even anywhere bold; but it is ' beautiful exceedingly.' Its boundaries are not mountains, but hills of sufficient elevation to form a picturesque and striking outline. The hill sides, which in some places rise abruptly from the water, and which, in others, slope more gently, are covered to a considerable elevation with wood; and the lake is adorned with twenty-three islands, almost every one of them finely wooded. Here too, as well as on Hazlewood domain, I found that the arbutus is not confined to Killarney. The extent of Loch Gilly is highly favourable to its beauty. The eye embraces at once its whole length and breadth; the whole circumference of its shores; all their varieties and contrasts at once; all its islands. One charm is not lost in the contemplation of another, as in a greater lake: the whole is seen at once and enjoyed. I remained many hours on Loch Gilly, rowing here and there, or not moving at all; landing on its islands, two of which—Church Island and

Hazelwood and Lough Gill

Ballina

93

Cottage Island—are full of beauty; putting ashore in little coves and inlets; and visiting a holy well, two or three hundred yards from the banks, where I saw eleven devotees, four of whom went from station to station on their knees. I also visited a house of public resort near the lake, which the citizens of Sligo frequent on Sundays; and tasted their favourite beverage, called *scolteen;* composed of the following *elegant* ingredients—whiskey, eggs, sugar, butter, caraway seeds, and beer."

The only point of picturesque attraction between Sligo and Ballina, is the small town of Balisedare, four miles on the road. A very fine stream dashes in rapids past the town, and a narrow and beautiful bay here indents the shore just at their outlet. The remainder of the road is only interesting for its fine sea-views. The town of BALLINA is pleasantly situated on the banks of the Moy, which runs through the centre of the town, separating the counties of Mayo and Sligo. The town nearly forms the head of the estuary, which puts in from Killala Bay. The part of the town on the Sligo bank of the river is called Aeduaree, but generally is included under Ballina. From the excellent fishing the Moy affords, and its proximity to Loch Conn, Ballina is the resort of many anglers during the summer season. The Moy is said to be second only to the Bann for its salmon; and, by an anecdote told in the Dublin Penny Journal, its amphibious productions are yet more remarkable. "Not a hundred years ago;" the narrator goes on to say, "there lived on the banks of the noble river, above named, a person, who, though neither a very well educated man or profound naturalist, was, what is perhaps of more consequence in the eyes of the world, a wealthy farmer, and a justice of the peace for one of the neighbouring counties. It happened that his worship, who was in the frequent habit of visiting his numerous farms on this beautiful river, was obliged to cross a small stream in its vicinity, and, although on horseback, he was apprehensive of wetting a portion of his dress, out of which he took no small pride, and which he denominated his 'yalla-gaiters.' He therefore divested himself of those useful and ornamental appendages, and, placing them across the shoulder of his horse, pursued his way; and, after some time, arrived at the town of Ballina. Here, to his great horror, he discovered that he had dropped his 'yalla-gaiters,' and was pondering on the propriety of returning immediately in search of them, when his magisterial attention was attracted by a crowd of gaping rustics assembled round the caravan of an itinerant Polito, on which were depicted, in glowing colours, the various animals contained within. The magistrate forced his way into the crowd, and got in front of the caravan just as the showman, who had been delivering to the bystanders a long catalogue of attractions, summed all up by announcing a pair of fine alligators found on the banks of the Nile. 'Yalla-gaiters,' roared the magistrate. springing from his horse, and seizing the astonished showman by the collar, 'you rascal, them is my yalla-gaiters; give them up to me this minute, or if you don't I'll cram you into jail, for I'm a magistrate.' 'Your alligators,' says the astonished and affrighted showman, 'why them there alligators were found on the banks of the Nile.' 'Found on the banks of the devil, said the magistrate, 'none of your tricks upon me, you rascal: I say they were found on the banks of the Moy. and they are my yalla-garters.' All the protestatons of the poor showman as to his innocence would probably have been vain, had not a friend of the worthy justice, who happened to pass at the time, and who was better skilled in natural history, explained to him his mistake, on which he slipped a crown into the hand of the terrified showman, and desired him to say nothing about the matter."

By a drive toward Killala, upon the old road leading from Ballina to that place, the traveller finds, at a few miles distance, the ruins of ROSERK ABBEY, romantically situated among the waving hills which stretch for several miles below Ballina, on the river Moy. Two miles further on lie the better preserved ruins of the once magnificent ABBEY OF MOYNE, erected in 1461. Even these, however, are fast "toppling to their fall." The abbey of Moyne lies in a sequestered pastoral district on the banks of the Bay of Killala, and the convent was watered by a small rill, which, dipping into the granular limestone, rises again under the abbey. The more prominent associations with the country between Ballina and Killala, are those connected with the famous expedition of the French, under General Humbert, in the Irish rebellion. Humbert landed at Killala," with a thousand and thirty private soldiers and seventy officers, from three frigates, two of fifty-four, and one of thirty-eight guns, which had sailed from Rochelle on the 4th of the same month, with design to invade the county of Donegal, in which they were frustrated by contrary winds. The garrison of Killala, consisting of only fifty men, (of whom thirty were yeomen, the rest fencible soldiers of the Prince of Wales's regiment,) after a vain attempt to oppose the entrance of the French vanguard, fled with precipitation, leaving two of their number dead and their two officers prisoners, together with nineteen privates. To compensate, as far as possible by the vigour of his operations, for the smallness of his numbers, seems to have been an object with the French general. He sent, on the next morning, toward Ballina, a detachment, which, retreating from some picquet guards or reconnoitering parties of loyalists, led them to a bridge, under which lay concealed a serjeant's guard of French soldiers. By a volley from these, a clergyman who had volunteered on the occasion, and two carabineers were wounded, the first mortally. This clergyman was the Rev. George Fortescue, rector of Ballina. The French, advancing to this town, took possession of it in the night; the garrison retreating to Foxford, leaving one prisoner, a yeoman, in the hands of the enemy." From Ballina, Humbert pushed on to Castlebar, where he obtained a victory over the royalist troops, but he was arrested in his further progress by Lord Cornwallis, who, in a battle at Ballinamuck, completely destroyed or took prisoners the whole French force. The battle of Killala, which took place soon after, is thus described by one of the historians of the rebellion, who adds to it some curious traits of the French army and officers.

Reserk Abbey

Abbey of Moyne

"On the 23d of September, thirty-two days after the landing of the French army, and fifteen after its capture at Ballinamuck, a large body of troops arrived at Killala, under the command of Major-General Trench, who would have been a day or two later in his arrival, if he had not been hastened by a message from the Bishop of Killala, concerning the extreme danger of his family, and the rest of the loyalists in that town. The peaceful inhabitants of Killala were now to be spectators of a scene which they had never expected to behold—a battle—a fight, which no person who has seen it once, and possesses the feelings of a human creature, would choose to witness a second time. A troop of fugitives in full race from Ballina, women and children tumbling over one another to get into the castle, or into any house in the town where they might hope for a momentary shelter, continued for a painful length of time to give notice of the approach of an army.

"The rebels quitted their camp to occupy the rising ground close by the town, on the road to Ballina, posting themselves under the low stone walls on each side, in such a manner as enabled them with great advantage to take aim at the king's troops. They had a strong guard also on the other side of the town, toward Foxford , having probably received intelligence, which was true, that General Trench had divided his forces at Crosmalina, and sent one part of them, by a detour of three miles, to intercept the fugitives that might take that course in their flight. This last detachment consisted chiefly of the Keiry militia, under the orders of Lieutenant-Colonel Crosbie and Maurice Fitzgerald, the Knight of Kerry; their colonel, the Earl of Glandore, attending the general. It is a circumstance which ought never to be forgotten by the loyalists of Killala, that the Kerry militia were so wrought upon by the exhortations of these two spirited officers, to lose no time to come to the relief of their perishing friends, that they appeared on the south side of the town at the same instant with their fellows on the opposite side, though they had a league more of road to perform.

"The two divisions of the royal army were supposed to make up about twelve hundred men, and they had five pieces of cannon. The number of the rebels could not be ascertained. Many ran away before the engagement, while a very considerable number flocked into the town in the very heat of it, passing under the castle windows in view of the French officers on horseback, running upon death with as little appearance of reflection or concern, as if they were hastening to a show. About four hundred of these misguided men fell in the battle and immediately after it; whence it may be conjectured that their entire number scarcely exceeded eight or nine hundred." To account for so great a slaughter, we are to observe from the same excellent narrative from which I have already transcribed, that they met with death on every side where they attempted to escape; for, when driven from their post outside the town by a flanking fire of the soldiery, they fled in all directions, they were furiously pursued by the Roxburgh cavalry, who slaughtered many in the streets, and were either intercepted at the other end of the town by the Kerry militia, or directed their flight to the shore, where also "the fugitives were swept away by scores, a cannon being placed on the opposite side of the bay, which did great execution."

The pursuit of the cavalry into the town "was not agreeable to military practice, according to which it is usual to commit the assault of a town to the infantry; but here the general wisely reversed the mode, in order to prevent the rebels, by a rapid pursuit, from taking shelter in the houses of the towns-folk, a circumstance which was likely to provoke indiscriminate slaughter and pillage. The measure was attended with the desired success. A considerable number were cut down in the streets, and of the remainder but a few were able to escape into the houses. Some of the defeated rebels, however, did force their way into houses, and by consequence brought mischief upon the innocent inhabitants, without benefit to themselves. The first house, after passing the bishop's, is that of Mr. William Kirkwood; its situation exposed it on this occasion to peculiar danger, as it fronts the main street, which was raked entirely by a line of fire. A flying rebel had burst through the door, followed by six or seven soldiers; they poured a volley of musketry after him, which proved fatal to Mr. Andrew Kirkwood; a most loyal and respectable citizen, while he was rejoicing at the victory, and in the very act of shouting out 'God save the king!' In spite of the exertions of the general and his officers, the town exhibited all the marks of a place taken by storm. Some houses were perforated like a riddle: most of them had their doors and windows destroyed; the trembling inhabitants scarcely escaping with life, by lying prostrate on the floor. Nor was it till the close of next day that their ears were relieved from the horrid sound of muskets discharged every minute at flying and powerless rebels. The plague of war so often visits the world, that we are apt to listen to any description of it with the indifference of satiety; it is the actual inspection only that shows the monster in its proper and full deformity."

Intelligence, activity, temperance, and patience, to a surprising degree, appeared to be combined in the soldiery that came over with Humbert, together with the exactest obedience to discipline. Yet, if you except the grenadiers, they had nothing to catch the eye. Their stature for the most part was low, their complexion pale and sallow, their clothes much the worse for wear: to a superficial observer they would have appeared incapable of enduring any hardship. These were the men, however, of whom it was presently observed, that they could be well content to live on bread or potatoes, to drink water, to make the stones of the street their bed, and to sleep in their clothes, with no covering but the canopy of heaven. One half of their number had served in Italy under Buonaparte; the rest were of the army of the Rhine, where they had suffered distresses that well accounted for their thin persons and wan looks. Several of them declared, with all the marks of sincerity, that at the siege of Mentz, during the preceding winter, they had for a long time slept on the ground in holes made four feet deep under the snow. And an officer, pointing to his leather small-clothes, assured the bishop that he had not taken them off for a twelvemonth.

Humbert, the leader of this singular body of men, was himself as extraordinary a personage as any in his army. Of a good height and shape, in the full vigour of life, prompt to decide, quick in execution, apparently master of his art, you could not refuse him the praise of a good officer, while his physiognomy forbade you to hike him as a man. His eye, which was small and sleepy, (the effect, probably, of much watching,) cast a sidelong glance of insidiousness, and even of cruelty: it was the eye of a cat preparing to spring upon her prey. His education and manners were indicative of a person sprung from the lower orders of society, though he knew how (as most of his countrymen can do) to assume, where it was convenient, the deportment of a gentleman. For learning, he had scarcely enough to enable him to write his name. His passions were furious, and all his behaviour seemed marked with the characters of roughness and violence. A narrower observation of him, however, served to discover that much of this roughness was the result of art, being assumed with the view of extorting by terror a ready compliance with his commands. Of this truth the bishop himself was one of the first who had occasion to be made sensible, as has been already related.

The officer left by Humbert at Killala, in command, Lieutenant-colonel Charost, had attained to the age of five-and-forty. He was born in Paris, the son (as the writer was told) of a watchmaker in that city, who sent him over early to some connexions in St. Domingo, where he was fortunate enough to marry a wife with a plantation for her dowry, which yielded him, before the troubles, an income of two thousand pounds sterling per annum. By the unhappy war, which still desolates that island, he lost everything, even to his wife, and his only child, a daughter; they were taken on their passage to France, and sent away to Jamaica. His eyes would fill when he told the family that he had not seen these dear relatives for six years past, nor even had tidings of them for the last three years. On his return to France, he had embraced the military life, and had risen, by due degrees, to the rank which he now filled. He had a plain, good understanding. He seemed careless or doubtful of revealed religion, but said that he believed in God: was inclined to think there must be a future state, and was very sure that while he lived in this world, it was his duty to do all the good he could to his fellow creatures. Yet what he did not exhibit in his own conduct, he appeared to respect in others; for he took care that no noise nor disturbance should be made in the castle on Sundays, while the family and many Protestants from the town were assembled in the library at their devotions.

Bondet, the next in rank to the commandant, was a captain of foot, a native of Normandy, twenty-eight years of age. His father, he said, was still living, though sixty-seven years old when he was born. His height was six. feet two inches. In person, complexion, and gravity he was no inadequate representation of the Knight of La Mancha, whose example he followed, in a recital of his own prowess and wonderful exploits, delivered in a measured language, and an imposing seriousness of aspect.

The writer ascribes to him vanity, pride, and an irascible temper; but believed him to have more than an ordinary share of feeling; and that his integrity and courage appeared unquestionable; and says, "on the whole, when we became familiar to his failings, we saw reason every day to respect his virtues."

Another French officer described by this writer was Ponson, only five feet and a half in stature, but actuated by an unremitted flow of animal spirits, and incessantly noisy. "He was hardy, and patient to admiration of labour and want of rest. A continued watching of five days and nights together, when the rebels were growing desperate for prey and mischief, did not appear to sink his spirits in the smallest degree. He was strictly honest, and could not bear the want of this quality in others; so that his patience was pretty well tried by his Irish allies;" but he expressed a contempt of the forms of religion, to an excess which is justly ascribed to "vanity, the miserable affectation of appearing to be more wicked than he really was." A fifth officer, named Truc, is described as a man of brutal behaviour, and of an appearance corresponding to his character; a front of brass, an incessant fraudful smile, manners altogether vulgar, and in his dress and person a neglect of cleanliness even beyond the affected negligence of republicans.

The characters of these officers may be little interesting to some readers, but they were far from being matters of no concern to the inhabitants of Killala and its neighbourhood. If they had all been of the same description as Truc, or even if they had not been men of active humanity, the county of Mayo might have exhibited scenes of massacre similar to those of the county of Wexford; since without their exertions the Protestants would have been imprisoned by the rebels as hostages, on whom the deaths of their associates, taken prisoners and hanged by the king's army, should be retaliated. Highly indeed to the honour of the French forces in general, the ingenious narrator of the transactions at Killala, gives the following testimony with respect to the behaviour of Humbert's army. "And here it would be an act of great injustice to the excellent discipline constantly maintained by these invaders, while they remained in our town, not to remark, that with every temptation to plunder, which the time and the number of valuable articles within their reach, presented to them in the bishop's palace, from a sideboard of plate and glasses, a hall filled with hats, whips, and great-coats, as well of the guests as of the family, not a single particular of private property was found to have been carried away, when the owners, after the first fright was over, came to look for their effects, which was not for a day or two after the landing. Immediately upon entering the dining-room, a French officer had called for the bishop's butler, and gathering up the spoons and glasses, had desired him to take them to his pantry. Beside the entire use of other apartments, during the stay of the French in Killala, the attic story, containing a library and three bed-chambers, continued sacred to the bishop and his family. And so scrupulous was the delicacy of the French not to disturb the female part of the house, that not one of them was ever seen to go higher than the middle floor, except on the evening of their success at Castlebar, when two officers begged leave just to carry to the family the news of the battle, and seemed a little mortified that the intelligence was received with an air of dissatisfaction."

This army, however, so respectful of persons and private property, had come into the kingdom destitute of money for the advancement of their enterprise. Its headers promised that "ready money was to come over in the ships expected every day from France: in the meantime, whatever was brought in voluntarily, or taken by necessity, to answer the occasions of the army, should be punctually paid for in drafts on the future directory of Ireland, of which the owners of the goods demanded were courteously invited to accept. For the first two or three days, many people did apply for such drafts to the French commissary of stores, whose whole time appeared to be taken up with writing them. Indeed the bishop himself was of opinion that the losers would act wisely to accept of them, not, as he told the people, that they would ever produce payment where it was promised, but because they might serve as documents to our own government, when, at a future period, it should come to inquire into the losses sustained by its loyal subjects. The trouble, however, of the commissary, in issuing drafts on a bank in prospect, was not of long duration. The people smiled first, and he joined himself in the smile at last, when lie offered the 'airy security.' Thus, though private plunder for the emolument of individuals was neither allowed nor practised, yet time necessitous condition in which this army landed, obliged its leaders to adopt this mode of public regulate d plunder for its subsistence. If cash had not been wanting to the rulers of France, they might be supposed to have acted from policy in sending none into a country which must remain hostile, if the invasion should prove abortive; and which otherwise they might think, ought to be obliged to sustain the expenses of its own revolution."

X.

ABOUT four miles from Ballina lies LOCH CONN, a large sheet of water, not much less than fourteen miles in length, and varying in breadth from one to three miles, except at the point of junction between the upper and lower lakes, where the breadth is contracted to the size of a river. It is a singular fact, that Loch Conn regularly ebbs and flows, though not at periods corresponding with the tides. The lake is situated considerably above the sea, and has no tide communication with it. The banks are, in many parts, of fine sand, which shows the high-water line. The shores of the lower lake on the west side, abound in little bays and creeks, and show some bold outlines. The PONTOON BRIDGE, crossing the channel between the upper and lower lakes, is a very beautiful spot, and the view from the rocky hill just above the inn at this place, is uncommonly fine.

From the point of Castlebar there is little to interest the traveller in search of the picturesque. Castlebar is a place of some stir and business, but having little or no attractions for the eye; and few tourists stop longer in it than to procure a fresh car for Westport. After passing the small but beautiful Loch Dan, the road begins to descend towards Westport, and the scenery becomes exceedingly attractive. In no part of Ireland, says Fraser, is there such an extraordinary combination of scenery as is here displayed, nor is there any town in it, the view of which strikes the traveller so forcibly as does that of Westport, when first seen under a favourable light from many parts of this road. The country around the town is very highly cultivated, the bay stretches out before the eye, with the town set in its curve like a jewel in a tiara, and to the right and left stretch away the ranges of mountains, the majestic Reek rising directly from the shore, and towering nobly over the surrounding landscape. The town of WESTPORT itself is embellished with a wall enclosing a stream, and running through the principal street, and at the further end of this is a gate entering to the grounds of Lord Sligo, the principal proprietor of the country. The best hotel in the west of Ireland is Robinson's, at Westport, situated on the side of the wall. The lofty eminence of the Reek, or Croagh Patrick, which is the conspicuous feature of all the views in this neighbourhood, is celebrated as a place of religious pilgrimage. Its sides and summit, at certain seasons, are climbed by devotees from all parts of Ireland, who "perform stations" as they ascend.

Just opposite Westport, at the entrance to Clew Bay, lies Clare Island, the residence of the ancient chieftainess of the county Mayo and its multitude of isles— Grana Uaile. One square and strong tower yet remains of her stronghold on the island shore. Of this "heroine of the west" Mr. Otway gives the following interesting account. "Grace O'Mealey, which has been corrupted into Grana Uaile, was the daughter of Breanhaun Crone O'Maille, tainst or chieftain of that district of Mayo surrounding Clew Bay, and comprising its multitude of isles. This district is still called by the old people the Uisles of O'Mealey; and its lord, owning, as he did, a great extent of coast, and governing an adventurous sea-faring people, had good claim to his motto, 'TERRA MARIQUE POTENS.' Breanhaun Crone O'Maille dying early, left a son and daughter—the son but a child—the daughter, just ripening into womanhood, seemed to have a character suited to seize the reins of government, and rule over this rude and brave people. Setting aside, then, at once the laws of tanistry, that confined the rule to the nearest male of the family, she took upon her, not only the government, but the generalship of her sept, and far exceeded all her family in exploits as a sea-rover; and from her success, whether as smuggler or pirate, as the

Lough Conn and Mount Nephin

case might be, she won the name of Grace of the Heroes. Acting in this wild and able way, she soon gathered round her all the outlaws and adventurers that abounded in the islands, and from the daring strokes of policy she made, and the way in which she bent to her purpose the conflicting interests of the English government and the Irish races—she was called the Gambler. As a matter of policy, she took for her first husband O'Flaherty, Prince of Connemara; and there is reason to suppose that the grey mare proving the better horse, the castle in Lough Corrib, of whose traditional history notice has been already taken, was nearly lost to the Joyces, by O'Flaherty the Cock, but was saved and kept by Grana the Hen, hence it got the name which it still keeps of Krishlane na Kirca—the *Hen's Castle* Be this as it may, Grana's husband, the Prince of Connemara, dying soon, she was free to make another connexion, and in this also she seems to have consulted more her politics than her affections, and became the wife of Sir Richard Bourke, the M'William Eighter. Tradition hands down a singular item of the marriage contract. The marriage was to last *for certain* (what said the pope to this?) but one year, and if at the end of that period, either said to the other 'I dismiss you,' the union was dissolved. It is said, that during that year Grana took good care to put her own creatures into garrison in all M'William's eastward castles that were valuable to her, and then, one fine day, as the Lord of Mayo was coming up to the castle of Corrig-a-Howly, near Newport, Grana spied him, and cried out the dissolving words—'I dismiss you.' We are not told how M'William took the snapping of the matrimonial chain; it is likely that he was not sorry to have a safe riddance of such a virago. We shortly after this find Grana siding with Sir Richard Bingham against the Bourkes, and doing battle with the English. The O'Mealeys, on this occasion, turned the fortune of the day in favour of the President of Connaught, and most of the M'William leaders being taken prisoners, six of them were hanged next day at Cloghan Lucas, 'in order to strengthen the English interest.' It is probable that it was in gratitude for this signal aid afforded to her lieutenant, that Queen Elizabeth invited Grana over to the English court; and it certainly confirms the Irishwoman's character for decision and firmness, that she accepted the invitation of the Saxon, of whose faithfulness the Irish nation had but a low opinion. Accordingly Grana sailed from Clare Island, and before she arrived at the port of Chester was delivered of a son, the issue of the marriage with M'William Eighter. He being born on ship-board, was hence named Tohaduah na Lung, or Toby of the Ship, from whom sprung the Viscounts Mayo. It must have been a curious scene, the interview at Hampton Court between the wild woman of the west, and the 'awe-commanding, lion ported' Elizabeth. Fancy Grana, in her loose attire, consisting of a chemise, containing thirty yards of yellow linen, wound round her body, with a mantle of frieze, coloured madder-red, flung over one shoulder, with her wild hair twisted round a large golden pin as her only head-gear, standing with her red legs unstockinged, and her broad feet unshod, before the stiff and stately Tudor, dressed

Pontoon Bridge, Lough Conn

out (as we see her represented in the portraits of that day) with stays, stomacher, and farthingale, cased like an impregnable armadillo— what a *'tableau vivant'* this must have been! and then Grana, having made a bow, and held out her bony hand, horny as it was, with many an oar she had handled, and many a helm she had held, to sister Elizabeth, (as she called her,) sat down with as much self-possession and self-respect as an American Indian chief would now before the president of the United States. Elizabeth, observing Grana's fondness for snuff, which, though a practice newly introduced, she had picked up in her smuggling enterprises, and perceiving her inconvenienced, as snuffers usually are when wanting a pocket-handkerchief, presented her with one richly embroidered, which Grana took indifferently, used it loudly, and cast it away carelessly, and when asked by Sir Walter Raleigh, why she treated the gift of her majesty in such a way, the answer of the wild Irish girl was of that coarseness that ought not to be read by eyes polite. Moreover, it seems Elizabeth was not happy in the presents which she proffered to the Vanathess; she ordered a lap-dog, led by a silken band, to be given to her. 'What's this for?' says Grana. 'Oh , it is a sagacious, playful, faithful little creature, it will lie in your lap.' 'My lap!' says Grana; "it's little the likes of me would be doing with such a thing :—keep it to yourself, Queen of the English, it is only fit for such idlers as you :—you may, if it likes you, fool away *your* day with such vermin.' 'Oh, but,' says Elizabeth, 'Grana, you are mistaken, I am not idle; I have the care of this great nation on my shoulders' 'May be so,' says Grana, 'but as far as I can see of your ways, there's many a poor creature in Mayo, who has only the care of a barleyfield, has more industry about them than you seem to have.' Of course, Elizabeth dismissed her soon: she offered, at her last audience, to create her a countess. 'I don't want your titles,' says Grana, 'arn't we both equals? if there be any good in the thing, I may as well make you one as you me. Queen of England, I want nothing from you—enough for me it is to be at the head of my nation; but you may do what you like with my little son, Toby of the Ship, who has Saxon blood in his veins, and may not be dishonoured by a Saxon title:—I will remain as I am, Grana O'Maille of the Uisles.' It was on her return from England, and when driven by stress of weather into the small harbour of Howth, that the often-told circumstance occurred respecting her abduction of the young St. Lawrence. Landing from her vessel, she and some of her followers proceeded to the castle and demanded admission, but were refused, on the ground that the noble owner was at his dinner and could not be disturbed. 'Oh, the Saxon churl!' says Grana, 'it's well seen he has not a drop of Irish blood in his big body; but he shall smart for it.' And so he did, for Grana, on her return to her vessel, entering into a comfortable cottage, and finding therein a beautiful boy, the eldest son of the baron, (who was out at nurse, according to the Irish fashion,) she carried him off, and brought him with her to her western land, where she kept him many a day, and did not restore him, until, besides receiving a large ransom, she made the stipulation that

Clew Bay from West Point

whenever a Lord of Howth sat at his dinner, his doors should remain open for the admission of all strangers. It is said that the St. Lawrences have kept to the covenant ever since; if so, the observance in its spirit of open hospitality may explain why the lords of Howth are not the wealthiest of our nobility. Grana continued on her return to strengthen her power, and had strongholds guarding all the harbours along the coast of Mayo; and so active and vigilant was she, that it is said that in her castle at Clare Island, where her swiftest vessels were stationed, the cable of her chief galley was passed through a hole made for that purpose in the wall, and fastened to her bed-post, in order that she might be the more readily alarmed in case of an attempted surprise. At her death it would appear that the power which was but concentrated by individual vigour and ability, dissolved with the spirit that gave it energy."

From Westport to the HEAD OF KILLERY HARBOUR, the road follows the coast. presenting fine views of the island of Grana Uaile and the opposite shores of Achill. The country commencing here, and lying immediately south, is inhabited by a "race of giants," the Joyces, who have given their name to a large district. Jack Joyce is its reigning king, and a visit to this personage is a necessary part of every western tour. Mr. Inglis says, "the Joyces are a large race, but Jack Joyce is huge, even among *them*. He is as near akin to a giant as a man can well be without being every bit a giant. In height, breadth, muscle, and general aspect, he is like a man—if not of another race— the descendant of another race. Jack Joyce looks upon himself as the greatest man for many a mile round; as a sort of king of that country, Joyce's country, as indeed he is. King Dan is a very inferior person to him there. But beware, reader! and address this individual in some phraseology more respectful than by the name he commonly bears. The salutation 'How are you, Jack! or Jack Joyce, my fine fellow, how do you do?' might be followed by an uncourteous reception. But Jack Joyce is really worth conversing with; he is a shrewed, intelligent, plain-spoken man; but not, of course, induced to favour with his conversation those who do not pay him the respect to which he thinks himself entitled." Perhaps a fairer judgment of Joyce's proportions may be got from a writer who is himself of a height and size which might, in his youthful days, have fitted him to be an "ugly customer" to Jack, the author of the Tour in Connaught. He thus describes his visit to the giant.

"I was determined to go and renew my acquaintance with my big friend, whom twelve years ago I found in all his might and glory as 'mine host,' at the head of the Killery—so I drove up to Jack's door, and enquired for Mr. Joyce, and was answered by a *very tall* young woman, not uncomely, who informed me that Mr. Joyce was within, but that as he had been out all night after cattle on the hills, he was on the bed asleep, but his daughter (for such she was) said, that if I desired it she would call him. I certainly did not like to go away without seeing BIG Jack, so he was called up, and as he came, loose, unclean, and frouzy, certainly my giant did not appear to advantage; for, some how or other, I had let my imagination play the rogue with my judgment, and magnify my retrospect with regard to this man.

"The first time I saw him, (as I say,) about twelve years ago, he made his appearance just as I drove up to his door, bouncing over the wall that divided the potato-garden from the front of his house, and, I think, a finer specimen of a strong man, tall and yet well-proportioned, I could not conceive. Such do not look as tall as they really are. The great bullet-head, covered with crisp curls, the short bull-neck, the broad, square shoulders, the massive chest all open and hirsute, the comparatively small sinewy loins, and pillar-like limbs, all bone and muscle. Milo, of Crotona, might have shaken hands with him as a brother, and the gifted sculptor of the Farnese Hercules might have selected Jack as his lay-figure. Such was my *beau ideal* of Mr. Joyce, from what I recollected of him since my former visit. But now, though I acknowledged the identity, yet certainly the man was greatly changed—but still, though I. am sure my fancy had been playing tricks, he yet was tall, stout, and able; but I am sure I know fifty English and Irishmen just as large. Having called for some liquor—reader, I hope you will believe me, not to drink, but just to put mine host in good humour—Jack and I got into chat, and, to be sure, he was full of the hard usage of the attorney who had put him out of Leenane; but he said he had got where he was a large and good farm, and all he wished was to see the head landlord, the provost of Trinity College, who was cheated *entirely, entirely,* by his middlemen, such as attorney R—— and others; but if he could but once get a sight of his *great reverence,* he would show him how acres, and hundreds of acres are kept from him.

"Upon acquainting him that I had the honour of an intimate acquaintance with *the greatest of all possible men,* EXCEPT LORD LEITRIM, you may suppose he was mighty civil; and taking advantage of that desire to please, I endeavoured to get from him an account of his family, but he really could not tell anything about them : he seemed to think that size was not so much the characteristic of the tribe or name as of his own immediate family; and to show me that he had not been the means of any degeneracy, he whistled to his son, who was in a distant field, who came at the call, and certainly a taller and more comely stripling, of about twenty years of age, I have not seen. He was at least six feet four inches in height, and I am sure, if fed on animal food as an English farmer's son would be, he would prove a grand specimen of the human race. I left *big* Jack and his *big* family, receiving from them a thousand thanks for promising to introduce him to the notice of the new provost.

"On my road towards Leenane, I met some persons with whom I entered into conversation about the neighbourhood, and about Jack Joyce. I found that he was not a favourite, that he was too apt to resort to his strength to settle disputes, when the *fist* he threw into the balance made the scale descend in his own favour. Indeed, he acknowledged to me on a former visit, that, as a justice of the peace was a great way off, he used to settle differences amongst the neighbours by taking the parties at variance by the nape of the neck, and battering their heads together until they consented to shake hands and drink a pint of *potteen* together, which, of course, it was Jack's office to furnish for a *consideration.*"

The author of this clever book will excuse us for extending our extract to the description of the scenery he noticed on his return from the visit to the Joyces.

"The descent is very rapid from the high grounds, on which Jack Joyce's new farm and public-house are situated, to the Killery Bay, and the inn of Leenane. As you descend, by a very good road, there are noble mountain-views, and the long Killery, stretching its dark and deep-cut line through the mountains, was certainly a fine sight, and very unlike anything I have seen elsewhere in the island; not, perhaps, presenting so grand a prospect as either Bantry Bay or Lough Swilly, but it has features all its own. About either of these fine estuaries there appears something that man has done—man has some share in the decoration, or even grandeur of the scene: but here at the Killery man and his works are out of the question; no sail upon the waters; no cultivation along the shore; all as rough nature has left it; even trees seem out of character with the place; and *there* is the deep bay, and *there* are the high mountains all around, the same, we may suppose, as when the first sea-rover turned inwards his prow for shelter or curiosity, and sought, and that in vain, for something that marked the occupation and dominion of man.

"Some have said that Killery Bay is like a Norwegian fiord. Never having been in the Scandinavian peninsula I cannot decidedly contradict; but it certainly does not meet *my* idea of a fiord, which supposes pine crowded precipices hanging and frowning over the deep blue wave; but this is not the case here; perfectly bare of any timber, the mountains, though rising all around, and assuming all manner of outlines, yet shelve gradually down to the shore, and I would say, that the character of the place is not *sublime* but *savage.*"

We arrived in good time at LEENANE, and found the new owner, or rather renter, a civil but inexperienced woman, who had lately taken possession, and who complained bitterly of her landlord, who had promised to put the house in good repair, and make it sufficiently decent to induce travellers to stop with her. This it was evident he had *not* done, and I was ready to partake in her vexation on observing the nice furniture and other accommodations intended for a good inn, stowed away in such a truly uncomfortable and dirty house. Having bespoke our dinner, we expressed a desire to go by boat to see Lord Sligo's SPORTING-LODGE AT DELPHI; and here it was well that we asked the price before engaging it, for the landlady, in order, perhaps, to compensate as she might for her as *yet* unsuccessful speculation, demanded more for a vile, dirty, leaky, brute of a boat, than we should have paid for the hire of one of the gayest and best-appointed cutters in Kingston harbour. However, by appearing to care little whether we should go or not, we by-and-by agreed on more reasonable terms, and went afloat. It was also well that the water was smooth, for the boat was not only leaky and heavy, but the fellows that undertook to row us seemed anything but expert. They were uncouth, creatures; the elder of the two knew but little English, and the other none at all, and they both seemed discontented and very much out of humour at being obliged to leave their potato-planting to go rowing a pair of idle Sassenach fools, as they evidently considered us to be.

I consider myself well paid for this boating excursion. Nothing can be finer than the mountain-scenery all around. When you are in the middle of the bay you seem locked in on every side, and were it not for the smell, and colour, and vegetation peculiar to the sea, the incomparable sea, you would imagine you were on a mountain-lake. But there is scarcely any lake that has not a flat, *tame* end, generally that where the superabundant waters flow off and form a river; but here nothing was tame; on every side the magnificent mountains seemed to vie with each other which should catch and keep your attention most. Northwards the Fenamore mountains— the Partree range to the east—Maamturc to the south—a little more to the south-west, the sparkling cones of the Twelve Pins of Binabola; then, a little more to the west, the Renvyle mountain, and off to the north of that again, the monarch of the whole amphitheatre, Muilrea, with its cap of clouds that it has caught, and anon flings fitfully off, as much as to say, I am the great cloud-compeller of Europe, and not one of you, ye proud rangers of the sky, shall come from the banks of Newfoundland without paying me tribute; and, no doubt ample tribute they *do* pay, and we had every reason to be fearful of partaking in the results of Mr. Muilrea tapping the American; but the alarm was false, the clouds only slowly rolled their huge masses along the topmost ranges, and we could see in their clear glory all the inferior hills as they rejoiced in the lights and shadows of the uncertain day.

After a row of more than an hour, we landed at the little pier at the entrance of the river Bondarragh, and passing a small fishing-village, we went along the river for about a mile and a half, until we reached this much-talked-of lodge of Delphi. Was it called so from any fancied resemblance to the oracular mountain in Greece? As far as a picture can give an idea of scenery, I have some notion of the farfamed throne of the solar god, but I could trace no similarity. I confess, altogether, I was greatly disappointed in this place. I think the mountains fine; I consider the sides of the hills, as they rise from the little lake, singularly picturesque and beautiful; for as the ranges of rock ascend, they assume a tortuous and wavy form, and between each wave of the uprising stratification, the fresh green grass of the young summer seemed to grow luxuriantly; there were then before you, as in manifold variegations, the green and the grey, tinting the whole sides of the mountains. There are two lakes in the valley, one close by the lodge, and the vale, a little above the small pleasure-ground, taking a turn at nearly right-angles, contains the other. By ascending a green eminence you can see both lakes; the upper and larger one, drawing its waters from the magnificent Muilrea, must present sublime views of the gorges of that noble

Delphi Lodge

mountain. I greatly regret that I had no time or opportunity to proceed along its banks. Having seen earls' and dukes' improvements in the Highlands of Scotland, England, and Wales, and what wonders in the way of planting have been done by Lords Fife, and Athol, and Breadalbane, I expected that this Irish nobleman, having this great mountain-district to himself, would have filled the glens and clothed the sides of the hills with his plantations, and that I should have seen masses of timber, becoming the purse and great mind of a most noble marquis; but it was no such thing. I think, that if a Dublin pawn broker had got possession of this valley, he would have stuck down about as many firs, and larches, and alders, and erected about as tasty a cottage, and decorated it with about as ornamental a verandah, which, by-the-by, is going fast to ruin, and that is not extraordinary, as the most "puissant" owner every year lets it to certain sporting lodgers, and, perhaps in imitation of some Italian marchese, makes the fishing and shooting of this place a means of increasing his revenue.

Altogether respecting this *show—place,* I may say nature's work is grand, and man s work pitiful; and I think it is worthy of the improvement, that it should be let *furnished, with the grass of a cow*! year after year.

I have heard it said, that in certain hot summers, residence here is made almost intolerable by insects larger than midges, but not quite the size of musquitoes, that bite bitterly, and make you wish by night for gauze curtains.

Having got as good a dinner as hungry tourists need desire at the inn of Leenane, we proceeded in the evening to Westport, going along the valley through which the Owen Erive river runs, and falling over many pretty cascades, feeds the head of the bay. This road is well laid out, is in excellent repair, and offers, I think, a succession of as fine mountain-views as are in Ireland; here dark and deep gorges, there, a bold, bare bulwark of a hill, presenting his huge shoulder—and now a long, deep, quiet glen, with its green sides covered with flocks; and the bleating of the lambs as they seek their dams along the ravines and precipices breaks sweetly on the lonely silence of all around, and gives a pastoral character to the district. The evening was peculiarly serene, the Partree hills (and, indeed, it is a noble chain, of great and singular variety,) were covered with light flocculent clouds, that under the tintings of the declining sun seemed as intended for a clothing of wrought gold, a raiment of heaven's own panoply, and so transparent was it, that every grey precipice and every beetling quartzose rock smiled in its turn under the sunshine as they were now revealed, and again veiled, by the golden-fringed clouds that moved so gently, so gracefully up the hill-sides, and then passed away in splendid masses eastward.

We just got out of this fine mountain country, and the sun was setting as we descended into Westport.

Leenane, Connemara

The Eagle Mountain, Killeries

XI.

CONNEMARA is rich in scenes of wild grandeur and beauty, but it has nothing in its secluded recesses more sublime and lovely than the LAKE OF KYLEMORE. It is very small, not more than two miles in , and its shores are better wooded than most of the neighbouring country. The horizon from every part of this lake is nobly broken up by mountains—Maam Turc, EAGLE MOUNTAIN, and other fine eminences breaking its low line in every direction. From Kylemore to Clifden the road follows the tortuous windings of mountain-valleys, and the base of the Twelve Pins, developes the finest variety of wild scenery in all Ireland. Clifden itself stands at the head of a narrow inlet of the sea, and the views of it from the eminences around are singularly fine. It has arisen something after the fashion of an American town, having attained its present growth in less than twenty years, and containing two or three streets, a chapel, a church, school-house, inn, &c. Twenty years ago not a house stood on its site. It is the property of Mr. D'Arcy, whose residence is Clifden Castle, two miles from the town; he has the merit of having founded the town. "He pointed out," says Inglis, "the advantages which would accrue to this remote neighbourhood from having a town and a sea-port so situated; and he offered leases for ever, together with four acres of mountain-land, at but a short distance from the proposed site of the town, at twenty-five shillings per annum. This offer was most advantageous, even leaving out of account the benefit which would necessarily be conferred by a town on a district where the common necessaries of life had to be purchased thirty miles distant, and where there was no market, and no means of export for agricultural produce, and so the town of Clifden was founded and grew." One of the most beautiful walks in Ireland is the two miles from the town to Clifden Castle. The path runs by the edge of a long narrow inlet, the banks of which are very rugged. "After reaching the entrance of the HARBOUR OF CLIFDEN and rounding a promontory, the Castle comes into view. It is a modern castellated house, not remarkable in itself, but in point of situation unrivalled. Mountain and wood rise behind, and a fine sloping lawn in front reaches down to the landlocked bay; while to the right the eye ranges over the ocean, until it mingles with the far and dim horizon." This part of the Emerald Isle is likely to rise to some consequence if the new schemes of improvement should be carried out, but it has been considered hitherto by the Irish themselves as almost a savage country. "Connemara," says a writer in the Penny Journal, "is a word which to English, and even to Irish ears, is expressive of nothing but the *ultima Thule* of barbarism. Yet its signification is most poetical— '*bays of the sea.*' Towards the north-east extremity of the county of Galway there is a portion cut off, as it were, by a natural barrier of lakes and mountains. If the map does justice to its subject, Connemara will appear black with mountains, dotted with lakes, and studded with bogs; its coast will be seen rugged, and indented with fine harbours; while the inland country, though wild, mountainous, and ill-cultivated, and so little known and visited that its name is a proverb, is yet equal to the finest part of Wales or of Scotland; and the traveller who ventures to enjoy its romantic picturesque scenery, and who from natural or acquired taste can relish 'the lone majesty of untamed nature,' may here have his feelings gratified to the full. As a proof how little is known of this singular part of Ireland, it may be mentioned, that a magistrate in an adjoining county, when he heard that a criminal had been arrested who had long lid himself in the mountain fastnesses of these Irish highlands, declared, that 'the poor fellow had suffered enough, in all conscience, for any crime he might have committed, by being banished seven years to Connemara.'"

The inhabitants of this part of the country are, of course, behind the rest of Ireland in knowledge and civilization. But if the reader understands by this that they are *barbarians,* and destitute of the feelings of humanity, he commits a very great mistake. The Irish highlanders are a warm-hearted, generous people, attached to their wild mountains and romantic glens, and, considering the few advantages which they enjoy, a lively, intelligent race. In the old times their "mountain land" was the retreat of those daring spirits who scorned to submit to the yoke of an invader; and here, preferring poverty and freedom to restraint and submission, they found a shelter amid the deep valleys and craggy rocks, like the ancient Britons in Wales, and the Highlanders in Scotland.

BALLYNAHINCH CASTLE is the first very attractive object on the road from Clifden to Oughterard, and is the residence of the principal land-proprietor in this part of the country, Mr. Martin. This gentleman is quite a king in his immense domain; and a person in the neighbourhood speaking of him to a traveller remarked, that Colonel Martin was the best Martin that ever *reigned.* His house stands upon the well-wooded bank of a long, narrow lake, and is backed by a range of dark and lofty mountains. The lake is one of a chain of waters that almost encircle the eminences called the TWELVE PINS or Binabola, said to be the most extraordinary and beautiful assemblage of mountains in the kingdom. In the course of Mr. Inglis's tour in Connemara, he was lucky enough to see a *pattern* in this neighbourhood , the description of which is too amusing to be passed over. He says, "It fortunately happened that on the second day of my sojourn at Maam a very celebrated pattern was to be held on a singular spot high up among the mountains, on a little plain on the top of the pass between Maamturc and the neighbouring mountain, an elevation of about one thousand two hundred feet, and I, of course, resolved to be present. A pattern was originally a religious ceremony, and was, and still is, always celebrated near to a holy well; but although some still frequent the pattern for devotional purposes, it is now resorted to chiefly as a place of recreation, where, after the better disposed have partaken of the innocent amusements of dancing and moderate hilarity, drunkenness and fighting wind up the entertainment.

"I was accompanied in my excursion by the innkeeper, and the road being rather toilsome, I was accommodated with a horse. This however was a luxury which I was soon obliged to disencumber myself of, for a great part, or rather by far the greater part of the road, being through bogs, I soon found the horse to be a dangerous companion, and was glad to leave him behind at a cabin door, and make my way through the bog on foot. It requires some practice to be an expert bog-trotter, to know where one may safely rest one's weight, where one must skip lightly from tuft to tuft, and where one must not risk an advance at all. I had had some experience of bogs before coming to Ireland, and proved so apt a learner in bog-trotting, that during the whole of my journey I never committed so great an error of judgment as to sink even knee-deep.

"The ascent to the spot where the pattern was to be held was picturesque in the extreme. Far up the winding way for miles before us, and for miles behind too, groups were seen moving up the mountain-side,—the women, with their red petticoats, easily distinguishable; some were on foot, some few on horseback, and some rode double. About half-way up we overtook a party of lads and lasses, beguiling the toil of the ascent by the help of a piper, who marched before, and whose stirring strains every now and then prompted an advance in jig-time up the steep mountain-path. Some few we met coming away—sober people, who had performed their devotions at the holy well, and had no desire to be partakers in the sort of amusement that generally follows.

"Everybody in this part of the country is called Joyce; and the spot where the pattern is held is claimed by the Joyces to be in Joyce's country: but this is not admitted by the Connemara boys, and accordingly two factions, the Joyces and their opponents, usually hold patterns near the same ground, though not close together; but yet so near as to make it impossible that the meetings should break up without a *scrimmage*. The Joyces are a magnificent race of men, the biggest, and stoutest, and tallest I have seen in Ireland, eclipsing even the peasantry of the Tyrol; and I believe, indeed, their claims on this head are universally admitted.

"When I reached the summit of the Pass and came in sight of the ground, it was about four in the afternoon, and the pattern was at its height; and truly in this wild mountain spot the scene was most striking and picturesque. There were a score of tents or more, some open at the sides and some closed; hundreds in groups were seated on the grass or on the stones, which lie abundantly there. Some old persons were yet on their knees beside the holy well performing their devotions; and here and there apart, and half-screened by the masses of rocks which lay about, girls of the better order, who had finished their pastimes, were putting off their shoes and stockings to trot homeward, or were arranging their dress, or perhaps, though more rarely, exchanging a word or two with a Joyce or a Connemara boy. All was quiet when I reached the ground, and I was warmly welcomed as a stranger by many, who invited me into their tents. Of course I accepted the invitation, and the pure potheen circulated freely.

"By-and-by, however, some boastful expression of a Joyce appeared to give offence to several at the far end of the tent; and something loud and contemptuous was spoken by two or three in a breath. The language, which in compliment to me had been English, suddenly changed to Irish. Two or three glasses of potheen were quickly gulped by most of the 'boys'; and the innkeeper who had accompanied me, and who sat by me whispered that there would soon be some fighting. I had seen abundance of fighting on a small scale in Ireland, but I confess I had been barbarous enough to wish I might see a regular faction fight; and now I was likely to be gratified. Taking the hint of the innkeeper, I shook hands with the 'boys' nearest to me, right and left; and taking advantage of a sudden burst of voices, I stepped over my bench, and retiring from my tent, took up a safe position on some neighbouring rocks.

"I had not long to wait; out sallied the Joyces and a score of other 'boys,' from several tents at once, as if there had been some preconcerted signal; and the flourishing of shillelahs did not long precede the using of them. Any one to see an Irish fight for the first time, would conclude that a score or two must inevitably be put *hors-de-combat*. The very flourish of a regular shillelah, and the shout that accompanies it, seem to be the immediate precursors of a fractured skull; but the affair, though bad enough, is not so fatal as it appears to be: the shillelahs, no doubt, do sometimes descend upon a head, which is forthwith a broken head, but oftener descend upon each other; and the fight soon becomes one of personal strength. The parties close and grapple, and the most powerful man throws his adversary. Fair play is but little attended to; two or three often attack a single man; nor is there a cessation of blows even when a man is on the ground. on the present occasion five or six were disabled, but there was no homicide : and after a *scrimmage* which lasted perhaps ten minutes, the Joyces remained masters of the field. The women took no part in the fight; but they are not always so backward; it is chiefly however when stones are the weapons that women take a part, by supplying the combatants with missiles. When the fight ended there were not many remaining, excepting those who were still in the tents, and who chanced to be of neither faction. Most of the women had left the place when the quarrel began, and some of the men too. I noticed after the fight, that some who had been opposed to each other shook hands and kissed, and appeared as good friends as before. The sun was nearly set when the pattern finally broke up; and with the bright sun flaming down the cleft, and gilding all the slopes, the scene was even more striking now than when we ascended. The long line

Garromin, Connemara

of pedestrians and horses stretched many miles down the lengthened defile; and the mountain-notes of the pipe, and the occasional burst of voices, and the lowing of the cattle, roused by these unwonted sonnds, filled all the hollow of the hills.

XII.

LEAVING Ballynahinch, the traveller passes through a district of the wildest and most gigantic scenery; upon his left rise mountains of stupendous height, upon whose bare and sterile sides the grey clouds rest in misty grandeur, while the chain of picturesque undulating hills, that skirt the Bay of Galway, stretch far away on his right. The remarkable hill of Cloonacartan stands at the entrance of the vale of Ina, from whose summit a magnificent view may be obtained of the most striking *fea*tures of the Connemara country. Glens and mountains extend on every side as far as the eye can reach; and bosomed in their deep solitudes may be seen that beautiful chain of lakes which lie between Ballynahinch and Outerard. Amongst these lovely pieces of water, the most beautiful is Garromin Lake, upon whose sequestered shores stands Glendalough, the residence of the late Dean Mahon, who chose this solitary spot for his house, and with great taste availed himself of the natural beauties of the scenery, to form there a highly romantic yet cheerful place of abode. On the left of Garromin these mountain-beauties, who, it must be confessed, were, at the time he wrote, a pair of exceedingly pretty and interesting-looking girls; one a dark haired, dark-eyed beauty, the other a laughing lass with rich brown hair and blue eyes; the Very Minna and Brenda of these wilds.

Before I quit the Connemara country, I shall briefly advert to the peculiar characteristics of the scenery, which distinguish this portion of Ireland from every other district in the island. The great and striking features of the Connemara land-scape are its mountains, whose peaks of quartz start up magnificently from lakes that want only the arbutus and holly of Killarney to rival the enchantments of Mucruss. The Twelve Pins, a stupendous group of these Titans of the land, lie between Ballynahinch and Killery Harbour; bare, but glittering with the aërial brilliancy peculiar to their formation, their peaked summits rush together,—in elevations of from two thousand to two thousand five hundred feet,—a splendid assemblage, to the clouds. But while their denuded peaks depend mainly on their own quartoze formation for their effect in the landscape, the sides and bases of the Pins, from which the violence of Atlantic storms has not yet been able to wash away their vegetable covering, take tints still more brilliant and various from their innumerable varieties of heaths and lichens.* What the arbutus is to Killarney, the heath is to Connemara, and in the absence of any breadth or depth of foliage, the eye rests most gratefully on a substitute so pleasing: for its streaks are of pale pink, rich brown, or glowing purple, mixed with the tender green of mountain-grasses, and occasionally alternating with the black stripes of uplying bogs, give a combination of colours, that, seen under the clarifying influence of western skies, is almost magical. Nor is all this brilliancy inconsistent with breadth. Connemara proper, though a mountainous is not an upland country; the plain from which its greatest elevations rise is little more, on an average, than one hundred feet above the level of the Atlantic; so that its masses lose not a tittle of their real altitude, but lifting themselves to their full height at a stretch, look over the plain with much greater majesty than many other mountains higher by a thousand feet. Lettery and Derryclare stand foremost, like an advanced-guard, to the group on the south; the others are formed in a solid square around Knockannahiggen, the captain of this grenadier company of Connaught Fencibles. In front, flank, and rear open four principal glens, each one with his torrent, and three of them with their proper lakes: Glen Hogan, with the lower Lake of Ballynahinch, looks southward on Roundstone and Birterbuy; Glen Ina, cradling its black waters under the tremendous precipice of Maam,—down which the stream that feeds Loch Ina goes twelve hundred feet plumb,—opens the gorge of its grand prison upon the east. Kylemore yawns westward and northward on Renvyle; and on the west and south, the ravine whose torrent waters Clifden grins horribly upon the Atlantic. The Joyce Country, or, as it may be termed, Upper Connemara, which stretches north of Connemara proper along the shores of Killery harbour, is a table-land, very different from the district of which I have been speaking, for the whole formation of the country is here changed; and instead of plains of granite and peaks of quartz, we have extended platforms of sandstone, cut into ravines rather than rising out of valleys , with few or no plains, till we descend their northern declivity into the bogs of Mayo. The deepest and the longest ravine in Joyce Country, is that occupied by the waters of Killery harbour, an elbow of the Atlantic,

* The wild district of Connemara furnishes several rare and interesting plants, of which the following are the most remarkable;—*Erica Mediterranea,* found in Urrisbeg, near Roundstone, and on the side of Muilrea mountain, near the Killeries; *Erica Mackaiana, Menziesia polifolia,* or Irish heath, which as well as the beautiful variety with white flowers, are now general favorites in garden collections, are to be seen between Clifden and Roundstone; the curious *Eriocaulon septanqulare,* which also grows in the Isle of Skye, in Scotland, is here to be found in almost every lake. The London-pride, *Saxifraga umbrosa,* is met with on several of the mountains in the greatest abundance, and the *Saxifraga oppositifolia* on the mountains which separate Connemara from the Joyce Country. The beautiful and delicate *Adiantum copillus veneris,* or true Maiden-hair fern, is found near Roundstone; the *Pimpinella magna* in great abundance in the Ross woods, and the *Silene Anglica,* in great profusion in corn-fields two miles west of Oughterard.

which some consider not inferior to any similar scene in Europe. Muilrea, the highest mountain in Connaught, rises in this district to the height (according to Mr. Bald) of two thousand seven hundred and thirty-three feet above the level of the sea. Its sides are of magnificent precipitousness from the water's edge to the crown of the ridge; and the northern declivities of the whole range, extending from Muilrea to the heights above Castlebar, are full of the most romantic hollows, and every hollow has its own lough and river. The absence of wood is the greatest drawback to the beauty of the Connemara scenery, and, it must be confessed, to the aspect of the country generally. The whole surface of Ireland presents scarcely a relic of a natural forest, and the few plantations to be met with rarely exceed a century in age. Yet, denuded of trees as it now is, it is certain that at no very remote period Ireland was far more abundantly furnished with natural woods than almost any European country. Noble forests once existed in every province, and even on these western shores, so exposed to the violence of the Atlantic gales, stately pines flourished in situations where it is now imagined that no tree can vegetate. The most authentic evidence of the antiquity of the forests and the nature of the trees which composed them, may he obtained from an examination of their remains, which have been inhumed in the bogs. Oak, fir, yew, and birch are the species of timber most abundant, and these are found under the bogs, sometimes at a depth of thirty feet from the surface. Indeed it has been conjectured that the decay of the immense forests with which the country was formerly covered, has been the origin of many bogs, and a strong degree of probability is given to the hypothesis from the fact, that in such situations the roots of trees have been often found resting upon each other. In the Parliamentary Reports concerning the bogs of Ireland, there is an account of a bog in which there is a succession of three layers of roots of firs, proving that three forests have flourished in succession in this spot. During the twelfth century, and long before it, extensive forests abounded throughout the country, affording shelter for wolves and all kinds of wild animals; the churches were built of timber, and, in short, until the commencement of the seventeenth century, Ireland had generally more reason to give premiums for the destruction of forests than to enact laws for their perpetuation. Dr. Boate, whose History of Ireland appeared in 1652, complains of the destruction of the Irish forests in his time; still many extensive woods, he says, remained. Wicklow, the King's County and Queen's County were throughout full of woods, some whereof were many miles long and broad. At this period there were also great forests in Donegal, in Tyrone, along Lough Erne, and in many other places in the province of Ulster. Peter Lombard, a Roman Catholic priest, who wrote an account of Ireland in 1632, states, that wild boars and wolves abounded in the woods, which also swarmed with martens, &c.; that the chief wealth of the country consisted in peltries. Such an abundance of wild animals required a corresponding extent of wooded country to afford them shelter. A vast quantity of timber was recklessly consumed in the smelting of the iron ore, which is abundant in many parts of Ireland. Sir William Petty, himself a manufacturer of iron, informs us, that there were six thousand iron-forges in Ireland, which gave employment to no fewer than twenty-five thousand persons, either in attending to the furnaces or cutting down the trees and preparing charcoal. It is easy to conceive the havoc such extensive iron-works must have caused in the forests, and the rapid change which the aspect of the country must have suffered from such a wasteful denudation, till at length the hills and mountains which were formerly covered with trees became bare, and then the iron-forges were obliged to stop working for want of charcoal.* Such was the fate of the woods in Ireland, and although the destruction of a vast quantity was necessary to the progress of agriculture and the general prosperity of the country, we must lament the barbarism which effaced so much of what was beautiful from its mountain scenery. The moistness of the Irish climate is one of the peculiarities by which it is distinguished from that of England, yet the medium fall of rain in Ireland is less on the average than in most parts of the sister island. But the great characteristic which makes the difference between the two countries lies in the colour of the scenery; for whether it be owing to the moisture of the atmosphere, or a soil resting upon a substratum of limestone, or to both causes conjointly, certain it is, that the Irish landscape presents a clearness, a brilliancy, a dewy serene and a vivid freshness essentially its own, and which has suggested the appropriately beautiful name of "The Emerald Isle,"bestowed with so much poetic truth upon this verdant land. The changeableness of the skies of Ireland is indeed amply compensated by the variety of effect imparted to the landscape. "I wish,"says the writer of the delightful 'Letters from the Irish Highlands,' "I wish you were here in Connemara, to enjoy, in rapid succession and in all its wild magnificence, the whirlwind, the tempest, the ocean's swell, and as Burns beautifully expresses it,

'Some gleams of sunshine 'mid renewing storms.'

* The perpetual warfare which existed in Ireland, must have also contributed materially to the destruction of the forests, which afforded shelter to the turbulent. The Irish parliament were at length induced to take some precautions to restrain the extermination which was being carried on against the timber; and in 1698, an act was passed in which we find the following clauses :—"Forasmuch as by the late rebellion in this kingdom, and the several iron-works formerly here, the timber is utterly destroyed, so as that at present there is not sufficient for the repairing of the houses destroyed, much less a prospect of building and improving in after times, unless some means be used for the planting an increase of timber-trees." It was also enacted, that persons having iron-works should plant five hundred acres every year; every person holding five hundred acres to plant one acre in seven years. The same act directed that two hundred and sixty thousand six hundred trees should be planted in thirty-one years from the year 1703. This legislation produced but little effect, and in the year 1703 another act was passed, repealing all duties on the importation of unwrought-iron and foreign timber, as such duties tended to the destruction of the woods of this kingdom. But the remedy came too late, the country had been despoiled of its forest honours, and it has never since recovered them.

To-day there have been fine bright intervals, and while returning from a hasty ride, I have been greatly delighted with the appearance of a rainbow, gradually advancing before the lowering clouds, sweeping with majestic stride across the troubled ocean; then, as it gained the beach, and seemed almost within my grasp, vanishing among the storm of which it had been the lovely but treacherous forerunner. It is, I suppose, a consequence of our situation, and the close connexion between the sea and the mountain, that the rainbows here are so frequent, and so peculiarly beautiful. Of an amazing breadth, and with colours vivid beyond description, I knew not whether most to admire this aërial phenomenon when suspended in the western sky, one end of the bow sinks behind the island of Boffin, while at the distance of several leagues, the other rests upon the misty hills of Innis Turc; or when, at a later hour of the day, **it** has appeared stretched across the ample sides of Muilrea, penetrating far into the deep blue waters that flow at its base. With feelings of grateful recollection too, we may hail the repeated visits of this heavenly messenger, occasionally as often as five or six times in the course of the same day, in a country exposed to such astonishing, and at times almost incessant, floods of rain."

This perpetual humidity of the climate of Ireland has most probably produced the attachment which the inhabitants are said to possess for their favourite spirit—whiskey. The practice of obtaining spirits by the distillation of malt is of very great antiquity, and it would appear that the Irish understood the art at the earliest period of the invention better than any other people. Sir James Ware believes that ardent spirits were distilled in Ireland much earlier than in England: he says, "the English *aqua vitæ*, it is thought, is the invention of more modern times. Yet we find the virtues of usquebaugh and a receipt for making it, both simple and compound, in the Red Book of Ossory, compiled nearly two hundred years ago; and another receipt for making a liquor then called *nectar*, made of a mixture of honey and wine, to which are added ginger, pepper, cinnamon, and other ingredients." Dr. Ledwich remarks, that the French poets speak of this nectar with rapture, as a most delicious beverage. The Irish produced two kinds of spirits, one distilled from the black oats of the country in a raw or unfermented state, which they called *builceann*, from *buille*, madness, and *ceann*, the head, indicating the intoxicating qualities of the liquor; the other, distilled from malted barley, and flavoured by the addition of aromatic ingredients, received the name of *uisge-beatha* or *uisge-bagh*, (water of life,) from whence *uisge* corrupted into the modern *whiskey*. Moryson, the secretary to Lord Mountjoy, who wrote a history of Ireland in 1599, says, that "the Irish *aqua vitæ*, vulgarly called *usquebagh*, is held the best in the world of that kind, which is made also in England, but nothing so good as that which is brought out of Ireland. The mingling of fennel seed and other things mitigating the heat, and making the taste pleasant, makes it less inflame and yet refresh the weak stomach with moderate heat and good relish." But the long train of evils which the pleasant demon, whiskey, has brought into Ireland, ought to make its very name accursed upon Irish lips. Every person who knows the ardent temperament of this people, their quick passions, which the slightest stimulant excites into madness, will, I think, agree with me, that more than half the feuds, the faction-fights, and the midnight outrages which have disgraced the country, owe their fosterage, if not their origin, to the baneful influence of intoxicating liquors. I feel satisfied that the manufacture of illicit whiskey has been one of the most formidable, yet lightly regarded obstacles to the moralization of the Irish peasantry. Like poaching in England, it is the first step in the road to the gallows,—the initiatory lesson in law breaking, which is almost invariably followed by the perpetration of acts of deeper guilt, until the arm of justice terminates the dark calendar of crime with the life of the offender. To escape the vigilance of the excise-officers, requires the exercise of great caution and considerable ingenuity, on the part of the persons engaged in the hazardous business of illicit distillation. For this purpose, the "still-house," as they term the miserable hut in which the whiskey is made, is frequently constructed on the side of a wild mountain, where the low roof, covered with *scraws*, or sods, assimilates so closely in appearance to the brown heathery surface of the mountain, that it is almost impossible to distinguish one from the other. Sometimes the private manufactory is placed in the centre of an extensive bog into which no gauger dare venture, except by day, at which time his approach can be descried at a great distance, and a perfect concealment of all the illegal apparatus and produce effected before he can reach the expected prize. A favourite site too for a still-house, is on an island in one of those lonely lakes with which Connemara and other mountain-districts in Ireland abound. In such a situation detection is almost impossible, as there is rarely more than one boat on the lake, and the whiskey makers take good care that their enemies shall not get possession of it. The smoke of the turf or peat employed in the process of drying the malted barley, gives that peculiar flavour to the illicit whiskey which is so much relished by native epicures in the article, though to a stranger, the *haut-gout* of a reeking tumbler of *potteen** punch, is generally far from being agreeable.

The features of the landscape are not less strikingly picturesque than the costume of the people, particularly the women of these Irish Highlands. Civilization and the increasing intercourse with strangers are, however, fast obliterating these peculiarities, and the traveller visiting Connemara will rarely perceive any difference in the dress of the people from that of the peasantry in other districts. Formerly a Connemara buck when dressed in his holiday attire, wore a pair of breeches open at the knee—his legs being encased in a pair of those soft, warm woollen stockings, of a light-blue or grey colour, for whose manufacture this place has been long celebrated,† and his feet inserted into a pair of stout leather brogues‡ with a fresh coat of grease of some kind

---

* Potteen, a name derived from the little pot in which the illicit whiskey is distilled.

† The Connemara stockings, manufactured from the fine soft wool of the mountain-sheep, were famous all over Ireland for their superior warmth and elasticity.

‡ The Irish brogue differs materially from the modern shoe, the sole of the shoe being stitched to the upper-leather with hempen threads twisted and waxed—while the sole and upper of the brogue are merely sewed together by a leathern thong. Ancient Irish brogues of very elegant form—composed of raw hides, tastefully ornamented—are not infrequently found in the bogs of Ireland. The brogue on the foot, and the coolin or long hair on the head, were for a length of time the distinctive marks of an Irishman—hence arose the saying, "He speaks with a brogue," when a person spoke with the Irish national accent.

or another. The blue frieze trusty, or great—coat—fastened like a mantle by a single button, or a strong clasp at the throat fell loosely from his shoulders, the vacant sleeves, into which he never dreamed of thrusting his arms, swinging idly on each side. A gay-coloured silk neck-handkerchief—a smart, narrow-brimmed hat, placed airily on one side of his head—and a good stout oak-sapling completed the appointments of a young fellow going to mass on a Sunday, accompanied by his sweetheart, who most probably would wear a scarlet linsey-woolsey petticoat—of sufficient brevity to show the proportions of a pair of handsome legs, set off, like the men's, with blue woollen stockings and brogues. A coloured cotton gown, drawn up in front, and pinned behind, displayed the scarlet petticoat to advantage;—the outer covering for the body being a blue cloak or mantle, with a hood, which might be drawn over the head at the pleasure of the wearer. The females also usually wear thin muslin caps, which come close to the face, and are profusely ornamented with showy ribbons. The frieze coat, of which I have been speaking, and the manner of wearing it loosely on the shoulders, are derived from the fashion of the mantle formerly worn by the Irish—which, according to the description of it, must have been the most commodious garment in the simplest form that could be devised. The poet Spenser, who resided in Ireland during some of its most troubled days, and who writes in a bitter and hostile spirit of the country, describes the mantle as answering the purposes of housing, bedding, and clothing to the turbulent Irish; "for,"says he, "it is a fit house for an outlaw, a meet bed for a rebel, and an apt cloke for a thiefe." He informs us how the outlaw, fleeth for his villanies into waste places, "where he maketh his mantle his house, and under it covereth himself from the wrath of heaven, from the offence of the earth, and from the sight of men. When it raineth it is his pent-house; when it bloweth it is his tent; when it freezeth it is his tabernacle. In sommer he can wear it loose; in winter he can wrap it close; at all times he can use it, never heavy, never cumbersome." Again he says, "yea, and oftentimes their mantle serveth them (the rebels) when they are neere driven, being wrapped about their left-arm instead of a target; for it is hard to cut thorough with a sword, besides it is light to beare and light to throw away."

In no part of Ireland is the national love for dancing more decidedly manifested than in the West of Ireland; the meetings for the purpose of indulging in this favourite pastime occur upon every occasion where business or pleasure draws a number of the peasantry to any particular neighbourhood. Fairs, markets, patrons, races, and hurling-matches are invariably accompanied by dances in the cabins near the spot, or in canvas tents erected for the occasion. The music is usually supplied to the dancers by an old fidler, or a blind piper, who receives a donation of a halfpenny or a penny from each couple as they stand up to *"welt the flure,"* to the music of "The Hare in Corner," or some other equally favourite jigg. A good piper has always been regarded as a person of no trifling importance in the district where he resides, or rather where he moves; for he is perpetually shifting his quarters from one place of merriment to another. Some of the pipers of the last century acquired considerable popularity amongst the higher classes of Society, and were much sought after, on account of their exquisite skill as musicians. O'Keefe in his *"Recollections"* relates a characteristic story of the pride of the famous Munster piper, Macdonnel, who, he says, lived in great style, keeping servants, grooms, hunters, &c. "One day that I and a very large party dined with Mr. Thomas Grant, of Cork, Macdonnel was sent for to play for the company during dinner; a table and chair was placed for him on the landing, outside the room, a bottle of claret and a glass on the table, and a servant waiting behind the chair designed for him—the door left wide open. He made his appearance, took a rapid survey of the preparation for him, filled his glass, stepped to the dining-room door, looked fill into the room and said, 'Mr. Grant, your health and company'! drank it off, threw half-a-crown on his table, saying to the servant— 'There, my lad, is two shillings for my bottle of wine, and keep the sixpence for yourself.' He ran out of the house, mounted on his hunter, and galloped off, followed by his groom."

Connemara, though it cannot boast a musician of such aristocratic pride as Macdonnel, possesses one of great local celebrity, in the person of Paddy Coneely, the blind piper. He is famous as the best player of jiggs and reels in the country, and no rustic dance would be thought to be complete in its arrangements that had not Paddy to give spirit to it by his admirable music. But it is not to his talents as piper that he owes all the interest that attaches to him; the extraordinary faculty, despite his blindness, which he possesses, of acquiring the most accurate topographical knowledge, is really astonishing. An ingenious writer upon Irish characteristics gives some striking traits of this singular individual. "Ask any questions respecting an old church or castle in his hearing, and ten to one he will give a more correct description of its locality, and a more accurate account of its size, height, and general features than, any one else; speak of a mountain, and he will break out with some such remark as this—' I discovered a beautiful spring on the top of that mountain, sir, that no one ever before heard of.'" His knowledge of atmospheric appearances and influences is equally, if not still more remarkable. He can always tell with the nicest accuracy the point from which the wind blows, and predict with a degree of certainty we never saw excelled, the probable steadiness of the weather, or any approaching change likely to take place in it. He is a perfect barometer in this way, for his conclusions are chiefly drawn from a delicate perception of the state of the atmospheric air, imperceptible to others, and are rarely erroneous. Paddy is extremely curious in his topographical examinations—nothing, however dangerous or seemingly inaccessible, escapes his observation; not a bridge, stream, river, glen, or mountain, within the circuit of his perigrinations, has been left unexplored by the *dark* piper. Paddy, in addition to his other anomalous tastes, is a keen sportsman, and enjoys a good coursing-match with as much relish as if he were in possession of sight as quick as his greyhounds. Indeed, he has never been heard to regret the loss of sight but once, and that was on the occasion of a country horse-race, when he was separated by accident from his friends, and being a considerable distance from the starting-post, he exclaimed, with great Irish *naiveté,* "Dear, dear, if I had my *sight* now, I might be able to *hear* the horses starting."

Near to Flynn's Inn—where we have halted with our readers during this digression —is a famous place of pilgrimage, St. Patrick's Well. The west of Ireland seems more particularly the inheritance of St. Patrick, for in this part of the island he spent much of the noviciate of his canonization. Respecting the birth-place of Ireland's apostle, there has been great difference of opinion; but his own confession—a work acknowledged of genuineness—proves him to have been a native of Armorica—a district of Gaul, now known as the territory of Boulogne. The time of his birth, according to the best authorities, may be assigned to A.D. 387. At the age of sixteen he was made a captive by the Irish monarch, Nial of the Nine Hostages, who, after ravaging the coasts of Britain, extended his conquest to the maritime districts of Gaul. In Ireland the young Patrick was purchased as a slave, and served six years tending the sheep of a man named Milcho; in the seventh year of his slavery he escaped to the coast from his master, and being received on board a merchant-Vessel was conveyed back to Gaul. Soon after his return he repaired to the college of St. Martin, near Tours, where his education being completed, he entered into the ecclesiastical state. The condition of Ireland, buried at the time in the darkest paganism, had doubtless left a strong impression on his enthusiastic mind, and being warned by a dream, he turned his thoughts to the conversion of that country. It was not, however, until he was upwards of forty years of age, that the long-coveted opportunity of undertaking his pious mission occurred; when he was sent by Pope Celestine as bishop to Ireland; and proceeding, after a short stay in Britain, to the scene of his labours, he arrived in the island, according to the Irish annals, in the first year of the pontificate of Sextus III. His first landing is supposed to have been in or near the harbour of Dublin; but being repulsed there and at some other places in Leinster, he steered his course to the coast of Ulster, and landed at a small port near Strangford. Here he succeeded in making some converts, and soon after he determined to celebrate the Christian festival of Easter in the very neighbourhood

Street in Galway

Abbey of Clare, Galway

of the Hall of Tara, where the princes and states of the kingdom were at the time assembled. The result of this bold but politic step was productive of the happiest results. The monarch Leogaire, the arch-druid Dubtach, and several of the lesser princes of the country becanie converts to Christianity. His spiritual labours from that time,—though dwelt upon with fond minuteness by his biographers, present only a succession of triumphs similar to that which marked his great effort in the mighty work of conversion at Tara. Multitudes flocked to him from every quarter, to receive baptism at his hands—churches were built, congregations formed, and priests appointed to watch over them, until the monstrous doctrines of Paganism were effectually rooted out of the land, and the benevolent truths of Christianity planted in their stead. Having thus filled the greater part of the island with Christians and with churches, the saint completed his labours by establishing a metropolitan see at Armagh; where, resting in the midst of the glorious work he had accomplished, he passed the remainder of his days between Armagh and his favourite retreat at Sabhul, in the barony of Lecale, the spot that had witnessed the first dawning of his apostolic career, and now shared the calm radiance which attended its setting; and where, on the 17th March, A.D. 465, he died, having then reached his seventy-eighth year.

XIII.

As you approach Galway, the universality of red petticoats, and the same brilliant colour in most other articles of female dress, give a foreign aspect to the population, which prepares you somewhat for the completely Italian or Spanish look of most of the streets of the town. It was a market-day when I arrived, and the large square in front of the inn was thronged with hundreds of people, shoeless and stockingless, but all with their "top-hamper," as the sailor would say, of this gayest of colours. Not only in dress, however, but in vivid gesticulation, and in a certain massiveness of feature, the Galwayians struck me as differing from all the other Irish I had seen. The noise of the potato and pig traders was perfectly deafening, and there seemed the promise of a fight in every group engaged in traffic. After wandering awhile among the baskets and carts, I turned down a well-thronged street, and was immediately struck with the singular architecture of some of the old SPANISH HOUSES, still in tolerable preservation. To me it seemed irresistibly like a street in Italy; and Inglis, who has travelled in Spain, says that at every step he saw something to recall Span to his recollection. "I found,"he says," the wide entries and broad stairs of Cadiz and Malaga; the arched gateways with the outer and inner railing, and the court within—

needing only the fountain and flower-vases to emulate Seville. I found the sculptured gateways and grotesque architecture, which carried the imagination to the Moorish cities of Granada and Valencia. I even found the little sliding-wicket for observation in one or two doors, reminding one of the secrecy, mystery, and caution observed, where gallantry and superstition divide life between them."

Galway was a famous town when its Spanish merchants were princes; but their fine dwellings were at one period usurped and defaced by the rabble, and little remains of the interiors to show their ancient glory. A gentleman who joined me in my walk took me to Lombard-street, to show me the antique front of the house of the far-famed Lynch Fitzstephen, the "Roman father" of Galway. It is a tottering old house with a tablet over the door, on which is sculptured a death's head over cross-bones, and a corresponding inscription. The story of his "stern virtue" is thus told.

"A few years before the battle of Knocktuadh, an extraordinary instance of civic justice occurred in this town, which in the eyes of its citizens elevated their chief magistrate to a rank with the inflexible Roman. James Lynch Fitzstephen, an opulent merchant, was mayor of Galway in 1493. He had made several voyages to Spain, as a considerable intercourse was then kept up between that country and the western coast of Ireland. When returning from his last visit he brought with him the son of a respectable merchant named Gomez, whose hospitality he had largely experienced, and who was now received by his family with all that warmth of affection which from the earliest period has characterised the natives of Ireland. Young Gomez soon became the intimate associate of Walter Lynch, the only son of the mayor, a youth in his twenty-first year, and who possessed qualities of mind and body which rendered him an object of general admiration; but with these was unhappily united a disposition to libertinism, which was a source of the greatest affliction to his father. The worthy magistrate, however, was now led to entertain hopes of a favourable change in his son's character, as he was engaged in paying honourable addresses to a beautiful young lady of good family and fortune. Preparatory to the nuptials, the mayor gave a splendid entertainment, at which young Lynch fancied his intended bride viewed his Spanish friend with too much regard. The fire of jealousy was instantly lighted up in his distempered brain, and at their next interview he accused his beloved Agnes of unfaithfulness to him. Irritated at its injustice, the offended fair one disdained to deny the charge, and the lovers parted in anger.

"On the following night, while Walter Lynch slowly passed the residence of his Agnes, he observed young Gomez to leave the house, as he had been invited by her father to spend that evening with him. All his suspicions now received the most dreadful confirmation, and in maddened fury he rushed on his unsuspecting friend, who, alarmed by a voice which the frantic rage of his pursuer prevented him from recognizing, fled towards a solitary quarter of the town near the shore. Lynch maintained the fell pursuit till his victim had nearly reached the water's edge, when he overtook him, darted a poniard into his heart, and plunged his body bleeding into the sea, which during the night threw it back again upon the shore, where it was found and recognized on the following morning.

"The wretched murderer, after contemplating for a moment the deed of horror which he had perpetrated, sought to hide himself in the recesses of an adjoining wood, where he passed the night a prey to all those conflicting feelings which the loss of that happiness he had so ardently expected, and a sense of guilt of the deepest dye could inflict. He at length found some degree of consolation in the firm resolution of surrendering himself to the law, as the only means now left to him of expiating the dreadful crime which he had committed against society. With this determination, he bent his steps towards the town at the earliest dawn of the following morning; but he had scarcely reached its precincts, when he met a crowd approaching, amongst whom, with shame and terror, he observed his father on horseback, attended by several officers of justice. At present the venerable magistrate had no suspicion that his only son was the assassin of his friend and guest; but when young Lynch proclaimed himself the murderer, a conflict of feelings seized the wretched father beyond the power of language to describe. To him, as chief magistrate, was entrusted the power of life and death. For a moment the strong affection of a parent pleaded in his breast in behalf of his wretched son; but this quickly gave place to a sense of duty in his magisterial capacity, as an impartial dispenser of the laws. The latter feeling at length predominated; and though he now perceived that the cup of earthly bliss was about to be for ever dashed from his lips, he resolved to sacrifice all personal considerations to his love of justice, and ordered the guard to secure their prisoner.

"The sad procession moved slowly towards the prison amidst a concourse of spectators, some of whom expressed the strongest admiration at the upright conduct of the magistrate, while others were equally loud in their lamentations for the unhappy fate of a highly-accomplished youth who had long been a universal favourite. But the firmness of the mayor had to withstand a still greater shock when the mother, sisters, and intended bride of the wretched Walter beheld him who had been their hope and pride approach pale, bound, and surrounded with spears. Their frantic outcries affected every heart except that of the inflexible magistrate, who had now resolved to sacrifice life, with all that makes life valuable, rather than swerve from the path of duty.

"In a few days the trial of Walter Lynch took place; and in a provincial town of Ireland, containing at that period not more than three thousand inhabitants, a father was beheld sitting in judgment, like another Brutus, on his only son; and like him too, condemning that son to die, as a sacrifice to public justice. Yet the trial of the firmness of the upright and inflexible magistrate did not end here. His was a virtue too refined for vulgar minds : the populace loudly demanded the prisoner's release, and were only prevented by the guards from demolishing the prison, and the mayor's house which adjoined it; and their fury was increased by learning that the unhappy prisoner had now become anxious for life. To these ebullitions of popular rage were added the intercessions of persons of the first rank and influence in Galway, and the entreaties of his dearest relatives and friends; but while Lynch evinced all the feeling of a father and a man placed in his singularly distressing circumstances, he undauntedly declared that the law should take its course.

"On the night preceding the fatal day appointed for the execution of Walter Lynch, this extraordinary man entered the dungeon of his son , holding in his hand a lamp, and accompanied by a priest. He locked the grate after him, kept the keys fast in his hand, and then seated himself in a recess of the wall. The wretched culprit drew near, and, with a faltering tongue, asked if he had anything to hope. The mayor answered, 'No, my son; your life is forfeited to the laws, and at sunrise you must die. I have prayed for your prosperity; but that is at an end—with this world you have done for ever. Were any other but your wretched father your judge, I might have dropped a tear over my child's misfortune, and solicited for his life, even though stained with murder : but you must die; these are the last drops which shall quench the sparks of nature; and if you dare hope, implore that Heaven may not shut the gates of mercy on the destroyer of his fellow-creature. I am now come to join with this good man in petitioning God to give you such composure as will enable you to meet your punishment with becoming resignation.' After this affecting address, he called on the clergyman to offer up their united prayers for God's forgiveness to his unhappy son, and that he might be fully fortifled to meet the approaching catastrophe. In the ensuing supplications at a throne of mercy, the youthful culprit joined with fervour, and spoke of life and its concerns no more.

"Day had scarcely broken when the signal of preparation was heard among the guards without. The father rose, and assisted the executioner to remove the fetters which bound his unfortunate son. Then unlocking the door , he placed him between the priest and himself, leaning upon an arm of each. In this manner they ascended a flight of steps lined with soldiers, and were passing on to gain the street, when a new trial assailed the magistrate, for which he appears not to have been unprepared. His wretched wife, whose name was Blake, failing in her personal exertions to save the life of her son, had gone in distraction to the heads of her own family, and prevailed on them, for the honour of their house, to rescue him from ignominy. They flew to arms, and a prodigious concourse soon assembled to support them, whose outcries for mercy to the culprit would have shaken any nerves less firm than those of the mayor of Galway. He exhorted them to yield submission to the laws of their country; but finding all his efforts fruitless to accomplish the ends of justice at the accustomed place and by the usual hands, he by a desperate victory over parental feeling, resolved himself to perform the sacrifice which he had vowed to pay on its altar. Still retaining a hold of his unfortunate son, he mounted with him by a winding

Galway

stair within the building, that led to an arched window overlooking the street, which lie saw filled with the populace. Here he secured the end of the rope, which had been previously fixed round the neck of his son, to an iron staple which projected from the wall, and after taking from him a last embrace, he launched him into eternity.

"The intrepid magistrate expected instant death from the fury of the populace; but the people seemed so much overawed and confounded by the magnanimous act, that they retired slowly and peaceably to their several dwellings. The innocent cause of this sad tragedy is said to have died soon after of grief, and the unhappy father of Walter Lynch to have secluded himself during the remainder of his life from all society except that of his mourning family."

There is a very good view of GALWAY FROM THE CLADDAGH, a suburb of rather a singular character. We strolled thither from our contemplation of the death's-head over the door of the unhappy Fitzstephen, and found enough in the oddity of the little fishing-town to divert us from the melancholy impression we had received. "The inhabitants of the Claddagh,"says Wright," about three thousand in number, speak a dialect of the ancient Irish, retain their pristine dress and customs, and, with an old-fashioned pride, boast of the separateness of their origin and race. Strangers, whom they call *transplanters,* they do not welcome with that hospitality that generally belongs to an ancient state of things, and they appear to have a timidity of forming matrimonial alliances beyond the limits of their own little dynasty. The marriage portion is peculiarly emblematical, and is, perhaps, the bearing adopted in the arms of the town; it is a small fishing-boat, or, amongst the poorest, a share in one, given to the son-in-law.

"Their dexterity in the management of the boat, and in encountering the dangers incident to the fisherman's life, is proverbial; and landsmen may view with surprise the happy results of skill, prudence, and propriety in the pursuit of a life so full of peril. Part of their time is devoted to the mending of their nets; another, but smaller, to the enjoyments of the alehouse: but when once they put out to sea, they become cautiously alive to their awful situation, and taking with them oaten cake, potatoes, water, and fire, never suffer any species of malt drink or spirits to form part of their store. The fisherman's return, however, is touched with different tints; safe ashore, he throws his cares overboard, commits the cargo to the happy wife and innocent children that hail his safe arrival, and withdrawing with his messmates to the fireside, makes joyous offerings to the god of wine. During the husband's festivities are the hours of industry of wife and children; to them belong the exclusive task of disposing of the fish, and the duties of purse-bearer and controller of the household.

"On the eve of St. John the election of a mayor and sheriffs is made by the Clad dagh boys. Their mock ceremony is accompanied by real mirth; fires are lighted up in various places through the town, round which boys and girls dance in joyous hilarity, armed with long-handled besoms made of dock stems, with which they gently touch each passenger who refuses to obey the mandate of 'honour the bonfire.' The attendants of the mayor and sheriffs are also armed with like rude *fasces* of authority, which in the plenitude of fun, are ultimately set on fire, and whirled round over the heads of the noisy corporation.

"The noble bay of Galway is the unfailing treasure of the Claddagh boys, and the origin and cause of the growing importance of Galway. The surface spreads over an area of two hundred square miles, the Arran Islands being taken as its sea boundary or breakwater. Its waters wash a coast of thirty miles, indented with secure and deep harbours, and possessing numerous roadsteads. In the deep water, sunfish, hake, cod, and turbot are taken in all their varieties, and on a ground that is believed to be an extension of the Newfoundland Bank. Along the shores crustaceous fish are caught, and large and delicious oysters at Pouldudy, Burrin, and Rinvarragh. Herrings abound here in the season, and their exclusive capture is claimed by the Claddagh boys. The salmon fishing yields an annual revenue of £500, although the retail price is trifling, and the entire draught consumed at home."

I left the crowded and foreign-looking streets of Galway most unwillingly, and passed my last afternoon in a visit to the fine ruins of CLARE ABBEY, beautifully situated on the banks of the Clare river near its entrance into Lough Corrib. Thence I kept on my way to Athlone and Clonmacnoise.

its fall—it is even surprising that it does not tumble; and I suspect that it would long ago have fallen a victim to the elements or to the barbarous violence of the people, were it not that it is considered as part of an expiating penance for the pilgrim to creep on his bare knees under this arch while approaching the altar-stone of this chapel, where sundry paters and ayes must be repeated as essential to keeping the station. Adjoining this is a holy stone on which St. Kieran sat, and the sitting on it now, under the affiance of faith, proves a sovereign cure for all epileptic people.

"Here is the largest enclosure of tombs and churches I have anywhere seen in Ireland. What a mixture of old and new graves! Modern inscriptions recording the death and virtues of the sons of little men, the rude forefathers of the surrounding hamlets;—ancient inscriptions in the oldest forms of Irish letters, recording the deeds and the hopes of kings, bishops, and abbots, buried a thousand years ago, lying about broken, neglected, and dishonoured, what would I give could I have deciphered! I should have been glad had time allowed, to be permitted to transcribe them. And what shall I do with all those ancient towers, and crosses, and churches, without a guide? I looked around : there were many people in the sacred enclosure; some kneeling in the deepest abstraction of devotion at the graves of their departed friends,—the streaming eye, the tremulous hand, the bowed-down body, the whole soul of sorrowful reminiscence and of trust in the goodness of the God of spirits, threw a sacred solemnity about them that few indeed, though counting their act superstitious, would presume to interrupt; he who would venture so to do, must be one indeed of little feeling. I saw others straggling through the place—some half intoxicated, sauntering or stumbling over the gravestones—others hurrying across the sacred enclosure, as if hastening to partake of the last dregs of debauchery in the tents of the patron-green.

"After looking about vaguely for some time, this church of St. Kieran was what caught my particular attention. It was extremely small, more an insignificant oratory than what could be called a church;—a tall man could scarcely lie at length in it; a mason would have contracted to build its walls for a week's wages; yet this, my mendicant guide said, was the old church of St. Kieran. The walls had all gone awry from their foundations; they had collapsed together, and presented a picture of desolation without grandeur. Beside it was a sort of cavity or hollow in the ground, as if some persons had lately been rooting to extract a badger or a fox; but here it was that the people, supposing St. Kieran to be deposited, have rooted diligently for any particle of clay that could be found, in order to carry home that holy earth, Steep it in the water, and drink it; and happy is the votary who is now able amongst the bones and stones to pick up what has the semblance of soil, in order to commit it to his stomach as a means of grace, or as a sovereign remedy against diseases of all sorts.

"From the little oratory of St. Kieran, the woman led us on to the largest of the ruined churches, which, after all, is of no great size; but still it is the most remarkable

Entrance doorway of Temple McDurmot, Clonmacnoise

of any, not only for its greater size, but for the beauty of its western entrance, and the exquisite and elaborate workmanship of its northern doorway. This church is said to have been originally erected by the M'Dermots, princes of the northern parts of Roscommon; a tablet on the wall, near the eastern window, records that it was repaired in 1647, by M'Coghlan, the lord of the adjoining territories.

"Whether the northern doorway into this church existed prior to the repairs of M'Coghlan, or whether executed by his direction, I am not competent to decide; but I am induced to believe that it was constructed in a more auspicious day of taste in Gothic architecture in Ireland. It is executed in blue limestone, marble it may well be called, and the elaborate tracery, on which the whole fancy and vagary of Gothic license is lavished, stands forth as sharp, fresh, and clean as if but yesterday from under the chisel.

"Amongst the other ornaments of this highly-finished doorway are figures in alto rilievo one evidently of a bishop giving his blessing, the other of an abbot; the third figure is much mutilated, and that apparently done on purpose."

"Proceeding from M'Dermot's church, our attention was directed to a very fine stone cross, the largest in the place, formed of one piece, and covered with carvings in basso rilievo and inscriptions, which had I the ability, my time would not allow me to decipher. 'Come, my good woman,' said I, 'tell what may be the stories told of these figures.' 'Why, then, myself cannot tell you anything about them, they are all out ancient; may be Darby Claffy yonder, the ouldest man about time churches, could tell you somewhat.' Now Darby Claffy was standing idle, leaning not far off against the wall of Dowling's church, looking up at O'Rourke's tower, and a finer studio for a sketcher than the head, face, and form of the venerable-looking man could not be seen : eighty winters had dropped their flakes as light as snow-feathers on his head; arid there he stood, with his hat off, his fine Guido countenance and expressive face, a living accompaniment to all the grey venerability that was around. 'Come over here, Darby Claffy, honest man, and tell the strange gintlemen all you know about them crosses and things—musha, myself forgets; at any rate I must run and show Judy Delancy, the simple crathur, where to find her father's grave. Heaven be wid yees, gintlemen, and don't forget poor Judy.' A shilling given to her seemed the source of unutterable joy; her little son that was beside her, appearing as if he never saw so large a coin, snatched it in raptures from his mammy, and danced about the gravestones in triumph. I was pleased to buy human joy so cheaply. The old man did not belie his fine countenance; his mind was stored with traditionary recollections concerning Clonmacnoise, which, if not according to recorded facts, were founded on them; and he spoke with perfect assurance in the truth of what he said, and of the sanctity of all around. 'Can you, my honest fellow, tell us anything about the figures carved on this cross?' 'A little, plase your honour; but *sartain* I'm no scholar. Come here now, mister, do you see that figure with the keys? That is St. Pether; and that there beside him is St. Kieran. Do you see a book in his hand? That is the Gospel of St. Matthew, which Kieran learned so well from holy Finian, of Clonard, in the county Meath, where in ould times there was a great school, somewhat the same as Maynooth now is, whence young Father Flinnerty has just come home edicated; well, plase your honours, Kieran was called Kieran of St. Matthew, because he knew that Gospel so well. And do now look below Pether and Kieran, and don't you notice young men smiling, and one playing the bagpipes? Well, this represents the young priests that Kieran brought with him to Clonmacnoise; and as well becomes the divil, he must needs envy their devotions, and he used to come by night and play his bagpipes to divart them there, and draw them off from their vesper duties; and up they'd get from their knees, when the ould boy, in the shape of a piper, would play a planxty, and set a bait, (they couldn't for their life help it,) jigging it away. Now St. Pether in Heaven saw, to be sure, all this, and so he comes down to tell Kieran of it; and, moreover he falls upon Satan in a thrice;—don't you see him there how he has tumbled the enemy of man? and, as you see there, is sending him headlong to hell.' There was certainly something like a man playing the pipes cut on the cross, and a representation of two persons contending, and one getting the better of thie other; but whether old Claffy was right in his reading I cannot say. This cross is certainly one of the finest I have seen in Ireland; I question whether it is even inferior to those immense ones that are at Monasterboice, in the county of Louth.

"From thence we proceeded, the old man following us, to the church and round tower, which stands in the north-western extremity of the cemetery, and which is usually called M'Carthy's church and tower. The round tower, though small, is one of the most perfect in Ireland; it is conically capped, and the ranges of stone forming the cover are of the most beautiful and singular arrangement. The tower stands on the south side of the chancel of the church; and the doorway of the tower, instead of being elevated ten or fifteen feet from the ground, is on a level with the floor of the chancel from which it leads; it is within a few feet of time altar : moreover the archway leading from the nave of the church into the chancel, which is of the most finished and at the same time chaste order of Gothic construction, is wrought into the body of the round tower, part of whose rotundity is sacrificed to give room and form to the display of its light and elegant span. Now these two circumstances convince me that, in the first place, the church and tower were built at the same time; moreover, that as the church was placed more remote than other churches, and nearer invaders coming across the Shannon, the tower was provided as a look-out station and place of ready retreat for the priests to retire to with their sacred vessels and books.

"M'Carthy's church, in the north-west corner of the cemetery, was built by the M'Carthy More of Munster, the greatest sept in Cork; he who held under his sway the O'Learys and the O'Sullivans and the O'Donohus, and I don't know how many

Ancient Cross, Clonmacnoise

Doonass Rapids near Castle Connel

147

more Melesian O's and Macs. It is a curious and peculiarly interesting ruin, because, as I said before, there is here evident proof that the round tower and church were built at the same time; for besides that they both are formed of the same kind of stone, and are constructed with the same range and character of masonry, there is part of the rotundity of the tower sacrificed to give play to the full span of the chancel-arch, and exhibits one of the most chaste specimens in the world of what is called the Saxon arch. This tower is not large or lofty; it measures but seven feet in diameter within, and is but fifty-five feet high; it has a conical cap, which is essential, according to antiquarians, to make a round tower perfect; and a free-mason, supposing he was master of his craft, would say, 'Well done,' to the artist who constructed the beautiful courses of cut stone by which the cut cap was brought to a point. As I have already said, the door of the tower is level with the ground, and I think I could discern the marks of stairs that rose spirally to the top; unlike all other round towers, which, though there are marks of floors, story over story, in no other instance present marks of spiral stairs."

The Shannon from Portumna to Castle-Connell, including Loch Derg, is very like an American river, and except that its banks are so poorly wooded, it is equal in majestic natural beauty to several of our large waters. There is no point very strikingly picturesque, however, till we reach the ruined castle of the Kings of Munster, the warlike O'Briens, and here the Shannon for a considerable distance resembles the Rapids of the St. Lawrence. At the RAPIDS OF DUNASS, as they are called, the whole body of the Shannon pours over a mass of rocks descending considerably for half a mile, and into this picture comes the town of Castle-Connell, with its fine mansions, green lawns, and lofty towers, which adds much to the natural beauty of the river.

From this point to Limerick the Shannon is not navigable by boats, but the road runs close to the river-bank, and the beauty of the scene may thus be enjoyed by the traveller. There is much finer wood below than above Castle-Connell, and the country-seats are numerous and fine; Mount Shannon, Lord Clare's residence, perhaps the finest among them. Lady Chatterton in her agreeable book mentions that there is a tradition among the peasantry in the neighbourhood of Castle-Connell, that the ruins of the old castle above the town will fall upon the wisest person in the world if he should chance to pass under. A gentleman of much consideration in the neighbourhood fancied himself entitled to the honour of being crushed by them. He never could be prevailed on to approach the ruins, and when obliged to ride along the high road to Limerick, which runs near, he always passed the dangerous spot at full gallop.

I think no American traveller would enter Limerick without exclaiming in the principal street, "How very like New York!" The tall and handsome brick-houses, the iron railings, the broad and clean sidewalks, and something, it struck me too, in the

The Shannon

The Castle of Limerick

dress and style of the people reminded me very forcibly of my country. There was a chapel-bell ringing for an evening lecture, (it was just twilight,) and well-dressed persons were coming to it from all quarters, and this church-going feature perhaps contributed its share to the resemblance. I had had two hours of daylight ramble through the town before the evening shut in; and I must record my agreeable surprise at the beauty and thriftiness of the fair town of Limerick. In the morning I rose early, and mounted to get a view of LIMERICK AND THE SHANNON FROM THE CATHEDRAL TOWER. This fine river, with its handsome bridges, gives a grandeur to the view which would otherwise be wanting to so flat a country; yet in the charms of cultivation and quiet loveliness, the panorama from this elevated point is well worth the seeking. My guide called on me to admire the size of the bells, and with the words "Limerick bells," the story connected with them at once, and for the first time since my arrival in the town, recurred to my memory. "The remarkable fine bells of Limerick," so runs the story, "were originally brought from Italy : they had been manufactured by a young native, (whose name tradition has not preserved,) and finished after the toil of many years, and he prided himself upon his work. They were subsequently purchased by the prior of a neighbouring convent; and with the profits of this sale the young Italian procured a little villa, where he had the pleasure of hearing the tolling of his bells from the convent-cliff, and of growing old in the bosom of domestic happiness. This however was not to continue : in some of those broils, whether civil or foreign, which are the undying worm in the peace of a fallen land, the good Italian was a sufferer amongst many. He lost his all; and, after thie passing of the storm, found himself preserved alone amid the wreck of fortune, friends, family, and home. The convent in which the bells, the *chef—d'œuvre* of his skill, were hung, was razed to the earth, and these last carried away to another land. The unfortunate owner, haunted by his memories and deserted by his hopes, became a wanderer over Europe. His hair grew grey and his heart withered before he again found a home and a friend. In this desolation of spirit he formed the resolution of seeking the place to which those treasures of his memory had been finally borne. He sailed for Ireland, proceeded up the Shannon; the vessel anchored in the pool near Limerick, and he hired a small boat for the purpose of landing. The city was now before him, and he beheld St. Mary's steeple, lifting its turreted head above the smoke and mist of the old town. He sat in the stern and looked fondly towards it. It was an evening so calm and beautiful as to remind him of his own native haven in the sweetest time of year—the depth of the spring. The broad stream appeared like one smooth mirror, and the little vessel glided through it with almost a noiseless expedition. On a sudden, amid the general stillness, the bells tolled from the cathedral; the rowers rested on their oars, and the vessel went forward with the impulse it had received. The old Italian looked towards the city, crossed his arms on his breast, and lay back in his seat; home, happiness, early recollections, friends, family—all were in the sound, and went with it to his heart. When the rowers looked round they beheld him with his face still turned towards the cathedral, but his eyes were closed, and when they landed they found him cold!"

Descending from the cathedral tower with more difficulty than I ascended, from the dilapidated condition of the narrow stone staircase, I kept down the Shannon on the old-town side, to visit the ancient Castle of King John, the fine round towers of which still show nobly in every view from the other shore. New walls are built in with the old, and if I remember rightly, the castle is now used as a police-station, but it preserves its grandeur amid all the modern tenements which surround it. The old town, through the narrow streets of which I had made my way, is a very different place from the newer Limerick, and as Mr. Inglis remarks, a person entering the city by this avenue, and taking up his quarters there, would infallibly set down Limerick as the very vilest town he had ever entered. "The city is composed," says an historical writer, "of the English-town, the Irish-town, and the New-town-Perry. The first stands on the northern side of the river, being separated from the latter by a narrow arm of the Shannon, which embraces the English-town in its entire circumference; and on the north-west side of the great branch of the river, in the county of Clare, is the extensive and populous suburb of Thomondgate. The English-town has all the antiquated appearance of a close-built fortress, of the latter part of the seventeenth century : its venerable cathedral, narrow streets, and lofty houses, chiefly built in the Dutch or Flemish fashion, are said to give it a considerable resemblance to Rouen in Normandy. This gloom is however relieved at various openings by a view of the cheering waters of the Shannon, while the vicinity of the canal, and thie verdant fields and gardens which skirt the borders of the Abbey-river, afford a pleasant promenade to its dense population. The ground on which the New-town is built is rather elevated, and the soil is general gravelly and dry. The streets are spacious, cut each other at right-angles, and are occupied by elegant houses and merchants' stores, constructed of brick and limestone, for which the neighbouring district supplies the finest materials. A more superb city-view can hardly be presented to the eye, than the range of buildings from the new bridge to the Crescent, a distance little short of an English mile, including Rutland-street, Patrick-street, George's-street, and the Tontine; and its interest will be greatly heightened when the line of buildings is continued from the Crescent along the military road, and the projected square built on its left. Shops, tastefully laid out and richly furnished, line these streets, while others diverge to the right and left, which are chiefly occupied by the residences of the gentry. At every opening to the westward salubrious breezes from the Shannon inspire health and vigour; and a walk to the quays is amply compensated by the scenes of busy traffic there presented, and the various enlivening prospects which meet the eye. Here the packet-boat from Kilrush is landing her joyous passengers, whose nerves have been braced and spirits exhilarated by some weeks' residence on the shores of the Atlantic at Kilkee or Malbay. There turf- and fish-boats are discharging their cargoes, which are rapidly conveyed by Herculean porters to the dwellings of the consumers, amidst various specimens of Munster wit, sometimes delivered in the native language, and sometimes in Anglo-Irish. on the west are seen the distant towers of Carrig-o-gunnell Castle, and the Pool, where the larger ships ride at anchor in perfect security, while many a skiff cuts the blue wave. On the east appear the mill of Curragour, built in 1672, and its rapid current, which roars and eddies amidst rocks of various shapes and sizes; the bridge of Thomond, hoary with age; and the ivy-mantled turrets of King John's Castle, backed by the mountains of Clare and Tipperary. The city contains nearly fifty public edifices, about one-half of which stand on the south-west side of the river.

"The liberties comprehend about sixteen thousand Irish acres, extending from three to four miles south, east, and west of thie old city walls.

"The parish of St. Michael's, or the New-town of Limerick, is divided from the old city by a branch of the Shannon : it is described as containing two thousand houses and ten thousand inhabitants, and as comprising all the wealth and trade of the city."

I returned to English-town by THOMOND BRIDGE, one of the oldest structures in this part of Ireland. There were several bridges thrown across thie Shannon in the twelfth century, two of them by King Turlough O'Connor. It is supposed, however, that these were of wood, and that thie first stone bridges were erected by the Anglo-Normans. Thomond Bridge ranks as the most ancient of these, having been erected by the English adventurers as a necessary step to their intended subjugation of the ancient province of Thomond. This simple and apparently unskilful structure is perfectly level, and is built on fourteen arches, under each of which some marks of the hurdles on which it was erected are still visible. According to tradition, the original expense of building it was but *thirty pounds*. There are also some picturesque ruins of BAAL'S BRIDGE, now pulled down. The new structure of WELLESLEY BRIDGE, lately finished, is very handsome—erected from the designs of the late Alexander Nimmo.

The piers near these bridges were crowded with vessels, and the river-side, for some distance, presented the aspect of busy and thriving trade. The capabilities of the Shannon as a medium of trade have been very much discussed of late, and they are well developed in an article in the Dublin Penny Journal, from which we extract a portion. "The name of the river Shannon is familiar to the people of this kingdom; but all else concerning it is known to very few indeed. Most persons have learned from the common geographies, that in the centre of Ireland there rises a river of about the same length as the Thames, which, flowing through ten counties in a wide and fertilizing course, pours its waters into the Atlantic Ocean. The great resources and remarkable peculiarities of this river are still, however, little thought of and little understood. To those who have witnessed the eagerness with which in England the

Old Baal's Bridge, Limerick

Wellesley Bridge, Limerick

favours of nature are seized on and rendered available, and the indefatigable zeal with which her difficulties are overcome, it may well be matter of surprise that the Shannon does not enjoy the common facilities of unaided river navigation. Yet not only is this the case, but its superior adaptation and vast capabilities for all the purposes of commercial communication, are but imperfectly known to those most interested in the subject. A good deal of attention has latterly been given to the question of the improvement of the Shannon.

"Lough Allen, in the county of Leitrim, supplied by streams from the high and rugged mountains by which it is surrounded, forms the source in which the Shannon is considered to rise. The lake is about ten miles long, and is deeply imbedded in lofty hills, which contain rich and copious stores of iron and coal. Out of Lough Allen the river flows in a narrow and rather shallow and impeded channel; occasionally however widening into small lakes, between the counties of Leitrim and Roscommon, to Savesborough, where it expands into the great Lough Allen, twenty miles long and in some parts four broad. For thirty-seven miles to Portumna, the channel is more confined; but it is still a bold and wide river. From Portumna to Killaloe, its course is through Lough Derg, the largest of the Shannon lakes, being twenty-three miles long. At Killaloe it resumes the character of an ordinary river; but the navigation thence to Limerick is contracted and difficult. From Limerick to its mouth, the Shannon is a tideway, and appears in fact a great estuary or arm of the sea.

"From this sketch of thie Shannon's course, it is manifest that it possesses characteristics altogether different from those of the chief rivers of England. Unlike the equable flow of the Thames through its confined bed, differing but little from a canal, and admitting in much of its length of tracking along its banks, the Shannon pours its waters unconstrained through a very various country : now, with many falls, hastening past its rugged and uneven shores; and now, with gentle stream, coasting the low and rich meadows, which in winter the flood overflows; sometimes with close and narrow channel, and then opening into great lakes, like inland seas, studded with islands. Towing with horses on the banks can therefore be but little employed, and steam-vessels must be used to drag the loaded boats across the numerous loughs. In one respect the Shannon is unequalled by any river that we know of. From the sea to its head, a course of two hundred and thirty-four miles, it is navigable throughout. After the removal of some obstructions, and increasing the depth of the water in a few places, a barge of fifty tons burden may pass along its entire length from Lough Allen to the Atlantic.

"Ten counties possess the advantage of the proximity of the Shannon, which, at the lowest average, waters fifty miles of shore of each. What incalculable benefits then must accrue to this extensive district, by rendering the navigation thoroughly available for the purposes of intercourse! The soils of the counties bordering on the river, and consequently their productions, are different. Hitherto, notwithstanding the existence at their doors of a noble river, there have been no means of inter-change. A famine may rage in Leitrim and plenty prevail in Tipperary, yet the river Shannon affords no aid for the conveyance of the surplus produce of the one to supply the wants of the other. Potatoes may be very cheap in the south, and yet hardly to be procured in the north; turf may be had in one county for little more than the trouble of cutting it, while in another, at no considerable distance, the people may be suffering intensely from the want of fuel. Yet the Shannon—intended by nature as a great artery for the conveyance of commerce, that life's-blood of a people's prosperity—is not merely useless for the purposes of mutual assistance and communication among the inhabitants of its banks, but is actually a bar and impediment to their intercourse. Mr. Rhodes remarks, that the grand designs of nature have been in a great measure frustrated, and the river may not unaptly be compared to a sealed book. Were the navigation completed, how valuable in its effects would be the ready interchange of commodities amongst the various districts along its shores, extending and making equal the comforts of the people; aiding to remove the dangers of famine by opening to each locality the resources of all, and increasing the wealth and knowledge of the peasantry by the introduction of trade and all its attendant benefits! The transport of agricultural produce throughout the country bordering on the Shannon, would, however, form a small portion of the commerce of the river. Considerable quantities of corn are now conveyed by thie Shannon and Grand Canal to Dublin, for exportation to Liverpool; and this trade would be vastly increased by the improvement of the river. The mountains of Leitrim, round Lough Allen, abound in iron and coal. Here are situated the Arigna iron-works, producing about sixty tons of wrought iron per week : the quantity might be much increased by the opening of the navigation. The extensive coal-beds of this valuable district could also produce sufficient fuel for the entire country along the Shannon, were roads formed and the river laid open to the workings of industry and enterprise. There are excellent slate-quarries at Killaloe and other places; and marble, lime, and stone of every description may be procured in several districts close to the river; besides many natural productions at present unknown or disregarded,—inaccessible they may be said to be from the wretched state of the navigation.

"The extent of the country which would be immediately affected by the completion of this great line of communication, has been estimated at two million acres, in the heart of the island, rich in its various soils and numerous productions; yet where the peasantry are in the most miserable state of destitution, scarcely sustaining life by the wretched resources of poverty, numbers of them annually emigrating to England to obtain that employment denied them at home. Many districts of this country have been among the most disturbed and disorderly in Ireland. The providing of occupation, and of profitable markets for the produce of the soil, will vastly promote the peace and wealth of the country; and the increased comforts of the people will dispose them to habits of order and civilization. The introduction of British manufactures must greatly tend to elevate the condition of the people, and to enrich the English merchant, very important considerations in the discussion of our subject. The imports from Great Britain increase progressively each year, and must be much advanced by introducing so extensive a tract to all the wants of civilized society. The advantages of a great homemarket, whose demands are unaffected by political circumstances, cannot but he appreciated by the manufacturer. The benefits attending the completion of the Shannon navigation cannot be anticipated : many years must elapse before they are fully in operation; depending, as they must, so much upon the concurrent circumstances of the general state of the country, as respects the condition and habits of thie people, as well as the progress of other public improvements. The opening of the river will have but a partial influence, unless followed by the formation of roads to its banks, and the execution of other works necessary to facilitate the transport of the productions of the country, and to promote the intercourse between the Shannon and the districts more remote from its shores. As the intelligence, the habits, and comforts of the people, and their mode of agriculture improve, the trade of the Shannon will advance; and in the present and disgraceful condition of the inhabitants, we cannot form any reasonable estimate of the valuable consequences of the too-long delayed completion of this great work.

"The general wants of the navigation of the Shannon are simple in their nature, and easily effected : the deepening of the channel in some places—the placing of beacons and buoys, so essential in a river liable to great floods, and consequently of such variable width and depth—the erection of piers and landing-places—the formation of a complete system of roads to its banks from the surrounding country and the neighbouring towns and villages. But above all, and without which all else is useless or impracticable, the entire navigation should be placed under the control of an efficient and active body, responsible for its maintenance in a perfect and available condition, who should be guided in their management, not by their desire of profit, but solely with the view of rendering the river as useful and accessible as possible to the public."

XV.

THE SHANNON below Limerick is a broad and noble stream, but the nakedness of the shores deprived it of all charm for me. It is besides flat and sterile-looking; and after losing sight of The fine ruins of Carrig-o-Gonnell, I found the passage wearisome enough till we reached the domain of the great benefactor of this part of the country, Lord Monteagle, and began to near my destination at Tarbert. The Knight of Flin has a fine castle in this neighbourhood on the left bank of the river, and these two form oases in the desert. The SHANNON NEAR TARBERT assumes the look of an estuary, and the view here is altogether finer than farther up. I confess to great disappointment in the Shannon however, *malgré* the occasional beauties at and above Limerick : my expectations were too highly raised. Moore's poem of St. Senanus, (whose "Sacred Isle" is just below Tarbert,) and Sir Aubrey de Vere's elegant sonnet, give a romance to the Shannon, which paints it, in the fancy, too flatteringly.

> "River of billows! to whose mighty heart
> The tide-wave rushes of the Atlantic sea—
> River of quiet depths! by cultured lea,
> Romantic wood, or city's crowded *mart*—
> River of old poetic founts! that start
> From their lone mountain-cradles, wild and free,
> Nursed with the fawns, lulled by the wood-larks' glee,
> And cushat's hymeneal song apart!
>
> River of chieftains, whose baronial halls
> Like veteran warders watch each wave-worn steep,
> Portumna's towers, Bunratty's regal walls,
> Carrick's stern rock, the Geraldane's grey keep—
> River of dark mementoes—must I close
> My lips with Limerick's wrongs—with Aughrim's woes?"

The steamer passes Scattery Island after leaving Tarbert, and a good view is obtained of this poetical spot, which is graced with a round tower, one hundred and twenty feet high, and various ecclesiastical ruins. St. Senanus is said to have established a place of worship here before the arrival of St. Patrick, and it is to this day a place of Catholic pilgrimage. "It is recorded in the annals of Munster, that in the year 975, Brian Boroihme recovered this island from the Danes; it also appears that Queen Elizabeth granted it to the mayor and corporation of Limerick and their successors, who lately established their right thereto by a suit at law. The present possessor, a gentleman of taste, has fitted up a handsome lodge, and added many improvements."

A very interesting book, called Two Months at Kilkee, written by "Mary John

Knott," and embellished with some clever drawings, gives an excellent account of this little watering-place, and we must be indebted to it for a description of the views taken by the artist on this coast. "KILKEE, or Kilqui, is situated at Moore Bay, on the western coast of Ireland, in the county of Clare, about fifty English miles from Limerick, one hundred and seventy from Dublin, and twenty-five from Ennis, and its shore is washed by the Atlantic. Comparatively but a few years since it was only known as the residence of fishermen, whose habitations formed the row of cottages now called 'Old Kilkee.' At present there are upwards of one hundred comfortable houses and lodges for the accommodation of visitors, independent of the cottages in which the natives reside. Since that period the town has been gradually rising into importance, and it is probable will ere long, from the safety of its strand, and other peculiar circumstances, be one of the most desirable watering-places on the coast.

"The town, which commands a fine view of the bay, is built close to the sea, and assumes a semicircular form from the shape of the strand, which presents a smooth, white, sandy surface of above half a mile in length, where the invalid can, without fatigue or interruption, enjoy the exhilarating sea-breeze and surrounding scenery. The principal street runs nearly from one end of the village to the other; these extend to the strand, and at every few steps afford a view of the Atlantic wave dashing into foam against the cliffs which circumscribe its power, and the rocks of Duggana, which run nearly across the bay. Some of the houses at the 'west end' of the town, as well as a few in the village, are modern, with sufficient accommodation (including stabling and coach-houses) for the family of a nobleman or gentleman of fortune; and every gradation can be had, down to a cottage with a parlour, two small bed-rooms, and kitchen, the rent varying according to the accommodation and demand. A few of the largest, fully furnished, pay from £15 to £20 per month; but the average for comfortable, good lodges is from £6 to £8, and the smallest from £3 to £4, including a plentiful supply of milk, potatoes, and turf, according to the custom of the place. One circumstance which strongly recommends this place is the prevalence of *cleanliness,* for which the houses, beds, and natives are remarkable. The walls of several new lodges are now built, and I am informed that upwards of thirty are in progress. It is however evident, that many of the people, anxious to possess a lodge and reap the summer fruits, have overbuilt themselves, to use their own words. A large Roman Catholic chapel has been lately erected near the road : the Protestant place of worship is but temporarily fitted up at the end of the Marine Parade. It is intended to build a handsome edifice for this purpose in the centre of the new square, at the west end. The surrounding country presents a very bleak aspect, without a tree, shrub, or garden-flower to enliven its surface. A number of poor cabins diversify the scene from the village to the hilly distance, to the extreme point of which the hand of man has carried cultivation.

"An extensive bog reaches to the skirts of the town, and affords a plentiful supply of fuel at a very low rate, which confers an incalculable benefit on the inhabitants : a cheerful fire generally enlivens the hearth of the poorest cottage. There are three hotels or boarding-houses in the town, where board and lodging are provided for about twenty-five shillings per week : tolerably well-appointed jaunting-cars are *now* amongst the advantages which this town affords. There are two chalybeate spas in and near Kilkee, which, it is said, possess properties similar to the celebrated waters of Castle Connell. One of them is situated, as already mentioned, about a mile distant; the other is adjoining the town, but from its present neglected state and difficulty of approach, we believe it is little frequented by strangers. These obstacles might, however, be removed at a trifling expense, if a path were made from the road along the stream, and the spa covered in and placed under the care of some deserving poor person, who, by a small allowance from visitors, might be able to gain something towards a livelihood : these healing waters could be made both attractive and useful to the invalid visitors of Kilkee.

"Near to this spot the antiquarian may gratify his taste by viewing a fine old Danish fort, the most perfect in this neighbourhood, where they may be said to abound. It lies behind the town, on a little hill, and has a thick bank thrown up all round, of about seven hundred feet in circumference : the moat or ditch is about twenty-five feet wide, the centre gradually rises from sixteen to twenty feet, the summit is about three hundred feet in circumference, and nearly level. on the south side are two rather small openings, which lead to subterranean chambers, and occupy the interior of the centre elevation : they are said to be extensive. The neighbourhood was thrown into consternation some time since by a ventriloquist, who caused sounds of distress and anguish apparently to proceed from these vaults. If the apertures were enlarged, it might afford an inducement to the curious inquirer to descend and explore the probable storehouses of the northern depredators. The lads of the village are now the chief visitors of this antique circle. One of our party was informed by a youth that it was a fine place to dry clothes in, 'for if all the rogues in the county Clare came, they could not steal them; that out of a joke some of them tried, but could not touch one, because of the spirits or ghosts which are said to frequent it; also that some time since the landlord wished to have the mound removed, but could not get the men to work at it, as they got afraid.' If it were really the landlord's intention to have it removed, we need not be surprised at the result, as a disposition prevails in most places amongst the country people not to level their favourite old circles.

"The strand this morning presented an unusual scene of bustle.

'Spring-tides returned, and Fortune smiled; the bay
Received the *rushing ocean* to its breast.'

161

Men and women were to be seen in all directions removing seaweed which they had cut from the rocks, and brought to the shore in canoes, together with large quantities of the long—weed, which they tied together in great bundles, and which floated in with the tide, propelling with them all that was loose between them and the shore. This scene brought to our recollection Capt. Cooke's description of the inhabitants of Otaheite. The women appeared quite as active as the men in leaping in and out of the canoes, standing in the sea up to their waists, and in that state filling carts and creels, which were placed contiguous to the sea to receive the loadings. There is one kind on which they set the highest value; it consists of many leaves, some of them three yards long, attached to a stalk of considerable strength : this they use for manuring potato-ground , the soil here being particularly poor and sterile. This was a scene of enjoyment to the young natives, especially the little girls, who, with their frocks drawn up, and neatly fastened round their waists to keep them dry, ran in and out of the water like amphibious creatures : to young and old it appeared like the joyous scene of a harvest-home.

"We were much amused in observing the dexterity of about a dozen young girls, who went to assist in pushing off a canoe with two men in it, who had long laboured without success to get clear of the land, owing to the resistance of the waves. With a considerable effort the little folks pushed it off; but whilst the men were congratulating themselves on getting clear of the land, and preparing to row away, the lighthearted lasses, bent on diversion, watched the returning wave, and archly uniting their efforts, drew the canoe and its cargo on dry land, and ran away highly delighted.

"The day being unusually fine, induced us to take an excursion on the water; but here, as in some other bathing-places, much cannot be said of boat-accommodation. The natives use canoes for fishing, which are the only description of boat to be found along this coast. About twenty of these comprise the fishing-establishment at Kilkee, they are composed of a frame of light timber or strong wicker-work, covered with sailcloth, rendered waterproof with pitch and tar. The best kinds have slight timber hoops to support the cloth, which is an improvement. A few years since they were covered with horse and cow-hides, after the custom of the ancient Irish. These little vessels have neither keel nor rudder; they are particularly calculated to skim over the surface of the waves, and pass safely amongst the rocks on this dangerous shore, where a timber-boat might be dashed to pieces. The expert rowers, with a light paddle or oar in each hand, glide very swiftly over the waves, and turn them with great dexterity. It is surprising at times to see them going along shore; when a breaker approaches that would fill the canoe over its side, they instantly turn the head, which from its being elevated, enables them to ride over in safety, and as quickly return to their course : they are considered much safer when well managed than timber boats of the same size. The weight of the latter would preclude their general use along the coast; as where there are not any sheltered harbours, the fishermen on landing have to carry their canoes above the reach of the waves. When the sail-cloth happens to be torn, it is most expeditiously repaired; a sod of lighted turf is held near the rent until the pitch is melted, a fresh piece is stuck on the aperture, and the canoe is immediately launched; the water hardens the cement, and without further ceremony the fishermen jump in and row off."

The fair authoress gives an equally interesting account of her visit to the NATURAL BRIDGES near KILKEE. "After a residence of seven weeks, an excursion was planned to visit the unfrequented village and bay of Ross, near Loof-Head, whose natural bridges of rock, over an inlet of the Atlantic, are considered amongst the greatest curiosities on this romantic coast; and finding my health and strength so much recruited, that instead of being unable to go a mile in a jaunting-car without feeling quite exhausted, I undertook a *ride* of twenty-four miles.

"Nothing worthy of note occurred, with the exception of an occasional caution from our careful driver, of 'Will you be *plazed* to *howld* fast,' or having to get occasionally off the car in passing over sundry hollows in the road; otherwise we might have found ourselves on the ground *without the trouble of alighting.* On stopping to inquire the shortest path to the 'Bridges,' the good-countenanced natives flocked around us; but as they could not speak English, we were at a loss for direction, until a little lad, who understood our language, came up and offered to act as guide. After passing over two fields we reached these remarkable objects—both picturesque, yet quite different—extending across the same natural canal or inlet, which appears as if cut out of the solid rock, and varies from fifty to sixty feet in width, and in its course it makes nearly a right-angle. The inner bridge next to the termination, and which is first seen, is beautifully arched, and formed of numerous thin strata of rock, like sheets lying closely over each other. The under side of the arch looks as smooth as if covered with a coat of dark plaster. It would appear that at some period the whole was a mass of rock, whose strata took an extraordinary curved or arched direction inland, which is likewise apparent in many other places here and along the cliffs to Loop-Head, and that by some convulsion of nature a portion of the under strata was forced out, as the broken edges can be seen at low water, appearing like a sort of abutment from which the perfect arch springs : lines of these indented edges are apparent in an undulating course along the side of the canal nearly to its mouth, and appearing as if chiselled out by the hand of art.

"This bridge, together with that now about to be described, 'are formed of coarse arenacious clay-slate, with crystals of quartz in the fissures.'

"The latter bridge is a remarkable structure, being nearly as level on the upper as the under surface. When we consider the span, which is forty-five feet, the thickness above the arch, nine feet, and the width, thirty feet, and reflect how impossible it would be for man, with all his boasted powers, to construct, or for a moment to support so great a mass, without a curve underneath, the mind can only contemplate this extraordinary structure as formed by the creative touch of nature's Divine Architect. From its exposed situation, close to the ocean, it has for ages withstood the force of the overwhelming billows during the westerly tempests. Nearly under this bridge are low caverns or openings between the rocks, as if caused by the coast having been shaken and rent into great fissures, into which the guide (who afterwards joined us) threw large stones, that were heard bounding and echoing to a great depth. Many of the fissures in some places are lined with minute crystals, which sparkle beautifully in the sun's rays. One of our party picked up a remarkably fine specimen. The guide attempted to disengage some good pieces, but failed for want of proper tools. The canal, or wild rocky valley, when the tide is out, is above a quarter of a mile in length, and when the visitor walks along the bottom of it he can only see naked rocks, the sky, and the breakers foaming in at the end. The bay is lined by a high bank of 'boulders,' or large rounded stones, which from their bulk appear to have been accumulating for centuries; they are similar to those of Forankeee Bay, near Kilkee, but in much greater quantity. The ruins of an ancient little chapel and those of a dwelling-house, for many years the residence of the Keane family, in whose possession the property still remains, are to be seen near the village.

"Although the weather was oppressively warm on the road, yet the sharp breeze from the Atlantic rendered our cloaks very acceptable. Whilst the remainder of the company amused themselves in taking sketches of the bridges, or wandering amongst the rocks in search of crystals, I was glad to take shelter in a fisherman's hut. The poor woman received me with a courtesy of manner, which cultivation may improve but nature alone can impart. The interior of this dwelling soon presented the most complete picture of an *Irish cabin* I had ever seen. Seated on the only chair in the house, in a short time I found myself surrounded by all the women and children belonging to the few contiguous huts, most of whom seated themselves on the floor. A numerous family of domestic animals, consisting of cocks, hens, cats, and a dog, quite at their ease, were interspersed amongst us; but at my particular request a *large pig* was not allowed to join the company, although extremely anxious for admission. From the fisherman's wife, whose propriety of manner as well as that of her neighbour's quite struck me, I learned many interesting particulars respecting the localities of the place, she being the only one present who could speak English, and acted as my interpreter. It appears they have a very good landlord, and that the tenants were tolerably well off: the poorest hut was not without a featherbed, and many of them had two, which bespeaks a degree of comfort seldom to be met with in an Irish cabin. In this one I observed a new style of 'wagon-roof' bedstead, with timber curtains (if I may use the expression) : the back, roof, and foot were covered with nice white deal-boards nailed on, as well as the side next the wall : the *tout ensemble,* however, looked most comfortable. She likewise informed me that her husband was a pilot, and then out in the bay; that they paid two pounds per acre, with liberty to cut as much turf as they chose. That they availed themselves of this privilege was pretty evident, from the fine fire that blazed on the hearth. Here also the women toil in the field, and draw seaweed for manure on their backs. A remark made in Irish by a sweet little boy, and interpreted by his mother, amused me. His sister was giving him a drink of water rather awkwardly out of a large wooden noggin, and looking innocently up in her face, he said, 'Don't spill it, *agra,* (my dear,) for 'tis *very good.'* How easily are the wants of *nature* satisfied! Finding that the women did not know how to make fishing-nets for their husbands, and for which they had to pay, and being furnished by them with a rude netting-needle and twine, I set to work to instruct them, at which they seemed much gratified. After pleasantly spending more than an hour with this interesting group, when about to take my leave, my new acquaintance asked if, when I got home, I should ever think of the people of Ross. I replied, there were too many agreeable circumstances connected with my visit to allow me soon to forget them. Being joined by my party, attended by a numerous escort, we reached our vehicle, and with mutual expressions of kind feelings, we bade each other farewell."

One of the CAVES ON THE ATLANTIC is thus described. "The sea has now become smooth by the wind blowing off shore for two or three days, and the weather is settled; and being kindly accommodated with a ship's small boat, which was picked up at sea by some fishermen, we this evening set out to visit a cavern about two miles from Kilkee. After rowing out of the bay, and finding ourselves on the mighty Atlantic, I may acknowledge we felt more at ease in a boat with a keel and rudder than we had done in a canoe, although the motion was much slower from the boat being heavier. We were accompanied by another party in a canoe, who soon got ahead of us. Having cleared the rocks of Duganna, the great expanse of water presented a magnificent appearance; the nearest point on the opposite shore was that of Newfoundland, two thousand miles distant. In passing along the dark cliffs, the Amphitheatre, the Puffing Cavern, the Flat or Diamond Rocks, in succession, arrested our attention and excited admiration. As we glided over the glassy surface of the water in Look-out Bay, we did not anticipate that it would so soon be the scene of a dreadful shipwreck, where a large number of our fellow-creatures who were on board the 'Intrinsic,' were instantaneously hurried into an awful eternity when she went to pieces.

"Having arrived at the mouth of the cave, we lay to. in order to take soundings, and to examine the majestic perpendicular cliffs, one hundred and fifty feet high, by which we were surrounded, throwing their dark shade on the water, which gave it the appearance of a sea of ink. The water here was thirty-three feet deep. We were gently wafted into this magnificent cavern, of which I can only give a faint sketch; but to enable the reader to form some idea of its size, I shall give the best computation we were able to make. The height of the rude arch at the entrance, by comparison with the cliff above, appeared to be about sixty feet, and lowered as it receded to thirty or forty; the breadth at the bottom was the same; there were great blocks and angles of rock projecting on either side; within the entrance to the left were a number of stalagmites, formed by the dropping from above, and standing on a sloping rock, like small brownish sugarloaves. The roof presented a beautiful variety of rich metallic tinges, from the copper, iron, and other mineral substances held in solution by the water, which kept continually dropping from the top, and gave increased effect to the light thrown in at the entrance, which formed a striking contrast with the darkness at the upper end : on the right a number of stalactites lined the side, having the appearance of a drapery of seaweeds, and produced a handsome effect. The echo here is astonishing. After proceeding inward about two hundred and fifty feet, the light becomes very dim, and the cavern narrower, making an angle to the left. A jutting rock at the entrance of this angle shuts out the little light, on which account the inner chamber is rendered nearly dark. Proceeding on slowly, and having a boat not liable to be injured by touching a rock, we allowed it to float in by the effect of the swell, until the awful and profound silence was broken by the noise of the boat touching the rock at the extreme end, which broke upon the ear with an indescribably deep and impressive sound, as it reverberated from the roof and sides. Whilst in the dark part we perceived, what was also noticed by another party, that the dipping of the oars and the dropping from the roof produced a sparkling appearance under the water—caused, no doubt, by the air-bubbles reflecting the little light, which we could scarcely perceive. on leaving this gloomy place and emerging into day, the sunbeams were shining outside the entrance of the cave, about two hundred and fifty feet distant, and hence reflected on the dark rippling water within; and again, being thrown upon the rougharched roof, rendered still more brilliant by its beautiful metallic tints, broke like a scene of fancied enchantment upon the delighted vision. We were followed into the cave by two men in a canoe, who brought some very fine fish just caught; and this curious coincidence probably occasioned the first market that ever was held in this magnificent cavern."

All this is very similar to the scenery of a watering-place near Boston in the United States, called Nahout, where there is a much-visited spot called a spouting-horn, which, with a change of name, is very well described in Mrs. Knott's account of the Puffing Rock near Kilkee. It is about fifty feet high and thirty feet square, and has an opening down through the middle to a large chamber beneath; and when the breakers are driven in by strong wind and tide, after filling the lower space, the water is spouted up through the aperture like graceful feathery plumes, and descending in mist, produces, when the sun shines brightly, a most vivid and beautiful iris, whose arch may be seen by standing with your back to the sun. The whole of the coast near the mouth of the Shannon is rather extraordinary, and by crossing the river, we come

Puffing Hole, near Kilkeel

to the CAVES OF BALLYBTJNIAN on the Kerry side. "This bay," says a traveller who visited them in 1833, "is about five hundred paces in width, and its sands, which are piled up the sides of its inner portion, are dry and firm, though the prevalence of westerly winds and the strength of its currents mar the pleasantness and security of the bathing. The cliffs, which front the northern side, extend about two hundred and ninety yards, and rise gradually from the east to the west, or towards the sea, where they attain a height of one hundred and ten feet. They preserve throughout great perpendicularity, and are composed of two great beds, from thirty to forty feet in thickness, of compact ampelite, divided by a seam of the same slate, but fissile and anthracitous, and pouring out streamlets of water which contain iron and salts in solution, and tinge the rocks with bright yellow ochreous colours. These cliffs are also penetrated by several caves of small dimensions, which open upon the bay, and are crossed in one place by a fissure, occasioned by the fracturing of a rock which dips at a small angle of inclination (four to five degrees) to the east. The last cave on the sea-side, which has also an entrance from the bay, immediately curves round, and allows the sea to be seen, breasting its foaming way with much impetuosity, even on calm days, up two distinct apertures, through which the light gleams with almost starlight brightness.

"Any attempt to describe the connexion and relation of all these minor caves would be obviously a tedious enumeration, not warranted by the importance of the subject. They are most easily navigated in a boat from the northern side, where the rocky passages may be traversed for a considerable distance, without any communication with the open sea : and during this navigation, which is chiefly carried on in a line parallel to the western face of the cliff, the various entrances are often crossed at right-angles, affording the most striking contrast of light and shade—the colour of the waters being often of a hue so sparklingly bright, and so extensively vivid, as to resemble molten silver; while the boat, hurrying through the deep and wave-worn arcades into light and airy arched or vaulted chambers, only in their innermost recesses dark and repulsive, and passing from cave to cave, and hall to hall, with inlets pointing to the sea, or high cliffs affording their protection against the waves, and occasionally well-like apertures, which open through the roof to yield a telescopic view of the heavens, assist, more especially with the sudden transitions from absolute darkness to the most brilliant light, in giving to the whole an appearance of fairy scenery."

W. Ainsworth having entered from the Kerry shore, does not allude to the entrance from the Clare side; and as I know that much disappointment occurred to a party from Kilkee, who went by the way of Carrigaholt, and attempting to get back the same way, were carried by the tide up to Kilrush, and did not reach home until next morning, I am enabled to give the following hints, as they were communicated to a friend of mine by James Patterson of Kilrush, from whose well-known nautical knowledge and experience the information may be useful to other visitors, and prevent danger and disappointment. This gentleman, it appears. was one of the first who explored the dark and extensive recesses of the great caves, into which he took with him blue-lights and torches. He says that it requires the wind to blow for two days off the land, say easterly or south-east, in order that the sea may be sufficiently calm; should it be at all from the west, the water is so rough that a boat could not enter. When the weather is favourable, he advises to take a boat at Kilrush, and go down with the first ebb of the tide, which may not be half out when the caves are reached, at ten miles' distance; three or four hours can then be spent in examining them; and on the boat coming out, the flowing tide rushing in brings them back to Kilrush with ease. Parties should also get the opinion of some person well acquainted with the place as to providing suitable boats; for large ones can get into but few of the caves, the entrances being low and narrow, and very small boats are unsafe to cross the river.

The cliffs of Ballybunian contain a great quantity of alum, iron pyrites, &c., which have occasionally taken fire from being exposed to the action of the atmosphere, and which fire was formerly supposed to be of volcanic origin. I shall insert a short account of this phenomenon from a tourist who visited them forty years since; his description is well worth the perusal of every lover of science.

"Some years back a part of these cliffs, between the castles of Sick and Dune, assumed a volcanic appearance. The waves, by continual dashing, had worn and undermined the cliff, which giving way, fell with tremendous violence into the sea; several great strata or beds of pyrites, iron, and sulphur were in consequence exposed to the action of the air and salt-water, the natural effects of which were that they heated and burned with great fierceness. The clay near it is calcined to a red brick, mixed with iron ore, melted in many places like cinders thrown from a smith's forge. Many who did not consider well the causes, and, the effects naturally to be expected from them, have supposed this to be volcanic."

To the kindness of Captain Sabine I am indebted for an account of the birds which he met with on these coasts. "Of sea-birds, I recognised in flight, of terns, the *hirundo* and *minuta;* of gulls, the *argentatus, fuscus,* and *tridactylus,* and I heard of a gull with very red legs, which was, I suppose, the *ridibundus;* of the guillemots, the *troile, brunnichii, grylle,* and *alba;* cormorants and oyster-catchers abundant; the oyster-catchers more frequently in groups than in pairs, although it was the breeding season; puffins and razorbills. Of land-birds, the only species worth particular remark is the chough, which breeds in the rocks at Ballybunian, as does the rock-pigeon."

"Before leaving Loop-head, the visitor is recommended to walk about a mile along the cliffs towards Ross, where their fancifully-curved strata present extraordinary appearances. In the face of the rock, one of the bays is the resort of thousands of sea-gulls, whose young in the autumn, ranged on narrow shelves of rock that line the bay, loudly scream for food, which the parent birds seem to answer as they skim along the surface of the water, looking down for their prey; altogether the noise was so great, that a party who lately visited it rushed forward in amazement to see what could have produced such extraordinary clamour. Near this is a conical hill, called Cahir Croghaune, situated a short distance from the road, and well worth ascending: the view all round will amply repay for the trouble.

"In the spring of 1834, one of the cliffs which had been undermined by the waves, fell into the sea with so loud a noise that the manager at the lighthouse thought it was thunder. When a party recently visited this place they found it dangerous to approach, as many of the fragments appeared ready to follow the fallen masses."

From the complete absence of ooze, and the exclusive sand and rock which form the western coast of Ireland, the sea-water at Kilkee is remarkably pellucid and bright; and the persons engaged in recovering the sunken cargo of the Intrinsic worked to great advantage, from being able to see objects distinctly at fifty feet below the surface. A very uncommon variety of curious sea-weed is also found here, particularly the Carrigheen moss, used by invalids, and said to be as nutritious as isinglass.

The antiquarian finds matter of interest at Kilkee, in the shape of two of the ancient *Raths,* one on each side of the village. That on the east seems of great antiquity. The circumference outside the rampart is two hundred and fifty-six yards, the top of the mound one hundred and twenty-six; the height of the top of the Rath, above the fosse, which has been filled considerably, is twenty feet; the height of the centre rampart ten feet, and twelve above the fosse. At the south side of the top of the mound is a passage covered with large flags, and leading into the interior. An inhabitant of Kilkee, who some years ago penetrated to the interior, found a chamber of twelve feet diameter, walled at the sides, and covered with broad thick flags. Within his memory, this person said, this and other raths had been the abodes of fairies. About thirty years ago, no gentleman in the south of Ireland could induce his men to open a rath, unless he would first take off the sod himself, and then he was obliged to ply some courageous fellows with whiskey in order to raise their spirits for the accomplishment of his object. A friend of mine informed me, that near Limerick, where he was educated, it was commonly believed that whoever disturbed a rath would die before the expiration of the year, and that his grandfather having ploughed one up in defiance of the superstition, and having chanced to die within the twelvemonth, had secured undisturbed repose to all the raths in the neighbourhood. Mr. Crofton Croker has written a very satisfactory chapter on fairies, expressed with his usual elegance, and a few extracts from it will be *apropos* to the superstitions of the raths. "In common with other countries," he says, "particularly the Highlands of Scotland, a traditional belief exists among the Irish peasantry in those romantic little sprites denominated fairies; and it is wonderful, considering their being creatures of imagination, that the superstitions respecting them should have remained so much confined, and so very similar. Whether the fairy mythology of Ireland has been derived from the East, and transmitted hence through the medium of Spain, or has, as some believe, a northern origin, it is of little import to inquire, particularly as nothing more than conjecture cain now be advanced on the subject. It is, however, evident that the present fairies of Ireland, if not Gothic creations, were at least modelled in the same school and age with the elves of northern Europe.

"There is an odd mixture of the ridiculous and the sublime in the prevalent notions respecting such beings. Nor could there have been invented a more extraordinary medium between man and his Maker. The most esteemed novelist of the present day has happily described these curious creations of the mind, as

"That which is neither ill nor well
That which belongs not to heaven or hell;
A wreath of the mist, a bubble of the stream,
'Twixt a waking thought and a sleeping dream :
A form that men spy
With the half-shut eye,
In the beams of the setting sun am I! "

Partaking both of the human and spiritual nature, having immaterial bodies, with the feelings and passions of mortality, fairies are supposed to possess both the power and inclination to revenge an affront : and the motive of fear, which induces some savage nations to worship the devil, prompts the vulgar in Ireland to term fairies good people,' and in Scotland guid folk;' nor is it uncommon to see a rustic before drinking, spill a small part of his draught upon the ground, as a complimentary libation to the fairies. Such as use the word fairy are often corrected in a whisper, which caution arises from conceiving that these beings are invisibly present, and the appellation is considered offensive, as denoting an insignificant object. Thus, hoping to deceive by flattery, the maxim most attended to in the intercourse with these little great ones' is, that civility begets civility.' Doubtless on the same principle the Greeks, as observed by Augustus Schlegel, called their fairies Eumenides, or the benevolent , and assigned for their habitation a beautiful grove. I cannot think of this policy,' said my friend C—, 'without fancying a grin on Medusa, and those little urchins, the northern fairies, holding their sides with laughter.' The same system of fear and flattery seems to have existed amongst the Irish even towards animals in the time of Elizabeth; for Camden tells us, they take unto them wolves to be their *godsibs*, (gossips,) whom they tearme *Chari Christ,* praying for them, and wishing them well, and so they are not afraid to be hurt by them.'

"The circular intrenchments and barrows, known by the name of Danish forts, in Ireland, are pointed out as the abode of fairy communities, and to disturb their habitation, in other words to dig or plough up a rath or fort, whose construction the superstitious natives ascribe to the labour and ingenuity of the good people,' is considered as unlucky, and entailing some severe disaster on the violater of his kindred. An industrious peasant, who purchased a farm in the neighbourhood of Mallow from a near relative of mine, commenced his improvements by building upon it a good stone house, together with a lime-kiln. Soon after he waited on the proprietor, to state the trouble he was come to by reason of the old fort, the fairies not approving of his having placed the lime-kiln so near their dwelling. He had lost his sow with nine *bonniveens,* (sucking-pigs,) his horse fell into a quarry and was killed, and three of his sheep died, all through the means of the fairies!' Though the lime-kiln had cost him five guineas, he declared he would never burn another stone in it, but take it down without delay, and build one away from the fort; saying, he was wrong in putting that kiln in the way of the 'good people,' who were thus obliged to go out of their usual track. The back-door of his house unfortunately also faced the same fort, but this offence was obviated by almost closing it up, leaving only a small hole at the top to allow the good people free passage should they require it. In these raths, fairies are represented as holding their festive meetings, and entering into all the fantastic and wanton mirth that music and glittering banquets are capable of inspiring. A fairy chieftain of much local celebrity, named Knop, is supposed to hold his court in a rath on the roadside between Cork and Youghal, where often travellers, unacquainted with the country, have been led astray by the appearance of lights, and by alluring sounds proceeding from within; but when

"The village cock gave note of (lay,
Up sprang in haste the airy throng;
The word went round, ' Away! away!
The night is short, the way is long;'

and the delicious viands change into carrion. The crystal goblets become rugged pebbles, and the whole furniture of the feast undergoes a similar metamorphosis.

"An eddy of dust raised by the wind is attributed to the fairies journeying from one of their haunts to another; on perceiving which the peasant will obsequiously doff his hat, muttering 'God speed ye, God speed ye, gentlemen;' and returns it to his head, with the remark, 'Good manners are no burthen,' as an apology for the motive, which he is ashamed to acknowledge. Should he, however, instead of such friendly greeting, repeat any short prayer, or devoutly cross himself; using a religious response, the fairy journey is interrupted; and if any mortals are in their train, the charm by which they were detained is broken, and they are restored to human society. on these occasions the production of a black-hafted knife is considered as extremely potent in dissolving the spell. This weapon is believed to be effective, not only against fairy incantation, but also against any supernatural being; and accounts of many twilight rencontres between shadowy forms and mortals are related, to establish its power, gouts of blood or jelly being found in the morning on the spot where the vision had appeared. A respectable farmer has been pointed out to me whose familiar appellation in Irish was, 'Kill the devil,' from the report of his having quelled, by means of a black-shafted knife, a phantom that long had haunted him.

"A stanza, containing the track of a fairy procession, is preserved by Dr. Neilson in his Irish Grammar; and as a curiosity the translation may be worth copying.

"Paying a fleeting visit to many an ' airy castle, rath, and mount,' Finsar and his troop hold their course from dawn of noon till fall of night, on beautiful winged coursers.

> ' Around Knock Grein and Nock na Rae,
> Bin Builvin and Reis Corain,
> To Bin Eachlan and loch Da-ean,
> From thence north-east to Sleive Guilin—
> They traversed the lofty hills of Mourne,
> Round high Sleive Denard and Balachanery,
> Down to Dundrin, Dundrum, and Dunardalay
> Right forward to Knock na Feadaled;'

the latter name signifying in English the Musical Hill, so called from the supernatural strains supposed occasionally to proceed from it.

"The most romantic dells are also pointed out as scenes of fairy resort, and distinguished by the term ' gentle places.' Beetling linen by the side of a rocky stream that murmurs through an unfrequented glen, is represented as a favourite , or rather common female fairy occupation, where they chant wild and pathetic melodies, beating time with their beetles. The herbs and plants with which such glens abound are considered as under fairy influence, and are collected, with many ceremonies, for charms, by cunning old women, termed 'Fairy Doctors,' or sometimes, from their professed knowledge of surgery, 'Bone-setters.' A confidence in superstitious quackery exists so strongly amongst the lower orders in Ireland, that many instances are known to me where patients have been carried a distance of several miles to a 'Bone-setter,' to whom a fee was given, when they might have received without removal, and free of expense, every attendance from the most skilful surgeons. 'I would not, if all the doctors in Ireland told me so, treat the poor sufferer thus,' is the prefatory sentence used by these 'wise women.' 'What do doctors know about sick people? but take the herbs which I shall give you, bury them at sunset in the north-east corner of the fort-field; and when you return, tie a thread three times round the left-hand upper post of the sick person's bed, and let it remain there for nine nights,' &c. Camden, it would seem, had some faith in the efficacy of these 'skilful women,' who, 'by means of charms,' to use his own words, ' give more certain judgment of the disease than many of our physicians can.

"Fairies are represented as exceedingly diminutive in their stature, having an arch and malicious expression of countenance, and generally habited in green, with large scarlet caps; hence the beautiful plant *Digitalis purpurea,* is named 'fairy-cap' by the vulgar, from the supposed resemblance of its bells to this part of fairy dress. To the same plant many rustic superstitions are attached, particularly its salutation of supernatural beings, by bending its long stalks in token of recognition.

"Old and solitary thorns, in common with the digitalis, are regarded with reverence by the peasantry, and considered as sacred to the revels of these eccentric little sprites, whose vengeance follows their removal. Any antique implement casually discovered by the labourer is referred to the fairies, and supposed to have been dropped or forgotten by them : small and oddly-shaped tobacco-pipes, frequently turned up by the spade or the plough, the finder instantly destroys, to avert the evil agency of their former spiritual owners. Amongst these remains may be noticed the flint arrow-heads, said to be sportively shot at cattle by the fairies; and in compliance with the popular superstition, termed, even by antiquarians, 'elf-arrows.

"The fairies are believed to visit the farm-houses in their district on particular nights, and the embers are collected, the hearth swept, and a vessel of water placed for their use before the family retire to rest. But these dubious divinities seem to preside more especially over cattle, corn, fruits, and agricultural objects. Milking the cows, upsetting the dairy-pans, and disarranging whatever. may have been carefully placed in order, are amongst their mischievous proceedings. Cluricaune or Leprehaune is the name given to the Irish Puck. The character of this goblin is a compound of that of the Scotch Brownie and the English Robin Goodfellow. He is depicted (for engraved portraits of the Irish Leprehaune are in existence) as a small and withered old main, completely equipped in the costume of a cobbler, and employed in repairing a shoe. A paragraph lately appeared in a Kilkenny paper, stating, that a labourer returning home in the dusk of the evening, discovered a Leprehaune at work, from whom he bore away the shoe which he was mending as a proof of the veracity of his story; it was further stated, that the shoe lay for the inspection of the curious at the newspaper-office. The most prominent feature in the vulgar creed respecting the Leprehaune is, his being the possessor of a purse, supposed to be, like that of Fortunatus, inexhaustible; and many persons who have surprised one of these fairies occupied in shoe-making, have endeavoured to compel him to deliver it : this he has ingeniously avoided, averting the eye of his antagonist by some stratagem, when he disappears; which it seems he has not the power of doing as long as any person's gaze is fixed upon him.

"Fairy children, I have been assured, are frequently seen in lonely glens, engaged in mimic fights and juvenile gambols. A story related by Gervase of Tilbury, in the Otia Imperialia, and mentioned in the Minstrelsy of the Scottish Border as current, with only slight variations, both in the highlands and lowlands of Scotland, is equally so in the south of Ireland, and is perhaps the most common of fairy superstitions. A woman, who had been abstracted to nurse a young fairy, during her residence amongst the supernatural community, accidentally anointed one of her eyes with a substance entrusted to her for the use of her infant charge. on being emancipated from captivity, the 'good people' still remained visible to the eye which had been touched by the magic ointment, and hence she daily beheld them engaged (like the Sylphs in Pope's Rape of the Lock) in their various fairy avocations. The woman, however, remained a silent spectator, until happening to recognize, sporting amongst others, the fairy child whom she had nursed, in all the delicate bloom and beauty of unearthly youth, her prudence forsook her, and at the sight she was betrayed by her feelings into an exclamation of delight; on hearing which the young fairy approached his nurse, and inquired by what means she was conscious of his presence. She pointed to the anointed eye, into which he instantly darted a spear that he held in his hand, and thus, by destroying the organ, shut out for ever the secrets of the invisible world from the mortal eye to which they had been revealed. When a child appears delicate, or a young woman consumptive, the conclusion is that they are carried off to be made a playmate or nurse to the young fairies, and that a substitute, resembling the person taken away, is deposited in their place, which gradually declines and ultimately dies. The inhuman means used by ignorant parents to discover if any unhealthy child be their offspring or a changeling, (the name given to the illusory image,) is, placing the child undressed on the roadside, where it is suffered to lie a considerable time exposed to cold. After such ceremony, they conclude a natural disorder has caused the symptoms of decay; and the child is then treated with more tenderness, from an idea that had it been possessed by a fairy, that spirit would not have brooked such indignity, but made its escape. Paralytic affections are attributed to the same agency, whence the term 'fairy-struck;' and the same cruel treatment is observed towards aged persons thus afflicted.

"A pleasing ballad by my friend Mr. Anster has been founded on this superstition; the mother is supposed to speak.

'The summer sun was sinking,
With a mild light, calm and mellow,
It shone on my little boy's bonny cheeks,
And his loose locks of yellow.

'The robin was singing sweetly, And his song was sad and tender;
And my little boy's eyes, as he heard the song,
Smiled with a sweet soft splendour.

'My little boy lay on my bosom,
While his soul the song was quaffing;
The joy of his soul had tinged his cheek,
And his heart and his eye were laughing.

'I sat alone in my cottage,
The midnight needle plying;
I feared for my child, for the rush's light
In the socket now was dying.

' There came a hand to my lonely latch,
Like the wind at midnight moaning,
I knelt to pray—but rose again—
For I heard my little boy groaning!

I crossed my brow and I crossed my breast,
But that night my child departed!
They left a weakling in its stead,
And I am broken-hearted.

Oh! it cannot be my own sweet boy,
For his eyes are dim and hollow;
My little boy has gone to God,
And his mother soon will follow.

The dirge for the dead will be sung for me,
And the mass be chanted meetly;
And I will sleep with my little boy,
In the moonlight churchyard sweetly.'

"Sometimes an intricate legal question arises in the case of a young woman being carried off by the fairies, and returning after an absence of several years, which is by no means uncommon, when she finds her husband married to a second wife. More than one instance of this unexpected reappearance has come within my own knowledge, and I select the relation contained in a letter which I received during the present year, from its being the most recent case. 'The day before I left Island Bawn,' says the writer, 'I heard of an Irish Kilmeny, in the person of the wife of a labouring cottager, who having died about twenty years since, and been buried with the usual ceremonies, the poor man allowed a reasonable period to elapse, and subsequently took unto himself another helpmate, with whom he had since continued to live; when one night last winter, (1820,) they were disturbed by a woman vociferously claiming admission into their cabin, and asserting her right to the full and undisturbed sovereignty of the same, inasmuch as she was the owner's true and lawful wife, whom he supposed deceased and interred, whereas she had only been with the fairies, from whose power she had now emancipated herself. So minute and clear (if not satisfactory) did she make out her title, that both the husband and his second spouse quailed before this unwelcomed visitant from the "good people." The first wife allowed her "*locum tenens*" to remain in the house while she behaved herself respectfully; and all went on smoothly for some time, the stranger supporting the truth of her story by mysteriously telling the fortunes of those who flocked to see so wonderful a woman. Being,' continues the writer, 'unable to pay her a visit myself, I requested a young lady who was staying at my sister's to do so, and who was much more qualified than I should have been, to elicit, if possible, the truth. With her usual kindness she undertook the task, and I cannot do better than copy her letter to my sister.

" 'My dear Mrs. L—,   *Ballyhogan, 6th January,* 1821.

" 'In compliance with your brother's request, I have sat down to give you an account of my visit to the fairy woman. On Thursday morning last, having procured a guide to show me the way to her house, I departed on my mission, and after a walk of about four miles, arrived at the little village of Castle Town, on the Shannon. "That white house *yonder,* Miss, is the one the fortune-teller lives in," said the guide. I was readily admitted, and found the inside thronged with visitors, to whom the diviner talked in the common gipsy strain. Being more anxious to hear her own story than anything she could tell me of myself, I asked her if the report respecting her having recently returned from the fairies was correct. Her reply was, that she had been with the "good people" many years, and as a reward for her conduct while among them, they had bestowed the gift of fortune-telling. I then begged her to inform me of some further particulars; and after considerable hesitation on her part, and persuasion on mine, she gave me the following history, which I will recount verbatim, as highly illustrative of fairy superstition and Irish manners.

" 'My father, whose name was Thady Donohoe, lived in a little place they call Mount Shannon, near Slain; he was a shoemaker, and supported his family by his work, until he lost his health through grief at my folly in not being led by his advice; and I'm *sartin shure* (certain sure, confident) I suffered all I did for going against my father. He loved me *bitter* (better) than any of his *childer* (children), because he had no *deaghter* (daughter) but myself; and at eighteen he thought to get me married to a neighbour's son, who was a *neat boy* (a handsome fellow); and, indeed, not that I say it, I was a neat, clean-skinned girl at that time, though I may deny it to-day; but I was fond of a young man who was working as a labouring boy at a farmer's house *handy by* (adjacent). Well, when I *tould* (told) Paddy Doody, for that was my lover's name, what my father wished me to do, he said, if I did not run away with him, my father and my brothers would make me marry the other boy, and he should kill himself or go distracted. So I went off with him *shure enough,* (without hesitation,) and we were married by his parish priest as soon as we came to Castle Town. I never saw my father till he was dying, which was about six months after : he gave me his blessing and a cow before he died. After the funeral I came back to my husband, and we lived very happily for some years. My eldest little boy died, and I was nursing my second, when one night about Midsummer, as we were sitting at our supper, I was fairy-struck and fell off my chair; so *with that* (instantly) poor Paddy ran out for one of the neighbours, who desired him to send for the priest, which he did *to be shure* (as a matter of course). But when he came he did not know what to do, but said prayers over me, and anointed me for death; and when the holy oil was put on me I was better, and continued to mend for several days; but I was still very weak and low. I had an *impression about* (oppression on) the heart, and a dimness in my eyes, and a ringing in my ears, and my face was greatly altered. Well, one night after we all lay down to sleep, it was about twelve o'clock, I heard a great noise, and saw a light in the room. I called Paddy, but he could not hear me. My little child was about three months old, and lay asleep by my side. In one minute the house was full of people, men and women, but no one saw them but myself; and one of the women came to the side of the bed, and said, "Judy, get up, you are to come with us, and I will put one in your place to nurse your child." So with that they dragged me out of bed, and put an old woman in my place, who took my *cratur of a child* (creature, a term of endearment,) in her arms. I thought I should die, but I could not speak a word. They took me off with them, and there were several horsemen, with red caps, outside the door; and the women who sat behind them on the horses had blue cloaks. There was a piper on a grey pony that led the way; and when I got to their dwelling I was given a child to nurse. I am not allowed to tell anything that happened while I was there; all I can say is, that I never ate one mouthful of their food, if I did I never could have left them. I came every night to my own house for cold potatoes, and I lived on them. Paddy buried, as he thought, the old woman that was put in my place, but she came away to us. I am twenty years from home, and my husband is married again : this is my son's house. When I came home Paddy would not own me, but I soon *made him sensible* (convinced him) I was his wife. I have suffered more than I can tell any one while I was with the "good people;" and I promised the Blessed Virgin if she would release me to do six months' *pinnance,* (penance) at a holy well in the King's County, where I am going next week : if I live to return, my son will let me pass the rest of my days with him, should my husband not allow me.'

"Dr. Neilson gives us, with every appearance of authenticity, a more intricate matrimonial case than the foregoing, where the woman on her return from Fairyland, finding her first husband married, marries again herself. The second wife of the first husband dies, and he having discovered his former spouse claims her; but her second husband, being unwilling to part with her, denies the claim. The question is referred to an ecclesiastical tribunal, where fairy agency will not be acknowledged, and which, under conflicting testimony, is unable to determine the matter. It however ultimately terminates in the friendly arrangement, 'that both doors of the woman's second husband's house should be set open; that Joyce (her former husband) should stand seven steps from the street-door, and Thady in the garden, seven steps from the back-door; that she should take her choice, and abide by it thenceforward.' The child was sleeping in the cradle, and as Mary was about to depart, she went to the child to take leave of it and shed a tear. She went then towards the street-door, when she heard the child arter her; presently she returned and remained without murmuring or uneasiness with Thady Hughes till her death.

"A curious spirit, and one I believe peculiar to Ireland, is the Banshee, or White Fairy, sometimes called the Frogh or the House Fairy. The derivation of both these names appears to me obvious from the credulous personification, that of a small and shrivelled old woman with long white hair, supposed to be peculiarly attached to ancient houses or families, and to announce the approaching dissolution of any of the members by mournful lamentations. This fairy attendant is considered as highly honourable, and in part of an elegy on one of the Knights of Kerry still extant, the family Banshee is introduced as deploring, with wailing accents, the knight's impending fate; when every trader at Dingle who hears the strain becomes alarmed lest it should forebode his own death; but the bard assures them, with an air of humorous sarcasm, they have no cause for uneasiness, such warning being given only to those of illustrious descent.

"Another species of Irish fairy is the Phooka; the descriptions given of which are so visionary and undefined that it is impossible to reduce them to detail. The name of many lonely rocks and glens in Ireland declares them sacred to this spirit. In the county Cork there are two castles, called Carrig Phooka or the Phooka's Rock, one near Doneraile, the other not far from Macroon; and in the county Wicklow, the celebrated waterfall Poula Phooka, or the Phooka's Cavern, is well known.

"Notwithstanding the universal belief in fairy influence, the credence given to witchcraft amongst the vulgar Irish is by no means, proportionate. Some few instances are historically preserved; but, considering the extent and reputation which witchcraft obtained during the reigns of Elizabeth and James I. in England, these may. be viewed as imparted rather than primitive superstitions. The admirable account of Moll White given in the Spectator, presents a collection of the popular notions respecting the sorcery of old women; and those who are inclined to investigate the subject further, may find some hundred volumes written upon it.

"The most remarkable Irish witch on record is Dame Alice Ketyll (whose history is to be found at length in Camden). Amongst the charges made against her, when examined in 1325, was the sacrificing nine red cocks to her familiar spirit or imp, named Robyn Artysson, 'at a stone bridge in a certain foure-crosse high-way.' 'Item, that she swept the streets of Kilkenny with beesomes, between Complin and Courefew, and in sweeping the filth towards the house of William Utlan her sonne, by way of conjuring, uttered these words :

' Unto the house of William, my sonne,
　Hie all the wealth of Kilkenny town.'

"And amongst 'the goods and implements of the said Alice, there was a certain holy wafer-cake found, having the name of the divell imprinted upon it; there was found also a boxe, and within it an ointment, wherewith she used to besmear or grease a certain piece of wood, called coultree, which, being thus anointed, the said Alice with her complices, could ride and gallop upon the said coultree withersoever they would all the world over, through thick and thin, without either hurt or hindrance.' These things, we are told, were notorious; and Dame Ketyll, to avoid punishment, escaped to England; but one of her accomplices, Pernill or Parnell, was burned at Kilkenny, who avouched that Alice's son William 'deserved death as well as herself, affirming that he, for a year and a day, wore the divell's girdle upon his bare bodie.' Kilkenny seems to have been peculiarly fatal to witches. In October 1578, dox relates, that Sir William Drury, the lord deputy, caused thirty-six criminals to be executed there, 'one of which was a blackamoor, and two others were witches, and were condemned by the law of nature, for there was no positive law against witchcraft in those days.'

"Some more recent account of witches is traditionally preserved in Ireland, particularly of Nanny Steer, whose malign glance produced madness, and the malady of many a wretched lunatic who wandered about the country was attributed to her baneful influence.

"In the Queen's county a young man, named Rutlidge, on the day of his marriage, is said to have become a victim to one of these dreadful looks, from his having neglected to invite Nanny Steer to the wedding, who appeared an unbidden guest, and casting an evil eye on the 'bridegroom, he immediately became a maniac.

" 'In no case,' says Camden, speaking of Irish superstitions, 'must you praise a horse or any other beast until you say "God save him," or unless you spit upon him. 'If any harm befall the horse within three days after they seek him that praised him, that he may mumble the Lord's Prayer in his right ear. They think that there bee some that bewitch their horses with looking upon them, and then they use the help of some old hagges, who saying a few prayers with a loud voice make them well again? This' belief in the fatal effects. of an evil eye is as. prevalent at the present day as when Camden wrote; and few, if any, of the lower orders will speak to or of a child without spitting out, and excusing himself should a superior be present, with ' It's for good luck sure—and God' bless the boy, and make a fine man of him.' So powerful is this superstition, that, even people of education and above the ordinary rank, are obliged from policy to accommodate themselves to it in their intercourse with the peasantry, as few things are considered more dangerous and unfriendly, or are longer remembered, than the omission of such ceremony.

"Another vulgar superstition regarding witches is, their power of assuming the shape of some insect or animal; the most favourite forms are, those of a fly or hare under the latter disguise they are supposed to suck the teats of cows, and thus either deprive them of their milk, or communicate an injurious effect to it.

Of the following story, numberless variations are in circulation amongst the Irish peasantry. A herdsman having wounded a hare, which he discovered sucking one of the cows under his care, tracked it to a solitary cabin, where he. found an old woman smeared with blood and gasping for breath, extended almost lifeless on the floor, having, it is presumed, recovered her natural shape.

"In churning, should not the milk readily come butter, the machinations of some witch are suspected. As a test, the iron coulter of the plough is heated in the fire, and the witch's name solemnly pronounced, with the following charm, on whom this spell is supposed to inflict the most excruciating tortures—

'Come, butter, come,
Come, butter, come :
Peter stands at the gate
Waiting for a buttered cake:
Come, butter, come.'

And if the milk has lost its good qualities by means of incantation, it immediately turns to excellent butter.

"In the sixteenth century, the same opinion existed in Ireland, somewhat tinged with a relic of Pagan or Druidical rites, fire being considered, before the introduction of Christianity, the immediate representative of the Deity, and the first of May as peculiarly sacred to those rites, many relics of which may still be discovered..

" 'They take her for a wicked woman and a witch, whatever she be that cometh to fetch fire from them in May-day, (neither will they give any fire then, but unto a sick body, and that with a curse,) for because they thinke the same woman will the next summer steale away all their butter. If they find an hare amongst their heards of cattell on the said May-day, they kill her, for they suppose she is some old trot that would fetch away their butter. They are of opinion that their butter, if it be stollen, will soone after bee restored againe, in case they take away some of the thatch that hangeth over the doore of the house, and cast, it into the fire.'

"Amongst some Irish manuscripts in my possession, the composition I apprehend of the sixteenth and seventeenth centuries, there is a long description, possessing considerable poetic. merit, of a contest between Eogan and ' Conn of the Hundred Battles,"part of which presents a picture of the appearance of some supernatural hags to the contending chieftains the night previous to the engagement : the translation is extremely literal.

"When Eogan came back. from the council, three witches stood before him;. frightful beyond description, with red and fiery-looking eyes, and long, lank, grizzly hair hanging down dishevelled over cadaverous countenances. The eye-brows of these fiends were large, rough, and grim, growing into each other, and forming two

181

curvatures. of matted bristles. Their cheeks were hollow, shrivelled, and meagre; and their beaked noses covered with parched skin, issued. forth prominently from the deeply-wrinkled and knobby foreheads of these monstrous and filthy she-devils! Their 'blasting' tongues, with flippant volubility, held ceaseless gabble; and their crooked, yellow, hairy hands and hooked fingers resembled more the talons of an eagle or a foul-feeding harpy, than the fingers of a human creature. Thus, supported by small inbent and bony legs, they stood before Eogan.

" 'Whence come ye, furies?' asked the chief.

" 'We come from afar by our powers,' replied they.

" 'I demand to know your powers,' said Eogan, leader of the mighty bands.

" 'We. cause the sea to run higher than the mountain-tops by our breath : we bring snow on the earth by the nodding of our white heads we spread flames in dwellings by our words, we alter and change the shape of every person, nay, of those in our own occupation, by the rolling of our eyes; we—'

" 'Enough!' cried the mighty Eogan 'I now demand your names.'

" 'Our names,' returned the bags, 'are Ah, Lann, and Leana : we are daughters of Trodan the magician, and we have come from remote countries to warn you of your approaching death; for Eogan shall die by the keen-edged and bone-cleaving sword of the ever victorious 'Conn of the Hundred Battles.' "

" 'on your own heads may this prophetic warning light, ye hags of hell!' returned Eogan. 'May your forebodings of Conn sink into nothing on the air, and be un-answered by the voices of the mountains. May the trees bear the brunt of your evil words, the venom of your lips fall harmless on the rocks of the valley, and your malice be given to the waves of the ocean.'

" 'It is inevitable destiny we speak,' said they : 'we have spoken without precipitation and without reward;' and muttering of their horrid spells, they vanished from Eogan.

"That night came the same three hags to the tent of the King of Spain's son, and they boded ill to him; and thence they came where the hosts of Conn of the Hundred Battles hay encamped, and they roused that hero with these words :

" 'In thy arm be thy strength; in thy sword be thy safety; in thy face be thy foes; in thy strides thy prosperity. The pride of Ireland is against thee, in life and in motion. Be thou restless as the treacherous light that gleams to benighted travellers.

"In the preceding part of the same poem the support and assistance received by Eogan and his tribe from a sorceress named Eadoin is mentioned, who, in a former engagement, so fascinated the eyes of Eogan's adversaries by her enchantments, that some rocks on the field of battle assumed the appearance of formidable bodies of armed men; and while Goll and the sons of Moirne, with their valiant associates, attacked these flinty phantoms, and were occupied in contest with invulnerable and senseless stones, the sorceress conveyed the unwilling Eogan and his followers from the scene of warfare, and embarked them for Spain. 'The rock,' adds an English note on this passage of the manuscript, 'which was converted into the resemblance of Eogan and his troops, is at this day called the Scalped Rock, in Irish "Cloch Bhearrha," in Glean Rogh, near Kinmare, from the indenture made in it by the arms of Goll, which were shivered and broken into pieces thereon.'

"As in England, a worn horseshoe nailed on the threshold, or near the entrance of a house, is considered as a security against witchcraft; but this remedy is used only in the better description of cabins.

"Many of the ancient Irish chieftains have received deification, and the credulous believe in their frequent reappearance on earth as the messengers of good tidings, such as a fine season or an abundant harvest. Other shades are compelled to perform certain penitential ceremonies in expiation of crimes committed during life; of the latter may be mentioned an Earl of Kildaire, doomed to ride septennially round the Curragh, an extensive ecommon, until the silver shoes of his supernatural steed are worn out. To the former class belongs O'Donnoghue, a chief of much celebrity, whose May-day visit on a milk-white horse, gliding over the Lakes of Killarney, to the sound of unearthly music, and attended by troops of spirits, scattering delicious spring-flowers, has been lyrically preserved by Mr. Moore, and is accurately recorded in a poem by Mr. Leslie on Killarney, and in Mr. Weld's account of that lake, as also in Derrick's Letters, where some additional particulars may be found from the pen of Mr. Ockenden. 'There is a farmer now alive,' says that gentleman, 'who declares, as I am told, that riding one evening near the lower end of the lake, he was overtaken by a gentleman, (for such he judged him by his appearance to be,) who seemed under thirty years of age, very handsome in his person, very sumptuous in his apparel, and very affable in conversation. After having travelled for some time together, he observed, that as night was approaching, the town far off, and lodging not easy to be found, he should be welcome to take a bed that night at his house, which he said was not very distant. The invitation was readily accepted; they approached the lake together, and both their horses moved upon the surface without sinking, to the infinite amazement of the farmer, who thence perceived the stranger to be no less a person than the great O'Donnoghue. They rode a considerable distance from shore, and then descended to a delightful country under water, and lay that night in a house much larger in size and much more richly furnished than even Lord Kenmare's at Killarney.'

"Second-sight, so common in the Highlands; I believe is unknown in the south of Ireland. Story relates a mysterious appearance of stars, accompanied by heavy groans, that preceded the landing of the rival monarchs William and James, seen by 'one Mr. Hambleton, of Tollymoore, a justice of the peace in his county, and a sober, rational man;' in company with others who were journeying towards Dundalk; adding, 'they have a great many tales of this kind in Ireland, and the Inniskilling men tell you of several such things before their battles.' I should, however, consider these visions, on account of their northern limits, as derived from Scotland, and not genuine Irish superstitions.

"I fear it may be considered that I have dwelt too long upon, and entered too minutely into the notions of the ignorant; but early associations have tempted me to linger over these marvellous relations, and have, perhaps, misled my maturer judgment.

> 'Such fancies are the coinage of the brain,
> Which oft rebellious to more sober thought
> Will these strange phantoms shape; the idle prate
> Of fools and nurses, who in infant minds
> Plant such misshapen stuff, the scorn and scoff
> Of settled reason and of common sense!'

"On the whole, from what may be collected, the present state of Irish superstition closely resembles that of England during the age of Elizabeth; a strong proof of the correct measurement of those who have stated a space of two centuries to exist between the relative degree of popular knowledge and civilization attained by the sister kingdom."

XVI.

THE ROCK OF CASHEL arrests the traveller on his road from Limerick to Kilkenny— a remarkable-looking eminence, the only one in an extensive plain, and crowned with a pile of the noblest assemblage of monastic ruins in Ireland. It resembles nothing that I remember except the citadel of Gratz, built on just such a rock, with a town at its base. The ruins are supposed by some to have been both a monastic and a regal edifice; and from the want of regularity in plan, as well as peculiarities in the workmanship and style of ornamenting, appear to have been the work of several periods. The town of Cashel, once the residence of the kings of Munster, has now dwindled into a place of very moderate pretensions. "The want of a navigable river," says Wright, "is the only assignable cause for the desertion of this royal seat, encompassed by a great extent of country, fertile as cupidity could desire, and diversified by gentle undulations. The most ancient structure in the group of buildings on the rock is called Cormac's Chapel, from the founder, Corinac-mac-culinan, King of Munster and Archbishop of Cashel, who flourished in the beginning of the tenth century, and was slain in battle by the Danes.

Approach to Cashel

185

Rock of Cashel

"The chapel, the first and perhaps the only edifice that graced the rock in ancient times, is entirely of stone, both walls and roof; the latter ridged up to an acute angle, the sides or legs of which are tangents to a counter-arch, springing from the inner front of the walls. The doorway is in the Saxon style, which pervades also the other parts of the chapel, and is adorned with zig-zag and bead ornaments. Above the archway is the effigy of an archer in the act of shooting at an ideal animal. The ceiling or roof is of stone, groined, with square ribs springing from stunted Saxon pillars, with enriched capitals. There is one rich Saxon arch, ornamented with grotesque heads of men and animals, placed at intervals all round from the base upwards, and a second arch within the recess or crypt, probably intended to receive the altar. The walls are relieved by blank arcades, and the ceiling by numerous grotesque heads. The pilasters, from which the blank arches spring, have been adorned with a variety sculptures, and their capitals anciently gilt over; but the imperfect view which the half-light of the interior admits is fatal to a minute examination. A small cell on the north side of the chapel is supposed to have been built over the remains of the founder, and a niche in the wall canopied his tomb. Above the doorway of the corresponding recess is another of those hieroglyphic emblems—a quadruped, the hind-quarters of which are marked with a cross. The exterior of the chapel preserves an exact uniformity of style, and is adorned with blank arches, separated by short pillars with grotesque capitals, and at the western end it is attached to a lofty square tower.

"The pillar-tower raises its tapering form at the eastern angle of the north transept of the cathedral, and unites with Cormac's chapel in confirming the superiority of our early ancestors in masonry and ornamental architecture.

"Between the deanery-house and the cathedral is a curious stone, raised on a rude pedestal: one side is carved with a crucifixion, and the other with an effigy of St. Patrick. On this stone the Toparchs of Munster were crowned, as the great monarch of Ireland was upon the *Lia-fail,* or stone of destiny, now placed beneath the coronation chair in Westminster Abbey.

"About the year 1495 the cathedral was burned by the Earl of Kildare, with the barbarous intention of destroying Archbishop Creagh, whom he supposed to have been within during the conflagration. This turbulent noble was afterwards impeached, and amongst the various charges brought against him was this, of having burned the cathedral of Cashel. He readily confessed his fault, and added, 'that he never would have done it, but that he thought the archbishop was within it at the time.' The candour and simplicity of his confession convinced King Henry that he could not be capable of the intrigues and duplicity with which he was charged; and when the Bishop of Meath concluded the last article of impeachment with the remark-able words, 'You see all Ireland cannot rule this gentleman;' the king instantly replied, 'Then he shall rule all Ireland,' and forthwith appointed him to the lord-lieutenancy of that kingdom.

"The rock of Cashel was regularly fortified in the year 1647, but stormed and taken by Lord Inchiquin, who put all the clergy he found there to death. Divine service continued to be performed here until the Gothic reign of Archbishop Price, who unroofed the choir, and commenced the Cromwellian mode of beautifying a country, by converting its noblest structures into picturesque ruins.

"Many other monastic ruins adorn the vicinity of the city, exceedingly deserving of antiquarian notice. lore Abbey retains some of its beautiful groined arches and slender tower, and Hacket's Abbey possesses considerable interest.

"Cashel was constituted a borough by Archbishop Donat in 1216, and enclosed by a stone wall in 1320. Archbishop O'Hedian repaired the several defences, and built a hail for the vicars choral in the year 1421. The city now returns one member to the imperial parliament.

"The great 'Magician of the North' arrived at Cashel on his way to the metropolis, and being unprepared for a spectacle so magnificent, one so suited to the peculiar habit of his soul, forgot his intended journey, and was found wandering amongst the lone aisles of the cathedral at the approach of night. Another eminent individual, an eloquent candidate for the suffrages of his countrymen, felt the inspiration of the ruined pile that, hanging over his rude forum, told him of the once proud pre-eminence of his country. 'Here,' he exclaimed, 'my cradle was first rocked, and the first object that in my childhood I learned to admire was that noble ruin, an emblem as well as a memorial of Ireland, which ascends before us, at once a temple and a fortress, the seat of religion and nationality, where councils were held, where princes assembled, the scene of courts and of synods, and on which it is impossible to look without feeling the heart at once elevated and touched by the noblest as well as the most solemn recollections.' The effect of such an address upon a people of such an enthusiastic temperament may readily be concluded. The orator obtained the reward of his poetic and eloquent appeal."

The view from the summit of the ruins of CASHEL is very extensive and beautiful. The county of Tipperary is spread out below,—one beautiful variegated plain, richly cultivated, and bounded by the Galtee and other mountain ranges; while at the foot of the rocks the beautiful pleasure-grounds of the archbishop spread out in lawn, clumps, and shrubberies, like (to use Mr. Inglis's simile) a piece of Mosaic work.

There is a legend which says, "that Cashel was first pointed out to the herdsmen of Core, King of Munster, by a heavenly messenger, who foretold the coming of St. Patrick, and that the king immediately erected a royal palace on the spot, now called Carrick-Phadring or Patrick's Rock, and from receiving here the rent or revenue of his kingdom, it was called Ciosoil (since corrupted into Cashel), cios signifying rent, and *oil* a rock.

"The remains of the old cathedral, which overlook the town, prove that it must have been a very extensive and beautiful Gothic structure, boldly towering on the

188

Ruins at Cashel

celebrated rock of Cashel, and forming with it a magnificent object, bearing honourable testimony to the labour and ingenuity, as well as the piety and zeal of its former inhabitants. It is seen at a great distance and in many directions. The extent of the nave and choir, from east to west, is about two hundred feet, and the steeple is in the centre of the cross. Divine service continued to be performed in this venerable cathedral till 1752, when Archbishop Price unroofed the choir, and it was speedily converted into a ruin. Archbishop Agar endeavoured to restore it to its pristine glory, but its dilapidated condition rendered the attempt fruitless, and a new cathedral was soon after erected. Near the east angle of the north aisle of the old cathedral is a round tower, from which to the church there is a subterraneous passage. This tower is supposed to be the oldest structure upon the rock of Cashel, from this circumstance, that all the erections upon the rock, which is limestone, are built of the same materials, except the tower, which is of freestone. It is fifty-four feet in circumference at the base, and the height of the door from the ground is eleven feet. It consists of five stories, each of which, from the projecting layers of stone, appears to have had its window. The stone on which the ancient kings of Munster were crowned still remains near this spot.

"Connected with the cathedral, on the south side of the choir, is King Cormac's Chapel, by some supposed to be the first stone building in Ireland. Dr. Ledwich considers it one of the most curious fabrics in the kingdom, and its rude imitation of pillars and capitals makes it appear to have been copied after the Grecian architecture, and long to have preceded that which is usually called Gothic. This chapel is fifty feet by eighteen in the choir, and of a style totally different from the church. Both on the outside and inside are columns over columns, better proportioned than one could expect from the place or time. The ceiling is vaulted, and the outside of the roof is corbelled, so as to form a pediment pitch. It is very probable it was built by Cormac on the very foundation of the church originally erected here by St. Patrick.

"Hore Abbey, called also St. Mary's Abbey of the Rock of Cashel, was situated near the cathedral church, and originally founded for Benedictines; but the Archbishop David M'Carbhuil, of the family of the O'Carrols, dispossessed them of their houses and lands, and gave their possessions to a body of Cistercian monks, and at the same time took upon himself the habit of that order. The noble ruins of this edifice still remain. The steeple is large, and about twenty feet square on the inside; the east window is small and plain, and in the inside walls are some remains of stalls; the nave is sixty feet long and twenty-three broad, and on each side was an arcade of three Gothic arches, the north side whereof is levelled, with lateral aisles, which were about thirteen feet broad; on the south side of the steeple is a small door leading into an open part, about thirty feet long and twenty-four broad; the side-walls are much broken, and in the gable-end is a long window : there is a small division on the north side of the steeple, with a low arched apartment, which seems to have been a confessionary, as there are niches in the walls with apertures.

"A monastery, called Hacket's Abbey, was founded in Cashel in the reign of Henry III. for Conventual Franciscans, by W. Hacket. In the. night of the 14th of February, 1757, the lofty and beautiful steeple of this friary fell to the ground. The edifice was situated at the rear of Friars'-street, but is now so much gone to ruin that it is difficult to trace its divisions.

"Amongst the ruins many ancient pieces of sculpture, containing interesting inscriptions, have recently been discovered."

Ours is an age of memoirs, reminiscences, autobiographies, and personal sketches, and we miss from the history of the romantic old Irish kings the material (which will be profuse in those of our own time) for forming a familiar idea of their characters, loves, frailties, and lighter qualities. In such a spot as Cashel, where kings have succeeded kings, each with a life of human passions and interests, and where little is left beyond the name and the habitation, the imagination longs for some data by which to paint the fancy-pictures of bygone times. One story has come down to us, the wrong of which it treats having prepared the way for the first conqueror of Ireland, and a poetical and well-told story it is. Lady Chatterton listened to it from the lips of one of the wandering bards of Erin, and she gives it us in his impassioned language. "In ancient days," he said, "when the Roman Emperor Adrian had a wall built across Britain to keep his hold over that country, we had a glorious king of our own, who reigned over the whole of Ireland; his name was Tuathal, and he was the greatest monarch who ever caused the golden stone to groan at their coronation.*

"His forefathers had governed Ireland for upwards of a thousand years, since the days of his great ancestor Milesius. In his time the royal palace at Tara was the abode of all the beauty and bravery, both of our own land and from foreign parts. The song of the bard and the music of harps were never silent.

"The king's two daughters, Daireen and Fithir, were so lovely that no prince in all the world was thought good enough to be their husbands. They had been instructed by the queen, their mother, who was the daughter of the King of Finland, in all the curious arts of the time.

"Daireen, the eldest, was like a swan; her voice was sweeter than any harp in the hall; and so full of wisdom were her words, that not only were those in the palace always watching to catch the sound, but it was said, that a voice from the kingdom

---

* "This stone," says Ware, "was brought by the Tuatha de Denains into Ireland, and was used at the coronation of their kings. It is pretended that during the ceremony an astonishing noise or groan issued from it. This wonderful stone was lent by a king of Ireland to Feargus, King of Albania in Scotland, in order to render the ceremony of his inauguration more solemn: unfortunately it never returned to Ireland. Keneth had it placed in a wooden chair, in which the kings of Scotland sat at the time of their coronation in the Abbey of Scone ; whence it was transferred by Edward I. of England, and placed in Westminster Abbey, where, they say, it is still preserved."

Interior of Castle Abbey

192

of souls' (that which we now call echo) used to repeat her sayings to those outside the walls.'

On her soft cheek with tender bloom
The rose its tint bestowed ;
And in her richer lips' perfume
The ripened berry glowed.

'Her neck was as the blossom fair,
Or like the cygnet's breast ;
With that majestic graceful air,
In snow and softness drest.

'Gold gave its rich and radiant die,
And in her tresses flowed,
And like a freezing star, her eye
With heaven's own splendour glowed.'

"Fithir, the youngest sister, was gentle as a cooing dove, and fairer and more modest than the snowdrop in spring'.

'Bright her locks of beauty grew,
Curling fair and sweetly flowing;
And her eyes of smiling blue—
Oh ! how soft—how heavenly glowing!'

She was several years younger than her sister, whom she adored with all the veneration due to a superior being. Indeed, so fond were these two royal maidens of each other, that it was said by some, that the reason they refused the hand of many illustrious monarchs was that they might never be separated. Others believed that they had made a vow to dedicate their lives to each other, and to the service of their God.

"Daireen, who was proud and haughty to all the world, was gentle as a lamb to her lovely sister, while Fithir would overcome the timidity of her disposition to accompany the more adventurous Daireen when she went to chase the wild deer in the forest.

"The most valorous and handsome youth of that glorious age was the Prince of Leinster. He often visited at the court of his royal kinsman, and was sure to win the prize of all martial exercises, as well as the oak-leaf crown, which was bestowed by the fair hands of the princesses themselves, for the best songs and poems.

"Above all, he excelled in calling forth tones from the harp, which were said to draw tears from the starry eyes of the haughty Daireen; and that this lady, who had never looked on any other man but to command, and who caused even the great king her father sometimes to quail beneath the glance of her dark eye, was seen once to smile on the young prince; and yet, strange to say, the Prince of Leinster was the only visitor at the court who had not sought the hand of either princess.

"Some thought that he was perplexed between the loveliness of both, and knew not which to choose. Fithir, indeed, looked on the handsome youth with admiratation, as well she might, but she seldom addressed a word to him, though she seemed to enjoy listening to his eloquent discourse with her sister.

"At last a change came over the Princess Daireen, she was no longer the oracle of the court; the roses forsook her cheeks, her harp became unstrung, and the heart of her father was sad. The noble youths who had been proudly refused by her, were delighted to see this, and many were the hopes her softening manner gave rise to.

"Some say, that about this time the Prince of Leinster declared his love for the gentle Fithir, and that he was rejected either by the maiden herself or the king her father, who would not suffer the younger to marry before the elder. How this was can never be known; but, however, it came to pass, that after a time the Prince of Leinster and the beautiful Daireen were married.

"The nuptials were splendid; for eight days and eight nights the sound of music and mirth never ceased in all Ireland; and the many brilliant colours of the robes worn by the joyful people, caused the face of the country to look like a rain bow.

"At the end of this time, the young prince conducted his bride to his own palace in Leinster ; and both he and Daireen implored permission to take the Princess Fithir with them, but the king was unwilling to part with her.

"Poor Fithir was inconsolable for the loss of Daireen; all the joyousness of her heart fled; she who had always till this moment been the light and life of Tara's halls, and the joy of her father's soul, now secluded herself from dance and song, and devoted her whole time to the service of her God.

"A gloom was cast on the hitherto brilliant court, and neither minstrels nor tournaments enlivened the silent palace.

"The king caused physicians and others noted for their skill in the healing art, to try and restore the spirits of his darling child, but nothing would succeed. At last the queen, who knew how little medicine can avail when the mind is sad, and who was well aware that the heart of Fithir was bound up in the absent Daireen, implored the king to allow them to visit the young pair in Leinster.

"He consented, and preparations were making for the royal progress, when the melancholy intelligence reached them, that the Princess Daireen had died in giving birth to her first-born son.

"Soon afterwards the Prince of Leinster visited Tara; he was attired in the deepest mourning, and every one was struck with the change his inconsolable grief had made in his appearance. He was gloomy and sullen; no one ventured to speak of Daireen in his presence ; the sound of her name seemed intolerable to him.

"When poor Fithir contemplated the change which sorrow had wrought on the countenance of her brother-in-law, she exerted herself to control her own anguish, that she might comfort him. He had brought with him the infant of her adored sister, and Fithir never suffered it to depart a moment from her sight. King Tuathal, though he suffered intensely from the loss of his beloved daughter, was glad to see that Fithir, though at first nearly overwhelmed by the agony of this sudden blow, seemed roused by it from the state of hopeless lethargy into which she had been plunged since Daireen's departure. The care of her sister's child had given her some object in life; and though her soft blue eyes were often bedewed with tears, she would smile on the beautiful infant, and caress it for hours.

"Soon the Prince of Leinster talked of returning to his own territory: Fithir joined her entreaties with those of the king, that he would leave his child at Tara ; but the youthful father refused; and indeed no one wondered at his unwillingness to part with all that remained to him of the beautiful Dair'een, the dear pledge of their love, the only object which could cast a ray of joy over his widowed days.

"On the day previous to the one fixed for his departure, he had a long interview with Fithir; many were the tears they sired together over the unconscious babe, who smiled innocently upon them both.

"Perhaps the widowed prince thought it cruel to separate Fithir from the object of her love, whose little arms were so often clasped round her snowy neck; and therefore he lingered day after day and month after month at the palace. It began to be surmised at last, that he was as much in love with Fithir as he had been with her beautiful sister, and had succeeded in gaining her affections, and obtaining her father's consent to their nuptials; and soon the rumour was confirmed by the preparations for the marriage.

"The wedding was as splendid as that of Daireen's ; but tradition says, there was a gloom over the whole scene. The harp of the chief bard suddenly broke, while he was chanting the marriage hymn; and the airs to which the guests danced at night sounded like mournful dirges; the brilliantly illuminated halls became dim, and the torches outside refused to burn.

"However, all these ill omens, which were considered to bode bad hick by the sages of the court, did not seem to attract the notice of the young couple, and if the Prince of Leinster was not so joyous a bridegroom as formerly, it was no wonder, considering how recently he had buried the beautiful Daireen.

"Fithir, though timid and retiring, had from childhood been of a joyous disposition; and the king and queen forgot all their sorrow in witnessing the restored health and beauty of the beloved princess. They saw her depart for her splendid home in Leinster without regret, resolving before long to visit her there.

"Fithir was received with enthusiasm by her husband's subjects; flowers were strewed beneath her steps, and she found everything in the palace as splendid as all she was accustomed to at her father's court; but nothing could cause her to forget the dear sister whom she had loved so deeply.

"Often did she visit the cairn which covered her remains, and she would take the infant prince to weep over it with her: but she could never prevail upon her husband to accompany her in her daily visits to the grave; indeed, he often chid her for allowing anything to disturb the serenity of her life, and never suffered Daireen's name to be mentioned.

"One evening, about six months after their marriage, as Fithir was returning through a lonely part of the garden from her sister's grave, she heard sounds of distress. They seemed to proceed from a tower which flanked the ancient part of the old castle, which she understood had not been inhabited since the death of the late prince.

"Fithir paused to listen; and then, urged by curiosity and a wish to relieve the sufferer, attempted to clamber up the steep bank on which the tower was situated. But the increasing darkness rendered this difficult; and the timidity of her disposition made her fearful of she knew not what. There was something, too, so melancholy in those plaintive sounds, that it inspired her with a vague apprehension. Could it be the spirit of her sister which hovered over this spot? She was accustomed to think of Daireen as in a state of bliss—she well knew the purity of her mind; her great comfort was in considering that she was in the enjoyment of the happy hereafter they had so often talked of together.

"Could that dear sister be suffering from the omission of some rite or sacrifice, and thus have incurred the vengeance of one of the offended gods?

"Full of painful and perplexing thoughts, she returned to the castle. There was a brilliant entertainment that evening, but Fithir's heart was sad; she longed for' the last guest to depart, that she might tell all her fears to the husband who knew and entered into her every thought and feeling.

"The time at length arrived; but no sooner had she begun her tale, than she was alarmed at the dark and gloomy expression that lowered on her husband's brow. He rebuked her angrily, and refused to listen to the excuses the trembling princess endeavoured to make for having offended him. He hurried out of the apartment, after having extorted from her a promise never to mention her sister's name.

"Fithir loved her husband with all the ardour of her affectionate nature ; but the memory of her sister was to her so hallowed, that she was miserable at his prohibition.

"It was no unusual thing in those pagan times to marry a kinswoman or sister of the deceased, which custom was probably derived from our ancestor's the Egyptians, who received many ideas of religion from Moses arid the Israelites. This being customary, Fithir never imagined that the prince's conscience could be troubled by the idea of having given a successor' to his first wife; nor had she felt any compunction herself at having stepped into her sister's place, because she was thereby fulfilling a sacred duty.

"There was in the castle an old attendant, who had accompanied Daireen to

Leinster, and who was ardently attached to both princesses ; but her spirits had never recovered the death of Daireen, and she seldom came into the presence of Fithir unless when summoned to attend her.

"To this old lady, whose name was Scota, the princess now confided her cares, and the next evening was accompanied by her in her pilgrimage to her sister's tomb. On their return, they passed near the old tower, but no sounds of lamentation were heard : days and weeks passed away, no mysterious sound again reached tire ear's of Fithir, and she began to reproach herself for having disturbed her' husband's mind by her vain imaginings. She redoubled her attentions to him, and peace arid happiness seemed again restored.

"To add to her joy, the king and queen were expected on a visit, and the delighted Fithir was busy in preparing for their reception. The day previous to that fixed for their arrival, the prince was absent on a hunting excursion in the mountains; and Fithir, attended by old Scota, was taking her diversion in the beautiful gardens of the palace. Her dear sister's child could now walk alone, and began to delight her with its innocent prattle. She was in expectation of soon being a mother herself, but she doubted whether her hove would he so intense even for her own offspring as for the little Heremon, who had quite the features of her adored sister. It was the first time the prince had been absent since their marriage; and with that tenderness, mingled with sadness, which a first separation from a beloved object sometimes causes, she indulged in reflections on the amiable points of her husband's character, and the blissfulness of her lot.

"As she gazed on the beautiful views and the distant mountains where her lord was sporting, little Heremon rambled towards the bank on which the ruined tower was situated, and in childish waywardness had clambered up almost to the summit of the precipitous bank. The old attendant Scota was the first to perceive his dangerous situation, and prudently abstaining from screaming, she called her lady's attention to him. They both followed as quickly as they could climb up the perilous ascent: Fithir's nimble feet first reached the boy, and clasping him in her arms, she returned thanks to the gods for his preservation.

"But to descend was not so easy; and, after a fruitless attempt, she desisted, and resolved to try and reach the summit. It was with considerable difficulty while holding the child on one arm, that she at last reached a sort of recess near the bank, but below the foundation of the old tower wall. This recess she found to be a grated aperture or window: it was too closely barred to allow of her passing through; and seeing no other means of escape, she called to Scota to send some attendants with a ladder to rescue her from this dangerous and dizzy height. Scota flew to execute her bidding, and Fithir sat down on the window-sill to repose after her fatiguing effort.

"Was it fancy, or did she really hear that plaintive voice within, which had once before met her ear's? No, it was not the wind—a dying voice seemed to pronounce her own name. Fithir shuddered : 'Am I so soon then to die?' said she, caressing the child; 'cannot I live to see thee a man?' Again, 'Fithir! dearest Fithir!' was distinctly pronounced. 'I will come to thee, my sister, my love,' said the weeping princess.

"You must know that in those old days, people were said to hear their own name pronounced before they died, by the voice of the dearest friend who was gone before them to the land of spirits. Fithir's first thought, therefore, naturally was, that her summons was come, and her days in this world were numbered. She listened breathlessly, expecting to hear once more the spirit's voice; but it was no sound from the abode of the departed that again met her ear. No, this time the conviction was too strong, that those were the living, suffering, plaintive accents of a mortal, to admit of a doubt.

" 'Fithir, my own darling sister, come to me, I am dying,' was uttered in still fainter and more imploring tones.

"At this moment the attendants arrived with a ladder. The first impulse of the bewildered Fithir was to cause the bars of the window to be broken in. Trembling with awe and apprehension, she entered the dark chamber and caused a diligent search to be made: a torch was procured, arid by its light a narrow staircase was discovered. A low moaning seemed to proceed from overhead. Fithir, in an agony of expectation, was the first to mount the stairs, and soon she found herself in a small low room, faintly illuminated by a narrow slit in the wall.

"On the ground lay a pale and emaciated form; and in this wreck of mortality, Fithir recognized her beloved sister. In a moment they were clasped in each other's arms. Neither spoke for a length of time. Old Scota and the astonished servants stood gazing with speechless horror, not knowing whether the wretched object they beheld was the real frame, or the spiritual shadow of their once beautiful mistress.

"The two sisters wept, and then smiled through their tears, as if for some time unmindful of anything in this world but the intoxication of meeting. Perhaps, indeed, both were instinctively afraid to speak, lest the charm of seeing each other should be broken; lest some fearful mystery should be unravelled, which might plunge them in unspeakable woe.

"It was as if they lingered on the brow of a precipice, down which they were destined to be hurled, resolved to make the most of the last moments of life before the blessed light of another day was quenched for ever.

"But at last the sinking frame of Daireen could no longer support itself: the joy which had been excited at the sight of her sister, had brought a glow to her hollow cheek, a hectic, like the fever-spot, which burns brighter the moment before it is extinguished. Her eyes closed: it was then that Fithir, in agony at the apprehension of losing again her beloved sister, exclaimed, 'Dearest Daireen, who has done this? who is the wretch that has inflicted this dreadful doom?'

" 'Ah! who indeed?' groaned Daireen; then starting up within supernatural force,

Holy-cross abbey

she exclaimed, 'Tell me who is my rival, that I may hurl the imprecation of Heaven upon her guilty head? Who—who has deprived me of my husband's love?'

" 'Rival! can it then be? the Prince of Leinster—can he know of this?'

" 'Know of it! it was his arms that dragged me here, that cast my struggling form into this horrid dungeon. It is for him I live—yes, for vengeance on him, the father of my child.'

"Stunned by the dreadful disclosure these words conveyed, Fithir sank upon the dungeon floor. Her husband—her idol—lie whom she thought so perfect! it was too much.

"They ran to raise her from the dungeon floor: she was dead!

"Daireen's shattered frame retained the weary spirit only long enough to learn that it was the prince's guilty passion for her dear sister had caused her sufferings. Too soon the fatal truth was told; but far from cherishing revenge against her innocent rival, she clung with the energy of despair to the lifeless form of her lovely sister, and her last sigh was breathed upon the bosom of her childhood's friend.

"The vengeance of King Thuathal was terrible: he invaded, at the head of a large army, the possessions of his guilty son-in-law; and not content with this, he desolated the whole province, and levied a tribute on the kingdom of Leinster, resolved that all the subjects for succeeding generations should suffer for the guilt of the prince.

"This tribute was the cause of most of the misfortunes and civil wars of Ireland. Though sixteen centuries have rolled, over our old country, we have still cause to lament the guilty passion of the Prince of Leinster; the fatal beauty of Fithir and Daireen."

Eight miles from Cashel, on the Suir, in a rich pastoral district, stands the village of HOLY CROSS, a humble hamlet enough, but interesting from the fine pile of monastic ruins mouldering to decay in the midst of it. "This abbey," says Wright, "was commenced in 1182, by Donald O'Brien, king of North Munster, and the charter of its foundation was witnessed by Gregory, Abbot of Holy Cross; Maurice, Archbishop of Cashel ; and Britius, Bishop of Limerick. The style of its dedication is said to be attributable to a piece of *the true Cross,* that was presented in the year 1110 to Murtagh, Monarch of all Ireland, by Pope Pascal II. This relic, set in gold and adorned with precious stones, was preserved in the abbey until the approach of the Reformation, when it was saved from annihilation by the family of Ormonde; by them it was committed to the Kanaught, who delivered it to the Roman Catholic hierarchy of this district, to which it anciently belonged. The holy relic measures only two inches in length, is very thin, secured in the shaft of an episcopal cross, and enclosed in a gilt case.

"Peculiar privileges and extensive demesnes were attached to this religious establishment. Its charter was confirmed by King John and by Henry III., who took the abbey under his royal protection. The abbot sat as a baron in parliament, was

Interior of Holy-Cross Abbey

Kilkenny Castle

styled Earl of Holy Cross, and was also vicar-general of the Cistercian order in Ireland. While the relic, from which the abbey takes its dedicatory name, continued here, numbers of all classes and ranks in society made pilgrimages hither; amongst whom the Great O'Neil and one of the proud Desmonds are mentioned. Soon after the general dissolution, however, the abbey and its valuable estates were granted to Thomas Earl of Ormonde, at an annual rent of £15.

"The architecture of the nave is inferior to that of the tower, transepts, and choir'. The tower is supported on lofty pointed arches; the roof groined in a style of superior workmanship, and pierced with five holes for the transit of the bell-ropes. The north transept, which is also groined, is separated into two chapels, one of which, the baptistry, was lighted by a window of peculiar design, and contains the baptismal font. Here are the fragments of an altar-tomb: to this the south transept is similar. The choir is adorned with two rich monumental relics, of designs entirely original, and unlike any sepulchral or ecclesiastical architecture to be seen in other countries : one, which separates two little sanctuaries, consists of a double row of pointed arches springing from pillars, enriched with spiral flutings, less rich, but resembling the Apprentice's Pillar in Roslin Chapel; the base is ornamented with trefoils and finials, and at one side is a small font for the reception of holy water. The interior dimensions favour' the idea that this curious piece of architecture received the remains of the deceased during the performance of the funeral mass; but it is also conjectured to have been erected as a shrine for the reception and display of the sacred remnant of the true cross, already spoken of.

"The second memorial alluded to is equally interesting from the beauty of its design; but its sepulchral appropriation is yet uncertain. A projecting canopy of stone is supported by three trefoil arches, springing from slender columns of black marble: the soffit of the canopy is groined, and the pedestal of the monument enriched with sculpture. Its. position on the south side of the high altar has led antiquaries to attribute this mausoleum to the original founder of the abbey, Donald O'Brien; but as the architectural decorations do not justify so early a date, nor the armorial bearings resemble those of the O'Brien family, the idea of its being a royal monument is no longer entertained. There are five escutcheons, three of which bear arms, beneath the canopy: the first shield on the dexter side bears a cross; the second, the arms of England and France, quarterly; the third, the arms of the Butlers; and the fourth seems to bear the arms of the Fitzgeralds. From an inspection of these heraldic proofs, and reference to the peerage, it is concluded that this elegant monumental struicture was raised to the memory of the daughter of the Earl of Kildare, wife of James IV. Earl of Ormonde, commonly called *The White Earl'*, who died about the year 1450."

The entrance into Kilkenny, and the romantic view of the castle of the Ormonds rising above the river, reminded me strongly of one of the views of Warwick Castle

The first impression of the town from a cursory glance is extremely fine; the cathedral of St. Canice, the castle and other very imposing structures, coming into almost every view, from the unevenness of the ground, and the happily chosen sites of all these edifices. Kilkenny is divided into two parts, called Irish-town, (the neighbourhood of the cathedral,) and English-town, (that of the castle,) the latter, thrifty-looking and well built, and having an air of gentility, in which many of the second-class of Irish towns are rather deficient.

The morning after my arrival, some friends were kind enough to accompany me to KILKENNY CASTLE, which is being modernized within and un-modernized without; the old furniture giving place to the luxuries of London in our own time, and the walls and towers undergoing castellation. We were first taken through the gardens and conservatories, laid out and supported in princely magnificence; and thence we crossed the public road to the castle, which we were most civilly shown "from turret top to donjon keep." You would scarce fancy yourself in a castle, however, in any part of it; and my own recollections are principally of the views from the windows, which were unequalled for picturesque richness, particularly one from a balcony overhanging the Nore. I should not forget, however, a picture of a Marchioness of Ormond, which struck me exceedingly, and one or two very choice old cabinets. Historically, this castle is one of the most interesting in Ireland. There is perhaps no baronial residence in Ireland that can boast at the same time of a foundation so ancient, a situation so magnificent, and so many historical associations, as the princely residence of "the chief butler of Ireland," Kilkenny Castle. It appears to have been originally erected by Richard de Clare (Strongbow) as early as 1172; but this structure having been destroyed by Donald O'Brien, King of Limerick, it was rebuilt in 1195, by William Lord Marshall, Earl of Pembroke, in the possession of whose descendants it remained till the year 1391, when it was purchased by James Butler, the third Earl of Ormond, from Thomas he Spencer, Lord of Glamorgan and Kilkenny, whose grandfather, Hugh, acquired it and the earldom of Gloucester in marriage with Eleanor de Clare, third sister and coheir of Gilbert, ninth Earl of Clare and Gloucester. From this period to the present it has been the chief residence of the illustrious house of Ormond; and we trust shall long continue so. Here, in 1399, the earl had the honour of receiving King Richard II., and of entertaining that sovereign for' fourteen days. In March 1650, when the city was invested by Oliver Cromwell, and its defence entrusted to Sir Walter Butler, the cannon of the former were opened on the castle, and a breach was effected on the 25th, about midday; but the besiegers were twice gallantly repulsed, and te breach was quickly repaired. On this occasion it was said that Cromwell, apprehending a longer' resistance than suited the expedition necessary in his military operations at the time, was on the point of quitting the place, when he received overtures from the mayor and townsmen, offering to admit him into the city. He accordingly took possession of Irish-town, and being soon after joined by Ireton with fifteen hundred fresh men, "Sir Walter Butler, considering the weakness of the garrison, few in number, and those worn out for want of rest by continued watching, and hopeless of relief determined to execute Lord Castlehaven's orders, which were, that if they were not relieved by seven o'clock the day before, he should not, for any punctilio of honour, expose the townsmen to be massacred, but make as good conditions as they could by a timely surrender. A parley was beaten, and a cessation agreed on at twelve o'clock the next day, when the town and castle were delivered up." The articles of capitulation were highly creditable to the garrison ; and it is recorded, that Sir Walter Butler and his officers when they marched out were complimented by Cromwell, who said, "that they were gallant fellows; and that he had lost more men in storming that place than he had in taking Drogheda, and that he should have gone without it, had it not been for the treachery of the townsmen.

Of the original castle, as rebuilt by the Earl of Pembroke, but little now remains. It was an oblong square, of magnificent proportions, with four lofty round towers at its angles. This castle was re-edified by the first Duke of Ormond, towards the close of the seventeenth century, in the bad style of architecture then prevailing on the continent, a taste for which had probably been imbibed by the duke in his repeated visits to France. It retained, however, three of the ancient towers, but changed in character, and disfigured by fantastic decorations to make them harmonize in style with the newer portions of the building. That structure has again been removed by the present marquess, and one of 'better' taste, the subject of our present Engraving, erected on its site, preserving, however, the ancient towers, and restoring them to something like their original character. The architect is Mr. Robertson of Kilkenny.

The interior of the castle will shortly be adorned with its original collection of ancient tapestries and pictures, valuable as works of art, but still more as memorials of some of the most distinguished historical personages of the two last centuries.

Nothing can be finer than the situation of Kilkenny Castle, placed on a lofty eminence immediately overhanging that charming river,

"The stubborn Newre, whose waters grey
By fair Kilkenny and Rosse-ponte broad."

From the military I went to the ecclesiastical eminence of the town, the hill opposite the castle, crowned with the noble CATHEDRAL OF ST. CANICE. This, to me, is one of the most beautiful masses of architecture in Ireland. The hill on which it stands is crowned with noble trees, which hide and disclose the old towers very picturesquely, the tall shaft of the famous Round Tower Waring above all, and the approach is by a long and ancient stone staircase, very like the ascent to some of the monasteries near Sorrento. The graceful proportions of the cathedral give it a lightness and elegance not common to buildings of that capacity, it being (among Irish churches) only

St. Canice, Kilkenny

inferior in size, I think, to Christ's Church and St. Patrick's in Dublin. "It was commenced," says the chronicler, "about the year 1180, by Felix O'Dullany, who translated the old see of Sagir from Aghaboe to Kilkenny. The greatness of the first design was such as its authors could never have expected to see completed, which induced them to cover in and finish the choir, and proceed at once to consecration, leaving to posterity the sacred task of conducting the noble plan to its consummation. This vast pile is cruciformed, extending two hundred and twenty-six feet from east to west, and the length of the transepts measuring one hundred and twenty-three. The nave is distributed into a centre and two lateral aisles, communicating by pointed arches, springing from plain pillars of black marble. Four pointed windows illuminate each aisle, and the upper part of the nave is lighted by five quatrefoil windows. Many ancient monuments, differing in degrees of pomp and costliness, are erected in the sideaisles, and augment the solitary graves of the venerable place, and the luxurious melancholy which such memorials inspire. The tower, much too low in proportion to the lengths of the choir and transept, is supported upon groined arches, springing from massive columns of marble. The western window is triplicated, and a cross and two Gothic finials crown the centre and angles of the great gable.

"The choir extends seventy-seven feet in length, and is uninterrupted in its simple grandeur by any of the trifling, though not unusual, decorations of cathedral churches. St. Mary's Chapel is situated to the north of the choir, communicating with the north transept ; and the chapter-house and bishop's court occupy corresponding positions on the south. The pillar-tower seems to claim admission amongst the venerable temples raised to the true religion, by its proximity to the church; but how far it is entitled to that respect, is still a matter of uncertainty.

"The present condition of the cathedral reflects much credit upon the learned incumbents of the see of Ossory for some years past; amongst whom, one of the chief in benevolence and in learning was Dr. Pococke, who raised and set up the inverted monuments, restored the shattered walls, and re-edified the whole structure. The tombs of St. Canice may be esteemed as so many historic records; and to a country whose history is still disfigured or obscured, such memorials are invaluable.

"The chair or throne of St. Kieran, a stone seat with arms of upright stone, having a graceful curve, stands in the north transept. This patriarch is believed to have preceded St. Patrick by thirty years in his holy mission, and to have been the first to preach Christianity in Ireland. Under the second window from the vestibule is a monument to the memory of Bishop Walshe, the unhappy manner of whose death has been, by political influence, unnoticed in the inscription. In the year 1585, the bishop cited one James Dullard, a profligate wretch, to appear in his court and reply to a charge of adultery, but the monster answered the citation by breaking into the palace of the bishop, and stabbing him to the heart with a skean. After the perpetration of this bloody deed he fled into Troy's Wood, and uniting himself to the banditti that then infested the vicinity, stated the mode in which he had qualified himself for his new vocation; but the banditti, shocked at the crimes, and disgusted with the confidence of Dullard, brought him to a formal trial amongst themselves, and finding him guilty, immediately twisted a gad around his neck, and hung him from a tree in the forest.

"Many sepulchral honours are here raised to the memory of the ancient and illustrious house of Butler; perhaps that of Peter Butler, eighth Earl of Ormonde, who died in 1539, and his countess, Lady Margaret Fitzgerald, are better known to the historian than others erected to the same illustrious family. The effigy of the earl is distinctly relieved in black marble, at full length, and in complete armour, his sword laid across his body, and his feet resting on a dog. The same monument entombs the mortal remains of his haughty countess, whose memory is perpetuated by the Irish, under the name of 'Moryhyhead Ghearhodh.' This extraordinary lady, inheriting the martial spirit of her ancestors, was always attended by numerous vassals, well clothed and accoutred, and composing a formidable army. She had several strong castles within the limits of her territory, of which that at Ballyragget was her favourite citadel, on the top of which her chair is still shown. Campion calls her a rare woman, and able for wisdom to rule a realm, had not her stomach overruled herself.' Her lord being appointed to the government of Ireland, is supposed to have discharged the high duties with honour and approbation; the latter owing to the prudent counsels of his lady, 'a lady of such port, that the estates of the realm couched to her; so politic that nothing was thought substantially debated without her advice; warlike and tall of stature, very rich and beautiful; a bitter enemy; the only means by which in those days her husband's country was reclaimed from the sluttish Irish customs to the English habits.'

"James Butler, eldest son of this remarkable lady, supposed to have been poisoned at a banquet, died at his house in Holborn, London. His biographer adds, that his death bred sorrow to his friends, little comfort to his adversaries, great loss to his country, and no small grief to all good men.'

"Dr. Pococke died in the see of Meath, to which he was translated from Ossory; but his public services, his eminent virtues, and great learning, are attested with an honourable gratitude by the erection here of a cenotaph, bearing a feelingly-written inscription to his memory. He not only caused those permanent repairs which a continuation of existence demanded, but exercised a vigilance in the detection of every fragment of antiquity in the cathedral that had escaped the ravages of time or barbarity. The eastern window was formerly adorned with stained glass of so much beauty, that Rimmini, a nuncro of the pope, offered £700 for it to Bishop Roth and the chapter, which they, valuing their honour above gold, very properly refused. During Cromwell's usurpation his fanatic followers broke in the window, allowing but few fragments to elude their sacrilegious hands: these Dr. Pococke gathered, and caused them to be inserted in the window above the western door."

There are one or two other very fine remains of architecture at Kilkenny, St. John's and the Black Abbey being in a very picturesque stage of decay. The former was called the Lantern of Ireland from the great number of its windows. It is now used as a parish church, somewhat to the detriment of its beauty. Kilkenny is a famous town for many reasons—one of which, and it will be no light honour, is its having been the birthplace of Banim, one of the first of the novelists. It is also famous, however, as the scene of the persecutions for witchcraft, which found a parallel in the horrors enacted at Salem in Massachusetts. "The Lady Alice Kettell," says one writer, "was summoned, in or about 1325, before the bishop, to answer the charge of practising magic, sorcery, and witchcraft. She and her accomplices, Petronilla and Basilia, were accused of holding nightly conferences with an imp or evil spirit, called Robin Artisson, to whom, in order to make the infernal thing obedient to all their commands, they sacrificed nine red cocks in the middle of the highway, and offered up the eyes of nine peacocks. The Lady Alice, by means of this imp and his associates, caused every night the streets of Kilkenny to be swept between the hour of complin-prayer and daybreak. And for 'what did she do this? To sweeten the town and make it agreeable? no such thing. Witches are not so benevolently inclined; but it was for the good of her greedy son that she did it, one William Utlan, a great land-pirate, an *avarus Agricola,* a fellow who monopolized all the town-parks, and grasped at great possessions. So the cunning mother had all the filth of the city raked to her son's door, to help him to manure his meadows; and such of the inhabitants as ventured to go out at night, heard unearthly brooms plying over the causeway, and fearful-looking scavengers were at their dirty work, who scouring away to slow chorus, chanted as follows:

'To the house of William, my son,
Hie all the wealth of Kilkenny town.'

But this was not all: the Lady Alice beat even Captain Freney the robber, and all his Kellymount gang, in riding amid the darkness of night. 'No sooner were the nine peacocks' eyes thrown into the fire, than up rose Robin the imp, and presented his potent mistress with a pot of ointment, with which she oiled her broomstick; and then mounting as gay as Meg Merrilies the Scotch hag, and having along with her Petronilla and Basilia, her dear friends, she performed a night's journey in a minute, and used to hold a *Sablat* with other enchanters on the *Devil's Bit,* in the county of Tipperary.

"This business made a great noise at the time. The Lady Alice Kettell, having powerful friends, escaped to foreign parts: her accomplice Petronilla was burned at the Cross of Kilkenny. William Utlan suffered a long imprisonment. On searching the Lady Alice's closet (as Hollingshed relates) they found a sacramental wafer, having Satan's name stamped thereon, and a pipe of ointment, with which she greased her staff, when she would amble and gallop through thick and thin, through fair weather and foul, as she listed."

To this account Mr. Crofton Croker replied by the following interesting letter, published in the Dublin Journal.

"The persecution of the Lady Alice Kettell, at Kilkenny, for witchcraft, is perhaps one of the earliest upon record. The Bishop of Ossory is stated to have been her accuser, and to have charged her and two companions with various diabolical acts; among others, that of holding a conference every night with a spirit called Robin Artisson, to whom, as you have related, they were said to sacrifice nine red cocks and nine peacocks' eyes.

"In this ecclesiastical persecution, the object of which appears to have been to extort money to cover the roof of St. Mark's Church, in Kilkenny, the connexion with the fairy creed is obvious from the name of the evil spirit. The appellation of Artisson, any Irish scholar will at once perceive has had its origin in the sacrifice said to be nightly offered up, as the translation of it is chicken-flesh and with respect to the name of Robin, I cannot help thinking, when Sir Walter Scott tells us that 'by some inversion and alteration of pronunciation' the English word goblin and the Scottish bogle come from the same root as the German kobold, he might as well have added poor Robin, if only for the sake of good-fellowship, as Robin's punning namesake, Thomas Hood, would have said.

"That Robin, however, was the popular name for a fairy of much repute is sufficiently well known; but since the mention of his name has accidentally occurred with that of Hood, I may be allowed to observe, that the title assumed by, or applied to the famous outlaw, was no other than one which had been appropriated to a denizen of fairy land; Hudikin or Hodekin, that is 'little hood,' or 'cowl,' being a Dutch or German spirit, so called from the most remarkable part of his dress, in which also the Norwegian Nis and Spanish Duende were believed to appear,

'Un cucurucho tamano,'

to use the words of Calderon. There is in Oxford-street a well-known coach-office, distinguished by the sign of 'the Green Man and Still,' but why so called I have never had satisfactorily explained by the curious in such matters. The derivation of tire Bull and Mouth, the Belle Sauvage, the Talbot, (old Chaucer's Tabart,) and many other signs, which may be quoted in proof of the mutability of things, are familiar to all, yet the origin of the aforesaid Green Man and Still remains involved in the most mysterious obscurity. I have, however, always been inclined to consider it as remotely derived from Robin Hood; and leaving fancy to fill up the chasm, have found myself willing to translate it as 'the forester and fairy,' or the green or woodman, and the still folk or silent people, as the supernatural beings we call fairies were not unusually termed; 'das still Volk' being the common German expression.

"This long digression, like the treacherous Friar Rush, might readily lead me on from 'the merry green wood,' until I became bewildered in the mazes of conjecture. Allow me, therefore, to return to Kilkenny, the scene of Alice Kettell's conjurations. That town appears to have been peculiarly fatal to witches. Sir Richard Cox, in his History of Ireland, mentions the visit of Sir William Drury, the Lord Deputy, to it, in October 1578, who caused thirty-six criminals to be executed there, 'one of which was a blackamoor, and two others were witches, and were condemned by the law of nature, for there was no positive law against witchcraft in these days.' From that it would appear that the statute of the 33rd of Henry VIII. against witchcraft had either become a dead letter, or had not been enacted in Ireland.

"Ireland has been, in my opinion, unjustly stigmatized as a barbarous and superstitious country. It is certain that the cruel persecution carried on against poor and ignorant old women was as nothing in Ireland when compared with other countries. In addition to the three executions at Kilkenny, a town the inhabitants of which were almost entirely either English settlers or of English descent, I only remember to have met with an account of one other execution for the crime of witchcraft. This latter took place at Antrim, in 1699, and it is, I believe, the last on record. The particulars of this silly tragedy were printed in a pamphlet, entitled 'The Bewitching of a Child in Ireland,' and from thence copied by Professor Sinclair, in his work entitled 'Satan's Invisible World Discovered,' which is frequently referred to by Sir Walter Scott in his Letters on Demonology."

On the same river, "the stubborn Nore," as Spenser calls it, stands JERPOINT ABBEY, founded by Donogh M'Gilla-Patrick, Prince of Ossory. In wealth, honours, and architectural splendours, Jerpoint was exceeded by no monastic institution in Ireland. The demesne lands extended over fifteen hundred acres of fertile ground, and the buildings included the abbey-church and tower, a refectory, dormitory, and offices, that occupied an area of three acres. The whole of this property, bequeathed for objects purely sacred, was granted at the dissolution to Thomas Butler, tenth Earl of Ormonde, at an annual rent of £49 3s. 9d.

"The style of architecture combines the Anglo-Norman and early English; and those parts that survive, and are approachable, display a beauty and perfection not inferior to anything of coeval structure in the kingdom; but from neglect and barbarity, this most splendid ruin is so injured and polluted, that the proportions of its vast choir and wide-spread arches, the shattered frames of the richly traced windows, with the mouldering fragments of sepulchral monuments, scattered over a surface of mire and filth, prohibit ingress or inspection. Exterior vestiges still appear of those buildings within whose shade the monks, on days of high solemnity, passed in their customary processions; but now they lie in masses of detached ruin, covered over with earth and grass, and distinguishable only by the eminence they form.

"The tomb of the founder is placed opposite the high altar in the south aisle and

Jerpoint Abbey

adorned with the recumbent effigies of a male and female in antique costumes. The male is represented holding a crucifix in his right hand, which rests upon his breast, while the left points to a harp hanging at his side. A full-length figure of an abbot, in his proper robes, reclines upon the marble torus of another tomb: in his left hand appears a crozier, in the volute of which an Agnus Dei is sculptured. Other monuments of exquisite workmanship present a melancholy disregard of proper feeling, and a wanton profaneness, by their shattered fronts and spoliated appearance; and the inscriptions of all are nearly effaced.

"The monument of Dullany lies obscured in the ruinous confusion and heaps of decay. He died in the year 1202, was interred on the north side of the high altar, and many miracles' are said to have been wrought at his tomb.

"The following stanzas," says Wright, from whom I get the information relative to this abbey, "feelingly and faithfully describe the beauties that linger round this decaying pile:

'I gaze where Jerpoint's venerable pile,
Majestic in its ruins, o'er me lowers;
The worm now crawls through each untrodden aisle,
And the bat hides within its time-worn towers.
It was not thus when, in the olden time,
The lowly inmates of you broken wall
Lived free from woes that spring from care or crime,
Those shackles which the grosser world enthrall.
Then, while the setting sunbeams glistened o'er
The earth, arose to heaven the vesper song;
But now the sacred sound is heard no more,
No music floats the dreary aisles along:
Ne'er from its chancel soars the midnight prayer;
The stillness broken by no earthly thing,
Save when the night-bird wakes the echoes there,
Or the bat flutters its unfeather'd wing.'

"The following stanzas allude to the involuntary resignation of the abbey and its vast domans by Oliver Grace Fitz-Oliver, of the Courtstown family the last Abbot of Jerpoint, in the year 1530:

'Nor let thy last lord, Jerpoint, be forgot,
Whose sorrows teach a lesson man should learn,
But fancy leads me to the very spot
From whence he parted, never to return.
I mark the venerable abbot stand
Beneath the shadow of his church's towers,
Grasping the wicket in his trembling hand,
Reverting to past scenes of happier hours,
And dwelling on the many years gone by,
Since first his young lips breath'd his earliest prayer,
To lisp of Him who lives beyond the sky,
And nurse the hope he might behold Him there.

213

And now he gazes ere his steps depart,
While earthly feelings wake that long had slept;
Then with a look that spoke a breaking heart,
He turned him from his hallowed home and wept.'

Lines written at Jerpoint Abbey, published in the
"Memoirs of the Family of Grace."

XVII.

I ENTERED WATERFORD over another of my countryman's wooden bridges, considered, like those built by the same man at Derry, Portumna, and Ross, rather as curiosities. The Guide-book says the bridge is eight hundred and thirty-two feet in length, and was built "by Mr. Samuel Cox of America." They might as well say, the road was invented by Mr. M'Adam of the eastern hemisphere. It was evening when I arrived, and the broad quay, lined with lamps, and the reflection of lights on the river, with the vague outline of tall buildings on one side only of the street, struck me as giving promise of a very fine city. Though my morning walk rather disappointed me, the quay is certainly a very spacious and well-constructed one, nearly a mile in length, and devoted partly to a promenade between the street and the river. After rambling about in vain to find anything in the other parts of the town to interest me, I called a car-driver, and asked if his horse was able to draw me to the top of the bill opposite the town. I had made my bargain and mounted the car, when the man turned to me before starting, and asked if I knew the toll over the bridge would be a shilling. Satisfied that I was willing to stick to my bargain with this additional expense, he whipped up, and began to chat away most merrily. I was pleased with the considerateness as well as the gaiety of my Jehu, and we were soon on excellent terms. No Yankee was ever more inquisitive, however; and after discovering by direct questions that I was not from Cork, nor Kilkenny, nor Dublin, but all the way from America, Pat said, "Then it's yer honour has a white skin and *spakes* like an Irishman, and looks intirely in the face like Mr. Power O'Shay, first-cousin to the mimber." After this compliment Pat could scarce do enough for me. He stopped several gentlemen on the road, somewhat to my annoyance, to ask where was the view, and to tell them I was come all the way from America to see Watherford, and couldn't "for ould Pope's big wall," which wall, by the way, he helped me over, by allowing me to step from the car to his shoulders, climbing up after me, that I might make a ladder of him also from the other side.

The Quay, Waterford

215

The view from the top of the hill quite repaid me for my trespass. Waterford is beautiful from this distance, and the banks of the Suir above and below the long bridge, are very bold and striking. The broad bosom of the river was covered with large vessels, steamers, and small sailing-craft; the quay was thronged with pedestrians and vehicles, the sun shone brightly, and the scene altogether, with its background of fine hills, was beautiful. There is said to be from twenty to sixty-five feet of water in the Suir at low tide, and vessels of eight hundred tons may come up close to the quay, a circumstance which has been found very favourable for the debarcation of cavalry and military stores. Waterford has always, from this and other reasons, been an important port of Ireland. Its ancient name was *Cuan-na-Frioth,* or Haven of the Sun. It was afterwards called *Gleann-na-Gleodh,* or Valley of Lamentation, from the tremendous conflicts between the Irish and the Danes. By old Irish authors, it is frequently named, from its shape, the *Port of the Thigh.* Its historical record states that it was founded in 155, but made a considerable town under Sitric in 853. It was still inhabited by the Danes in 1171, the time of King Henry's invasion. There are other historical events connected with King John, Richard II., (who remained nine months at Waterford to assuage his grief for the death of Queen Anne,) the Desmonds, &c. &c. Its great feature to antiquarians, however, is REGINALD'S TOWER, a fine old remnant of Danish architecture, standing near the lower end of the quay. It was built by Reginald, Son of Imar, in 1003. In 1171 it was held as a fortress by Strongbow; in 1463 a mart was established in it; and in 1819 it was partly rebuilt in its original form, and appropriated to the police establishment. Besides these various uses, it has been used as a prison. After the successful storming of the town by the English forces of Strong-bow, led on by the redoubtable Raymond le Gros, in 1171, when the city was plundered, and all the inhabitants found in arms were put to the sword, Reginald, Prince of the Danes, and Malachy O'Faelan, Prince of the Decies, with several other chiefs who had confederated to resist the invaders, were imprisoned here after they were condemned to death. They were saved, however, by the intercession of Dermot MacMurrogh, who, with many other Welsh and English gentlemen, came to Waterford to be present at the marriage of Earl Strongbow with Eva, the King of Leinster's daughter.

I walked back over my fellow-townsman's "bridge of American oak," enjoying very much the beauty of the banks of the river on the side opposite the town: with the exception of the banks of the Suir, however, the neighbourhood of Waterford looked bleak and uninviting. The hotel was but indifferent, and I was not sorry to curtail my stay somewhat, and hurry on by the first conveyance towards Lismore.

The views of LISMORE CASTLE, which have been taken always from the most favourable points, prepare a disappointment for the traveller who chances to approach it first from the side toward the town, the insignificant buildings of which

216

shoulder it rather too closely. From all other points, however, it is a most striking and noble object, and justifies its reputation as one of the first of the noble residences and demesnes of Ireland. Its position, overhanging the Blackwater, is very commanding; its gardens, lawns, and walks are laid out with exquisite taste; its antique towers and its modem habitableness are beautifully harmonised; indeed, it is a spot which one's heart aches to leave—capable, to the imagination at least, of all that a residence can do for the happiness of the most luxurious. This castle was the property of Sir Walter Raleigh, at whose death it was forfeited, and purchased by the ancestor of the Duke of Devonshire. The town of Lismore adds to this historic interest the fact that it was the birthplace of Boyle and Congreve. "Lismore Castle," says Ritchie, "was founded on the ruins of an abbey by King John, in the year 1185. After being destroyed by the Irish, and undergoing various other fortunes, it was rebuilt, and became an episcopal residence; till at length, in 1589, it passed with the rest of the manor to Sir Walter Raleigh, on consideration of a yearly rent of £13. 6s. 8d., and was afterwards sold by him to the Earl of Cork. In 1626, the famous Robert Boyle was born within its walls. In the rebellion of 1641, it withstood successfully a siege by five thousand Irish, under Sir Richard Beling. On this occasion it was defended by Lord Broghill, the earl's third son, whose letter to his father is well known, but still worth reprinting here.

" 'I have sent out my quarter-master to know the posture of the enemy; they were, as I am informed by those who were in the action, five thousand strong, and well armed, and that they intend to attack Lismore. When I have received certain intelligence, if I am a third part of their number I will meet them tomorrow morning, and give them one blow before they besiege us; if their number be such that it will be more folly than valour, I will make good this place which I am in.

" 'I tried one of the ordnances made at the forge, and it held with a pound charge; so that I will plant it upon the terrace over the river. My lord, fear nothing for Lismore; for if it be lost, it shall be with the life of him who begs your lordship's blessing, and styles himself your lordship's most humble, most obliged, and most dutiful son and servant,   BROGHILL.

"Two years after, the castle was attacked again by a still greater fore, and again remained triumphant; but in 1645, it was at length taken by Lord Castlehaven. The defenders on this occasion were Major Power, and a hundred of the earl's tenants, who are said to have been allowed honourable terms of capitulation, after expending all their powder, and killing five hundred of the enemy. This sounds like one of Napoleon's bulletins.

"From the Boyle family, Lismore passed into that of Cavendish, in 1748, by the marriage of Lady Charlotte Boyle, daughter of the fourth Earl of Cork, to the fourth Duke of Devonshire. The present Duke has done much to improve and beautify the

217

Lismore Castle

The Valley of the Blackwater

was made in vain, for Kelly struck off his head and conveyed it to the Earl of Ormond, by whom it was sent over, 'pickled in a pipkin,' to England, where it was spiked on London Bridge; and his body, after eight weeks' concealment, obscurely interred in the little chapel of Killanamana, in Kerry. For this service Elizabeth's 'well-beloved subject and soldier, Daniel Kelly,' was rewarded with a pension of twenty pounds yearly, which he enjoyed for many years, but was ultimately hanged at Tyburn.

"The account given by Spencer of the state of Desmond's country, who was a spectator of it, exhibits a dreadful and impressive picture of the calamitous effects of civil warfare. He tells us, that 'any stony heart would rue the same. Out of every corner of the woods and glynns, they' (the people of Munster,) 'came creeping forth upon their hands, for their legs could not bear them; they looked like anatomies of death. They spake like ghosts crying out of their graves; they did eat the dead carrions, happy when they could find them, yea, and one another soon after, insomuch as the very carcasses they spared not to scrape out of their graves; and if they found a plot of watercresses or shamrocks, there they flocked as to a feast for the time, yet not able to continue there withal,—that in short space there was none almost left, and a most populous and plentiful country suddenly became void of man and beast.'

"In the Earl of Ormond's services against Desmond, the destruction of forty-six captains, eight hundred notorious traitors, and four thousand common soldiers is enumerated; yet a letter that has been preserved in the Scrina Sacra, from Desmond to Lord Ormond, is written in that tone of submission which renders it but too probable that vindictive motives alone urged the latter to refuse every overture of Desmond's to obtain mercy.

"Neither the death of Desmond, nor the depopulation of the country, restored tranquillity to the south of Ireland; and Elizabeth, by the advice of Sir Robert Cecil, sent over James, the only son of the late earl, who had been educated in the Tower under the eye of the English government, in expectation that the adherents of his father would rally around their young lord, and become peaceable subjects. This was the more desirable, as a remaining member of the family, termed in history the Sugan Earl, had assumed the title of Desmond, and appeared in arms against the queen.

"Reared in confinement, inexperienced in popular tumult, and ignorant of political intrigue, the young Earl James arrived at Youghal on the 14th of October, 1600, under the guardianship of Captain Price, and submissively waited on the Lord President of Munster, to whom he delivered despatches explanatory of the purpose of his journey into Ireland, and his patent of creation as Earl of Desmond, copies of which may be found in the Pacata Hibernia. The president sent the young earl to Kilmallock, whither the news of his coming had preceded him, and the followers of the Desmond family crowded to welcome their chief, 'insomuch as all the streets, doores, and windowes, yea the very gutters and tops of the houses were filled.' 'That night the earle was invited to supper to Sir George Thornton's, who then kept his house in the town of Kilmallock; and although the earl had a guard of soldiers which made a lane from his lodgings to Sir G. Thornton's house, yet the confluence of the people that flockt thither to see him was so great, as in half an hour he could not make his passage through the crowd; and after supper he had the like encounters at his returne to his lodging.' Old and young hurried into Kilmallock from the surrounding districts; the former showered their blessings on the earl, the latter offered their vow of allegiance; and according to an ancient custom, every one flung upon him wheat and salt, as a prediction of future peace and plenty, so powerful was the bond of feudal clanship.

"James, the young earl, had been brought up a Protestant in England, and the day following his arrival at Kilmallock, being Sunday, he attended service in the parish church. On his return his followers collected around him, and with tears and groans reproached him with his apostasy. They implored him on their knees not to forsake the religion of his fathers. James meekly urged, in reply to their vehement entreaties, the plea of religious freedom to be the true spirit of the Gospel: but this reasoning did not satisfy his adherents; they looked on him as an agent of the English government, sent amongst them to sap the foundation of their faith; and the very voices that yesterday were loudest in acclamations of joy, swelled the uproar of imprecations poured upon James Fitzgerald; for they denied his right to the title of his ancestors, whose religion he had renounced. Every mark of ignominy and insult was heaped upon him by the infuriated crowd: they cursed him, they spat upon him ; and abandoning Kilmallock, left the Earl of Desmond to return to England, where he died in obscurity a few months after. His dissolution is announced in the Pacata Hibernia, with an air of the greatest *sangfroid*. 'The eleventh (January, 1601) the lord president had intelligence from England that James (the late restored Earle of Desmond) was dead, and that eighteen hundred quarters of oates were sent into Munster for the reliefe of our horses.'

"The fate of the Sugan Earl, as lie is styled, was little more fortunate than that of his predecessor. After one or two defeats, he was hunted from place to place, and so closely followed that it was often known to his pursuers where he had been concealed the preceding night.* The Galtee mountains were the chief retreat of the Sugan Earl; and his kinsman, the White Knight, being induced by money or fear, perhaps both, betrayed and seized him as he lurked in the cave of Skeenarinky, not far distant from Mitchelstown. Being forcibly carried to Kilmallock, he was thence conveyed to Cork, where he was tried and found guilty of being a traitor, on the 14th of August, 1601. But his life was spared by a piece of state policy; and the earl, transmitted to the Tower of London, died there a prisoner, after seven years' confinement, and was buried in its chapel. His brother John emigrated to Spain, and was distinguished as Earl or Count of Desmond, which title was also given to his son, Gerald, who died in the service of a foreign court, without issue, about the year 1632."

The view of the small town of Lismore from the highly picturesque bridge, which was built by the Duke of Devonshire, if not the most striking, is the most beautiful in this district of country. The Blackwater, both above and below the bridge which leads into the town, flows through one of the most verdant of valleys, just wide enough to show its greenness and fertility; and diversified by noble single trees and fine groups. The banks bounding this valley are in some places thickly covered, in other places thinly shaded with wood. Then, there is the bridge itself, and the castle, grey and massive, with its ivy-grown towers; and the beautiful spire of the church; and the deep-wooded lateral dells that carry to the Blackwater its tributary streams. Nothing can surpass in richness and beauty, the view from the bridge, when at evening, the deep woods and the grey castle, and the still river, are left in shade, while the sun streaming up the valley gilds all the softer slopes and swells that lie opposite.

There is, besides the cathedral, a large Roman Catholic chapel, a small Presbyterian meeting-house, a court-house, and good inn, a classical school, and schools for poor children, endowed and supported by the Duke of Devonshire. Lismore, in former ages, was a place of great learning and piety; it is now reduced to a small town, yet kept in good repair by the proprietor, the Duke of Devonshire, whose large venerable castle, rising from the wooded rocks hanging over the river, forms the principal feature of the town.

Lismore is the best halting-place for those who are anxious to see the beauties of this part of the Blackwater and the adjacent country. The river Mr. Inglis describes as equal to the finest parts of the descent of the Rhine; and as boats can always be hired, we would advise tourists in fine weather to proceed by Water. Though from a little below Lismore, to its' *embouchure* at Youghal, it is a tidal river, wanting the constant current which constitutes one of the charms of river scenery, and presenting at ebb-tides, disagreeable muddy, sides, yet these drawbacks are amply compensated by the bold banks, extensive improvements, and striking natural features along its course. At and above Lismore, it is a fine deep inland river, pursuing its peaceful course, and gliding among ,the trees and underwood which adorn the lovely valley. The newly-made roads across the Knockmel-down and Kilworth ranges
to Clogheen and Mitchelstown, now also afford great facilities to those who wish to ascend the mountains, or to explore the dells, glens, and table-lands of this interesting district.

* Sir Richard Cox, in the narration of one of his escapes, strongly depicts the wretched state of the country. "The president having notice that the Sugan Earl and Dermod Magragh, titular Bishop of Cork, were at Lisbarry, in Drumfinin Woods, sent a party thither, who were so near surprising them, that the Sugan Earl was fain to run away barefoot; and the bishop got some old rags about him, and so well personated an old impotent beggar, that the English who met him *did not think him worth a hanging*, and therefore suffered him to pass."

XVIII.

IN no part of Ireland will the tourist in search of the picturesque receive more ample gratification, than in travelling through the south-western portion of the island. Lakes, which, in romantic beauty, vie with the boasted ones of Switzerland or Cumberland: mountains, that, for sublime grandeur, might be proudly claimed by Scotland herself: rivers and unregarded streams, whose sylvan charms are as deserving the homage of the poet's pen and the painter's pencil as the more favoured banks of the pastoral Wye,—continually surprise and enchant the wanderer through the counties of Cork and Kerry. But in what other country under heaven will he meet with such magnificent scenery, as that which presents itself along the extensive line of coast, lying between Cork harbour and the mouth of the Shannon? There nature has placed her everlasting barriers of rock to oppose the rage of the Atlantic, whose mountain billows vainly lash the huge and jutting headlands, that shelter within their Titan arms noble bays and lovely creeks,—or in the happier words of Ireland's poet:—

> "Glens, where the ocean comes,
> To 'scape the wild winds' rancour;
> And harbours—worthiest homes,
> For freedom's fleets to anchor."

The general character of this portion of Munster is hilly. In the more western districts the lofty mountain ranges exhibit a wild and beautiful aspect—delightful to the lovers of sublime and picturesque scenery, but generally barren and unproductive, except in the deep vallies that lie between the gigantic hills, where prolific nature revels in her richest attire. The most equable and fertile tracts are found in the eastern part of the county of Cork; nothing can exceed the richness and abundance of the land in the neighbourhood of Doneraile, Fermoy, and along the banks of the Blackwater down to Youghal. From the great diversity of the scenery, it need hardly be said that the western parts of Ireland furnish the most favourable field that an artist could select for the application of his talents, while, for the gratification of the antiquarian examiner, the County of Cork alone will yield him a rich harvest of subjects, particularly in the mounds, raths, cromlechs, pillars, excavations, circles of upright stones, and other vestiges of the gloomy mysteries of the Druidical worship, which thickly overspread this country. Of churches and other ecclesiastical edifices, there are few to be found of striking architectural importance, although many examples occur of small churches, constructed of great stones piled together without the use of cement, with inclined walls, and doors narrower at the

227

its name from the little river Glanmire, which, stealing like a coy virgin from its leafy covert, unites with the broad Lee, about three miles from the quay of Cork. A delightful walk open to the public, and not unaptly termed the "Lovers Walk," adjoins the town on the Glanmire side. It runs parallel to the river amidst a wilderness of trees and flowering shrubs—through whose interlacing branches, glimpses of the Lee, with numerous white sails flitting over its bright waters, may he occasionally caught. It is truly a place made for the heart's sweet converse—and, to use the language of a native bard,

> "'Tis there the lover—may hear the dove or
> The gentle plover—in the afternoon."

Although the road under the brow of the Glanmire hills, crowned as they are with superb country seats, and overlooking the winding arm of the bay, combines more points of the picturesque than is often to he met with; it is from the river that the finest views of its enchanting shores can be had. I shall not therefore dwell on their beauties here, but request my readers to accompany me in my pilgrimage to the far-famed Blarney Stone.

Blarney village lies within five miles of Cork; the principal object of curiosity that it boasts is its old castle, which stands on a precipitous lime-stone rock, at whose base flows the Awmarteen, a small river of considerable beauty. A massive square pile, about one hundred and twenty feet in height, which formed the donjon or great tower, all that now remains of the extensive outworks and defences which bztenderof old around it in every direction, and covered, it is said, a space of ground, whose interior area or court-yard measured eight acres. The walls are of immense thickness, and must, before the introduction of artillery, have been impregnable. The roof and all the floors have long since disappeared; but the curious visitor may, by a little worming through the narrow spiral staircase, and occasionally putting his neck in jeopardy, succeed in exploring all the chambers, particularly that called the "Earl's Chamber," which is still pointed out as the favourite apartment of one of the earls of Clancarty, the former possessors of the castle. It is a cheerful room, lighted by a large bay window, commanding a pleasing prospect of the adjacent country; the floor is tiled, and the fragments of tapestry still attached to the walls show that it was fitted up with some regard to comfort as well as elegance. Sir Walter Scott, when he visited Blarney in 1808, entered this chamber, and afterwards was present at the ceremonial of kissing the "Blarney stone." To this stone the castle owes more of its celebrity than to its historic recollections. A curious tradition attributes to it the power of endowing whoever kisses it with the sweet, persuasive, wheedling eloquence, so perceptible in the language of the Cork people, and which is generally termed *"Blarney."* This is the true meaning of the word, and not as some writers have supposed, a faculty of deviating from veracity with an unblushing countenance whenever it may be convenient. Milliken, the Blarney laureate, thus describes its virtues :—

> "There is a stone there—whoever kisses
> Oh! he never misses—to grow eloquent,
> 'Tis he may clamber to a lady's chamber,
> Or become a member of the Parliament."

Notwithstanding the celebrity of this stone, a perplexing doubt exists as to its identity. Some of the guides point out as the real stone, one placed on the highest part of the battlement at the north—east corner of the tower, upon which the date 1760 has been cut. We, however, incline with those best acquainted with the anitiquarian traditions of the castle, to concede the tongue—sweetening virtues to a stone which forms part of the face of the wall a few feet below the parapet. A ball from the cannon of Lord Broghill, who in 1643 attacked and took the castle, struck and displaced this celebrated stone, but it has been subsequently secured in its position by means of a strong iron cramp. Persons desirous of kissing it must submit to the unpleasant operation of being suspended by the heels, and lowered, head downwards, from the summit of the tower at the alarming height of one hundred and twenty feet from the ground, before they can reach it; and as this is the only way by which access can be gained to the genuine stone, it is not strange that the majority of those who visit Blarney, should prefer performing the osculatory ceremony on the more accessible stone, to risking their necks in the highly perilous, and certainly not very graceful mode of reaching the other, The grounds attached to the castle are still remarkable for their beauty and before man's avarice had obliterated many of its charms, must have been a perfect little Eden. Trees, whose venerable beauty might have stayed the ruthless axe, have been felled; statues, (humorously alluded to in Millikin's song,) have been removed: the winding walks are choked with rubbish, and overgrown with brambles—the grottoes are damp and desolate—the inviting seats are gone, and the luxuriant laurels that overshadowed them have grown into straggling disorder. Everything betokens neglect and ruin; and the Rock-Close, as this spot has been called, now presents a melancholy spectacle of its former beauty. A few years more, and the last vestiges of the improvements which a refined and judicious taste made here will have passed away, and the traveller may wander amongst these ruins, vainly seeking the charming scenes from whose altered features,

> "Decay's effacing fingers
> Hath swept each trace where beauty lingers."

From the Rock-Close, a flight of rude steps formed in the solid rock, and called "The Witches' Stairs," leads downwards by a gloomy passage, from which the visitor emerges suddenly upon the banks of the river. The transition, when unexpected, has all the effect of a change to a fairy scene in a theatre: it delights and surprises the stranger, and even those accustomed to behold it view it with undiminished admiration. The old castle of Blarney was built about the middle of the fifteenth century, by Cormac M'Carthy, surnamed *Laider,* or the Strong, who was also the founder of the castle and abbey of Kilcrea. Blarney remained in the possession of the "Lords of Muskerry" and the Earls of Clancarty, descendants of Cormac the founder, until it became forfeited, along with the other estates of these haughty chieftains, at the Revolution, after which it came into the hands of Sir James Jefferyes, in whose family it has continued to the present time. Adjoining the castle on the east side is the mansion-house, built at a more recent period than the castle, but, like that edifice, it is now a complete ruin, having been unroofed and dismantled by the present proprietor. Blarney Lake, a pretty sheet of water, lies about a quarter of a mile from the castle; it, however, would be scarcely worth noticing, were it not connected with some old tradition of a herd of enchanted white cows, that at certain seasons are said to come up out of the lake to graze amongst the luxuriant pastures on its banks. There is also a story generally current amongst the peasantry, that the last Earl of Clancarty who possessed Blarney, cast all his plate and treasures into a certain part of the lake, and that *"three of the M'Carthys inherit the secret of the place where they are deposited;* any one of whom dying communicates it to another of the family, and thus perpetuates the secret which is never to be revealed until a M'Carthy be again Lord of Blarney."

A very remarkable *Cromlech* or Druid's altar of immense size stands on the banks of the river Coman, within the pleasure-grounds of the castle, and numerous single pillar-stones, inscribed with ancient Ogham characters, and other Druidic relics, abound in the neighbourhood. These monolith pillars, so commonly met with in Ireland, are now generally admitted to be of Pagan origin, and as they are frequently to be found in the neighbourhood of those circles of stone, which are supposed to have been consecrated to the purposes of sun-worship, there is every reason to conclude that they were in some way connected with the religious mysteries of the primeval inhabitants of Ireland, although the precise nature of that religion still remains buried in obscurity, in order, it might seem, to give to the antiquarians a debatable ground on which to create numerous fanciful theories. The resemblance of the single stone pillar to the Round Towers of Ireland appears to favour the hypothesis of their affinity, in being both intended to represent visible images of the Deity; and should a perfect elucidation of the early system of religion in Ireland be ever obtained, there is little doubt that it will afford a key to the origin and intention of the *cromlechs,* stone circles, pillars, temples, rocking-stone and other gigantic but apparently objectless works, usually termed Druidical, so abundantly scattered over the country. Besides those massive stone pillars, which it is imagined were devoted to the ceremonies of religion, there are others which seem to have been merely sepulchral monuments;* but these latter are distinguished by being wrought by man's art into a conical summit, whereas the former are wholly unwrought. Urns, containing human bones, ashes, and other funeral remains, are found in the base of the monumental pillars, and sometimes within the circles of upright stones. Dr. Ledwich quotes a laxv of Odin, which directed "great stones to be erected Orb and round the sepulchre of the deceased; and the rule was, that a single circle round the base of the barrow indicated it to be the tomb of some chieftain or general, and there sacrifices were performed in memory of the deceased." But it is apparent that these sepulchral stones were of a totally distinct character from those erected for the celebration of religious rites, and also from those circles and stones which it is believed were used for purposes of inauguration and judicature.

The road from Cork to Bantry Bay by Bandon and Dunmanway is agreeably furnished by the hand of nature, and adorned with several rich demesnes and handsome villas, but presents no feature of remarkable interest until we reach Bandon. a This is a large, well-built, and thriving town situated on the Bandon a gently winding river, which Spencer describes as

"The pleasant Bandon, crowned with many a wood."

After passing the town it increases in magnitude, and is navigable within four miles of the town for vessels of light burthen. The place owes its prosperity to the enterprising spirit of that extraordinary man Richard Boyle, afterwards the first Earl of Cork. The site upon which the town stands formed part of the extensive forfeited estates of O'Mahony, a chieftain who had engaged in the rebellion of the Earl of Desmond. The greater portion of the forfeited district was purchased in 1602 by the then Mr. Boyle, whose foresight and sagacity enabled him to discover the natural advantages of the spot, on which, in the year 1608, he commenced building the present town of Bandon. It was originally surrounded by fortified walls, but in consequence of the towns-people rising upon, and disarming a garrison which was placed over them in the interest of James II., the town was heavily fined, and the party then in power caused the walls to

---

* *Sepulchral pillars.*—Mr. Beaufort, an intelligent investigator of Irish antiquities. makes the following remarks on this singular kind of monument: lie says, "The *Gobhlán* or beaked stone. is time only Pag an monu ment found inn Ireland, amid appearing to be sepulchral, that has been formed by a tool. These pillars are round, terminating in a kind of beak or snout, on which are marked a few characters resembling an inscription. Such monuments are found not only in Ireland, but in Germany, Poland, Persia, Batavia, and Hindostan; in all which countries they exhibit the same size, form, and character; and in the East are supposed to have been erected in honour of the sun. In Ireland they are found erected on level ground, on hills, and on tumuli. Under some are signs of humation, under others none; such being probably *termini.*" It is not my intention here to enter into a disquisition on these rude but impressive works; but I must remark, that there appears no foundation whatever for Mr. Beaufort's conjecture, that those prodi ious monuments could have been intended for such a trivial purpose as he assigns to them. Nothing short of a powerful morah ineenmive could have urged a people, in a state little removed from barbarism, to have designed or accomplished such immense structures.

Scene from Sugar-loaf Mountain

be levelled to the ground, since which time they have not been rebuilt. Under the influence of the enterprising and active spirit of the Earl of Cork, Bandon soon became a place of some importance. He commenced reclaiming the large tracts of bog and moorland, which lay in the immediate vicinity of the town, and succeeded in planting a race of industrious tenantry in a district, that, before it came into his possession, wore an aspect of rude and cheerless desolation. Much, however, as one must admire the energy and perseverance of this great man, the cruel rigour with which he persecuted all those opposed to him in warfare or religion will always darken the page upon which his history is written. In a letter to Secretary Cook, speaking of his new town of Bandon, he says, "No Popish recusant, or unconforming novelist, is admitted to live in the town at all." Following the example set them by the over-zealous earl, the town authorities subsequently caused the following illiberal inscription to be placed over the principalgate :—

"JEW TURK OR ATHEIST
MAY ENTER HERE,
BUT-NOT A PAPIST."

I am happy to say that the good taste and better sense of a later generation caused the removal of this obnoxious inscription. Dunmanway, a small town of little note between Bandon and Bantry, lies embosomed amidst hills of rugged and sterile aspect; offering few objects to attract the traveller's attention. A short distance beyond the town, the road enters a dark and lofty defile, which winds for nearly a mile through savage but picturesque mountains, that occasionally exhibit vestiges of the natural woods, with which they were formerly covered.

BANTRY BAY has so often formed the subject of the tourist's pen, that little has been left to me to describe. Viewed from Knuck-na-fiach, a favourable point on the mountains, it presents to the eye an expanse of land and water, a panorama of bold and magnificent scenery, not perhaps to be equalled in the world. Overwhelmed by the novelty and immensity of the objects by which the stranger finds himself surrounded, his eye wanders from point to point of the vast picture with a painfully pleasurable distraction; now resting upon the placid surface of that island-studded bay, within whose capacious bosom the navies of England might ride in safety: now vainly straining to reach the dimly defined horizon of the more distant

"World of waters wide and deep;"

now wandering along the graceful and picturesque shores of the Bay, or following the bold outlines of the hills and mountain-ranges, that sweep almost around this noble haven. Hungry Hill,* the loftiest of his giant brethren, towers in stupendous grandeur before us. The Sugar-loaf, Bere Haven, and Glengariff mountains claim our admiration; while more distant still, Priest's Leap, the Reeks, and Mangerton, show

243

betimes their huge proportions through the cloudy veil that shadows them. The town of Bantry is little better than a fishing-village; it possesses no trade, and the remoteness of its situation affords little hope that it ever will have any. In a historical point of view, it is remarkable as being the place at which, forty-five years ago, one of the finest appointed armies that ever sailed from the shores of France attempted a landing. In December, 1796, a fleet of seventeen sail, ten of which were of the line, anchored in Bantry Bay. The fleet originally consisted of twenty-five ships of the line, but they had been scattered and dispersed by violent storms, and when the remnant of this proud armament reached the Irish coast, the dissension and jealousy which existed amongst the leaders of the expedition prevented them taking advantage of the opportunity that offered, of landing the troops without opposition. Humanly speaking, had this army landed, nothing could have opposed them: the city of Cork would in three days have been in their hands, and Ireland would have been lost to England, for a time at least. But Providence decreed it otherwise; on Christmas-eve, 1796, a tremendous hurricane came on, by which the French fleet were driven out to sea, and the kingdom saved from the horrors of an invading warfare.

GLENGARIFF attracts almost as many pilgrims as the Giant's Causeway. It is usually reached by boat from Bantry, and the peculiarly wild scenery of the bay is thus seen to great advantage. But another way, affording bolder varieties of landscape, is to cross the range of hills which spring from the bay by a road which is very difficult except to the pedestrian. Glengariff as its name signifies, is a rough or craggy glen, about three miles in length, shut in by magnificent mountains. Its breadth seldom exceeds a quarter of a mile. The sides of the precipitous rocks which inclose it, are clothed with yew, holly, arbutus, and a variety of other trees and plants, that flourish here in the luxuriant abundance of a southern climate. Through this alpine valley a lonely mountain-stream forcing its way over every impediment that presents itself, rolls seaward, murmuring as it goes its troubled song to the woods and rocks, that answer in hoarse echoes the wild music of the torrent. The beauties of Glengariff are not to be viewed in a day, nor appreciated in a morning's walk: to be properly felt, they must be examined leisurely, and in all their various lights and distances. An eloquent writer on the scenery of this fairy vale says : "It is by treading its tangled pathways, and wandering amid its secret dells, that the charms of Glengariff become revealed in all their power. There the most fanciful and picturesque views spread on every side. A twilight grove, terminating in a soft vale, whose vivid green appears as if it had never been violated by mortal foot—a bower, rich in fragrant woodbine,

---

* *Hungry Hill* has acquired some notoriety as being the place where Mr. Crofton Croker laid the scene of *Daniel O'Rourke's* Adventures in his flight to the Moon. This humorous legend appeared long before Mr. Croker appropriated it, in one of the volumes of The *Bee,* a periodical published about fifty years since, now in the library of the British Museum.

Glengariff Inn

Cromwell's Bridge, Glengariff

intermingled with a variety of clasping evergreens, drooping over a miniature lake of transparent brightness—a lonely wild suddenly bursting on the sight, girded on all sides by grim and naked mountains—a variety of natural avenues leading through the embowering wood to retreats, in whose breathless solitude the very genius of meditation would appear to reside, or to golden glades sonorous with the songs of a hundred foaming rills." The wildness of the glen-scenery is happily and effectively contrasted with the cultivation and art displayed in the beautiful grounds of Glengariff Castle, which is the point generally chosen by artists from which to make their sketches of the mountain valley. The most extensive view of the glen is to be obtained from the steep on the old Berehaven road, near Cromwell's Bridge, from whence the spectator beholds the dark woods, hills, and rushing streams of Glengariff, the lofty mountains of Berehaven, the bold shores of Bantry Bay, and, afar off, the line of ocean, bounding all with its dark blue cincture.

XIX.

KILLARNEY, the Mecca of every pilgrim in search of the sublime and beautiful in nature, the mountain Paradise of the West, will form the subject of the present chapter.

The road from Glengariff to Killarney lies through a mountain district, which once belonged to the O'Sullivans and M'Carthys,—in whose deep solitudes may be found scenes of romantic beauty; stupendous cliffs, lofty mountains, thrown by the hand of nature into the most picturesque disorder, the rushing torrent, the placid lake, the broad sea, and the rocky shores, all combine to form a succession of glowing and magnificent pictures, whose effect upon the spectator exceeds the power of description. Kenmare is a neat town, pleasantly situated on the northern shore of a noble estuary, called Kenmare River. The town is the property of the Marquis of Lansdown, under whose fostering care it has within the last few years assumed a thriving and prosperous appearance. Between Kenmare and Killarney the savage aspect of the country begins to mellow into the softer traits of the lake

scenery; the hills are partially wooded, and the crags, which overhang the road, are tufted with rich verdure. Shortly after passing through a short tunnel which forms a part of the road, the traveller obtains the first view of the Upper Lake, spread before him in its calm beauty, like a broad mirror set in the bosom of the majestic mountains. The town of Killarney,—in the Irish language *Kill-airné,* or the church of

the sloe-trees,—is a small, regularly-built town, within a mile of the shores of the
lake, deriving its principal support from the strangers who come to visit the lakes and
the surrounding scenery.

Ross Island is usually the first place visited by strangers at Killarney; the Castle,
a highly picturesque building, formerly the residence of O'Donaghoe, Prince of the
Lakes, stands on the largest island in the Lower Lake, separated from the shore by a
narrow channel, across which a bridge of a single arch connects it with the mainland.
The neighbouring ground has been improved and made the site of a cottage *orneé*, by
Lord Kenmare, and the walks, young woods, and lawns give a delightful air of
refinement to the vicinity. The sun was near setting when I reached Ross Castle, and
a soft and golden flood of light covered the bosom of the lake; and the background
of mountains and islands, with a glory inexpressibly beautiful. The side of the ruined
castle towards me lay in deep shade, and its one square and tall tower cut the glowing
sky with an effect which made me wish I had been an artist. The scene altogether,
for softness of atmosphere, richness of light, singular beauty of outline, and
combination of island, mountain, and water, seemed to me quite incomparable. I
ascended the top of the ruin, and sat watching the fading light on the lake, till the
colour was dissolved in twilight : it was a rare moment of natural beauty, sufficient of
itself, without legendary or other interest. I enjoyed it to the depths of my heart.

The next morning I returned to this same spot, which is the usual place of
embarkation for persons desirous of visiting the Lower Lake. The day was fine, but it
looked cold after the glowing light in which I had seen it the evening before. The
castle is built on a limestone rock, and must at one time have been a place of
considerable strength; but, except the large quadrangle, which I ascended the night
before, and two flankers in a ruined state, nothing remains of this once important
fortress. In the great rebellion Ross Castle was garrisoned by the Irish, and in 1652,
resisted for some time the attacks of Ludlow, one of Cromwell's generals. But the
Parliamentary commander having launched a number of boats on the lake, attacked
the castle by iand and water, and forced the besieged to capitulate. Ware records the
event in his Chronological Table in the following words : "Ross, in the county of Kerry,
a castle in an island, is yielded up to Ludlow, after he had caused a small ship to be
carried over the mountains and set afloat on the lough, which terrified the enemy.

From Ross Island I took boat to Innisfallen Island, and on the way was shown
a small islet of rock, with one side nearly twenty feet perpendicular above the water,
called O'Donaghoe's Prison. Here the famous old prince, immortalized in song and
legend, is said to have confined a disobedient son and some of his rebellious
associates. In what age this great dynast of the lakes flourished cannot be easily
determined, but that a distinguished hero of that name once did reign over this
favoured region it would be heresy to dispute. According to tradition, he was a
powerful and beneficent monarch; his arm was strong in the fight, and the words of

Ross Castle, Killarney

Innisfallen, Lake of Killarney

wisdom were on his lips in the council. But the life of this good prince was doomed to terminate while still in the pride of his manhood and the full lustre of his renown and glory. There are two traditions in which the manner of his death are differently related; one asserts, that, while sitting surrounded by his subjects at a banquet, he became suddenly spiritualized, and descending "as some light vision," to the neighbouring lake, plunged into its crystal waters and vanished from their sight. Another legend ascribes his death to the removal of a stone which covered a fairy well in the valley, the waters of which rose in the night, inundated the district, and involved the prince and his people in one common doom. It is believed that he quits, at times, the regions of immortal bliss, and appears in person among the descendants of his people. His appearance is regarded as an omen of prosperity to whoever beholds him; he is generally seen mounted on a gallant white steed, bounding over the lake; but he is sometimes beheld on the green shores contending in the mimic fight, or treading the stately measure of the ancient Irish dance. As we approached Innisfallen, the woods, which at a distance seemed impenetrably dense, opened in glades and alleys. The trees are of larger growth than common, the ash and holly apparently thriving to the best advantage; the arbutus also flourishes here in abundance, and not only contributes to the beauty of the lakes, but to the wealth of the people, who manufacture a variety of pretty toys of its wood, and endeavour to convince the traveller that salmon broiled over an arbutus fire possesses a delicious flavour, which cannot be imparted to the fish by any other mode of cooking; the consent to the experiment involving employment for half a day, with other etceteras, to the well-practised boatmen of the lake. Innisfallen, though a mere ruin at present, was once the seat of an order of monks, distinguished in the ecclesiastical history of Ireland. It was founded by St. Finan *Lobhra,* or the Leper, some time about the commencement of the seventh century. The abbey church consisted of a single aisle, seventy feet long and twenty wide; and from the narrowness of the few windows which can now be traced, it must, like most of the very ancient churches in Ireland, have been extremely dark. The architecture of the cloister is exceedingly rude, but though much dilapidated, the limits of its covered walk, and the apertures opening into the interior area, may be still distinctly traced. At a short distance from the principal ruins there are three other buildings which it is said belonged to the abbey; but the most interesting of all the remains of antiquity at this place is a small chapel or oratory, covered with ivy, which stands on a mass of rocks close to the water.

From Innisfallen I pulled over to Mucruss, the charming demesne of Mr. Herbert, which stretches from the foot of the Turk Mountain along the eastern borders of the Middle and Lower Lakes. The old abbey of Irrelagh or Mucruss stands on a slight eminence, on the right of the road leading to the mansion-house, and as seen brokenly through the trees, is an object of the highest picturesque beauty. A well-kept, good road, lying through very highly-cultivated park-scenery, conducts to the abbey, of which I made a cursory examination, deferring to another day the pleasure of a leisurely survey of these beautiful ruins. Having ordered my boat to meet me at the head of the Upper Lake, I took a car, and proceeded by a capital road along the shore to TURK CASCADE, a very picturesque fall, formed by the Devil's Stream in its descent from Mangerton. The waters are precipitated in a sheet of white foam over a projection of the mountain, from a height of sixty or seventy feet. After breaking on the rocks in mist and spray, the torrent resumes its impetuous course through a deep narrow ravine, and soon mingles with the waters of the lake. Mr. Herbert has a pretty cottage, romantically situated on the borders of the ravine, amidst young plantations and tastefully arranged pleasure-grounds. After ascending a winding path to a lofty spot above the cascade, where I got a very fine view of the LOWER and TURK LAKES, I resumed my route along the smooth road leading past Mucruss Cottage, admiring the splendid purple tints on the mountain sides, and the wonderful variety in the shapes and groupings of the noble mountains around me. On reaching a very spacious tunnel, which lets the road through a cliff on the shore, I found my boatmen sitting on the rocks, engaged with a wooden noggin of goat's milk and a bottle of whiskey. Leaving them to their agreeable employment, I drove on a mile further to see the DERRICUNNEHEY CASCADE. The driver stopped at the ruins of a small cottage, situated on a stream, which I crossed by a rustic bridge, and obtained an excellent view of a fine waterfall, some thirty feet high, surrounded with picturesque adjuncts of wood and rock. The artist, whose beautiful drawings embellish this work, was fortunate enough to witness the taking of a stag just below the Derricunnehey Cascade. Of this sport, for which Killarney is so famous, Mr. Weld gives a graphic account.

"On the day preceding the hunt those preparations arc made which are thought. best calculated to ensure it a happy issue. An experienced person is sent up the mountain to search for the herd, and watch its motions in patient silence till night comes on. The deer which remains the most aloof from its companions is carefully observed, and marked as the object of pursuit, and it is generally found at the dawn of the ensuing morning, in the vicinity of the evening haunt. Before the break of day the dogs are conducted up the mountain as silently and secretly as possible, and are kept coupled until some signal, commonly the firing of a small cannon, announces that the party commanding the hunt has arrived in boats at the foot of the mountain; then the dogs are loosed and brought upon the track of the deer. If the business, previous to the signal, has been silently and orderly conducted, the report of the cannon, the sudden shouts of the hunters on the mountain, which instantly succeed it; the opening of the dogs, and the loud and con tinned echoes along an extensive region of woods and mountains, produce an effect singularly grand.

Turk Cascade

Taking a Stag near Derrycunnihy Cascade

"Tremble the forests round; the joyous cries
Float through the vales; and rocks, and woods, and hills
Return the varied sounds."

"The deer, upon being roused, generally endeavours to gain the summit of the mountains, that he may the more readily make his escape across the open heath to some distant retreat. To prevent this, numbers of people are stationed, at intervals, along the heights, who by loud shouting terrify the animal, and drive him towards the lake. At the last hunt which I attended, a company of soldiers were placed along the mountain-top, who, keeping up a running fire, effectually deterred him from once ascending. The hunt, however, begins to lose its interest after the first burst, and the ear becomes wearied with the incessant shouts which drown the opening of the hounds, and the echoes of their mellow tones. The ruggedness of the ground embarrasses the pursuers; the scent is followed with difficulty, and often lost altogether, or only resumed at the end of a long interval : much con fusion also arises from the emulous efforts of the people on the water to follow the course of the hunt, especially if it should take a direction towards the upper lake, when the contending boats are frequently entangled among the rocks and shoals of the river which leads to it. Those who attempt to follow the deer through the woods are rarely gratified with a view, and are often excluded from the grand spectacle of his taking the sail, or, in other words, plunging into the lake. It is therefore generally recommended to remain in a boat; and those who have the patience to wait as long as five or six hours are seldom disappointed. I was once gratified by seeing the deer run for nearly a mile along the shore, with the hounds pursuing him in full cry. On finding himself closely pressed, he leaped boldly from a rock into the lake, and swam towards one of the islands; but terrified by the approach of the boats he returned, and once more sought for safety on the main shore; soon afterwards, in a desperate effort to leap across a chasm between two rocks, his strength failed him, and he fell exhausted to the bottom. It was most interesting to behold the numerous spectators who hastened to the spot; ladies, gentlemen, peasants, hunters, combined in various groups around the noble victim as he lay extended in the depth of the forest. The stag, as is usual on these occasions, was preserved from death.

"Whether the red deer will long preserve their numbers, after the woods of Glena, which have hitherto afforded them such shelter, are cut, appears very questionable. For a series of years past they have continued much in the same proportion. Very few are destroyed in the chase, with which parties are indulged; for, when the animal enters the water, as he generally does, it is easy for the persons in boats to take him alive and uninjured. It appeared from the marks on the ears of the last I saw taken, that the same mischance had befallen him twice before. The day after the hunt, he was a third time, to the amusement of a large party of ladies and gentlemen, turned out of a stable at Colonel Herbert's, and liberated in Mucruss demesne; from which place, it was presumed, he would soon escape, and by swimming across the lake, regain his favourite abode on the side of Glena."

On my return from Derricunehy, I walked some distance up the hill from which the cascade descends, to get a view of THE LAKES AS SEEN in the APPROACH FROM KENMARE. From this elevation the three bodies of water appear spread out below the eye with their islands and mountain shores, in a landscape of which no description can convey an adequate idea. Fortunately in this case, the pencil "takes up the burthen," and in the wonderful perfection of the arts, description can be conveyed through the eye almost with the reality and enjoyment of nature.

On again reaching the tunnel, where I had left my boat, I was recommended by the driver to ascend the cliff through which it is cut, and on a platform, now smooth by the feet of travellers who had climbed there before me, I stood a few minutes and admired a smaller VIEW OF THE UPPER LAKE, enjoyable from the nearness of the objects which compose it. The mountains which hem it in, are of a bolder and more rugged cast, and the small rocky islands in its bosom rise very high from the water, and are covered with trees and vegetation. One of the largest of these is called Ronayne's Island, after a recluse who occupied it for some years. He built himself a cottage on the rocks near the water, the ruins of which are still visible, and, avoiding all society, employed himself wholly in reading, hunting, and fishing. He became exposed, of course, to the visits of curious people, and was on such occasions exceedingly savage and morose; but his name, says Wild, is still mentioned with respect and even admiration, at Killarney.

From Ronayne's Island, the prow was pointed homeward, and with the warm sun creating an atmosphere of mid-summer on the tranquil bosom of the lake, I lay in the stern-sheets, and watched the magnificent changes in the mountain-groups as we sped onward, and wanted nothing but some congenial friend to share my happiness. We soon entered on the narrow river which connects the two lakes, and after some winding through a channel, where the current ran very strongly, we came in sight of a picturesque old bridge, and the boatmen requested me to steer directly for the centre of the arch, with a caution to be careful and steady. They then shipped their oars, and the current increasing to great rapidity, we shot under the bridge with a velocity that rather surprised me. By another direction from the bow-oarsman, I steered in to the right, and ran up to a landing-place, where fifteen or twenty people stood around some object, with which they were so engaged as not to observe our approach. I jumped ashore on the island (Dinis,) and, to my horror, discovered the body of a drowned man, whose feet an old woman was tying together after straightening the corpse for burial. He was a boatman, who had fallen overboard in towing his boat against the stream, and had been dead about two hours. It was the body of a powerful man, and I heard from the boatmen that he was commonly called Big Rob, and was very much given to intoxication: he left a wife and ten children,

Approach to Killarney from the Kenmare Road

Upper Lake, Killarney

who were entirely dependent on him. The horror of this sight and the melancholy of the whole event saddened the remainder of my day on Killarney. This WEIR BRIDGE is a dangerous spot, and many accidents have occurred in shooting the rapid. "The rapidity of the current," says Wild, "forms an impediment to the ascent of boats not to be counteracted without considerable efforts, and never fails to occasion much delay in proceeding to the Upper Lake. To render the boats more manageable, the passengers are always required to land, and walk through the woods till they get above the bridge; and, even after being thus lightened, it required the united strength of nine or ten men to drag a large boat against the stream. The bridge consists of two arches, of which one alone affords a passage for boats; the other is obstructed by a wall, built across the stream from the central pier to the shore. It was intended formerly as part of a fishing weir, and is now left for the purpose of deepening the channel at the opposite side.

Leaving the spot where we had been met by this melancholy spectacle, we kept down the narrow channel to the opening of Glena Bay, and turning round a point to the left, landed in a small and lovely crescent of the shore; in the centre of it stood a *Cottage ornée*, the close-shorn lawn of which descended everywhere to the edge of the water. Rocks behind it, trees around, the forest extending up the mountain behind, and the solitude of lake and mountain burying it in silence and beauty. Glena cottage is a place to remember with a heart-ache when one is weary of the world. I landed and strolled through its gardens and shaded walks, and re-embarking unwillingly, steered across the lower lake toward Ross Island.

The romantic legend of O'Donoghoe and his phantom stud recurred to my mind as we skimmed across the still waters of the lake. Moore's beautiful song called "O'Donoghoe's mistress," is, as he informs us, founded upon one of the stories connected with this legend of the lakes : it relates, that a young and beautiful girl, whose imagination was so impressed with the idea of this visionary chief that she fancied herself enamoured of him, at last in a fit of insanity, on a May morning, threw herself into the lake.

The approach to Ross Island by water is remarkably picturesque. The grey towers and ivied walls of the castle appeared as if emerging from the waters of the lake—and glittering as they were at the moment I beheld them, with the rich rays of the evening sun, nothing could be imagined more strikingly beautiful. It was long after I returned to my inn at the village before I could think of anything but the delightful scenery I had been viewing; and even after slumber had "steeped my senses in forgetfulness" I was in fancy wandering through the fairy scenes of this enchanting region. On the following morning I determined to make another review of Innisfallen, and Mucruss Abbey, whose beauties I had not sufficient time to examine on my former visit. Accordingly I took boat at an early hour in the day, in order to have full leisure to admire those interesting places. The character of the scenery of

Old Weir Bridge, Killarney

the Lower Lake is totally distinct from that of the Middle, or Upper Lakes; it is distinguished for its elegance and beauty, being studded with rocks and wooded islands, covered with a variety of evergreens. The Upper one, on the contrary, is remarkable for its wild sublimity amid grandeur, while the Middle Lake combines in a great degree the characteristics of the other two. There are lakes in Switzerland, which, for single views, perhaps excel either of the Lakes of Killarney;—but, taking the peculiar atmosphere, the variety and grouping of the mountains, the interest of the ruins on the shores, and (above all to my thinking) the exquisite mingling of art with nature, and Killarney has no rival. Of the numerous islets with which the bosom of the Upper Lake is studded, and which have all received names, there are only four or five worthy of any consideration, except as accessories to the splendid picture which nature here spreads before us. Ross Island in extent claims superiority, but for beauty it cannot compare with

> "— Innisfallen, of the islands queen."

It is in truth an isle of beauty and repose, where a man, weary of the storms of the world, might spend in calm tranquillity the evening of his life. I cannot better describe the scene than in the words of a fair poetess, whose enthusiastic admiration of the magnificent scenery of the lakes gives a vivid freshness to her delineations:—

> — "Here nature dwells
> 'Mid laughing vales, 'mid rosy smiling bowers
> And velvet lawns, embroidered o'er with flowers;
> Fantastic shores, that varied charms display,
> Of cliff, and bower, and many a shady bay,
> Where waving groves o'er crystal mirrors rise,
> And ope to heav'n their variegated dyes.
>
> "Bright, through the vistas of the pensile woods,
> Burst on the view the mountain's glassy floods,
> Glena's rich groves, that up its steeps advance,
> And lave their shadows in the lake's expanse;
> The peak of Tomish* rising o'er the clouds,
> Above the mountains that the blue mist shrouds."

Viewed from the water, Innisfallen appeared to be covered with an impervious wood; but after penetrating the leafy screen which fringes the shore, I found the interior of the island spread out into beautiful glades and lawns, embellished by thickets of flowering shrubs and clumps of magnificent trees, amongst which the boasted

---

* To the west of Glena stands a lofty pile, called Tomish, (or Tomies,) variegated half way to its top with a waving forest; and down whose sides, especially after rain, run very considerable cataracts into the great lake. There are many other hills still running more west, as far as the eye can trace for many miles; the nearest and most surprising for their loftiness are the Reeks, whose tops resemble so many pinnacles or rather spires lost in the clouds.—*Smith's History of Kerry.*

arbutus, with its dark shining leaves, stood conspicuously distinct.† From these delightful openings the lofty peaks of the distant Tomies and Glena, with the misty summits of the purple mountain, which form the southern boundary of the lake, are distinctly seen; while between the dark stems of the trees glimpses are caught of the sparkling waters below, and the more distant sunny shores.

Innisfallen, like every spot in this region of romance, has its legends. It is, indeed, a marked trait in the Irish character, and one strikingly illustrative of the imaginative genius of the people; that general tendency to associate the wild and marvellous with the sublime and beautiful in nature. Every glen and rath—every lake and island possesses its legendary tale; but, alas! they remain almost unknown. England has the philosophic annalist of her smiling plains and ancient towns; she has the poets of her lawns and rivers. Scotland can exult in her gifted soils, who have made her romantic land known to fame : she has had her Burns in song, and her Scott in those stirring tales that celebrated her picturesque mountains and storied lakes. Who has done— who will do so much for the interesting traditions, the neglected scenery of Ireland?

But to return to our legend of Innisfallen, the substance of which, as related by the peasantry of the place, is as follows : In ancient times, it is said, a friar of the Abbey of Innisfallen had wandered, on a fine summer's day, to an adjacent grove, where the silent tranquillity of the scene and its perfect seclusion disposed his mind to religious meditation and prayer. Prostrate on his knees, his thoughts abstracted from the contemplation of all earthly things, his soul exalted with visions of a better world, he perceived not the flight of time; hours passed unheeded away, until at length fatigue threw him into a profound slumber, which lasted (on the authority of the legend) *seven hundred years.* During so very protracted an afternoon nap, many a change took place in a world where everything is perishable and transitory. The pious brotherhood of his convent had been all consigned ages past to their native dust ere the good friar awoke from his sleep of centuries. On opening his eyes and looking around him, his senses were overwhelmed with the deepest amazement. The whole face of nature was altered it was no longer the scene he had been accustomed to

† The arbutus, which is found in such abundance upon the shores and islands of these lakes, has been long celebrated for its beauty, particularly as it is rarely found growing in any other part of the kingdom. Sir Thomas Mollyneux, in the Philosophical Transactions, No. 227, says, that it "is not to be found anywhere of spontaneous growth nearer to Ireland than the most southern parts of France and Italy; and there, too, it is never known but as a frutex or shrub; whereas, in the rocky parts of the county of Kerry about Lough-Lane, and in some of the rocky mountains adjacent, where the people of the country call it cane-apple, it flourishes naturally to that degree as to become a large tree." In another place the doctor adds, "the trunks of these trees in Ireland have been frequently four and a half feet in circumference, and they grow to about nine or ten yards in height, and in such plenty, that many of them have been cut down to melt and refine the ore of the silver and head mines discovered near Ross Castle." Upwards of forty islands in this hake are covered with beautiful trees and shrubs, intermixed with the arbutus, which is frequently found growing high above the water on the bare rock, without any apparent means of sustenance but what it derives from the roots penetrating into the fissures of the hard marble."

contemplate. A beautiful lake burst on his astonished sight where no lake had been before : rubbing his eyes, amid tweaking his nose, to assure himself that he really was awake, he began to imagine that all he saw was the effect of a miracle, which heaven had worked while he slept. With this conviction he arose and repeating an *aye,* entrusted himself to the waters of the lake, which bore him in safety to Innisfallen. Directing his steps to the abbey, he entered the open gate, with the hope of having all these wonders explained; but, alas! a fresh cause of astonishment awaited him there; the monks whom he found inhabiting the abbey were all strangers to him, and ridiculed his improbable story. Amazed and confounded, the poor friar turned sadly from the place where he was regarded as an impudent impostor; and retiring soon after to one of the rocky islands of the lake, lived for many years a holy life, and died at length in the odour of sanctity.

The place where it is said this marvellous event had occurred is called Ross View, at about the distance of a mile from Killarney : by the simple country people it has always been esteemed a hallowed spot, and, with implicit faith, they point out three small indentations in the rock, as being the impressions of the friar's chin and elbows during his enchanted slumber, when compelled by extreme weariness he sank down there while engaged at his devotions. There is a small well close by, which it is said possesses a miraculous power in curing all disorders : thither the afflicted, who have sufficient faith in its healing virtues, resort for relief of their bodily ailments. On these occasions, or indeed at any other time that they visit this spot, they never fail to strew the ground with corn or crumbs of bread, as a repast for those birds who they believe are blessed spirits, sent by an invisible power to be the peculiar guardians of this scene. Now all this, though it may seem ridiculous to the matter-of-fact reader, is rife with the spirit of poetry, and the legend related as it was to me, amidst the romantic scenes with which it was associated, possessed an indescribable charm, which it would be impossible to convey under other circumstances. But even in this remote district the age of romantic fiction is passing fast a way : the "good people" are deserting their ancient raths and green rings; the Banshee's boding voice is now rarely heard wailing upon the midnight blast;* the "old grey man" has forsaken his lonely glen, and the comic little Leprechaun is no longer heard at his cobbler's work in the deep dry ditches by the blackberry-hunting urchin, whose heart beats with quicker motion as he advances with stealthy pace to seize the little fellow and his coveted red purse, and who is nearly frightened out of his wits by the sudden whir of a blackbird through the rustling leaves. Perhaps it is better that it should be so;

---

* It is a popular superstition in the southern and western parts of Ireland, that a little time prior to the decease of any individual connected with the ancient families of the country, a spirit, whom they call "the Banshee," appears to give warning of the approaching calamity, and that this apparition assumes the form of a woman clothed in white, with dishevelled hair, seated, on these occasions, somewhere in the neighbourhood of the house where the melancholy event is to take place, and singing, in tones of predictive sadness, a wild and mournful ditty.

and though the poet and the romancist may regret the disappearance of the fairy and legendary lore of Ireland, it is to be hoped that the progress of civilization, by bringing in its train peace and plenty to these shores, may cause the philanthropist to rejoice at the change.

Leaving Innisfallen, I directed my boatmen to pull across to O'Sullivan's cascade, which lies at the south side of the lake, and which is shown to strangers as one of the greatest beauties of Killarney. The shore here exhibits a sweep of wood so great in extent and so rich in foliage, that it is impossible not to be struck with its beauty. High overhead rise the magnificent Tomies but while I was admiring the sublimity of the scene, our boat glided into a small bay, in the centre of which is a chasm in the wood : this is the bed of a considerable stream which forms O'Sullivan's cascade. Landed to the right of it, I walked under the thick shade of the wood, over a rugged declivity close to the torrent-stream, which breaks impetuously from rock to rock, with a roar that kindles expectation in the mind of a person visiting this scene for the first time. The picture I had formed in my fancy did not exceed the reality : on a sudden I beheld rolling headlong from the mountain,—

> "Th' ungovernable torrent loud and strong,
> In thunder roaring as it dashed along;
> Leaping with speed infuriate, wildly down,
> Where rocks grotesque in massive grandeur frown.
> With ocean strength it rushes on its way,
> 'Mid hoary clouds of everlasting spray;
> To its rock-basin, with tremendous roar,
> The brown hills trembling round the wizard shore."

The stream, which bursts from the deep bosom of a woody glen, throws itself over the face of a high perpendicular rock into a basin concealed from the spectator's view; from this basin it forces itself impetuously between two rocks into another reservoir : this second fall is of considerable height, but the third and lower one is the most striking in its appearance. Each of these basins being large, there appears a space of several yards between the three falls; and the whole being as it were embowered within a woody arch, the effect is exceedingly picturesque and beautiful.

Before quitting Killarney I resolved to pay a second visit to the ruin of Mucruss Abbey, which though not comparable in extent or architectural grandeur to many similar edifices in Ireland, is, from the beautiful seclusion of its situation, one of the most interesting monastic remains I have met with in this country. The abbey, of which I have already spoken, overhangs the lake in one of the finest parts of Mucruss demesne. Embosomed in the shade of lofty and venerable ash, oak, yew, elm, and sycamore trees, festooned with trailing plants, and garlanded with ivy of the darkest and most luxuriant foliage; it is more beautiful in its loneliness and decay than it could have been in its pristine state of neatness and perfection.

The exact period of the foundation of Mucruss Abbey has not been well ascertained, but that a church was situated here from a very remote time, appears from a record in a manuscript collection of Annals in the library of Trinity College, Dublin, which states, that the church of Irrelagh (Mucruss) was burned in the year 1192. The present ruins are, however, altogether of a later date, and are the remains of a monastery of Conventual Franciscans, erected by the M'Carthys, Princes of Desmond, and dedicated to the blessed Trinity. It owes its present state of preservation to the repairs which it received in 1602, and subsequently in 1662, as appears from a black letter inscription placed on the north side of the choir. The church consists of a nave and choir, separated by a small belfry, which is pierced by a narrow Gothic door, connecting the nave and choir. On the south side of the nave there is a small chapel; on the north side lies the cloister, which is the most perfect and interesting portion of the building. Within the walls of Mucruss Abbey some of the Irish kings arc supposed to be interred : the vault of the M'Carthy Mores is placed in the centre of the choir, and is marked by a flat stone in the floor, on which the coronet and arms of the Earl of Glencare are rudely sculptured : a more stately monument designates the resting-place of O'Donoghoe of the Glens, who is buried in the same vault. The portion of ground on the south of the church has for ages past been the favourite cemetery of the peasantry of the surrounding district; and it is not uncommon for persons who die at great distances from this place, to lay their injunctions on their friends and relatives to have their remains conveyed thither for sepulture, firmly convinced that their spirits would not enjoy rest if their mortal part was consigned to any earth but that of the blessed Mucruss! Such requests are always religiously complied with by the survivors of the deceased, though the expense incurred often utterly ruins the person who executes the pious task. The cloisters consist of an arcade of Gothic arches; the pillars and mouldings of which are of grey marble : the solemn and imposing effect they produce is greatly heightened by the venerable and majestic yew-tree,* which rises, like a stately column, from the centre of the enclosure, and spreading its dark and lofty branches overhead, suggested to Mr. Smith, who wrote the History of Kerry, to compare it, with more truth than poetry, to "a great umbrella." This remarkable tree, which there is no reason to doubt is coeval with the abbey, has ever been regarded with the deepest religious veneration by the peasantry, many of whom shrink back with terror on entering within its precincts, and few can remain long without feeling impatient to escape from

---

* Cambrensis informs us, that the Irish church-yards of his day were generally planted with yew. That this tree was indigenous to Ireland there can be no doubt. It has been found in a fossil state in many parts of the country, and its trunk has been frequently dug up from the Irish bogs of very large dimensions. One of these found in the Queen's County, indicated, by its annual rings, a growth of five hundred and forty-five years. One of the Irish names for this tree, *Ioghadh* or *Iodha* pronounced *Ioga* or *Eega,* had been given to the sixteenth letter of the Irish alphabet a long time before Christianity was introduced into the island.

its oppressive influence. An old woman who had been praying, according to the custom of the country, beside the grave of some deceased relative, observing me examining the tree with some degree of attention, volunteered to relate to me a legend concerning it, which had been handed down from generation to generation, and which is firmly believed by all the country folks for miles around. Having an hour to throw away, and being well pleased to avail myself of the protection which the thick foliage of this wonderful tree offered against the fervid rays of the noontide sun, I seated myself upon one of the moss-grown tombstones, and invited my ancient *skanahus** to take a seat beside me : with a multitude of apologies and thanks for my "honour's civilitude," she at last consented to accept the proffered accommodation, and smoothing down her apron with critical nicety, commenced her recital in the usual Irish method, by asking a question.

"May be your honour knows the Fineens of these parts?"

"No," I replied, "I am unacquainted with any person in this neighbourhood."

"Well, it don't much matter :—any how they're come of the right ould stock, and has some of the rale O'Sullivan blood in their veins; but, as I was sayin', there was one Frank Fineeen lived, I don't know how long ago, over at the other side of the lake : a nater boy than Frank you couldn't pick out from here to Doneraile, and it ishe that was the darling among the *cailleens* : many a purty red cheek grew redder when he walked into the chapel of a Sunday morning; and it's little of the prayers or sarmins the poor girls minded with thinking of Frank Fineen and his pair of roguish black eyes.

"But amongst them all there was not one, barrin Honor Hennesey, that could plase Frank's fancy. Honor, to be sure, was as likely † a girl as ever shook a foot on short grass; tall and comely she was, and straight as a rush; and when she moved it was like a slender ash-tree waving in the summer wind. Then, hadn't she a beautiful blume upon her cheek like the blush of an opening rose? and as for her eyes, *wissha!* I can't tell your honour how they sparkled with the life and joy that was dancing in her young veins. Any how she put poor Frank Fineen's heart into a terrible flustration; and more besides him, I can tell you; for there was hardly a boy in the parish, ould or young, that wasnt ready to break his neck after her. If Honor had a fault, it was, that she delighted in bewilderin' the poor souls with her deIndia' ways; for it can't

---

* The *Shanahus,* or professional story-teller, was in times past the historian and genealogist of great families in Ireland : he recorded the heroic acts of the chiefs and princes, and preserved the memory of illustrious names; but as the changes of society hurried on, and the feudal power of the ancient houses began to decay, the records of fallen greatness became a theme ungrateful to the ears of the gentry, and, to use the words of Carleton, that first-rate painter of Irish manners, "from the recital of the high deeds and heroic feats of by-gone days, the *Shanahus* sank down into the humble chronicler of hoary legends and dim traditions." The profession, if it may be so called, is now exercised indifferently by old persons of either sex.

† *Likely,* good-looking.

be denied that her smile wor like the priest's blessing, every body got a share of it, and each one thought he himself had the biggest ind of it. In troth, it was a shame for her; but sure it's the way with all the *cailleens,* they like to make fools of the men; and by what I understand, sir, it's much the same amongst the quality ladies. Hows'ever, there was only two of all her sweethearts for whom Honor really cared a *trawneen,** and these were Frank Fineen, and a wild young chap called Neal Connor, who had been out sogering in the horse-dragoons, and fighting agin ould Boney and the black king of Morawco in furrin parts, and who had lately come home to see his ould mother, and get cured of a wound in his arm that happened to him by axcidence in the wars.

"Neal was a smart good-looking fellow enough, with an uncommon gift of the gab, and a free and asy way that made him, like a tinker's dog, at home wherever he went. His dress, too, was enough to take the sight out of one's eyes, and he wore a little cap like a skimmin-dish, with a bit of gold band round it, stuck on one side of his head, as if he thought everybody should admire him. Of course, lie had nothing to do but *stravaige* up and down the village, showing his fine clothes, and divarting himself with making love to all the purty girls that came in his way, and, amongst the rest, to Honor Hennesey, whose head was fairly turned with all the murdherin stories he told her of; his fights and battles, where the colours wor flying and the drums bating, and the trumpets blowing, and the cannons tundhering, and the generals shouting out, 'Feigh a baillagh! † Fair play for ould Ireland! 'while the Connaught Rangers, the darlins, wor making lanes through the French *corps* with their swoords and bag'nets. Any how these fine discoorses made Honor begin to fancy she liked the young soger better than Frank Fineen, who had been coorting her for nigh hand a twelvemonth, and who she knew doted down upon the very ground she walked upon; so that between Frank's honest love and Neal's fine speeches, poor Honor didn't know which of them to choose, and, like many a girl in her situation, would fain have kept them both. Hows'ever that could not be, at laste in these parts; and so as the time was fast drawing on that Frank should return to his regiment, Honor found that she must decide one way or the other. I believe it was only two or three evenings before the day that Frank was to leave the village, that a meeting was held at the public-house above at the cross-roads, where all the boys and girls of the neighbourhood were gathered to have a fling of a dance together. It was understood that on this night Honor was to make her choice between her lovers, so becoorse they both came

---

* *Trawneen,* the stem of the grass.

† *Feigh a baillagh!* "Clear the way," or more literally, "Clear the pass," was often the watchword to victory in the Peninsular campaign amongst the Connaught Rangers, who formed a portion of the brave Picton's "fighting division." Those who have served amongst those gallant fellows cannot forget the magical effect which this national battle-cry produced amongst the Irish regiments; and with what dauntless resolution they rushed to the charge amidst shouts of "*Feigh a baillagh.*"

prepared to do all they could to win the hand of the purty *cailleen*. Neal, it was remarked, never talked so fast, laughed so loud, and whispered such *slewthering** speeches into Honor's ear as on that evening. Frank, who was no match for the soger at the *blarney,* sat by without opening his lips, but every now and then he threw such mournful and reproachin' looks over towards Honor, as caused her cheek to turn pale, and made her wish in her heart that Frank could spake to her like Neal. Well, as the night grew late, some of the ould people began to talk of ghosts and sperrits, and holy places, and laygends, and the like; and, amongst the rest, of the yew-tree of Mucruss, which was planted by the blessed hands of St. Columbkill himself, who left a strict order and command to all thrue believers not to touch so much as a leaf from it. I don't know what put it into Honor's head, but says she, quite suddenly,

" 'I wish I had some of the leaves of that tree : I hear they are good for the tooth-ache; and last night I had it so bad I could not get a wink of sleep.'

Then giving a side-glance at her sweethearts, she added, in a careless way,

" 'I wondher is there anybody here fond enough of me to go to the abbey tonight and fetch me a handful of the leaves.'

" 'I'll go,' cried Neal and Frank, jumping up together.

"Honor looked from one to the other in a laughing way.

" 'I won't make little of either by preferring one to the other,' says she, 'but if you're both so eager to oblige me, I'll give him who first brings me a branch from the yew-tree that grows in the church'—here she smiled one of her deludin' smiles, and purtended to look for a pin she had dropped on the flure—' I'll give him,' says she, 'whatever he asks that 'tis in my power to bestow.'

"The words had hardly passed her lips, when the two young men, without the laste warning, started off, like a brace of greyliounds, down the hill towards the abbey.

" 'Blessed mother! 'cried Honor, turning as pale as a shroud, 'they don't mean to touch the blessed tree! Sure they might know I was only joking to try their sperrit. Shawn M'Garry, *achree,* run afther them, and don't let them attempt such a thing. Run, Shawn, *asthore.'*

"But Shawn should have had the foot of one of the mountain-deer to be able to overtake the rivals, who were already half-way down the hill. The night was as black as pitch, but both the lovers knew every inch of the path, and you may be sure neither of them let much grass grow under their feet on the way. On they kept running for the bare life, till Neal, who was the lightest of the two, got a good piece ahead of Frank, and was crossing the last ditch between him and the abbey, when he hard a voice calling to him in the pitifullest manner you can consave,

" 'Neal Connor, Neal Connor! 'says the voice, 'stop and help a poor ould woman that's fallen into the ditch.'

---

* *Slewthering,* flattering.

" 'I haven't time,' says Neal, 'at the present.'

" 'For the love of heaven! for the blessed Vargin's sweet sake, don't lave me to perish here,' says the ould woman.

" 'Don't bother me,' says Neal, 'I wouldn't stop now for an univarse of ould women;' and away he run.

"Just then up comes Frank.

" 'Help a poor ould crather out of this, Frank Fineen, and my blessing will attend you,' cries the same voice.

" 'That I will and welcome, poor woman,' says Frank, 'though every minnit is worth gold to me now.—Where are you at all?'

" 'Here I am, in the ditch : give us your hand, *acourneen*.

"Frank reached out his hand to her, which she caught hoult of; but when he tried to pull her up she was so mortial heavy he could hardly stir her.

" 'Pull away, Frank, *abouchal,—pull* away, *asthore*! 'says the ould woman from the bottom of the ditch.

" 'I'm pullin' my best,' says Frank, making a great heave, and raising her about half-way up the bank, when his foot slipped and down he went, head over heels, along with her into the mud and sludge of the ditch. After struggling and sliddhering about for a long while, he at last got himself and the ould woman upon dry land.

" 'You've done one of the blessed works of mercy, Frank,' says she : 'A poor ould woman like me has little to give; but here's something at laste for you to remember me by,' and tearing a bit off the corner of her cloak, she gave it to Frank, who put it in his pocket, and walked off towards the abbey quite melancholy, for he knew he had lost so much time that his chance of being first back with the yew-branch was gone. Surprised at not meeting Neal on his return, he entered the cloisters; and there what did he behold, but the soger stretched upon one of the tombstones, with a large branch of the blessed tree in his hand. Frank at first thought he was dead, but after a while he began to recover; and at last, with Frank's help, he tottered to a neighbour's cabin, where he was put to bed— and the priest sent for; but before Father James could arrive poor Neal Connor was a corpse. Before he died, however, he tould Frank, that the instant he cut off the branch of the tree, he heard a dreadful screech!— heaven presarve the hearers— and at the same time felt a sudden blow from something he couldn't see, which struck him sinseless to the ground."

"Indeed ?"

"Aye, sir, but the most particular part of the story ain't tould yet; for the next day, when the people went to look at the yew-tree, they found the ground around it steeped in blood from the wound that Neal Connor had made cutting off the branch; and since then the ghost of the soldier is said to haunt this ould place, followed by a big dark man, who every night whips him three times round the abbey walls."

I suppose my ancient chronicler perceived an incredulous smile lurking about my mouth, for she hastily added, as if replying to my thoughts :

"In troth, sir, it is a mighty remarkable laygend, and has some hard parts in it; but still an'all, it's as thrue as that your honour is sitting there upon that flagstone."

I assured her that I placed as implicit belief in her narration as I did in any similar marvellous tradition.

"But, said I, who was the old woman that Frank helped out of the ditch?"

"I knew your honour would be curious about her. Well, then, that ould woman was no other than the blessed Saint Bridget herself; and if Neal Connor had shown a pitiful heart towards the cries of the distressed, she would have pursarved him from the misfortune that happened to him. As for Frank, he had his reward for the ducking he got that night; for in less than a month he was married to Honor Hennesey—and, by all accounts, there was lashins of whiskey at their weddin; but that was before the Teetotallers was hard of in these parts."

The simple moral of the woman's story pleased me exceedingly, and having acknowledged the gratification I had received by a small douceur, I quitted the abbey, overwhelmed by a shower of blessings, poured forth with that energetic eloquence in which the Irish peasant gives expression to the emotions of a heart warm in its gratitude and bitter in its hate.

I had already obtained a view of the Upper Lake from the cliff above the tunnel in Turk Lake but I resolved to devote another day to exploring its numerous beauties more closely, and also in visiting the extraordinary mountain-pass, called the Gap of Dunloe.

The wild grandeur of the Upper Lake strikes the observer on first beholding it with feelings of awe and admiration. Perfectly distinct in the character of its romantic scenery from that of the Turk and Lower Lake, it combines many of the softer beauties of wood and water, with all the stern sublimity of mountain scenery; possessing in a surpassing degree every variety of landscape that can delight the eye or gratify the imagination. Embosomed amidst majestic mountains, whose fantastical summits seem to pierce the sky, the lake appears to be completely landlocked. On the south lie the Derricunehey mountain ranges, and on the left the lofty Reeks

> "Lift to the clouds their craggy heads on high,
> Crown'd with tiaras fashioned in the sky;
> In vesture clad of soft etherial hue,
> The Purple Mountains* rise in distant view,
> With Dunloe's Gap—."

This mountain cincture imparts to the Upper Lake an air of solitary beauty and intensity of interest, not to be found to the same extent in either of the other lakes.

---

* *Purple Mountains.—This* lofty range of hills has acquired its name from a beautiful heath of a bright purple colour which clothes them nearly to the summits, and gives them, when viewed at a distance, a peculiar rich tint.

The Lower and Turk Lakes, Killarney

Nature here sits in lonely and silent grandeur amidst her primeval mountains. Solitude—stillness, the most profound, rest upon the woody shores and the tranquil lake, filling and overpowering the mind with a deep sense of the perfect seclusion of the scene. A stranger visiting these lakes should therefore commence his tour with the lower, and proceed, step by step, to this lake, whose solemn beauties form a crowning scene to the splendid panorama on which his eyes have been feasted and an impressive object for the termination of his pleasant labours. The shores here seem to have been fashioned by the hand of nature in one of her most whimsical moods. "Numerous," says an intelligent writer, "are the projecting headlands some, whose rocky fronts dip down abruptly into the water; others with gentler shores, and summits finely waving with wood, form the sides of deep receding bays, and present to the explorer at every turn, new and highly picturesque views."

At various points bright mountain-streams may be seen pouring down the glens and deep ravines—now leaping from rock to rock, and flashing, like living silver, in the broad sunlight—now glittering in the shade of the dark foliage, till they are lost in the shining waters of the broad lake. A number of islets of the most picturesque forms are also scattered over its surface some of them are mere masses of naked rocks; others, on the contrary, are redundant in vegetation, producing trees, shrubs, and plants in the wildest profusion; amongst which the arbutus, with its tempting berries, and the mountain-ash, with its scarlet clusters glowing through the dark shining foliage of the holly-tree are prominently conspicuous in the autumn season. The surprising natural architecture of several of these islands has been noticed by almost every writer who has described the beauties of Killarney : and by the aid of fancy are brought to resemble temples, pillars, and fortresses. Smith, in writing of them, says, "some of them are of such stupendous height that they resemble at a distance so many lofty towers standing in the water, and being many of them crowned with wreaths of arbutus, represent the ruins of stately palaces." In several instances the action of the water has worn away the lower parts of the rocks composing these islands, giving to the overhanging portions the resemblance of masses of giant architecture, thrown confusedly together by some convulsion of nature. In other places the rocks are completely perforated; forming natural arches, sufficiently large for boats to pass through; though I must confess, while our boatmen rested on their oars for a few moments in one of these singular chasms, in order to our examining it at our leisure, that the threatening appearance of the huge impending rocks, supported upon disproportionately slender columns and crumbling foundations, considerably abated the pleasure that I should have enjoyed in the contemplation of these strange freaks of nature at a more respectful distance. There are three principal islands in the lake, known as Ronayne's, M'Carthy's, and the Eagle's; besides the several lesser islets, to which the lake-boatmen have given names. The first mentioned, the centre of a cluster of five lying near the western shore, I have alluded to slightly in another place. It is finely wooded, with precipitous shores, and covered with the richest verdure. From the summit of a rock in the centre of this island, a new and magnificent view may be obtained of the whole scenery of the Upper Lake, with all its splendid accessories of mountains, rocks, and woods. The spectator there beholds the cloud-crowned peaks of the surrounding mountains, piled up like the eternal barriers of a vast amphitheatre, of which the sparkling waters of the lake form the smooth arena; producing a *coup-d'œil,* which for beauty and grandeur cannot be surpassed by the most favoured spots on earth. Brandon Cottage is the principal object of interest on the western shore of the lake. A modern antique tower, erected by the late Lord Brandon, stands in the gorge of the rugged glen of *Coom dubh,* or the dark valley. When viewed from the lake, with its majestic mountain back-ground, it forms a bold and prominent feature in the picture. The situation of the cottage is highly romantic, and the noble possessor has enhanced the natural beauties of this picturesque retreat by his tasteful improvements.

Derricunehey Cascade, which I have already described, forms the great point of attraction for visitors on the eastern side of the lake. In the vicinity of this fall is a lovely creek or inlet from the lake, whose entrance is between two lofty crags. Within these lies a spacious and beautiful sheet of water, hemmed in by rugged precipitous rocks, and thick overhanging trees. Behind this is a deep, wooded ravine, through which a rapid stream rushes with considerable force from a cataract, concealed in a sequestered glen at a short distance from the shore. This charming place has received from the boatmen the very unexpressive and commonplace name of Newfoundland. I had now nearly completed my tour of the Upper Lake, having reached Coleman's Eye, the point at which its superabundant waters begin to descend, by a narrow outlet nearly five miles in length, to the Lower Lake. Coleman's Eye has received its name from some legendary hero of that name, who in his eager pursuit of the chase, or flying from an enemy, (for tradition is not clear on the point,) leaped the stream about thirty feet in width at this place, leaving his footmarks deeply imprinted in the rock where he alighted. Giving to this legend all the credence it deserves, I agree with the ingenious author of the "Historical and Descriptive Notices of Cork," that those footprints in rocks, which are by no means uncommon in Ireland, are "in their origin Druidic, many of then being connected with the ancient policy of the country, are regarded with traditional reverence by the peasantry, who preserve various legendary recollections of them, attributing some to the Fenii or to giants, others to holy men, and more to animals of a superior character." Spenser, the poet, mentions having seen stones in Ireland on which the ceremony of inaugurating the chiefs or tanists was performed. On these, he says, that he found "formed and engraven, a foot, which they say was the measure of their first captain's foot, whereon bee, standing, received an oath to preserve all the ancient former customs of the country inviolable."

273

One of the most remarkable objects to be visited in passing down the river from Coleman's Eye to the Weir Bridge, is "the Eagle's Nest," which every curiosity-hunter makes a point of seeing before leaving Killarney. It is a rugged cone-shaped mountain, nearly one thousand seven hundred feet in height, thickly wooded at its base, but presenting to the spectator's eye as it travels upwards a succession of broken crags, thinly covered with trailing plants and flowering mosses. Amongst these inaccessible precipices the golden eagle *(Falco chrysætos,)* makes its eyry, and from this circumstance time mountain derives its name. This noble bird, though formerly common in the western parts or Ireland, is now rarely to be found, and only in remote and mountainous districts, where it breeds amongst the loftiest cliffs. Mr. Maxwell, in his "Wild Sports of the West," narrates several amusing anecdotes of the Irish eagle, illustrative of its predatory habits; amongst others, he relates, that some years past "a herdsman on a very sultry day in July, while looking for a missing sheep, observed an eagle posted on a bank, that overhung the pool; presently the bird stooped and seized a salmon, and a violent struggle ensued : when the herd reached the spot, he found the eagle pulled under water by the strength of the fish, and the calmness of the day, joined to drenched plumage, rendered him unable to extricate himself. With a stone the peasant broke the eagle's pinion, and actually secured the spoiler and his victim, for he found the salmon dying in his grasp."

It is said by the peasantry (with what accuracy I know not) that the eagle is particularly attached to black fowls, but that it never carries off turkies. The proximity of an eyry to a mountain village is a serious misfortune to the inhabitants; the eagles being ever on the watch to sweep through the cabins and seize on any prey that offers. The havoc they commit in this way is astonishing : the writer quoted above, endeavouring once to examine an eagle's nest, came to the bottom of the cliff on whose face the eyry was situated. That the eagle's dwelling. was overhead was quite evident; for, says he, "the base of the cliff was strewn with bones and feathers, and the accumulation of both was extraordinary. The bones of hares, rabbits, and domestic fowls were most numerous; but those of smaller game and various sorts of fish were visible among the heap." But it is not from its being the lofty station of the king of birds that this cliff has obtained all its celebrity; it is also remarkable for its fine echoes, which may be heard to the best advantage at a station selected on the opposite shore. To produce the effect desired, a small cannon is sometimes discharged; each explosion awakening a succession of echoes like peals of thunder, breaking on the startled ear with a deafening crash, that seems to shake the mountain to its granite foundations, and followed by another and another till the reverberations are lost in the hoarse and indistinct murmurs of the distant hills. A bugle sounded under the Eagle's Nest produces on the contrary a series of wild and solemn melodies; the plaintive and lonely voices of the rocks and glens, fill the soul with "sweet sadness," and, as Inglis says, "makes our imagination endue the mountains with life; and to their attributes of magnitude, and silence, and solitude, we for a moment add the power of listening and a voice.

But these and all other artificial means of awakening the mountain voices sink into utter insignificance, when compared with the sublime effect produced by a thunder-storm, which I had the good fortune to witness amongst these rocks and glens. The giant hills seemed to battle with the elements. To use the impressive language applied by Byron to a similar scene amongst the Alps :—

> "Far along
> From peak to peak, the rattling crags among,
> Leaps the live thunder! Not from one lone cloud,
> But every mountain now hath found a tongue,
> And Jura answers, through her misty shroud,
> Back to the joyous Alps, who call to her aloud!"

There are many other objects of minor interest to which the stranger's attention is always directed in his voyage down the channel; each possessing some strange tradition or amusing anecdote, and many of them, I suspect, owing their existence to the creative fancy of the guides, who endeavour to gratify the appetite for the marvellous of the lion-hunters who visit the lakes, by inventing the wonderful stories they relate.

The GAP OF DUNLOE, which I next visited, is a wild mountain defile or pass, lying between the Reeks and the Purple Mountain, a shoulder of the Tomies range. The glen, which is about four miles in length, presents a most extraordinary appearance. On either hand, the craggy cliffs, composed of huge masses of projecting rocks, impend fearfully over the narrow pathway, and at every step threaten with destruction the adventurous explorer of this desolate scene. In the interstices of these immense fragments, a few shrubs and trees shoot out in fantastic shapes, which, with the dark ivy and luxuriant heather, contribute to the picturesque effect of the landscape. A small but rapid stream, called the *Loe,* (from whence the name of the ravine,) traverses the whole length of the glen, expanding itself at different points into five small lakes, each having its own proper name, but which are known in the aggregate as the *Cummeen Thomeen* Lakes. The road, which is a mere rugged footpath, constructed on the frequent brink of precipices, follows the course of the stream, and in two instances crosses it by means of bridges. One of these stands at the head of a beautiful rapid, where the water rushes in whitening foam over the rocky bed of the torrent. The part of the glen which attracts most admiration is that where the valley becomes so contracted as scarcely to leave room between the precipitous sides for the scanty pathway and its accompanying strand. The peasantry have given to this romantic pass the name of "the Pike."

Keeping onward, the visitor begins to ascend the Purple Mountain until he reaches an elevated point, from whence he obtains a sudden view of the Upper Lake, and the

275

The Gap of Dunloe

rich scenery in its neighbourhood. The unexpected suddenness with which this splendid prospect bursts on the sight, the complete transition from the wild and gloomy scenery of the valley, to the smiling landscape that has sprung up, like the fabled gardens of Armida, entrances the mind of the beholder with admiration and delight. Beautiful, surpassingly beautiful, is the prospect before us! "On our right," says Mr. Windele, in describing it, "lies the deep, broad, desolate glen of *Coomduv;* an amphitheatre buried at the base, and hemmed in by vast masses of the mountain, whose rugged sides are marked by the courses of the descending streams. At the western extremity of the valley, gloomily reposes amidst silence and shadows one of those lakes, or rather circular basins, of dark still water, *Loch an bric dearg,* the lake of the charr or red trout.' Other lesser lakes dot the surface of the moor, and, uniting, form at the side opposite the termination of the gap, a fine waterfall of considerable height, enjoying the advantage not common to other falls in Ireland, of being plentifully supplied with water at every season of the year. The characteristics of the scenery of the Gap of Dunloe are generally admitted to be, magnitude, sternness, and lonely sublimity. I cannot, therefore, understand how Mr. Inglis, whose perceptions of natural beauty were generally very correct, could have said in his 'Tour,' that he did not deem it worthy its reputation, and though confessing, that, 'it presents many features of the picturesque,' adds, that 'its approaches to sublimity are very distant."

I did not ascend the Reeks, or more properly, M'Gillycuddy's Reeks; named from an ancient sept or branch of the O'Sullivans. They are reputed the highest of the Irish mountains : the altitude of *Carran-tuel,* (the culminating point of the range,) according to the late surveys of Nimmo and Griffith, being three thousand four hundred and ten feet, making it eight hundred feet above the height of Mangerton, which had previously been considered the loftiest mountain in Ireland.

The ascent of *Carran-tuel* is both difficult and dangerous, requiring an active and experienced guide to conduct the courageous traveller by the fearful precipices which lie between him and the dizzy summit of this monarch of the hills, and is only to be encountered by strong lungs, cool heads, and feet accustomed to those perilous mountain-paths. But the peak of the ridge once attained, the prospect from thence will, I have been assured, richly repay the toil of the way. The scene is magnificent beyond conception. Beneath the spectator's feet lies "sea of terrene billows, each with its own blue lake, amongst which Lough Carra is distinguished as the broadest and fairest. At every turn they are seen in the sunlight or shadowed by overhanging precipices. Of the Killarney Lakes, a small portion only of the Lower Lake is visible, owing to the interposition of the Tomies Mountains." A vast and uninterrupted view is also obtained from this elevated point, extending beyond the Shannon on the north, and embracing in a westerly and southerly direction the bays of Tralee, Dingle, Castlemaine, Kenmare, Bantry, Dunmanus, with Cape Clear, and far beyond all the waters of the Atlantic Ocean, forming a dark line of horizon to the immense picture.

These mountains formerly harboured vast herds of red deer, but from various causes their numbers are now greatly thinned. Another gigantic species of the same animal existed in Ireland in far distant ages, as is evident from the enormous bones and antlers, which are so frequently dug up in various parts of the island, that the peasantry are acquainted with them as the "old deer," and in some places their remains are found in such quantities that they are thrown aside as valueless. A splendid relic of this noble animal, which was dug up at Rathcannon, near Limerick, is now to be seen in the Museum of the Dublin Society. It consists of a perfect skeleton, with beautifully expanded antlers, extending six feet on either side. The height from the ground to the highest point of the antler is ten feet four inches, and the length from the end of the nose to the tip of the tail is ten feet ten inches. The immense size of these antlers must have given the animal a most majestic appearance: while viewing them, I have often fancied that I beheld the dry skeleton clothed again in life's vesture, and saw the magnificent creature bounding, in the pride of his strength, over the hill tops, or bursting through the thick woods; while the hunter "chief of Eri, with a crown on his brow," attended by princes, cheered on with shout and horn, the stalwart Irish wolf-hound, (meet enemy for his noble game,) to the warfare of the deer.

> "Wild mirth of the desert—fit pastime for kings,
> Which still the rude bard in his solitude sings,
> Oh! reign of magnificence, vanished for ever,
> Like music dried up in the bed of the river.

It is extremely probable that the chase of this gigantic creature formed part of the business and pleasure of the early inhabitants of Ireland. The poetic remains of Ossian—not the M'Pherson forgeries—but those fragments of Ossianic song, which are still to be found amongst the peasantry in the remote districts, abound with allusions to the hunting of the tall deer, and the Irish wolf-dog, *(sagh cluin,)* which was employed to hunt the deer as well as the wolf, is frequently spoken of. This noble animal, uniting all the strength of the mastiff with the speed of the greyhound, and depending on its eye, its foot, and its wind, would hunt down the game that the scent-hound started for it. It was anciently so much prized that two of them were deemed a gift worthy of being sent from one sovereign to another. So far back as the fourth century Irish wolf-dogs were exhibited at the Circensian games at Rome, and were an article of export from Ireland in our own middle ages. But with the extirpation of the wolves and the destruction of the deer, the race of high wolf-dogs disappeared, and though not completely extinct, it has become so rare that there are not more than one or two families in Ireland that now possess specimens of the true breed. The last wolf seen in Ireland was killed in the neighbourhood of Dingle, in the county Kerry in 1710; the place is still known by the name of "the Wolf's Step."

Maryerton Mountain and its vicinity remained only to be visited now; and the following morning, accompanied by a guide, I commenced ascending it. Its height is calculated at two thousand six hundred and ninety-three feet. It is not by any means so difficult of ascent as *Carran-tuel,* being easily accessible on horseback. Though not so wildly picturesque in its appearance as the monarch of the Reeks, Maryerton possesses sufficient interest to repay the traveller for a day's visit to it. As he ascends, a vast and commanding prospect is gradually revealed : mountains, plains, and lakes seem spread like a map beneath him in pleasing distinctness of outline and position. The great object of attraction to the visitors of this mountain is the *Devil's Punch-bowl,* which lies near its summit, and usually forms the limit of their examination. This "Bowl," which is a small lake about a quarter of a mile in diameter, is contained in a deep chasm of the mountain. Its waters, which appear of an inky blackness from the dark nature of the surrounding peat-soil, and the overhanging shadow of the perpendicular rocks, are intensely cold, yet they have never been known to freeze. The supply is principally from springs, and the overflow of the water discharges itself under the name of the *Devil's Stream,* down the side of the mountain, and after forming the Turk Waterfall flows into the Turk Lake. The Bowl has been conjectured by many persons to be the crater of an extinct volcano; this opinion seems, however, to have been formed on very slight grounds, for there are not the most remote traces of volcanic action anywhere in its vicinity; and if the hypothesis were founded merely on the shape of the Bowl, the same supposition might with equal correctness be extended to every other lake or tarn, to be found in such numbers amongst the entire chain of these mountains. The Punch-bowl, independent of the natural interest it possesses, has gained an additional celebrity from the circumstance of the great statesman, Charles James Fox, when on a visit to Lord Kenmare, in 1772, having swam round the bason, a feat, like that of Lord Byron's swimming across the Hellespont, which subsequent travellers feel more disposed to admire than imitate.

XX.

The route which I selected for my return to Cork runs through the valley of the Flesk and the romantically situated village of Ballyvourney, and is much more interesting than the mail-coach road by Milistreet.* The Flesk river, which is formed by the junction of two mountain-streams, after a rapid and tortuous course through the valley to which it gives its name, enters the open country about seven miles from Killarney at Killaha Castle, and after a brief but interesting career through woods and plains, savage rocks, and flower-enamelled banks, mingles with the waters of the Lower Lake at Castlelough. Killaha Castle, now in ruins, was formerly a stronghold of the O'Donoghoes, erected some time about the close of the fifteenth century, for the protection of the important pass of Glenflesk, at the southern extremity of which it is situated. A slender square tower is all that now remains of this once proud edifice; every portion of the outworks and external defences having long since yielded to the destroying tooth of time and the depredations of the country people. Running parallel to the high-road, the river, which is here narrow, but deep and winding, traverses the valley. The sides of the glen on either side are composed of sterile, rocky mountains, exhibiting continuous ranges of weather-beaten rocks, rising in terraces one above the other, interspersed with patches of coarse heather and scanty pasturage for a few goats and poor-looking cattle. In the lower parts of the glen and along the banks of the river the soil is rich, and abundant, and the traveller's eye is relieved by the sight of cultivated plains, verdant meadows, and

---

* *Millstreet.* The mention of this place brings to my mind a curious legend, which was related to me respecting a little village called Cullin, in its neighbourhood, which had the misfortune of incurring the displeasure of a Saint Latereen, who left her curse upon the smiths' forges in it; so that, according to the popular tradition, "all the coals of Cork and the bellows of Munster would not be able to heat iron there." The story runs thus : Saint Latereen, who by the way was a female saint, and by far too handsome for such a profession, lived a holy and retired life in a lonely glen near the village. The saint prayed a great deal and fasted still more, and whenever she did indulge in the luxury of a meal, she cooked her own dinner, probably through a beautiful spirit of humility; or it might be, because her household did not include a servant. However, on these occasions it was her custom to repair to a neighbouring smith's forge for a coal of fire, which she carried home in a little cup in the folds of her petticoat. The smith, who was a man of taste, and moreover a good judge of female symmetry, could not forbear admiring the beautiful legs of the young saint, which in her simple forgetfulness she allowed him to see every time she took the coal in her petticoat. Respect for the sanctity of her character kept the man silent a long time; at last, tempted by the devil while she was taking the live coal as usual, he said, "Latereen, you have a pair of beautiful legs." The flattered saint, who never thought of her beauty before, looked down to see if the smith spoke truly, when the coal set fire to her garments and they blazed up around her. In her grief and vexation for this fault, she prayed that Cullin might never again have a smith to tempt the innocent to sin. It is gravely added, so powerful was the saint's ban, that it is impossible to heat iron to a red heat in Cullin; and though the place is well situated for a smithy, every attempt to establish a forge there has been ineffectual.

waving fields of yellow grain, chequered by the vivid green of the frequent potato-garden, that invariable appendage to the Irish peasant's cottage.

The population of this remote valley preserve in a striking degree the personal characteristics of their Celtic race warmly attached to their native glen, they have seldom wandered beyond its limits, and more rarely have been intruded on by strangers; the consequence is, that, in their appearance, manners, and customs, they are still pure Celts : compelled by the advance of civilization to forsake their old marauding mode of life, they submitted to the laws, but refused to mingle in the society of the stranger. An observing writer remarks, that "The modern Glenfleskean is generally a quiet, hardworking, honest, and inoffensive member of society; sobered down to habits of peaceful industry, preserving only the memory of the old mode of his life, its dangers and its spirit-stirring vicissitudes; and content by honest toil to seek and to retain the means of existence, which his ancestor sought by the strong hand, and despised if not so obtained." At the southern extremity of the valley, opposite to the entrance from Killarney, a series of precipitous rocks have received the name of *Plaii-a-dhawn*, or the Cliff of the Demon : they form the face of the *Crochawn* Mountain at the opening of the valley. About midway up, a fissure in the rock, called *Labbig-Owen,* or Owen's Bed, is pointed out as the place of refuge of a notorious outlaw, who formerly had his head-quarters in this district. The passage to this mountain retreat is intricate and toilsome; but after some difficult scrambling over loose stones and broken crags, the visitor reaches the foot of the Outlaw's rock, and by means of a ladder gains access to what is called his bed, which is only a rough platform, overhung by a portion of the cliff, that effectually shelters it from the rain and the crumbling of the rock above. Here, armed and provisioned, and accompanied by only one faithful follower, Owen, secure in his impregnable lair, defied for a time all attempts of his enemies to seize him. His fireplace, table, stool, &c. hewn from the rock, are still pointed out by the guides, who delight in recounting numerous anecdotes of the prowess, courage, and generosity of the Irish Rob Roy. The history of this outlaw is variously related : it would appear by the most authentic accounts, that he was of the M'Carthy race, and, as in duty bound, a follower of O'Donoghoe of the Glens. Mr. Croker says, that he was a mere cattle-stealer, and that his marauding propensities brought him under the grip of the law, and obliged him to take refuge at Labbig. There for a long time he baffled the pursuit of his foes, until becoming weary of his irksome situation, or for some other reason not now known, he quitted his favourite haunt, and retired to Iveleary, amongst whose mountain-crags he fancied he would be in perfect security.

The following version of the manner in which Owen met his death has been adopted by Mr. Windale; the account given by Mr. Croker ot this outlaw's career differs from it in many respects. "In an evil hour," says the narrator, "he sought the shelter and protection of an old friend, as he imagined, but in reality of his bitterest enemy. Reardon, for that was the name of his host, rejoiced in his soul that he had now got possession of one whom he had long wished to have within his grou; and regardless of every law, and of that of hospitality, held sacred even by the most barbarous nations, he treacherously devised his destruction. To open violence he dared not resort, for the strength and vigour of Owen were too well known to him; he had therefore recourse to stratagem. He placed the bed of his intended victim over a kind of trap near the fireplace, which sinking in the night, Reardon and his selected accomplices attacked its sleeping occupant with *graffauns,** and slew him; after which they cut off his head." This treacherous action brought lasting odium on the Reardons in the neighbourhood where it occurred, and they are still called reproachfully, *Reardane na ceean,* or "Reardon of the head." Owen's attached follower, on hearing of his master's fate, threw himself, in a paroxysm of grief, over the face of the cliff, and was dashed to pieces on the rocks beneath.

Macroom is a considerable market-town, lying nearly midway between Cork and Killarney. It is placed on a neck of land formed by the junction of the river Lee with the Sullane : the latter, though a fine river and every way equal to the Lee except in the length of its course, bride-like resigns its name as soon as they become united. There is little to interest the antiquarian or tourist in Macroom; the town consists of a long straggling street, and contains no pub buildings worthy of notice. The surrounding country is diversified in its character large tracts of bog lie in close proximity to it; but the bold mountain range which stretches to the north makes an agreeable variety in the features of what would other wise be a very monotonous landscape. The Irish name of Macroom *(Maigh-cruim)* is of great antiquity, signifying the plain of *Crom,* who, according to antiquarian was the supreme deity of the ancient Irish. Mr. Windele says, he was "adored under the name of *Crum Cruagheoir,* and is supposed to be the same worshipped Zoroaster. His altar was the *Cromleac,* and his priest the *Cromthear."* It is certain that Macroom was the head-quarters of the followers of the Druidic religion West Munster : here the bards, who were the second order of the Pagan priesthood, held their bardic meetings, even after they had embraced Christianity. The Castle of Macroom, now the property of R. Hedges Eyre, Esq., adjoins the town. It is a huge baronial structure : tradition assigns its foundation to King John, but of this there are some strong doubts. The probability is, that it was built by the family of the O'Flyns, from whom it derives the Irish name *Caslean-i-Fhlionn,* "O'Flyn's Castle." This ancient family once held extensive possessions in the baronies of Carbury and Muskerry, to the latter of which they gave the name of "O'Flyn's pleasant country." A great part of this extensive tract between Macroon and Inchageelah belonged to another very ancient and once powerful family, the O'Learys. The name is still common amongst the peasantry; but all the

---

* Graffaun, a three-pronged pitchfork.

282

broad possessions that once appertained to the family, not, a solitary acre now remains to it. Its last lineal representative, "the O'Leary," lived upwards forty years since in the village of Millstreet. He possessed, I am told, a moderate fortune; was a justice of the peace for the county, and supported the old style profuse hospitality beneath his roof. His dwelling was a small house in the village more recommended by the contents of its larder and cellar, and the kind and courtly manners of its owner, than by its external appearance. No door require the protection of a lock, as he said it was useless to secure the contents of his cellar in that way, when any person who sought it might partake of them. O'Leary as well by virtue of his magisterial authority as his local and personal influence maintained the peace at the neighbouring fairs and markets. His commands were in most instances obeyed without a murmur; but if any proved refractory, submission was promptly obtained by the vigorous application of the long and weight pole which he ever carried. His figure was lofty, athletic, and commanding : his latter days extremely venerable and patriarchal. He generally stationed himself in Millstreet in the morning of each succeeding day, his long pole supporting his steps, and ready if necessary to maintain his authority. There he introduced himself to every passing traveller of respectability, and invited him to enter his ever-open door and partake of his unbounded hospitality. "The O'Leary" was one of the last, perhaps the very last, who kept up the unlimited hospitality which was once the boast of his countrymen.

I may also mention in this place the following particulars relating to another gentleman, residing in this part of the country a few years back, who retained more of the dignity appertaining to an Irish chieftain than the jovial personage I have just noticed. His name was M'Carthy, and being lineally descended from M'Carthy Mor, king or prince of this province, he was still regarded as the titular king of Munster. He had in his possession the crown, sceptre, and other regalia which had been worn by his ancestors; and also possessed a cup, said to have been made from the cranium of an ancestor of Brian Boirohme, whom a M'Carthy chief had slain in battle. It was highly polished, and had a lid of silver. It was usual among the old Irish to decapitate their vanquished enemies, and was also a custom of the chiefs to form drinking-cups of their skulls, and to retain them as trophies. Numbers of such cups have been found in the bogs, and several are still in possession of ancient Irish families. The name of M'Carthy is very common amongst the people in this part of the province: those who bear it are not, however, distinguished by their name, but by the place of their residence or some other accidental circumstance. Thus, John M'Carthy does not bear that name amongst his neighbours, but is called *Long* John, *Short* John, *Black* John, *White* John, or John of the *Hill,* John of the *Glen,* &c.; the name of M'Carthy being borne by the chief alone.

Near to Millstreet is the Hill of Knockaclashy, an object of some interest to the historian and tourist, as the scene of a celebrated battle between the English

Parliamentary forces under Roger Lord Broghill and the Irish, commanded by Lord Muskerry, which was fought on the 26th of July, 1651. A detailed account of this battle, in the hand-writing of Lord Broghill, is preserved amongst the manuscripts at Lismore; and, as this action was one of the most important which occurred in the county of Cork during the wars of the seventeenth century, an abridgment of this curious document cannot fail being interesting to the general reader:—

The Republican general Ireton, who was besieging Limerick, having heard that Muskerry was advancing with his troops to relieve the place, dispatched Lord Broghill to intercept him : this nobleman, on the second night after his departure from the camp, discovered the fires of the enemy, and attacking their advanced guard at midnight in the midst of a violent storm, compelled them to retire in confusion about five miles from their head-quarters. At an early hour the following morning the English crossed the river Blackwater, near Clonmene, and directly after landing, the events of the day commenced with a prophecy in their favour. "We here met," writes Lord Broghill, "with ninety Irish, who were under protection. I asked them what they were assembled for? they answered, they had a prophecy, that there was a battle to be fought on that ground one time or another, and they knew none more likely than the present. Upon which I again asked them, on which side was the victory to fall? they shook their heads and said, the English were to get the day."

There was at that time much woodland in the vicinity of the field of battle, and Lord Broghill, by a skilful movement, drew the enemy from the wood in which they had taken shelter, and enticed them into the plain. As the enemy outflanked him both ways, he drew to the right with his right wing, "upon which the enemy advanced that way with one thousand musketeers, and with their horse fought horse-head to horse-head, hacking with their swords." After an obstinate resistance he routed their left wing. A body of the enemy then appearing on his rear, he faced about and charged through them. Then charging a second time, he practised an ingenious device, which greatly assisted in obtaining the victory for him. When they began to charge he caused his men to exclaim, "*They run! they run!*" On hearing the cry, the first rank of the enemy looked back to see if their friends in the rear were really running away. The troops in the rear *seeing the faces* of the front rank, thought they were the men who had turned their back, and, seized with a panic, began to run "in good earnest," so that, in fact, the whole of that division fled together. One thousand Irish pikemen still "stood firmly and fought stoutly;" but Lord Broghill "ordering their angles to be attacked, they were put into disorder and broken, upon which most of them were cut to pieces." The fugitives were pursued until nightfall with great slaughter. The sun had shone during this sanguinary day with unwonted splendor; but (as was the case at the battle of Naseby) the weather altered as night approached, and the work of destruction was performed upon the unhappy remnant of the Irish troops —who had retired to a neighbouring hill—amidst thunder, lightning, and a deluge of rain. I am inclined to believe, that it is to this circumstance that Moore alludes in the following opening stanza of one of his beautiful Irish Melodies:—

" Night clos'd around the conqueror's way,
And lightning show'd the distant hill,
Where those who 'seaped that fatal day
Stood few and faint—but fearless still."

In consequence of this victory Limerick surrendered to Ireton. Amongst the plunder acquired on this occasion, Lord Broghill mentions "a peck-full of charms, relics, &c. found in the baggage, besides a vast quantity taken from the slain, with a peculiar one on paper, said to be the exact measure of our Lady's foot, and written in it, "Whoever wears this, and repeats certain prayers, shall be free from gun-shot, sword, and pike respectively, as each desired."

The belief which the peasantry in many parts of Ireland still entertain of the efficacy of charms, in preserving. them from spiritual and bodily danger, is unbounded. To enumerate the different kinds of protective talismans, which knavery has invented to impose on the credulity of the superstitious, would fill a volume : every parish once had its "fairy doctor," as he or she was called, whose business it was to prepare charms and counter-charms for all manner of uses : to preserve cattle from murrain, and children from the *good people*—to bring back lost affection or stolen butter—to keep a household from "plague, pestilence, and famine"—or to guard the cows from being sucked by an old woman under the form of a hare. Scapulars— pieces of brown cloth, in which were stitched certain verses from the Gospel of St. John, written on paper or parchment, still continue, to be a favourite preservative against all perils by flood and field to the wearer. Education amongst the people is, however, gradually overthrowing these absurd superstitions, and before many years it is probable that they will be only remembered as the idle. fancies of an ignorant age. From Macroom I again turned westward out of my direct route to Cork, for the purpose of visiting the Lakes Allua and Gougaune Barra, near to which the river Lee takes its rise, in a country of such peculiarly romantic beauty as well entitles it to a visit from every traveller possessing the least taste for nature in the rude grandeur of her solitary retreats. The road, which at first is not very interesting and rather circuitous, runs through the valley of Garra and the rugged tract called "O'Leary's Country;" but as I approached the village of Inchageela it assumed a wilder and more striking aspect, being everywhere broken up into craggy hills, clothed with heath, furze, and numerous other shrubs and plants that flourish in these rocky regions. Emerging from a deep glen, I came in view of the village, which is only an irregular assemblage of poor habitations, and of the ancient Castle of Carrignacurra, formerly a place of some strength belonging to the O'Learys, but now reduced to a single lofty tower, whose moss-covered walls, surrounded by thriving plantations, afford an

Gougane Barra

agreeable relief to the eye amidst the wild and cheerless scenery in which it stands. Leaving Inchageela I found myself entering into the deep solitude of the mountain district, where the Lee expands itself into a beautiful sheet of water called Lough Allua (from *Lough-a-Laoi,* the Lake of the Lee,) about three miles in length, and in some places nearly a mile in breadth. This lake is picturesquely dotted with clusters of islands; but the natural beauty of the scene has been considerably impaired by the destruction of the woods which clothed the islets, and skirted the shores of the lough. The road which has been recently constructed lies on the northern side of the lake, following the indentations of its winding shores, through scenery of the most diversified yet solitary character, which will gratify the warmest expectations of the tourist who has leisure to investigate all its various beauties. After passing the lake, the river contracts itself into a narrow stream, and the traveller approaches , through narrow defiles and deep glens, the sequestered lake of Gougaune Barra, the first pausing place of the infant Lee, which bursts from the deep recesses of a rocky mountain a short distance from this spot. Antiquarians have assigned different etymologies to the name of this lake; some translate it, the *Hermitage* or *Trifle* of St. Barr or St. Barry. Mr. Windele, who is generally accurate in his derivations, says, that *Gougaune* is taken from the Irish words *Geig-abhan,* i.e. the gorge of the river. How he could have fallen into such an error is surprising, when it is evident that the name is derived from the artificial causeway, which connects with the shore a small island in the centre of the lake, where St. Fineen Barr lived a recluse life before he founded the Cathedral of Cork. The word *gougaune* is applied in the south-western districts of Ireland to those rude quays of loose stones jutting into the sea or river, constructed for the purpose of fishing. The lake, which is situated in a deep mountain recess, is enclosed on every side except the east with steep and rocky hills, down whose precipitous sides several mountain-streams pour their bright tributes into the placid waters beneath. The sanctified character of Gougaune Barra has, according to popular tradition, preserved it from that legendary monster, which, under the form of an enormous eel, infests many of the lakes in Ireland. One of these enchanted worms had in past ages taken up his quarters in this lough, where he remained un-molested until, by an act of daring sacrilege, he provoked the anger of St. Fineen Barr, and caused his own expulsion from the pleasant waters he had so long inhabited. The story was told to me by an old man whom I found fishing in the river, where it issues from the lake; and, as I should only detract from the simplicity of his legend by giving it in other language than his own, I shall, as nearly as possible, repeat it in the manner in which it was told to me.

"There was wanst upon a time, sir," said he, "a great saint, called Saint Fineen Barry, who lived all alone on the little island in the lake. There he built an illigant chapel with his own hands, and spent all his time in it day and night, praying, and fasting, and reading his blessed books. So, sir, av coorse, his fame went about far and near, and the people came flocking to the lake from all parts; but as there was no ways of getting into the island from the shore—barrin' by an ould boat that hadn't a sound plank in her carcash—there was a good chance that some of the crathers would be drownded in crassing over. So, bedad, St. Fineen seeing how eager the poor christhens wor for his holy advice, tuck pity upon them, and one fine morning early be gets up, and, afore his breakfast, he made that pathway of big stones over from the land to his own island. After that, the heaps of people that kem to hear mass in his chapel every Sunday was past counting; and small wondher it was, for he was the rale patthern of a saint, and mighty ready he was at all sorts of prayers that ever wor invinted. But I forgot to tell you, sir, that there was living at that time, snug and comfortable, down in the bottom of the lake a tundhering big eel; some said he was a fairy, more that he was a wicked ould inchanther, that the blessed St. Patrick had turned into that shape. Any way, he used to divart himself now and then with a walk upon the green shores of the lake, and those that saw him at these times said, that he had the ears and mane of a horse, and was thicker in the waist than a herring-cask. But with all that, the crather never milisted nobody, till one fine Sunday, after St. Fineen had finished saying mass in his little chapel, and was scatthering the holy water over his congregation, all of a sudden the ould eel popped up out of the lake, and, thrusting his long neck and head into the chapel window, caught hoult of the silver holy wather-cup betune his teeth, and without so much as 'by your lave,' walks off with it into the wather. Of course, there was a terrible *pillalieu* riz in the chapel when they seen what the blaggard eel was afther doing, and in half a minute every mother's son had run down to the wather-side pelting him all round the lake. But the plundhering ould rogue only laughed at their endeavours, till St. Fineen himself kem out of the chapel, drest in all his vistmints, ringing the mass-bell as hard as he could. Well, no sooner did the eel hear the first tinkle of the blessed bell than away he swum for the bare life out of the lake into the river, purshued by St. Fineen, till he got to the fall of Loneen, when he dropped the cup out of his mouth. The saint however hadn't done with him yet, for he kept purshuing him to Lough Allua, where he thought to hide; but the sound of the bell soon forced him to leave that, and swim down the Lee to Rellig Barra, and there St. Fineen killed the oudacious baste with one kick of his blessed fut, and afterwards built a church on the spot; which, as your honour may perhaps have heard tell, is now the cathedral of Cork. At any rate, sir, there has never been another of them big eels seen in the lake from that time to the present."

The little island to which St. Fineen Barr retired, alluded to in the legend, was, indeed, an admirably chosen place for the enjoyment of undisturbed solitude, and the indulgence of devout meditation. Several aged trees of the most picturesque forms grow upon its shores, and overshadow the ruins, of the chapel, the court or cloister, and other buildings appertaining to them, which cover nearly half the area of the island. In the centre of the court stands the shattered remains of a wooden cross, on which are nailed innumerable shreds and patches, the grateful memorials of cures performed on the devotees who have made pilgrimages to this holy retreat, and by whom this sacred relic is held in extraordinary veneration. Around the court are eight small circular cells, in which the penitents are accustomed to spend the night in watching and prayer. The chapel, that adjoins it, stands east and west; the entrance is through a low doorway at the eastern end. The length of the interior is about thirty-six feet, and its width fourteen. The side-walls, however, are not more than four feet in height, so that when roofed it must have been extremely low; not probably exceeding twelve feet. The walls of the convent adjoining are similar in height to those of the chapel. Mr. Windele says, its entire extent "is fifty-six feet in length by thirty-six in breadth; it consists of four small chambers, and one or two extremely small cells; so that when we consider their height, extent, and the light they enjoyed, we may easily calculate that the life of the successive anchorites who inhabited them, was not one of much comfort or convenience, but much the reverse—of silence, gloom, and mortification. Man elsewhere loves to contend with and emulate nature and the greatness and majesty of her works; but here, as if awed by the sublimity of surrounding objects, and ashamed of his own real littleness, the founder of this desecrated shrine constructed it on a scale peculiarly pigmy and diminutive." Indeed, while contemplating this and many other unworldly recesses in different parts of Ireland, it is impossible to avoid a conviction, that the wild scenery of those solitary islands and untrodden glens must have had considerable effect in nurturing an ascetic tendency in the minds of religious enthusiasts.

On the shores of the lake, near to the Causeway leading into the island, a few narrow mounds indicate the unpretending burying-place of "the rude forefathers" of this remote district; and in this solitary spot, the broken remains of an arched recess mark the last resting-place of a religious recluse, named O'Mahony, who terminated his life here sometime about the commencement of the last century. Smith, the historian of Cork, mentions having seen a tombstone with the following inscription, *"Hoc sibi et successoribus suis, in eadem vocatione monumentum imposuit Dominus Doctor Dionisius O'Mahony presbyter licit indignus."* The flag is not to be discovered now, it either has been removed or is buried in the rubbish of the place. Dr. Smith adds, that O'Mahony was buried 'in the year 1728.

A charming description of Gougaune Barra has been left us by a young poet named Callanan, a native of Cork, who, had he lived to realize the promise that his early writings held out, would have proved himself one of the most distinguished lyrists that Ireland has ever produced. The simple beauty of the style and freshness of the language induce me to transcribe the commencement of his poem :—

There is a green island in low Gouganne Barra,
Where Allus of song rushes forth as an arrow,
In deep vallied Desmond, a thousand wild fountains
Come down to that lake, from their home in the mountains.
There grows the wild ash, and a time-stricken willow
Looks chidingly down on the mirth of the billow;
As like some gay child, that sad monitor scorning,
It lightly laughs back to the laugh of the morning.
And its zone of dark hills—oh! to see them all bright'ning;
When the tempest flings out its red banner of lightning,
And the waters rush down 'mid the thunder's deep rattle,
Like the clans from the hills, at the voice of the battle;
And brightly the fire-crested billows are gleaming,
And wildly from Maolagh the eagles are screaming.
Oh! where is the dwelling, in valley or highland,
So meet for a bard as this lone little island?"

It would be impossible to convey by language, a more vivid and truthful picture of the "lone island" than that contained in these vigorous lines.

A very large and celebrated *Patron* is held on the island and the shores of the lake on St. John's day, when numerous tents are pitched, and a kind, of carnival is. held, in which dancing and singing, interspersed with love-making, praying, and fighting, form the principal business of the meeting. As many of my readers may have never. heard of the Irish *Patron,* or, as it is more generally pronounced, *Pattern,* it may be as well to explain to them that it is an assemblage of persons of both sexes at a particular place, for the performance of certain religious ceremonies and penances. The locality usually chosen is a "Holy Well," in all probability one of those which in the early Christian ages had been used by the priests for the purposes of baptism. Many. of these have in their vicinity a hermitage, chapel, or tomb of the pious man whose sanctity attaches itself to the well, and whose waters in consequence are said to possess miraculous virtues in healing the sick and maimed. The time at which the believers in those wonderful cures resort to the health-giving fount is on the anniversary of the *Patron* Saint of the well. On such occasions it is not unusual to see several thousand persons collected at a celebrated fountain, many with pious, but mistaken zeal, performing their painful penances on their bare knees around the holy well, for themselves or on behalf of their friends; for it is not unusual, when the penance is too severe for the strength or inclination of the principal, to have "*the stations,*" as they call the routine of the performance, executed by proxy. The original intention of the *Patron* was evidently of a religious character, but in process of time it degenerated into a scene of gross riot and debauchery; which at length caused the suppression of these meetings by the Roman Catholic clergy.

While upon the subject of holy wells, I may be permitted to state, that the profound veneration which the peasantry of Ireland, particularly in the provinces of

Scene at Gougaune Barra

Munster and Connaught, entertain for these sacred fountains, and the singular religious ceremonies practised by the devotees, who resort to them, form a most curious and interesting subject of inquiry to the philosopher and antiquarian. The late Dr. Charles O'Conor, an enlightened Roman Catholic divine, who wrote a learned Essay upon the practice of Well-worship in Ireland, satisfactorily proves that it is of Pagan origin. Its introduction into the island he attributes to the Phœnicians, and he adduces several authorities to show, that, if it did not arise amongst the Chaldeans, it can at least he traced back to them; and that from Chaldea it passed into Arabia, thence into Egypt and Lybia, and, lastly, into Greece, Italy, Spain, and Ireland. In all these countries the vestiges of well-worship are still discovered by the antiquarian, but in none of them are they so numerous, or preserved with such reverence, as in Ireland, where the attachment to ancient customs and usages is so strong as to have become a national characteristic. The practice of attaching to the trees in the neighbourhood of these wells bits of rag, and other offerings of propitiation or gratitude to the patron saint of the spot, is also an undoubted relic of Paganium Travellers in the East frequently meet with trees beside fountains, covered with similar votive offerings. Hanway, in his "Travels in Persia," says, "We arrived at a desolate caravanserai, where we found nothing but water; I observed a tree with a number of rags to the branches. These were so many charms, which passengers coming from Ghllan, a place remarkable for plagues, had left there, in a fond expectation of leaving their disease also in the same spot."

The testimony of the early historians of Ireland also establishes the conclusion, that the worship of fountains in that country was derived from Paganism. In Tirechan's Life of St. Patrick, preserved in the Book of Armagh, it is related, that the Irish apostle, in his progress through the island, came to a well, called, *Slan* or Health, "because it was indicated to him, that the Magi honoured this fountain, and made gifts to it as to God." It was further reported to him, that, beneath a flat stone in the well, "a certain Magus, who worshipped water as a divinity, was interred." Patrick thereupon caused the stone to be raised up, and consecrated it to the true God. It is worthy of remark, that this identical well is still reverenced, though under a different name and a purer faith than formerly. Archbishop Usher says, that St. Patrick baptized his converts, including Alphin the king's son, in a well near Patrick's Church, Dublin, which in after ages became an object of devotion for the faithful, and so remained until it was inclosed in the foundation of a house in the seventeenth century. In like manner, the other holy wells of Ireland, though owing their early religious character to idolatrous worship, from being subsequently applied to the purposes of Christianity, have acquired an additional claim to the attachment of the simple peasantry.

A little to the east of the island, the waters issue from the lake, and form the head of the River Lee, which at this point is so shallow that it may be crossed by a few stepping-stones. From thence it pours its irregular course over huge ledges and masses of rock—now sweeping onward headlong, and now pausing in dark eddying pools through the rugged valley, until it reaches bough Allua, of which I have already given a description. Before quitting this neighbourhood I visited the Pass of Keimaneigh, which, for picturesque though gloomy grandeur, I have never seen surpassed, even in this region of romantic glens and mountain defiles. Through this Pass runs the high road from Macroom to Bantry, having the appearance of being excavated between the precipitous crags, that, rising on either hand, assume the resemblance of fantastic piles and antique ruins, clothed with mosses and lichens, with here and there the green holly and ivy, contributing by the richness of their tints to the beauty of the scene. Even the arbutus, which by many is supposed to be peculiar to Killarney, is found here interspersed through the overhanging rocks. "We behold with wonder," says an agreeable writer, "this and the ash , and other hardy plants and shrubs, growing at immense heights overhead, tufting crags, inaccessible to the human foot, where we are astonished to think how they got there. The London-pride grows here, and on the surrounding mountains, as well as amongst the ruins of Gougaune Barra, in the most astonishing profusion. On the mountains of Turk and Mangerton, near Killarney, It is met with in great abundance; but its plenty in the neighbourhood of the Lee far exceeds all comparison." Having completed my examination of Keimnanheigh, I began to retrace my route to Macroom highly gratified with my visit to these romantic scenes; which, had they been thrown in almost any other part of Europe, would have been a favourite pilgrimage for those lovers of the picturesque, who haunt the Rhine and traverse the Alps, in search of nature in her wild and beautiful solitudes.

From Macroom I proceeded by the Cork road along the right bank of the Lee—here a sweet and sylvan stream. About nine miles from Cork, a little to the left of the high road, stand the ruins of the Abbey and Castle of Kilcrea. The abbey occupies a retired and picturesque situation on the margin of the Bride, a small river which takes its rise in the neighbourhood of Kilmurry, and for several miles winds through a long valley, in the midst of which was formerly the dreary morass, known as the Bog of Kilcrea; rendered almost impervious to the traveller by the matted underwood, and other rank vegetable productions, with which it was overgrown. The numerous remains of large oaks still found in the neighbourhood, show that the greater part of this vale and the lofty uplands by which it is surrounded, were in more ancient times covered by a vast wood.

The friary, as well as the church which adjoins it, are worthy the attention of the antiquarian and the artist : an avenue of venerable ash and elm trees conducts the visitor to the church, and prepares the mind for the solemn impressions that the gloomy appearance of the ruins are calculated to inspire. It is said, that a nunnery existed on this spot at a very early date, of which St. Cyra or Cera, was abbess; and the anniversary of that saint is celebrated on the 16th of October but all traces of such an institution have long since disappeared. The Ulster Annals state that the friary was founded in 1478. Its church was dedicated to St. Bridget or Bride. In 1614, Sir Arthur Chichester, then lord-deputy, committed the care of the friary to Cormac Lord Muskerry, upon condition that he should not permit the friars to live in it. It does not appear, however, that this rigorous injunction was obeyed; for in 1621 a brother of the house, Philip Sullivan, published an historical work on Ireland, and it was not until the wars of the Commonwealth, that the friars were driven from their pleasant retreat. In 1641 Cromwell gave the lands and friary of Kilcrea to Lord Broghill, the conqueror of Muskerry on the field of Knockiclashy. The buildings, which had sustained considerable injury in the struggle between the conflicting parties, were ultimately converted into a fortress for the Republican troops under the command of Captain Bailey. There is a tradition amongst the peasantry in the neighbourhood, that, on the expulsion of the hospitable old' friars,* a colony of *black* crows, which until that time had been strangers to Ireland, established a rookery in the avenue, and held a solemn chapter in the belfry. It would appear from the ruins, that the buildings were never of any great extent, nor very remarkable for architectural embellishment; their principal interest arises from the melancholy contemplation of the gloomy and neglected aisles, where the dust of prince and peasant lie mingled in undistinguishable confusion beneath the ruinous tombstones, which are scattered over every portion of the church and convent. Most of these stones bear the names of the old families and septs of the district.

M'Carthy, M'Swiney, and Barrett are the most numerous. In the choir are many decaying monuments; Smith, Ware, and other historians speak of the tomb of *Cormac, M'Carthy, Lord Muskerry, surnamed Laider, or the Strong*, founder of

---

* *Hospitality of the Monks.*—*The* following stanza from a short Poem, entitled "THE THREE MONKS," which appeared in the Irish Penny Journal, describes very accurately a practice followed in this old monastery, whose hospitable gates were ever open to the poor as well as the rich.

> "Three monks sat by a bogwood fire!
> Shaven their crowns, and their garments grey;
> Close they sat to that bogwood fire,
> Watching the wicket till break of day,
> Such was ever the rule at Kilcrea.
> For whoever passed, be he baron or squire,
> Was 'free to call at that abbey and stay;
>
> Nor guerdon or hire for his lodging pay,
> Though he tarried a week with the Holy Quire."

the convent, which is stated by Ware to have been in the middle of the choir, with the following inscription on it :—"Hic jacet Cormacus fil. Thadei, fil. Cormaci, fil. Dermith magni M'Carthy, Dnus. de Musgraigh Flayn ac istius conventus primus fundatur. An. Dom., 1494." Besides this chief, several of his immediate descendants, lords of Muskerry, were interred in this sanctuary It is the last resting-place of the notorious Roger O'Connor, who made himself So obnoxious to the English government by the active part he took in the disturbances of 1798, in connexion with his brother Arthur O'Connor, and others of time revolutionary party. He was the author of several works, of which the most remarkable was the "Chronicles of Eri," a tissue of absurd fiction which he endeavoured to make the world receive as an authentic history. He was an extremely vain and turbulent man— proud of his princely descent; for which reason he Styled himself in his writings *"Kier Reige"* or "Chief of his name and race." He ended his life in retirement, not far from Kilcrea, and was interred, according to his request, in the burial-place of the M'Carthy's. In the nave of the church lie also the mortal remains of "Arthur O'Leary the outlaw."* A low altar-tomb covers his grave, upon which we read the following inscription :—

"Lo! Arthur Leary, generous, handsome, brave,
Slain in his bloom, lies in this humble grave.
Died May 4th, 1778, aged twenty-six years."

* *O'Leary, the Outlaw.*—*The* history of this unfortunate young gentleman, who fell a victim in the prime of life to the barbarous penal enactments against Catholics, which for centuries disgraced the statute books of England, is given by Mr. Windele, from whom I have abridged the following account of his untimely death. Mr O'Leary was a Roman Catholic of considerable personal property, (the laws not allowing persons of his religious faith to hold real estates). He had been an officer in the Hungarian service, and on his return to Ireland his influence over the tenantry of his old patrimonial estate excited the jealousy of Mr. Morris, one of its landed proprietors. A horse of O'Leary's having won a race against a horse of Morris's, inflamed the already kindled jealousy, and the latter, availing himself of the then existing laws, which disabled a Roman Catholic from keeping any horse exceeding five pounds in value, attempted a legalized robbery by publicly claiming from O'leary the very animal that had won the race, tendering him at the same time five pounds, the price awarded by the law for a Papist's horse. O'Leary indignantly refused compliance, declaring "he would surrender him only with his life." A scuffle ensued, out of which he was glad to escape with his life. By a summary process he was proclaimed an *outlaw* on the spot, and soldiers were sent out to intercept him on his return to his residence. Two of them placing themselves in ambush fired at him as he approached his house, but without effect; O'Leary returned the fire from a gun which he carried, when another shot from the soldiers laid him dead on the road. The brutal penal laws followed him even in death, and prohibited his interment in consecrated ground; his body was accordingly buried in a field outside the abbey, where it lay several years before it was removed into the church. Morris was tried in Cork for O'Leary's death, but was acquitted. As might have been expected, a bloody vengeance was taken by a brother of the slain gentleman, who, watching his opportunity, fired three shots at Mr. Morris through the window of his lodgings in a public street in Cork. One of the shots inflicted such a wound in his side, that he soon after died of it. O'Leary the brother escaped to America after the perpetration of the deed, where, it is said, he lived to a good old age. Such was the state of Ireland seventy years ago!

There are, doubtless, other interesting monuments to be found here; but the accumulation of mould, hones, and other relics of mortality within the precincts of the ruins, renders it impossible to discover them without considerable labour. The passage from the church to the convent is on the north side of the nave, through an enclosure, called the "Earl's Chamber." From thence the visitor proceeds to the different chambers of the convent, the names and uses of each being furnished by the guides, who point out, with confident volubility, the kitchen, refectory, dormitory, penitentiary, &c. The corbels, which supported the joists of the second-floor, may still be seen in the walls. All the chambers were pleasantly lighted by numerous oblong side lights. The cloister which adjoins the north wall of the choir is a large square court, around which ran a covered-in ambulatory, where the brotherhood were wont to walk in wet weather. The other portions of the convent communicated with the cloisters by five doors, which opened into it.

At a short distance from the convent stands the Castle of Kilcrea, said to have been built in the fifteenth century by the same Cormac M'Carthy, Lord of Muskerry, who founded the church and friary. The ruins evince it to have been a place of considerable extent and rude magnificence. A staircase, composed of dark marble—of which there are extensive quarries in the neighbourhood—leads, by a flight of seventy-seven steps, from the ground-floor to the summit of the building, becoming spiral as it approaches the higher chambers. The upper apartment, which was spacious and well lit, formed the state-room; its floor, which is now unsheltered by a roof is overgrown with grass, from which circumstance it is called the *parkeen-glas,* or "little green field." Traces of outworks are still visible around the castle; and on the east side is the bawn, a small fortified area, defended by curtain walls and two square towers. This enclosure in former times served by day as a place of recreation to the inhabitants of the castle, and by night as a secure retreat for the cattle of the estate, which were in no less danger from their natural enemies, the wolves, than from the plundering bands of kernes or gallowglasses of the various hostile septs, who, as opportunity or hope of prey allured them, swept the country with whoop and shout, rifling and burning the dwellings of the unprotected peasants, and carrying away their cattle to their impregnable mountain fastnesses. There they enjoyed their triumph until the chief whose lands had been robbed, watching his time, rushed out with his enraged followers, and in the darkness of night retaliated upon the aggressors, by committing infinitely more mischief than he had sustained, and driving off if possible, double the number of cattle which his clan had lost.

The Castle of Kilcrea was once surrounded by thick woods; but, save a few young plantations near the walls, it is now totally denuded of its lovely forests, and stands in stern and lonely desolation,—a monument of departed greatness. Gazing at its dismantled towers and lofty battlements, I felt the melancholy force of an Irish bard's address to the ruins of Donegal Castle, who, bewailing the destruction of "the fortress of the once bright door's," utters a beautiful apostrophe to it in Iris native language, of which the following extract us a literal translation :—

"In lieu of thy rich wine-feasts, thou hast now
Nought but the cold stream from the firmament.

Over the mouldings of thy shattered windows,
The music which to-day breaks forth,
Is the wild songs of birds and winds—
The voices of the stormy elements.
O many-gated Donegal!
What spell of slumber overcame thee—
Thou mansion of the board of flowing goblets—
To make thee undergo this rueful change?"

From Kilcrea the road runs through Ballincollig, a neat little town, five miles from Cork. It is a military station, and contains a cavalry barrack and a police depôt for the province of Munster; also an extensive gunpowder manufactory, which gives employment to a number of persons in the neighbourhood: it was formerly in the hands of government, but is now worked by a private company. The neat-looking offices and buildings attached to this manufactory, and the numerous seats of the gentry on the banks of the Lee, give an air of cheerful comfort to the village and its vicinity. The castle of Ballincollig, near the town, was formerly a stronghold of the Barretts, an Anglo-Irish family,* who at one time possessed large estates in this county, and gave their name to the adjoining barony. It is a plain quadrangular tower, about forty feet in height, in the centre of a walled enclosure, defended by towers. A natural cave, which runs some distance into the rock beneath the keep, is still shown as the place where the former possessors of the castle confined their prisoners.

* *Anglo-Irish—The* jealousy with which the native Irish regarded the English intruders, even after a lapse of time which might be supposed sufficient to have extinguished all acrimonius feelings towards them, is strikingly exhibited in the following anecdote of O' Neal, Earl of Tyrone Marching by *Castlemore,* the principal seat of the Barretts, in the northern extremity of the barony of their name, he inquired, who lived in that castle? On being informed that it was Barrett, a good Catholic, who had been possessed of the estate above four hundred years; exclaimed, with an oath, "No matter, I hate the English churl as if he had landed only yesterday." It must be admitted, however. that the English settlers were equally bitter in their hostility to the Irish, and that they sought to maintain tire footing they had obtained in the island by studied barbarity of example, rather than by setting a precedent of mercy and forbearance. Can anything more sanguinary be imagined, than the sentiments expressed by the Earl of Cork in a letter to the Earl of Warwick, giving an account of a skirmish, in which his second son, Lord Kinalmeaky, was engaged against the Irish insurgents during the civil wars? After mentioning the number of the slain, he adds this barbarous comment, "And now the boy has blooded him-self upon them, I hope that God will so bless him and his majesty's forces, that as I now write but of the killing of an hundred, I shall shortly write of the *killing of thousands!*" Such were the feelings that animated both parties: a thirst for blood prevailed on either side, and the cruelties practised by the invaders served only to provoke a fierce spirit of vengeance and retaliation in the hearts of the injured party.

The edifice cannot boast any great extent or architectural beauty, nor is there much to interest the antiquarian in its ruins, although it is said to have been built as far back as the time of Edward III.

Within a mile of the village of Ballincollig the beautiful river Bride unites with the Lee. The rich lowlands adjoining the junction of the rivers, is called Inniscarra, (the beloved island) where the pious St. Senan* founded a monastery in the sixth century. It is a sweet secluded spot, admirably adapted for meditation and the alienation of the heart from worldly concerns. Not a vestige of this establishment is now to be discovered. There are some reminiscences which render Inniscarra a place of great interest to persons conversant with Irish history. It was there that the Earl of Tyrone encamped his numerous native forces at the close of the rebellion of the Earl of Desmond, commonly called the *Sugawn Earl;* and it was while here with the army that the President St. Leger was killed in a skirmishing excursion, not far from the city of Cork. A succession of several natural caves are to be seen near "The Ovens," a small hamlet in this neighbourhood, that derives its name from those subterranean chambers, some of which are said in shape to resemble ovens. Two of them are accessible to the curious; but there is little to render them worthy a particular description here. Like all caves found in lime-stone countries, they are merely a succession of irregularly-sized chambers, hung with spars and stalactites, and connected by narrow and intricate passages. Travellers who have visited the caves of Mitchelstown, or that of Dunmore in the county Kilkenny, will find these at Ovens much inferior to the former in romantic beauty, and in size and extent; although the country people say that they extend underground as far as the Castle of Carrigrohan, a distance of four miles from the place. The great number of those singular caverns

---

*   *St. Senan* or *Senanus,* according to ancient tradition, had introduced Christianity, and founded a church upon Scattery, a small island at the mouth of the Shannon, before the arrival of St. Patrick. The ruins of some old churches and an ancient round tower, one hundred and twenty feet high, seem to offer corroborative proof of the great antiquity of the place. An incident in the life of this saint, who it appears was celebrated for severe chastity, has afforded Moore the subject of one of his charming Irish melodies, called "St *Senanus and the Lady,"* to which he appends this curious note*:* "In a metrical life of St. Senanus, which is taken from an old Kilkenny MS., and may be found amongst the *Acta Sanctorum Hiberni* we are told of his flight to the island of Scattery, and his resolution not to admit any woman of the party: he even refused to receive a sister saint, St. Cannera, whom an angel had taken to the island for the express purpose of introducing her to him. The following was the ungracious answer of St. Senanus, according to his poetical biographer :—

> Cui Præsul, quid fœminis
> Commune est cum monachis.
> Nec te nec ullam aliam
> Admittemus in insulam.

According to Dr. Ledwich, St. Sensanus was no less a personage than the river Shannon; but O'Conner and other antiquarians deny this metamorphosis indignantly."

found in Ireland, is owing, in almost every instance, to the calcareous or lime-stone strata, of which the island is composed: to the same cause may be attributed much of the picturesque charms of its scenery—its numerous waterfalls—deep glens—subterranean rivers—natural bridges, and precipitous cliffs, which are not to be met with in the same extent, variety, and beauty, in any other country.

On the summit of a steep rock overhanging the river Lee, stand the picturesque ruins of the Castle of Carrigrohan. It consists of two distinct piles; one, the more ancient—built in the early feudal times, when the security of the chieftain depended on the number of his followers and the strength of his castle walls—is now a mere heap of ruins, whose massive architecture, narrow, gloomy chambers and vaulted dungeons, show that it must formerly have been a place of some importance. The other building, which is in better preservation, belongs to that era when the ancient castle began to assume the more peaceful characteristics of the modern manor-house. Its form is oblong, and three of the original high-pitched gables, surmounted with clustering chimney-shafts, still remain; which, with the ornamental projections at the angles, and the Tudor label mouldings over the windows, give a picturesque appearance to the building. The M'Carthys are said to have been the founders of the ancient portion of this castle, from one of whom, surnamed *Rohuin* or *the Nobleman*—the name of the fortress, *Carrigrohan,* (the Rock of Rohan,) is derived. It is mournful, while wandering through this part of southern Ireland, to meet everywhere the crumbling relics of the greatness of this once powerful family, whose very memory is now nearly forgotten, or remembered only by those to whom they are endeared by the traditions of the country, on who find a sad pleasure in turning over the pages of ancient Ireland's eventful history. While viewing those mouldering ruins, I could not forbear pie-turing to myself, that, perhaps within these very walls the ancient kings of Munster—the proud M'Carthys *Mor*—sate surrounded by warriors and statesmen, bards and chieftans, receiving embassies from foreign princes, though it may be said of the last of this noble race—that,

" In the fields of their country they found not a grave." *

---

* Robert, the fourth Earl of Clancarty, the lineal descendant of the Kings of Desmond, was the son of Donogh, whose estates were confiscated for his adherence to James II. Having vainly sought a restitution of his patrimony from George II. he retired in disgust to France, where he was allowed by Louis XV. apartments in the palace, rank in the army, and the privileges of the higher nobility. Notwithstanding which, he was haunted by an ever-yearning love for England; and in order, as he often said, "to die in sight of his native country," he retired to Boulogne, where, on a handsome pension from the French king, he was enabled to live in that hospitable convivial style which stiited his disposition, and to indulge in the society of the English and Irish refugees who resided there. lie died in 1770, at the advanced age of eighty-four, at his *chateau,* leaving two sons, who left no legitimate issue,

After the M'Carthys lost this castle it was possessed by the Barretts, of whom I have spoken in my descript ion of Ballincollig Castle; it is believed that the modern structure at Carrigrohan was erected by the latter family. The Barretts, like many English families, bad become, as I have elsewhere remarked, "more Irish than the Irish," that is, they were more turbulent and rebellious than the natives themselves— ever ready for a foray—and watching opportunities for plundering the peaceable inhabitants of the towns and cities. Amongst the records of the transgressions of these Barretts we read, that, in 1377, one Edward Perys was paid one hundred shillings as a recompense for his horse slain in an expedition against the Barretts, then in rebellion; and in the same year Richard Oge Barrett and his son William were obliged to send into Cork one thousand cows, as fines for their various seditions. In 1599, William Barrett, described as "a chief of a small countrie," who had been in rebellion with the Earl of Desmond, submitted to the queen's mercy. The extensive estates of this family were forfeited at the time of the Revolution by Colonel John Barrett. Carrigrohan was destroyed in the great rebel lion, though it was afterwards occupied by a Captain Cape, the notorious leader of a band of robbers, who infested this part of the country, and were the terror of the neighbourhood for a long time. West of the castle, at a sudden bend of the river, it forms a deep pool, which has obtained the fearful name of *Poul-an-lifrin* or Hell-hole; and is said to be the abode of one of those monstrous eels that the traditions of the peasantry describe as the terrible guardians of vast treasures, which lie concealed in the numerous fairy lakes of Ireland.

I remember it was after a day spent in wandering through the beautiful scenery which embellishes the banks of the Lee, that I was attracted by the sounds of music. guided by them I proceeded along a by-road until I came to a *sheebeen,* or small public-house, in front of which a number of persons of both sexes were assembled; the younger portion of the company were seated, some on the grass and others upon deal forms arranged around a small reserved space, in the centre of which an active, clean-limbed young fellow was dancing with an indefatigable energy that put every muscle and fibre of his frame into motion, opposite to a pretty modest-looking girl, who, with her eyes fixed upon her shoestrings, footed it, less vigorously perhaps, but with no less determination, to the popular jigg tune, "The Rakes of Mallow," perpetrated by a blind piper, who had been planted by "the boys" on an upturned *cleave,** on which a bundle of fresh straw had been laid by way of a cushion. A churn-dash stuck into the earth supported on its flat end a cake, which was to become the prize of the best dancer. The contention was carried on for a long time with extraordinary spirit; at length the competitors yielded their claims to a young man, the son of a rich farmer in the neighbourhood, who, taking the cake, placed it gallantly in the lap of a pretty girl, to whom I understood he was about being married. The visitor, to show his generosity, ordered a large supply of whiskey to be

* Cleave,—A large kind of basket, carried by the peasantry on the back.

distributed to those present; and as this acknowledgment is always expected from the dancer who gains the cake, it is generally conceded to him who is considered to be best able to pay for the honour.

The love of dancing appears to be inherent amongst the Irish, and constitutes a striking feature in the national character. Even poverty and its attendant evils, which might be supposed sufficient to depress the most elastic spirit, have not been able to extinguish the love of the peasantry for this amusement, that may be said to form an important part of their education. With them it is a natural expression of gaiety and exuberance of animal spirits—indicative of their ardent temperament; and I question whether a more accurate test could be found to judge the character of a people, than by their national dances. Carleton, the popular author of the "Traits and Stories of the Irish Peasantry," whose pictures of humble life are drawn with a thorough knowledge of his subject, says, that no people dance so well as the Irish, and gives the following excellent reasons for what he advances. "Dancing, every one must admit, although a most delightful amusement, is not a simple, nor distinct, nor primary one: on the contrary, it is merely little else than a happy and agreeable method of enjoying music; and its whole spirit and character must necessarily depend upon the power of the heart to *feel* the melody to which the limbs and body move. Every nation, therefore, remarkable for a susceptibility of music, is also remarkable for a love of dancing, unless religion or some other adequate obstacle arising from an anomalous condition of society interposes to prevent it. Music and dancing being dependent the one on the other as cause and effect, it requires little argument to prove that the Irish, who are so sensitively alive to the one, should in a very high degree excel at the other, and accordingly it is so." No person who has witnessed the enthusiasm with which an Irishman listens to a favourite piece of music; the different emotions it excites in his breast, according to the gay or mournful tendency of the strain, can doubt for a moment the truth of the above observations. It is the music that exhilarates and puts him into motion; the dance is the expression—the music the cause of his ecstatic delight. The skill acquired by the peasantry in this their favourite exercise, is regularly exhibited at weddings and other rustic festivals. A native buoyancy of spirit distinguishes their performance, and there is frequently to he found a grace and ease in the simple motions of the youthful peasant girl that would be the theme of admiration in the lofty ball-room.

Of the ancient dances of Ireland little is now certainly known those of a serious character are either entirely forgotten or rarely practised. Carleton mentions two which he has seen, one was called the Horo *Lheig*, danced only at wakes, funerals, and other mournful occasions; the second was a dance executed by one man. "It was not," he says, "necessarily performed to music, and could not be performed without the emblematic aids of a stick and a handkerchief." He adds, that this dance was addressed to an individual passion, and was doubtless a remnant of the old Pagan mysteries. There is a curious account of a dance, called the *Rinceadh Fadha* or Long Dance, traditionally said to have been the dance of the ancient Irish, in Walker's Memoirs of the Irish Bards. On the landing of James II. at Kinsale, the friends of that ill-fated prince, who awaited his arrival on the seashore, received him with the *Rinceadh Fadha*, the figure and execution of which delighted him exceedingly. The figure is thus described : "Three persons abreast, each holding the ends of a white handkerchief, first moved forward a few paces to slow music; the rest of the dancers followed two and two, a white handkerchief between each; then the dance began. The music suddenly changing to a brisk tune, the dancers passed with a quick step under the handkerchiefs of the three in front, wheeled round in semicircles, formed a variety of pleasing animated evolutions, interspersed at intervals with *entrechats* or cuts, united, and fell again into their original places behind, and paused." Mr. Walker conjectures that this might have been the dance of the Pagan Irish during their festivals. It is certain that all the nations of antiquity had different dances for different occasions. The old Greeks, who esteemed dancing not only an honourable but a necessary accomplishment, had religious dances and war dances; dances for marriages, for funerals, and for a great variety of occasions; and some of these have survived in a land where everything else has perished, or been changed. At the distance of nearly three thousand years, we can trace the Dædalian or Cretan dance, as described by Homer, in the Romaika of the Modem Greeks; and it is not straining a resemblance to say, that the character of the Cretan dance is to be found in the Irish *Rinceadh Fadha*. The ancient Pyrrhic dance exists still in the Albanitico, and in a dance peculiar to Candia, in which the performers, who are always men, are furnished each with a target and short sword, which can differ little in form from that described in the Iliad. Byron alludes to this when he makes a Greek poet thus reproach his effeminate countrymen :—

> "Ye have the Pyrrhic dance as yet,
> Where is the Pyrrhic phalanx gone?
> Of two such lessons, why forget
> The nobler and the manlier one?"

Byron never omitted an opportunity of sneering at the practice of dancing; but as it is well known his dislike arose from a morbid sensibility of his own unfortunate disqualification to join in its pleasures—his censure is of little consequence. How would the poet's self-esteem be mortified had he consulted an old Italian author, who says, that there is, or ought to be, as much immortality in a good dance as in a good Epic poem! But the evidences of the esteem in which dancing was held by the ancients are too numerous to require repetition. Plato, the divine philosopher, "thought it meet that young children be taught to dance." The severe lawgiver, Lycurgus, enjoined, dancing to the Spartans. Eschylus, the great tragic poet, did not think it unworthy his genius to turn his attention to the national dances of his country, which he improved considerably. Lucian claims the honour of the invention of dancing to the goddess Rhea, who, he says, taught the art to her priests in Phrygia and Crete. Homer makes honourable mention of dancing, and Herodotus relates how a certain noble Athenian lost his bride, the beautiful daughter of the king of Sicyon, by making some false steps in dancing for her. If we come nearer to our own times, we find dancing in high repute in England. Sir Christopher Hatton danced himself into the favour of Queen Elizabeth, who was passionately fond of dancing, and it was no unusual thing to see the staidest statesmen, judges, and senators taking part in the revels, when

"My grave lord-keeper led the brawls."

It is also related of a young Irish chief, (whose name I cannot at this moment recollect,) that coming to the court of Elizabeth to petition for some boon, he so captivated his royal mistress, with the grace and spirit with which he performed before her some of his country's national dances, that she not only granted his request, but loaded him with marks of her regard on his return home. To proscribe dancing, as many well-meaning but mistaken persons would fain do, would be to deprive the Irish peasant of one of the few blameless and healthful recreations that are left him to enjoy. Channing—the eloquent and truly Christian Channing—in his Lectures upon Temperance, advocates dancing as an innocent pleasure, and a means of improving the manners of the labouring classes. "The exercise," he says, "is amongst the most healthful. The body as well as the mind feels its gladdening influence: no amusement seems more to have a foundation in our nature. The animation of youth naturally overflows in harmonious movements. The true idea of dancing entitles it to favour. Its end is to realize perfect grace in motion; and who does not know that a sense of the graceful is one of the higher faculties of our nature?"

The mirthful dances of Ireland are the jigg, reel, hornpipe, country-dance, and *cotillon.* Of these the jigg is the dance peculiar to the country. The music of the jigg, and the steps used in dancing to it, being totally different from every other known movement, entitle it to be distinguished as the national Irish dance. I have, I fear, dwelt upon this subject at too great length, but the popularity of the amusement amongst all classes in Ireland may, I hope, justify me for having devoted to it an additional page.

The approach to Cork from Ballincollig is through a fertile and highly improved country, and the entrance to the city by the western outlet is exceedingly beautiful, and worthy of the second city in the kingdom. About a mile from the town the view is very imposing; the most striking objects that present themselves to the traveller's notice are the county jail and house of correction. The front of the latter,—the part of the building seen from the road,—is adorned with a portico of Doric columns, which stands out in beautiful relief : the whole is characterized by a noble simplicity of design, and a pleasing unity of its parts. The spacious well-formed road, the venerable trees of the Mardyke walk, the mansions of the gentry exhibiting taste and comfort united in a remarkable degree, and the richly cultivated fields which stretch along the banks of the river, give to this side of the city a character of wealth and grandeur (unfortunately but rarely to be seen in the suburbs of an Irish town) which prepossess one in favour of the place before he has entered it.

XXI.

ONCE more a sojourner in "the beautiful city," I availed myself of the invitation of an intelligent friend to spend a few days with him at his house, situated near the ancient town of Cloyne, to visit the eastern shores of the harbour. The road from Cork to my destination lay for some distance through the beautiful valley of Glanmire, which forms part of the environs of the city. This delightful vicinity is finely wooded, and thickly dotted with handsome villas and mansions; but, as I shall have occasion to notice its beauties when describing the harbour and river on my return, I shall only observe, in passing, that the beautiful mansion and demesne of Dunkittle are charmingly situated near the mouth of the little creek, where the Glanmire rivulet unites its waters with those of the Lee. Mr. Townsend, who many years ago wrote a description of Cork, says, that "all the situations of the Lee are fine, but none of them enjoy so extensive a combination of beauties as Dunkittle."

Keeping the Little Island on the right, I passed the pretty hamlet of Little Glanmire, and several handsome residences of the gentry, until I reached the island of Foaty, which is almost entirely occupied by the mansion and demesne of John Smyth Barry, Esq. The situation of Foaty is flat and uninteresting; but the labours of art, guided by excellent taste in planting and laying out the grounds, have rendered it a very beautiful residence. A handsome tower, which has been erected by the water-side, commands a fine view of the river and the beautiful scenery of the opposite shores. The village of Carrigtohill has little to recommend it to the notice of the tourist, except the subterranean chambers and circular entrenchments, of which no less than fifteen or sixteen have been discovered at different times in this neighbourhood. Earthen mounds, raised by human labour, are very numerous throughout Ireland, and amongst the peasantry are called indiscriminately *Raths* in the Irish language, and *Danish Forts* in English; the construction of them being popularly attributed to the Danes. This is an error into which many writers upon Irish antiquities have inadvertently fallen; the word *rath*, strictly speaking, should be applied only to those earthen works intended for purposes of military defence, and never to the mounds which are evidently sepulchral tumuli. Mr. Chalmers, in his "Caledonia," makes the following remark :—"*Rath* in the Gaelic and *rhath* in the British signified originally a plain, or cleared spot, such as the Celtic inhabitants of the British isles fixed their habitations on. *Rath* in the Gaelic also signified a *surety;* hence the term was applied by the old Irish, and by the Scoto—Irish to the villages in which they lived; to the seats of their flaiths or princes, and to a fortress or *place of security.*" Now it must be apparent to any one who has examined any of the Irish raths, that they correspond in every particular with the description given by Mr. Chalmers. They are found to vary greatly in size, some being merely slight elevations of moderate dimensions, surrounded by a single ditch; while in many instances they rise to a considerable height, comprising within their area from ten to twenty acres. These spacious raths are encompassed by ramparts and deep intrenchments, and bear a close resemblance to the ancient fortresses found in different parts of England, and ascribed to the ancient Celts or Belgæ. Doctor Ledwich says, that the woods and marshes served the Celts for camps and ditches, but that they learned from the Belgæ to take refuge on the hills, as Cæsar says was the practice of the Britons. Thus, in the opinion of this antiquarian, the Belgæ had the merit of teaching the art of earthen fortification to the Celts. It is therefore highly probable, that the knowledge of this mode of defence must have been possessed by a people deriving their customs and manners from the same source, and that a great number of the Irish raths were constructed by the inhabitants before the Danes obtained a footing in the country. Giraldus Cambrensis, who wrote on the Topography of Ireland in the early part of the twelfth century, adopted the vague tradition that ascribed these earthen forts to the Danes, and says, that they were constructed by Turgesius and his followers in the beginning of the ninth century. Now it is well known that Turgesius conquered only a portion of Ireland, yet these raths are to be found in every part of the island. "It is highly probable," observes Brewster in discussing this subject, "that many raths were altered and occupied by the Danes as places of defence, whilst some mounts, designed for military works, were, perhaps, entirely constructed by that people."

The subterranean chambers at Carrigtohill, which led to the foregoing remarks, are situated within one of those circular forts or raths. The descent to them is by a narrow sloping passage, which leads into a small excavated chamber, of about seven feet in diameter, formed without any masonry. Four of these chambers, connected by narrow and difficult passages, have been examined; but one or more remain still unexplored, in consequence of the passage conducting to the fifth chamber being built up with large stones. Similar underground works have been discovered within the boundaries of several of the ancient forts, some being regular sets of chambers, as is the case at Carrigtohill, others are simply long galleries, with an entrance in the centre of the intrenchment; while in many instances, no trace can be found of any passage to the inside. Various conjectures have been advanced as to the uses of these raths and chambers; by the best informed they are supposed to have been the sites of the dwellings of the ancient inhabitants, before they exchanged their rude habitations for castles of stone and walled towns. The vestiges of buildings still found on some of the more extensive raths, and the decayed bones, (chiefly those of the ox,) and charcoal, which are often discovered in large quantities on turning up the ground, are strong corroborative evidences that these places once formed the defensible places of abode, or retreat for the old Irish chieftains and their dependents. The close neighbourhood in which these mounds are usually found, as if for the purpose of ready communication in time of need, shows, that though divided into chieftainries, each under the separate command of its particular head, the septs united upon great occasions to repel a common enemy, or resent a common insult. This form of government by which every petty chief, although ruling his own vassals with arbitrary power, was obliged to render certain service to the great head of the state, is so generally known as the principle of the feudal system, that it is unnecessary for me to explain it further here. If, as it has been conjectured, these intrenchments were the rude defences of the habitations of the native Irish, it is extremely probable that the subterranean chambers might have been used as storehouses for the provisions of the little community: and the fact, that the entrances to these underground chambers have, in most instances, been discovered by accident, is only a further proof that they were intended as places adapted for concealment in time of danger. The popular tradition amongst the peasantry is, that after the Danes had been conquered at the battle of Clontarf, they constructed these forts and secret chambers to escape the pursuit of the Irish; but such a supposition is too absurd to obtain a moment's belief, as it is evident such works could not have been effected by a scattered force, flying before an active and victorious enemy. If the Danes *did* take refuge within these intrenchments it must be concluded that they were in existence for ages before their time.

These raths have time out of mind been an object of superstitious veneration to the Irish peasantry, who believe that the mysterious inclosures are the abodes of the fairies or "good people;" hence it is that few of the country folks will approach one of them after night-fall without trembling, lest they should incur the anger of the irascible pigmy gentry, by intruding on their revels, or disturbing their moonlight festivities. And to the same feeling of superstitious awe may be attributed their reluctance to disturb, by the operation of the spade or axe, these interesting relics of antiquity, which may be frequently seen overgrown with aged trees and underwood in nature's wild simplicity. Numerous are the tales related by the peasantry of daring individuals who have watched the midnight revels of the fairies in these places, which for long ages have been the favourite haunts of the tiny race. Children of mortals, who have been stolen by the "good people," are, it is believed, conveyed by them into these raths, on which it has been remarked the verdure is always greener and brighter than on any of the neighbouring fields. I remember, while sketching one of them in a remote part of the county Waterford, some years ago, being accosted by a young cowherd, who had been for a considerable time watching me at a short distance. He was evidently curious to know what I was doing, but a fear of intruding had kept him from approaching too closely, till seeing that I noticed him, he pulled off his hat, and addressed me with the usual salutation—"God save you, sir."

The ready response of "God save *you* too, my good man," spoken, perhaps, in a familiar tone, removed the formality of further introduction, and placed him instantly at his ease. Viewing attentively the sketch on which I was engaged, he pronounced the following criticism upon it, in a kind of half soliloquy:—

"Well, well, that hates all I ever seen in my born days! tth—tth—tth! Praise be to God; there's no telling what we'll live to see after that. There's the bigh ash three, and the ould ditch, and Ned H orrigan's red cow grazin', with the spanshil on her leg; and tare an ounties! as sure as turf, that's *me* in the corner, there sittin upon a lump of a stone. Wissha, don't I know myself by the hole in my coat and the crucked stick in my fist, all as nattral as life. Why then, if I don't make too bould, sir, what for is it you're putting us all down upon the paper?"

"I 'm making a sketch of this place."

"A skitch, sir ! troth I never heard of the like afore."

" 'Tis merely," said I, "a picture of this old rath I wish to have."

"I persave, sir," he replied, instantly comprehending my design, "and a mighty ancient ould place it is. Some people says it's haunted by a sperrit of a beautiful young lady, mounted on a white horse, that gallops every night three times round the rath; and by all accounts there's a power of the good people' *keep* * inside of it."

"Have you ever seen any of them ?" I asked.

"If I haven't I know them that has, sir: there's Katty Ryan, a dacent woman, though she's a first cousin of my own, had an aunt's father that once seen plenty of them."

"Ah! I should like to hear how that happened."

"Why, then, you needn't wish twicet, sir; I'll tell you all about it, just as I hard it from Katty's own mouth. It was about a month afther Katty's aunt Nelly was married to Tom Duggan, that Tom sot off airly one morning for the fair of Kilmac-thomas, to buy a *bonnieen*. Of coorse, there was no scarcity of pigs at the fair, and Tom soon shooted himself with as purty a shlip as ever you'd wish to behould. Well, towards

---

* *To keep,* as used by the southern peasantry in this sense, means to live or reside in any dwelling. *Bonnieen,* a little pig.

evening as Tom was driving his bargain home, whistling to keep the crathur from feeling lonesome on the road, he was overtook by a wizzen-faced little ould man, who looked very hard at the *bonnieen*.

" 'That's a fine pig,' says he.

" 'He's the makings of a fine one,' says Tom.

" 'You may say that,' says the old fellow, with a grin; 'what'll you take for him?'

" 'I don't want to sell him,' answers Tom.

" 'I'll give you your own price for him,' says the other, putting his hand in his pocket, and pulling out a big leather purse.

" 'Put up your money, my good man,' says Tom; 'I tell you I'm not going to part him.'

" 'You're not?'

" 'I'm not. Now, will that answer sarve you?'

" 'Parfectly,' says the ould chap, looking as cross as two sticks; 'but mind what I'm saying to you, Tom Duggan—its bad to make little of a fair offer, and may be you'd have cause to regret you refused my bidding for your *rootieen** afore long.'

"With that, throwing a contimptible look at the pig, he marched away as grand as a prince, and Tom druv home his bargain, but before he lay down himself, he put the crathur to sleep in a warm corner of the cabin, snug and comfortable, on a wisp of clane straw. Next morning Nelly, who was in bed when Tom came home, got up at cock-shout to admire the new mimber of the family.

" 'Arrah, Tom, honey,' says she, as soon as she clapped her eyes upon the baste, 'what sort of a poor starved divel of a pig is this you've brought me home?'

" 'Starved divel!' cries Tom in a huff, jumping out of bed; 'the pig's as iligant a pig as ever stood upon a poor man's fiure; that I'll maintain. Let me see him.'

" 'Och, murdher alive! what's this at all?' says he, when he saw a little ill-thriven animal, with a wizzen face the very moral of the ould man's, in the place of the pig he had brought home. 'That's not my pig; it's no more like the one I bought than I'm like Finn M'Cool.'

"However, it was a folly to fret; Tom and his wife knew there was no help for spilt milk, so they determined to make the best they could of their bargain; and 'who knows,' says Nelly, 'may be the crathur is like as swinged cat, better nor he looks, and that he only wants a little feeding?'

"But they soon found out, to their sorrow, though the strange pig ate as much as six, that instead of getting fatter or bigger, it was growing more *dawney* and wizzen-faced every day. This was a heavy hardship to poor Tom, who counted on selling the

---

* *Rootieen, a* little rooter.
† *Fin M'Cool* or *Comhal,* was a celebrated Irish giant, of whose strength and prowess many wonderful stories are related.
‡ *Dawney,* small and delicate.   § *Rooskiah,* a blazing fire.

pondhering on what pig when fat to make up the rint; and as he was lying awake one night, thinking and was best to be done, he thought he hard a rustling noise upon the floor, and lifting up his head softly, he saw by the light of the fire on the hearth, the wizzen-faced pig dragging over a *bresnagh* from the corner, and clapping it upon the fire as ordherly as any Christhen could.

"'Why then, conshumin to your impidence, you ugly baste; may be its a shin-hate you want,' says Tom, in to himself, for he didn't care to let the pig know he was watching him. Well, sir, afther the chap had made a good *rooskiah,*§ he sot himself up, saving your honour's presence, upon his hind-quarthers forninst the fire, and began unbuttoning his skin all down in front; and before Tom could make the sign of the crass upon himself, out of it walks the little ould man that overtook Tom on his road from the fair. Tom, you may be sure, lay as quiet as a mouse in a male-tub; but for all that he kept a sharp eye upon the motions of the ould fellow, who, afther foulding up the pig-skin as carefully as if it was his Sunday-coat, hid it behind a chest in the corner, and opening the cabin-door quite softly, went out of the house. As soon as he was gone Tom tumbled out of bed, and hurrying on his clothes, pulled the skin from where the ould man had put it, and tucking it under his arm, ran after the ould boy, who was marching at his ase along the road. Tom now resolved to find out who he was; so keeping a little way behind him, he walked on until he came to this very rath, where he stopped at a beautiful glass-door in the side of the hill, and knocked three times at it. Then somebody inside asked,

"'What's your business here?'

"'I'm come for my share of Tom Duggan's pig,' says the ould man, making answer, and immaydiately the glass-door opened, and in he wint.

"Presently up comes a train of little men, some wearing red caps with *deeshy** silver bells in them, that tinkled with a sound like the singing of birds; and every one of them knocked at the glass-door, and the same question and answer passed afore they were let in.

"'Bedad,' says Tom, as soon as he saw the last of them go into the hill, 'I'll thry and get a slice of my own bacon; so here goes for luck.'

"With that he marches to the glass-door and knocks three times at it, and when the porther inside axed him what he wanted, he answered as the others did, that he was come for his share of Tom Duggan's pig; upon which the door was opened, and in Tom walked as bould as brass. Well, sir, on he went till he came to a big room; but being timmersome of going in among strange company, he peeped through a slit in the door, and there, sir, he saw a fine roasted pig upon the table, and a power of the little people sitting round it, eating and laughing away for the bare life; and may be there wasnt a beautiful smell of the vittals enough to timpt the Pope o' Rome himself to ate mate upon Friday. Any way, poor Tom was near dropping with wakeness and hunger, while the company inside were splitting their sides, eating and laughing, till

309

they had nearly finished the pig, and the little wizzen-faced rascal was sticking his fork into the last morsel on the dish, when Tom, forgetting where he was, baweled out,

" 'Tundher an' turf! gintlemen, won't ye lave me even a *cruibeent* of my own pig?'

"The words were hardly out of his mouth when a terrible screech was raised, and the little chaps went tumbling one over the other to get out at the door.

" 'The devil take the hindmost,' says Tom, trampling and kicking the little people in his hurry to be off with himself; and without stopping to give the porther at the door a thrifle for his civilitude, he boulted out, and never looked behind him till he got back to his own cabin.

" 'But,' said I, 'I always understood that mortals venturing into these fairy habitations are not allowed to return into the world, being obliged to become the servants of the little gentry.'

" 'True enough, sir, and that would have been Tom's case, too, if he hadn't the luck to have the ould man's pig-skin under his arm at the time, for 'tis well known, that the fairies can do nothing to harm you if you have anything belonging to one of them about you. But the best of the story is to be told yet, sir. The wizzen-faced chap came the next morning to Tom, begging and praying for his skin, but he wasnt the fool to give it back until he had paid him the full of a pot of gold for it, and glad enough the ould fairy was to get it at the price."

From Foaty I proceeded to the town of COVE, delightfully situated on the south side of the Great Island. The town, which is neatly built, has a busy, lively look, and is cleaner than the generality of sea-ports. It can boast but few objects of antiquarian interest, being merely an insignificant village at the beginning of the present century, its subsequent importance has been in a great degree owing to the late war, during which Cork harbour was made a rendezvous station for the British navy. But the town of Cove owes its greatest celebrity to the mildness of its climate and its excellent situation, being open to the sea on the south, and encompassed on every other side by high hills, which effectually shelter it from the cold winds. This happy position, and the picturesque beauty of its environs, have for many years past made Cove a favourite resort for numbers of invalids, who, as a medical writer* remarks, "would otherwise have sought the far-off scenes of Montpellier or Madeira, with their vehement suns and less temperate vicissitudes of clinnate. The many recoveries here have justified the selection, and proved the restorative and invigorating principle of its atmosphere. An admirable equability of climate, and an absence of sudden and violent interruptions, are the great characteristics which have so beneficially marked out this town to the ailing and debilitated, and established its reputation."

---

* Dr. Scott, of Cork, whose 'Medical Topography of Cove' is in the hands of every invalid visiting this place.

The Cove of Cork

From the steepness of the site on which Cove is built, the invalid is afforded a variety of climate, tempered to his wishes, and attainable according to the elevation of the different ascending terraces; and for all purposes of exercise the neighbourhood abounds with exhilarating walks and drives.

But it is not to the valetudinarian alone that Cove offers attractions: its proximity to Cork, the beauty of its scenery, and its favourable situation for sea-bathing and for boating excursions, draw a great influx of gay and fashionable visitors here during the summer months. The town, as I have observed, is built partly on the margin of the shore, and on the stages of the steep hill that overhangs the harbour. It is from these terraces that the most extensive prospects over the harbour may be obtained, and, undoubtedly, it is a noble sight to look down upon the broad expanse of that land-locked haven, with its fortified isles, encompassed by lofty hills, crowned with numerous villas and mansions: and should, as is frequently the case, a fleet be lying at anchor under the shelter of the land, nothing can be conceived more lovely and magnificent than time effect of the *coup d'œil* In the valley, to the rear of the hill which overlooks the town, is the small ruined church and burying-ground of Clonmell. A large proportion of those interred there are strangers: many a storm-tossed mariner lies there, who has struggled with death upon time ocean, that he might breathe his last upon the land, and instead of the dark billows rolling over his cold remains, have the bright green grass and the young flowers springing from his grave. Many a youthful victim too, whom fell consumption had marked for its prey, but who, with self-deluding hope, sought too late to arrest its progress in this mild and genial climate, has found his last resting-place in that lonely church-yard. In this cemetery reposes the mortal part of the Rev. Charles Wolfe, an elegant though almost unknown writer, who, in 1823, at time early age of thirty-two, died in Cove, whither he had removed for the benefit of its air. He was the author of the "Lines on the Death of Sir John Moore," which, had he never written anything else, was sufficient to stamp him as a poet of tIne highest order. Here also, in an undistinguished grave, is buried "Tobin," the author of the popular comedy of "The Honeymoon," who died in the harbour on his passage to the West Indies.

In order to reach Cloyne from Cove I took a boat to Saleen, a small inlet about four miles from the latter town, on the eastern shore of the harbour. The boat was pulled by a crew consisting of four young athletic men. I thought as I watched them bending to their oars, their sinewy arms and ample chests fully developed by the motion of their bodies, and their honest countenances, bronzed by exposure to the sun and air, beaming with health and good-humour, that I never beheld four finer or more resolute looking fellows; just the sort of daring spirits for boarding a frigate or storming a fort that a Nelson or a Wellington would have chosen. The course we took was under the shores of Rostellan, the seat of the Marquess of Thomond. The castle is delightfully situated on a wooded promontory, commanding an exceedingly fine view of the grand and animated harbour with its beautiful shores. The demesne is rich in luxuriant beauty, and the judicious manner in which the grounds are laid out speak highly for the elegant taste of the noble owner. The present mansion is a modern erection, built on the site of an ancient castle of the Fitzgeralds, seneschals of Imokilly. An ancient sword, said to have been once wielded by Brian Boroihme, the great ancestor of the O'Briens, and the monarch who defeated the Danes at the memorable battle of Clontarf, is preserved in a small armoury of the castle, and shown to strangers as a genuine relic. The depth of water in the little creek into which we glided after passing Rostellan, does not permit boats proceeding more than a mile from its entrance; I therefore landed and commenced my walk to Cloyne, distant about two miles from thence. The path, which at first leads along a thickly-planted shore by the water-side, is extremely beautiful; by a sudden turn it brings us to the sweetly secluded little hamlet of Sleen, bosomed amidst the shade of hawthorns, and presenting such a picture of quiet pastoral beauty, that one might easily imagine Goldsmith had it in his mind when describing the beauties of "the Deserted Village,"

> "Where smiling spring her earliest visits paid,
> And parting summer's ling'ring bloom delayed."

The house and demesne of Castle Mary, contiguous to the village, form a prominent feature in the landscape; but the chief interest which attaches to this spot is the existence of a huge Cromlech* or Druidical altar, standing in a field at ashort distance from the house. It is an immense mass of limestone of an oblong shape, one end resting on the ground, and the other extremity supported by two large upright stones. Adjoining this great altar is a smaller one of a triangular shape, and, like the other, it is supported by two uprights in an inclined position. It is supposed that this lesser stone might have been used for the purposes of common sacrifice, while the greater altar was reserved for occasions of extraordinary solemnity. The incumbent stone or slab of the cromlechs is sustained in some cases by rows of upright pillars; in other instances the table is supported by two or more large cone-shaped rocks,

---

* *Cromlech.*—I have already spoken of the gobhláns or pillar-stones, (page 15,) so frequently found in Ireland. Like these, the Cromlech owes its origin to the idolatrous system of worship which there is every reason to suppose pervaded a great portion of the world before the existence of profane history; in its appearance, however, the Cromlech is totally different from the pillar-stone.

† The length of the incumbent stone is about fifteen feet, its breadth between seven and eight feet, and its thickness three and a half feet.

‡ The Irish and British word *Crom-leach*, which signifies a crooked or bent stone, it is sup-posed was applied to those rude altars from their inclining position; although it is equally pro-bable that they derived their name from being the stones on which sacrifices to the god *Crom* were offered. An ingenious conjecture has been advanced, that they were placed in an inclined position, to allow the blood of the victims slain upon them to run off freely.

313

but on none of the stones used in the construction of these altars can the mark of any tool be discovered. Numerous other *cromlechs* are known to exist in the County Cork,* but the description of this one may suffice to give an idea of all the others.

Cloyne, distant about a mile from Castle Mary, is pleasantly situated on a gentle eminence that rises from the southern vale of Imokilly, was formerly the seat of the bishop of the diocese of that name; but now, shorn of the honours of an episcopal residence, it has little besides its antiquarian interest to invite the attention of the traveller. The ancient name of the place was Cluaine-uamhach, or—the retreat of the caves—the propriety of the designation being evident from the numerous caves of great extent which exist in the neighbourhood: one very considerable cavern may be seen in a part of the episcopal demesne, called the Rock Meadow. The bishopric of Cloyne was founded in the sixth century by St. Coleman, a disciple of St. Finbar, the Bishop of Cork. The ancient cathedral is a small, low building, of an exceedingly plain and simple style of architecture, that refers its erection to a very early period: true it is, that modem innovations have disfigured the character of some parts of the building, and the repairs latterly bestowed upon it have been executed with as little regard to taste or propriety as the patches upon a beggar's cloak. The re-edification of the choir in 1776, under the direction of Bishop Agar, offers a striking evidence of this fact, in the absurd way in which light Italian ornaments have been blended with the more austere lineaments of the edifice, The form of the building is cruciform, consisting of a nave, choir, and north and south transepts; but the tower, if it ever possessed one, has entirely disappeared. Within the adjoining church-yard, which is surrounded by numerous venerable trees, that give to it a solemn and secluded aspect, are the remains of a small building, called by some "the Fire-house," by others, St. Coleman's Chapel. It is evidently of great antiquity, and tradition asserts that the bones of that holy man were preserved there until the beginning of the last century, when a bishop of Cloyne caused them to be removed, and the building nearly levelled to the ground.

The episcopal residence at the east end of the village is a spacious but irregular building, having been improved and altered according to the different tastes of the bishops who occupied it. The grounds and garden attached to it are extensive, and have been laid out with a considerable degree of elegance. In this house the celebrated Doctor Berkeley, a man illustrious for his learning, but more illustrious for his virtues, passed many years of his life, dividing his time between his pastoral duties, his garden,* and his books, and endearing himself to his flock by his gentle manners, and his earnest endeavours to promote the prosperity of the town.

A monastery was founded at Cloyne in the year 707, around which the town gradually grew up; the reputation of the monks for learning and piety attracting crowds of scholars and devotees to the place. At a short distance from the church, towards the west, stands one of the most remarkable specimens of the ancient

Turaghans or *Round Towers* of Ireland. The original height of the tower was ninety-two feet, but the conical roof having been demolished by lightning, an embattlement was placed round the top, which has increased the height to one hundred and two feet. It is divided into six stories, the first of which is eleven and a half feet from the ground, at which height the door of the tower is placed. The distance of each floor from the other is eleven and a half feet. The tower is built on a limestone rock; but with a strange disregard for that material, of which there is abundance on the spot, the stones which compose the tower have been brought from some distant quarry: this singularity is observable in many of the Druidic remains in both England and Ireland. The tower is now used as a belfry, and the name by which it is known amongst the peasantry is *Clogach-Cluina,* i.e. the House of the bell of Cloyne.

The existence of these Pillar Towers is one of tine most extraordinary circumstances connected with the history of Ireland; and notwithstanding all that has been written about them, and the innumerable conjectures which have been advanced on their origin and use, the question still remains unsolved. The writers who have discussed the subject have been, no doubt, fully satisfied each in his own mind of tine soundness of his own conclusions on the point; each is convinced that he has solved the riddle; but those who read and think without the bias occasioned by a predisposition to a favourite hypothesis, must still remain in doubt. It might have been expected that the recent discoveries in geography, which have disclosed every spot on the face of the globe, would have detected, in some region or another, buildings of a similar description. But no such thing; nothing that could justify the inquirer to connect the state of society in any other part of the world, with that which existed in Ireland at the time these singular edifices were constructed, has yet been brought to light. The state of the case relative to them, both as to facts and to conjectures, now rests nearly in the same position as it did when they first became a subject of philosophical investigation.Nevertheless, as objects peculiarly characteristic of the Scenery and Antiquities of Ireland, I may be permitted to offer here a few comprehensive reniarks upon a subject of such acknowledged interest, with reference to the opinions of various writers,

---

* *Bishop Berkeley.—The* fondness of the philosophic Berkeley for his garden is alluded to in one of the letters of Bishop Bennett to Dr. Parr. "The garden," he writes, "is large—four acres—consisting of four quarters full of fruit, particularly strawberries and raspberries, which Bishop Berkeley had a predilection for, and separated, as well as surrounded by shrubberies, which contain some pretty winding walks, and one large one of nearly a quarter of a mile long, adorned for great parts of its length by a hedge of myrtles six feet high, planted by Berkeley's own hand, and which had each of them a large ball of tar put to their roots. The doctor', belief in the sanatory effect of *tar* upon animal and vegetable life was unbounded; he wrote *a Treatise on Tar Water,* which caused a great sensation at the time.

Dr. Smith, in his History of Cork, relates, that on the night of the 10th of January, 1794, a flash of lightning struck the tower, rent the conical top, tumbled down the bell and three lofts, forced its way through one side of the building, and drove the stones, which were admirably well joined and locked into each other, through the roof of an adjoining stable.

concerning the date of the erection and intended use of these remarkable structures.

The main facts connected with them are as follow :—they are of a date beyond all traces of history or tradition; no record in existence notices the foundation of any one of them. They were built at a time when the art of architecture must have been in a very improved state. "A striking perfection observable in their construction, is the inimitable perpendicular invariably maintained. No architect of the present day could observe such regularity. Nelson's Pillar (Dublin,) has been proved to vary somewhat from the perpendicular line; but the keenest eye cannot trace a deviation in a single instance from amongst the whole of the Sabæan monuments. Even the tower of Kilmacduagh, one of the largest in the kingdom, having from some accident been forced to lean terrifically to one side, yet retains its stability as firm as before, such was the accuracy of its original elevation; while the cement employed in giving it solidity, and which is the direct counterpart of the Indian chunam, bids defiance to the efforts of man to dissever, except by the exertion of extraordinary power. These facts prove a highly advanced state of architectural knowledge. The number of these buildings is not less remarkable. Upwards of ninety have been ascertained either as existing at present, or at a period within historical memory. Their situation is also another remarkable peculiarity. They are generally in low and sheltered spots, never upon places of great elevation, and are also, with few exceptions, found in the immediate vicinity of some ecclesiastical building.

The existing towers have frequently suffered injury; but their altitude in their present condition varies from *twenty-five* to *one hundred and thirty-three* feet. Their usual circumference near the base is from forty to fifty feet. They frequently, but not uniformly, spring from a projecting plinth, and diminish gradually-as they ascend. In some remaining towers the roof is of a conical shape, and there is every reason to conclude that this was originally the shape of all. Battlements now crown the summit of several of them, but appear to have been added long after the erection of other parts of the structure. The door-way is raised to the height of several feet, generally from ten to twenty above the level of the ground. There are seldom any apertures for admitting light, except near the summit, where four small windows, pointing to the cardinal points, are to be seen in some of them. Both doors and windows are in general oblong openings, of less breadth at the top than the bottom a feature which designates the old Pelasgic and Egyptian style of architecture. Arched windows, with carved mouldings and sculptured decorations, are sometimes to be met with; but these deviations from the general mode of building may, with great probability, be ascribed to the early Christian priests, who, in later years, converted them to the purposes of Christianity: for, as I have observed elsewhere, it was the policy of the Christian Missionaries not to destroy the reverence which the people entertained for their ancient places of worship, but to change the object of their adoration from a false to a true God. There are no traces of stairs in any of these towers, yet the interior has in many instances projecting rests at different heights, as if for flooring-joists to rest on. These pillar-towers are almost exclusively confined to Ireland. Two have been met with in Scotland,* but it is easy to imagine that the prevalent taste for such buildings in Ireland, would lead to their imitation in one or two instances in a country so nearly adjoining, and peopled from it. A few buildings somewhat resembling them, that is, long narrow towers, have been seen in the eastern countries, but none of them are of the construction which an observer acquainted with those in Ireland would pronounce at once, and without hesitation, to be a *Turaghan*† or Pillar-tower.

Such are the leading facts connected with them: the conjectures on their use are equally numerous and vague. They have been pronounced by some to have been the residences of hermits, like the *stylites*‡ of the eastern countries, who spent their lives on the tops of elevated pillars; but history affords no grounds on which to rest the opinion. If such had been their use, the names of some of the inmates of buildings, in whose construction so much expense and ingenuity had been employed, could not have passed away unnoticed. They are supposed by some to have been Danish watch or signal-towers; ** but their situation in low and sheltered places at once contradicts his supposition. They are also said to have been belfries; but it is apparent that their application to such a purpose must have been long subsequent to their erection, and only in a few instances, as the greater number of perfect towers now remaining exhibit no traces of the insertion of beams in the mason-work for the suspension of a bell : besides which, the silence of history, as to the period of their erection,

* One is situated at Brechin, the other at Abernethy.

† The name *Tur-aghan,* literally "the tower of fire," warrants the supposition, that these pillars were connected with the ancient worship of fire. The word *agh* signifying "fire" in the Irish language, is frequently found compounded in the names of places in whose vicinity traces of Druidic structures may be discovered; as *Aghadoe,* "the field of fire," near to which stands one of these towers.

‡ Mr. Harris conjectures that the round towers were erected for the reception of the "An chorite Monks, termed *Stylites,* from the practice of living in a pillar. Simeon an enthusiast of the fourth century, was the first who adopted this singular mode of penance.

* Peter Walsh and Doctor Molyneux, as well as Doctor Ledwich, who has examined all that has been written on the subject with much critical severity, are of opinion, that the first specimens in Ireland were erected by the Ostmen or Danes, and that the towers constructed by that people were "imitated by the Irish." A conclusive objection to this hypothesis is, that no towers of this description are found in the country from whence the Ostmen or Danes proceeded.

** Walsh and Ledwich agree, also, that these Danish-built towers were converted by the Christian Irish into "steeple-houses or belfries." The latter writer believes them to have been "common appendages to wooden churches," and thinks it probable that they served as belfries from the beginning, as some of them at this day certainly do. The absurdity of supposing that a church should be constructed of wood and the belfry of stone, is too palpable to require any refutation. General Vallancy, though he attributes them to Pagan origin, believes that they may have been applied to the use of bells before Christianity was introduced. "The same cause" he says, "existed, namely, that of calling the people to devotion. The Egyptians had their bells, and the Irish Ceol *(Keol)* a bell, was certainly derived from the Egyptian *Kel,* a bell.

furnishes undeniable negative evidence on the opinion, that they were originally built in the early ages of Christianity, for any ecclesiastical purpose whatever. The founding of cathedrals, churches, abbeys, hospitals, and even belfries, are carefully noted in the annals. The erection of a structure so singular as that of a Round Tower would surely not have been passed over in silence in every instance; we should have some note of a few of them at least. Although, therefore, they may have been applied to ecclesiastical uses by those who introduced Christianity into Ireland, or by some of their successors, there are no data for connecting their foundations or originality of purpose with that era.

The want of a satisfactory solution to this question, involving so much of the ancient history of Ireland, has not arisen from neglect; it has been often and laboriously mooted—much learning and research have been brought to bear upon it; indeed, no writer, affecting to treat of the antiquities of the country, would presume to pass an opinion on them, without taking cognizance of these great indexes of the antiquity of the national civilization. Every writer, therefore, from Cambrensis* down, has noted them more or less largely, and most have hazarded a theory upon them. Within the last few years the Royal Irish Academy offered a gold medal as a prize for the best Essay upon the subject. The bonus drew forth two candidates, Mr. O'Brien, a learned and enthusiastic young writer, and Mr. George Petrie, a gentleman distinguished as an artist and as a cautious inquirer into the native antiquities of his country :—to the Essay of the latter the Academy awarded the prize. It will be sufficient to observe on these papers, that Mr. Petrie contends for the Christian origin of the Round Towers, to which he does not assign an earlier date than the sixth century, founding his opinion upon the similarity of their architectural style with some authentic monuments of ecclesiastical construction, and also from the sculptures found upon several of them, which he insists were executed at the time of their being built: he also makes the period of their erection subsequent to the introduction of Christianity into Ireland. Mr. O'Brien, on the contrary, supports the opinion, that they were erected in the remote ages of Paganism. His theory supposes that all the various theological systems, which have divided the world up to the present time, are founded upon an allegory; and the Pillar-towers are an emblem of

---

* Giraldus Cambrensis, who wrote in 1185, is the earliest writer who notices these singular towers. He describes them as *"Turres ecclesiasticas, quæ, more patrio, aretæ sunt et altæ, necnon et rotundæ,"* i. e. *Ecclesiastical towers, built in a manner peculiar to the country, narrow, high, and round.* Beyond this meagre information, that they were considered as appendages to the ecclesiastical edifices of the twelfth century, we have no certain record of them; all the rest is entirely the offspring of conjecture and hypothesis.

General Vallancy was the first who broached the bold theory of attributing the erection of these towers to the Indo-Scythæ, a people from the borders of the Indus, who worshipped fire, and were the early colonists of Ireland. He contends, that, in ancient Ireland, as in ancient Persia, there were two sects of Fire-worshippers; one that lighted fires on the tops of the hills and mountains, and others in towers. The Pagan Irish worshipped *Crom-cruaith,* the same deity that Zoroaster adored in fire, first on the mountains, then in caves, and lastly in towers.

that allegory—multiplied personifications of the great object of worship, which has led away the bulk of mankind from the spiritual worship of the invisible God. It is not very easy, and still less desirable, to convey a palpable idea of the theory of this very learned, very ingenious, and very visionary writer; but it will suffice to say, that he has discovered an identity in the form of the towers to the Hindoo *Lingam,* and that their use "was that of a cupboard," to hold those figures, sacred to the Indo-Irish *Budha.* Mr. Windell, a recent writer, who has devoted much attention to the subject, rather coincides with Mr. O'Brien's opinion; he says, the Irish names of these towers "are of themselves conclusive, amid announce at once a fane devoted to that form of religion, compounded of Sabæism, or star-worship, and Budhism, of which the sun, represented by fire, was the principal deity in all the kindred mythologies of Persia, India, Ph Phrygia, Samothrace, and Ireland. This idolatry, in many respects, differed from, that of Gaul and Britain. Zoroaster was its grand reformer in Persia, and the reformation seems to have been accepted in Ireland."

The round towers of England, which are found chiefly in Norfolk and Suffolk, attached to the churches, and which, from a faint similarity to the pillar-towers of Ireland, have caused Ledwich and other antiquarians to believe they were identical in character, and all of ecclesiastical origin. A very slight inspection will, however, convince any person that these English towers, which are uniformly constructed in a. rude manner, and composed of flints, rough stones, chalk, and other coarse ingredients imbedded in mortar, are extremely unlike the well-executed pillar-towers of Ireland.

An opinion, which bears with it some show of probability, has been advanced latterly, namely, that these pillars were monuments erected over the graves of celebrated kings, priests, or heroes. Such a belief would not be at variance with the character of the Irish towers—human bones having been found interred beneath one at Ram Island, in Antrim; and similar relics, which had undergone the process of burning, have also been recently discovered under the tower at Timahoe. When we behold the stupendous pyramids of Egypt, which were doubtless intended only as sepulchres for. the dead; we need not feel any great surprise if these aspiring pillars of Ireland should have been devoted to the same monumental purpose. *

I shall now dismiss this interesting but perplexing inquiry, which there is little probability will ever lead to a solution of the enigma that has puzzled so many antiquarians.

Although several splendid views may be obtained of the Harbour and River of Cork from different points on the land; the tourist who wishes to behold them in perfection will step on board a boat, or one of the steamers which ply daily between Cork and Cove, as this course gives a perfect command of the picturesque scenery on both sides of the river, with infinitely superior effect. Arthur Young, an intelligent traveller, who visited Cork at a time when the shores of the river had received little improvement from the hand of art, remarks, "that the country on the harbour he thought to be preferable in many respects to anything he had seen in Ireland." Inglis yields to the scenery the full tribute of his admiration. And Milner speaking of it, says, "that neither the Severn at Chepstow, nor the sea at Southampton, are to be compared to it." Another writer adds, that "no part of the scenery is barren or uninteresting; a perpetual variety is presented along the whole course. The eye, whilst lingering over some happy picture, is continually attracted by some new succession, possessing all the charms of the most romantic landscape."

Leaving the quay at Cove, we pass the islands of Spike and Hawlbowline; the former is the larger and more important. It faces the entrance of the harbour, and acts as a breakwater, to shelter it from the violence of the southerly winds and the strong flood-tides. It is also happily situated for the defence of the harbour, and has been strongly fortified for that purpose. This island is at present garrisoned by a small military force.

Hawlbowline is a small, rocky islet to the west of Spike, which affords the same protection to the vessels in the harbour from the strong ebb-tides that Spike island does from the flood. At the commencement of the French war, government erected on Hawlbowline immense naval and ordnance stores, warehouses, and a barrack, which, in these "piping times of peace," are perfectly useless.

The southern shore of the great bason now extends on our left-hand, from the harbour's mouth to the village of Monkstown. The scenery here is exceedingly beautiful; demesnes rich in cultivated lawns, woods, and green pastures, stretching down to the water-side, arrest and charm the eye; while the broad expanse of the harbour, encircled by undulating hills, assumes all the features of a broad lake, and completes the noble picture.

Monkstown is a pleasant little village, delightfully situated in the opening of a lovely glen. Some modern cottages, built in the Swiss style, and a church of light and

---

* The following paragraph which appeared this year (1841) in an Irish Journal, is strongly corroborative of the theory above stated. "We learn that some time since, Mr. O'Dell, the proprietor of Ardmore, in the County of Waterford, intended to erect floors in the tower there, and explored the inferior of the tower down to the foundation. With considerable difficulty he caused to be removed a vast accumulation of small stones, under which were layers of large masses of rock, and having reached as low down as within a few inches of the external founda-tion, it was deemed useless, and dangerous to proceed any further; and in this opinion some members of the society, who had witnessed what had been done, coincided. In this state of the proceedings, a letter from Sir William Betham was forwarded to Mr. O'Dell, intimating that further exploration would be desirable; upon which the latter gentleman, at great peril, 'commenced the task again. He now found another series of large rocks, so closely wedged together, that it was difficult to introduce any implement between them. After considerable labour, these were also coved and at length a perfectly smooth floor of mortar was reached, which he feared must be regarded as a ne plus ultra, but still persevering, he removed the mortar, underneath which he found a bed of mould, and under this, some feet below the outside foundation, was discovered, lying prostrate from east to west, a human skeleton."

graceful proportions, on the slope above the town, give a highly picturesque appearance to the place when viewed from the river. The ancient castle of Monkstown—

"Bosomed deep in tufted trees"

stands in a commanding situation on the overhanging hill. It is a plain, square structure, and was founded by an ancestor of the Jephson family, in the reign of James I. A popular tradition exists in this neighbourhood, that the castle was built for *two-pence*. It is explained in the following way. Anastasia, the wife of Sir John Jephson, during the absence of her husband, who was serving in the army of Philip of Spain, resolved to surprise him on his return by building a stately castle, without diminishing his funds. To accomplish this, she compelled her tenants and workmen to purchase milk, vegetables, and other provisions, which were formerly given to them gratuitously by the former possessors of the estates: and, by this traffic, she realized a sum of money which enabled her to build the castle, and left her, on reckoning up the expense, a loser of only *two-pence*. The shore from Monkstown to Passage is extremely beautiful. Rock Lodge, the residence of Mr. Galwey, midway between these places, occupies one of the most picturesque situations on the river; viewed from thence, the wooded hill, rising precipitously from the water, has a noble appearance: a white walled bathing-lodge a rustic bridge, thrown across the deep channel of a brawling stream, a tea-house, and a mimic fortification, placed in different conspicuous parts of the wood, give a peculiar pleasing effect to the landscape; but the most remarkable features of this "romantic" spot are those immense masses of rock which nature has piled up from the water's edge, with such apparent regularity as to present, when viewed in profile, a striking resemblance to a succession of huge steps, from whence they have received the name of "The Giant's Stairs." Here, too, tradition has been busy; and the tales of the peasantry assign to a powerful giant, called *Mahoon,* the construction of these stupendous steps: they implicitly believe that he resides in a cave beneath the cliff, and they gravely relate the adventures of persons who have had the hardihood to enter his subterranean abode. Carrick Mahon, the seat of Mr. O'Grady, next attracts our attention: the house, though an unpretending building, forms, from its elevated situation, a pretty and remarkable object from the river. The improvements around it, I have learnt, are entirely owing to the taste of the present possessor; and the luxuriant trees and shrubs that now clothe the rich slopes to the water's edge, are the immediate successors of the unprofitable heath and ragged furze, which a few years since were the sole possessers of the uncultivated soil.

The town of Passage now meets our view; it is situated at the base of a steep hill, and is principally supported by the strangers who assemble here during the summer, and by the occasional resort of merchant-ships of large burthen, the river being too shallow to admit vessels drawing a great depth of water to proceed up to the quays

Cove Harbour

of Cork. The town, which extends about half a mile along the banks of the river, has a pretty effect viewed from the water; but it is irregularly built, and the streets are narrow and dirty, with the exception of the terraces at the northern and southern extremities of the town, which are occupied by bathers and strangers, and are healthful and picturesque locations. The distance between Passage and Cork being much shorter by land than water, a constant intercourse is kept up between these places by means of vehicles—inclosed with oilskin-curtains and drawn by one horse—called *jingles*. But for those who prefer a trip by water, boats of the best description, manned by hardy and expert fellows, may be had at a moment's notice. Indeed, this facility of procuring boats, and the beautiful scenery on the river, is a main cause of the general taste for aquatic amusements, which distinguish the inhabitants of Cork.

Although a passion for music is one of the striking characteristics of the Irish people, in no part of the country is the taste for this delightful accomplishment more generally cultivated than in this city. Music almost invariably forms a portion of their entertainments at home; and in their excursions on the river, it is rare, indeed, to find a party without vocal and instrumental performers amongst them. Nothing can be more delightful than to stand on the Glanmire shore on a calm summer's evening, when the last breath of the dying breeze, and the last motion of the flood-tide are rippling the little waves on the strand; and listen to the voices of the singers from the pleasure-boats gliding along the placid river, at greater or lesser distances. Sometimes, like the Venetian gondolas, the musicians in one boat join in concert with those in another; and, as their voices are generally harmonious and their taste correct, the effect of the melody is perfectly delicious, almost realizing Moore's fanciful simile, of those sweet sounds that come

— "Like the stealing
Of summer wind through some wreathed shell."

An extensive view of the river and the surrounding country may be obtained from the telegraph-station, which is situated on the summit of the steep hill that overhangs Passage:—the ascent to it is rather difficult, but the toil of the walk is amply compensated by the delightful prospect which it presents. Hill and dale, wood and water, noble mansions and lowly cottages, green fields and rugged rocks; the deep blue sea, stretching far away to the southward in immeasurable expanse; the silvery Lee beneath our feet, winding placidly between its picturesque banks;— beautiful islands, bays, and headlands, momentarily arrest our attention, and appear to compete for the tribute of our admiration. Such are generally the impressions that a spectator receives when the varied and imposing picture from this spot first meets his eye.

On the northern point of the Great Island, facing Passage, Merino, the residence of T. French, Esq., is beautifully situated close to the shore, and is surrounded by lofty trees, which grow down to the water-side. Doubling the point, you enter the little bay of Foaty. The water being shallow here, the ebb-tide leaves a great extent of muddy shore exposed, which materially disfigures the beauty of the scene; but, visited at high-water, the view of the bay and the adjacent scenery is really delightful. On the right, the woody point of Merino bends gracefully inward, as if wooing the truant waters to its fond embrace. On the left-hand, the fruitful fields of the Little Island and the handsome mansion of Captain Roche rise to view : further inward, on a low, sandy point, which at high tides becomes perfectly isolated; stands one of the Martello Towers, which the government engineers, during the late war, caused to be erected, at an enormous expense to the nation, along the coasts of the British islands, apparently as a means of defence, but in reality of no manner of use, except to serve as monuments of the folly of the men who projected them; and, like the Round Towers of Ireland, at some future day to puzzle posterity with vain conjectures as to their original use. At the upper end of the bay, in the demesne of Foaty, * a handsome castellated structure, built by J. S. Barry, Esq, forms a very striking feature in the landscape. It is designed as a pleasure-house for the accommodation of that gentleman and his friends in their aquatic excursions. Several long guns are planted in battery round the castle near the water, and others of smaller size frown threateningly from the battlements of the castle; but in justice to these peaceful days, when a man's house need not be turned into a domestic fortress, I may remark, that the greater number of these formidable pieces of ordnance are perfectly inoffensive, being what sailors call "Quakers."

Keeping along the northern shore of the bay from this point, we enter the east channel of the Great Island, which is not navigable at low-water, except for the smallest boats. About half a mile up, the channel is crossed by Belvelly Bridge, the only way by which land-travellers can enter the island or reach Cove. Near to the bridge on the island are the ruins of the old castle of Belvelly, erected by the Hodnett family in the fourteenth century. It consists of a single square tower, still in tolerable preservation; but it appears never to have been a place of much strength or consequence.

Let us now retrace our course down the channel and across the smooth bay of Foaty, until we regain the centre of the river, and pause a few moments to admire the picturesque appearance of the town of Passage, stretching in detached clusters of houses along the shore, or dotting the sides of the hills :—then resuming our progress on ward, we pass the mansion of Boland, Esq., pleasantly situated in an extensive lawn studded with noble trees, which shelter and beautify the place. We next reach a conspicuous promontory, called Horse Head, crowned with handsome villas, which have a noble and elegant appearance. A pretty little

* I have already slightly alluded to the demesne of Foaty, as seen from the land on the road from Cork to Cove, p. 68.

cottage *ornée* occupies a charming nook near this spot; it is tastefully embellished, and sheltered by the picturesque rocks which overhang it, forming a most pleasing object in the landscape.

We now enter upon a part of the river lying between the Great Island and Black Rock, called Lough Mahon, from the ancient family of the Mahonys having formerly held large possessions in its vicinity, as well as from the resemblance it bears to a broad lake when sailing across it. "The whole," says Mr. Windle, "seems landlocked, enclosed on several sides by high hills, and on others, by wooded slopes stretching far inland to the foot of other chains of hills. Turn which side you will, the scenery is of the most charming description. Looking up towards the city, Black Rock Castle stands finely out, backed by woods and distant hills. The wood-crowned eminences of Lota and Dunkettle appear beside it with the finest effect."

Old Court, the seat of Sir George Gold, is magnificently situated on a *finely*-wooded eminence on the southern shore of the lough, and near it lies a little islet covered with trees, which has received the whimsical name of *Hop* Island, from its being the property of a Mr. Delamaine, the son or descendant of a man who formerly kept a *dancing* academy in Cork.

The Castle of Black Rock, a conspicuous and beautiful object, as we approach the city, is picturesquely situated on the extremity of a peninsula. It was originally intended as a fortress for the defence of this part of the river, but the taste of the good citizens of Cork being more pacific now than formerly, the corporation have latterly converted it, at considerable expense, into a handsome structure, where they hold a court of Admiralty annually, and assemble at certain periods in summer for the discussion of the more important business of eating and drinking. Adjoining to the castle is a lofty tower, in which a light is exhibited at night for the guidance of vessels coming up the river. The shores on the right-hand increase in beauty as we proceed upward. Opposite to the village and castle of Black Rock, the romantic river of Glanmire mingles its waters with the Lee. From this point the hills are thickly clothed with woods, groves, gardens, parks, plantations, and tasteful pleasure-grounds. Handsome villas are seen peeping through the tufted trees in every direction; many of them splendid, and all picturesquely situated; but the most conspicuous are Lota, the seat of D. Callaghan, Esq.; Lotamore, the residence of W. Green, Esq., and Tivoli, the seat of J. Morgan, Esq. The Lee, near Cork, is confined by a navigation-wall on the left-hand, for the purpose of narrowing the current of the river, which would otherwise waste itself over the extensive shallows that extend at the back of the wall, towards the village of Douglas. We are now arrived at the quays of Cork, and after having glanced at the principal beauties of this interesting river, we return to the point from whence we started, and find ourselves again at the mouth of the harbour.

Cork harbour being the most important, not only with regard to its commerce, and as being the embouchure of a beautiful river, but as being excelled by no other in its advantages as a spacious and secure port. I shall, from this point, as from an eminence, take a rapid glance at those noble havens which indent the southern and western coasts of Ireland. In doing so, some of the places that I shall have occasion to mention may be found noticed in another part of this work; however, as a great portion of the beauties of the country lie on the coast, and in the numerous and picturesque islands with which it is studded, I trust that none of my readers will feel indisposed to accompany me in my progress. Sailing eastward from Cork harbour, the first opening that presents itself to our notice is Ballycotton Bay; bleak, low, unsheltered, and almost devoid of scenic beauty, but abounding with fish of excellent quality. We next arrive at Youghal Harbour; the bold outline of the beetling cliffs, jutting out in dark defiance of the ocean swell, is extremely fine; and the effect is heightened by the beacon-towers with which the heights are crowned. These are so placed, that a train of signal-lights can be illuminated almost instantaneously along the whole range of the northern coast. They consist, in addition to the low-built residences, of an officer and a few soldiers, of a lofty tower, surmounted by a tall staff, on which a flag by day, and coloured lamps by night, may be raised in case of alarm. Each was also provided during the late war with a large pile of furze, for the purpose of being set fire to, in case of the appearance of an enemy's fleet. Youghal is a place of little maritime trade; as a harbour it is chiefly resorted to by fishing-boats. These craft, called *hookers,* are generally from ten to twenty tons burthen, and are open, with the exception of a few feet of deck in the forepart of the boat, beneath which is a small cuddy or cabin, in which the crew repose during the brief intermission of their toil while engaged in fishing. The boats are rigged cutter-fashion, with a large fore-and-aft mainsail, a foresail, and a jib; and though without the defence of a deck, it is almost incredible in what a heavy sea they will live. The Youghal *hookers* are esteemed the best and most seaworthy boats built on this coast. The Nymph Bank, an immense shoal lying some leagues out at sea, and extending as far eastward as Waterford Harbour, feeds an inexhaustible stock of fish of every kind, both round and flat; yet, strange to say, little advantage is taken of it by the fishermen of the coast, although great numbers of them go yearly from the counties of Waterford and Wexford to Newfoundland on the other side of the Atlantic, to procure a livelihood by the capture of the very same kinds of fish that are sporting about untouched and unthought of, almost within view of their native cottages and home. Why is this so? Not from want of enterprise or industry. Newfoundland proves this; yet there must be reasons for it. These might be analyzed, but my purpose at present is to explore, not to speculate. Rounding a bluff promontory called Helvoeck Head, we enter Dungarvan Bay, which, though open and safe, is shallow, and therefore useless, to vessels of large burthen. Thirty or forty years ago, Dublin derived its principal supply of potatoes from this port; the coasting craft in which they were carried, also brought

The Cork River

Yonghall Abbey

large quantities of heath-brooms. Hence it became a standing joke with the waggish crews of these traders, when they were hailed by the revenue-officer at Ringsend, on their entering the river Liffey, and asked,what cargo they had on board, to answer "Fruit and timber." Dungarvan was a place of some note during the civil wars, and the remains of the ancient walls may yet be traced. The castle, of which vestiges are still visible, is situated in the centre of the town, and is used for military purposes. Dungarvan is much frequented during the summer months by sea-bathers; but, like all the small towns on the coast, it draws its chief support from its fishing-resources. There are at present upwards of two hundred boats, and from one thousand four hundred to one thousand six hundred persons engaged in the trade, which would, under proper regulations and encouragement, become a means of great wealth to the poor inhabitants of the maritime counties of the south and west of Ireland.

Continuing our course along this iron-bound coast, a succession of magnificent scenes, formed by a number of deep bays, separated from each other by headlands projecting boldly into the ocean, present themselves to the eye of the spectator. Some of these havens, however beautiful to the eye, are carefully avoided by experienced mariners. Of this description is Tramore Bay, lying about four miles west of the harbour of Waterford, which has become infamous from the immense number of shipwrecks that have occurred in it. The bay is extremely shallow, and at low water a level sandy beach, nearly three miles in length, is left completely exposed. A vast ridge of sand, which has been accumulated by the action of the wind and waves at high-water-mark, forms a semicircular boundary to the bay on the land side. Behind this sandy belt is another great extent of land, rendered waste and profitless by the constant inroads of the sea through a narrow inlet, called Rineshark, at the eastern extremity of the bay. The rapidity with which the flood-tide rushes into this inlet, and spreads over the adjacent flat sands, operating jointly with the heavy sea, renders it almost impossible for a ship, when caught in the bay, to extricate itself by working to windward: and the ground is so foul and rocky, that the cables of vessels anchoring outside are frequently cut, and the ships lost. A melancholy shipwreck took place in this bay in 1816, when the Sea-horse transport, having on board the second battalion of the fifty-ninth foot, was driven on shore, and two hundred and ninety-two men and seventy-one women and children perished in the open day under the eyes of thousands of spectators, who were unable to afford them the slightest assistance. This shocking catastrophe created general consternation, and such was the sympathy felt for the fate of the brave fellows who had escaped death in many a bloody and well-fought battle in foreign climes, to meet it on the shores of their native land, that, for many years after the calamity, Tramore was almost completely deserted by the visitors, who, previous to it used to resort to it annually as an agreeable and fashionable watering-place. A plain unpretending monument has been erected in the church over their less fortunate companions, by the officers who escaped with life on that fatal day.

The next opening of the coast displays the noble harbour of Waterford, formed by

Waterford

the estuary of three great rivers: the Suir, the Nore, and the Barrow :—they all derive their sources from the same range of mountains in the central district of Ireland; diverge from each other, and water various parts of the rich champaign counties of Tipperary and Kilkenny; after which, approximating as they approach the termination of their meandering course, they unite and discharge an immense body of water into the Atlantic. The coasts of this noble bay are studded with the remains of ancient civilization, both religious and military; and the fine city of Waterford, which lies on the southern bank of the river Suir, about sixteen miles from the entrance of the harbour, forms the centre of commercial and manufacturing industry for this part of the kingdom.

The little village of Dunmore East lies in a sheltered bay inside the great western headland of Waterford harbour. This place was merely an obscure little fishing-hamlet twenty-five years ago; but an immense sum having been expended by government in constructing there an artificial harbour, and making it the station for the Post-office packets between Milford and Waterford, it has risen rapidly into importance, and aided by the improving care of the Marquis of Waterford arid the Earl of Fortescue, to whom the greater portion of the land in this neighbourhood belongs, it is likely to become, before long, a thriving and prosperous town. The shores here are extremely picturesque, and the natural caves formed by the action of the waves in the stupendous cliffs, are numerous and extensive: their principal tenants are marine birds, and occasionally seals; though they are said to have not unfrequently afforded asylums to the bands of smugglers that formerly infested this coast, and secure store-houses for their contraband merchandize, which, on being landed from the smuggling vessels, was generally deposited in these natural caverns, until it could be safely carried inland, and disposed of in various channels.

On the opposite point of the bay stands the Light-house of Hook, situated at the extremity of a narrow peninsula, which projects about four miles from the main land, and forms the eastern shore of the harbour. This light-house, which is very ancient, is an important feature in the navigation of this coast. It is upwards of one hundred feet in height, and has evidently been erected upon the remains of a still more antique building. It has been conjectured that one of the old Irish

Round Towers was converted to this purpose; but there is nothing in its structure to warrant such an opinion : it is more likely that it owes its origin to the Danes, who, it is known, formed a settlement at Waterford under their leader Yvorus, at a very early period, and whose maritime habits would naturally induce them to erect a beacon or light-house at the entrance of the principal seaport which had come under their sway.

I must not, however, omit a romantic and affecting story that has been related respecting the foundation of this light-house, upon the veracity of which I do not, however, mean to insist. The tradition states that an ancient castle once stood on this spot. It belonged to a noble Irish lady, who resided in it, and had two sons. When grown up to manhood they went abroad, and continuing absent a long time, the mourning mother often looked from her castle,

" O' er the dark waters of the deep blue sea,"

for their coming; but in vain. At length, apprised that they were on their voyage home from some distant land, she made joyful preparations to receive them. In a dark and fearful night their vessel approached the treacherous shores on the eastern side of Hook. No light in the castle appeared—nothing warned them of their danger. Need I relate the fatal catastrophe?—they perished! From that time the widowed and disconsolate mother carefully exhibited a light in her castle of Hook on dark and dangerous nights; a memorial of her own lamentable loss, and a pious endeavour to preserve other distressed mariners from the cruel fate of her sons. The modern light-house is a fine building, and from its commanding situation, can be seen at a great distance from sea. A dangerous reef of sunken rocks, called St. Bride's Bridge, stretches to the south-east from Hook Head : when the wind blows towards the shore, the sea breaks over these rocks with prodigious violence.

About four miles from Hook Tower* is Bag-en-bon Head, a small promontory, celebrated as the spot where Robert Fitzstephen landed; "the first of all English-men, after the conquest, that entered Ireland," as Hollingshed quaintly observes. In the summer of 1169, he embarked at Milford Haven in three ships, with thirty knights, sixty men-at-arms, and three hundred men-at-arms, and, after a speedy and prosperous voyage, landed at Bag-en-bon, a small creek at the mouth of the river Banna,† or Bannow, as it is now written. His first care was to secure himself and his followers from a sudden attack, by establishing his temporary quarters upon the extremity of the promontory, and throwing a rude ditch in front of this camp across its neck. With this small expedition came Hervey de Montmorency, the uncle of Strongbow, a wise and valiant commander. The following day Maurice de Pendergast, a Welsh gentleman, landed at the same place with a reinforcement of ten knights and two hundred archers, and Maurice Fitzgerald, with ten knights, thirty horsemen, and about one hundred archers, shortly after came to their assistance. These troops, few in number, but well disciplined, immediately entered on active

* It has been conjectured by the Chevalier de Montmorency, that the name is properly *Hougue* tower, and that it is so called after an Anglo-Norman knight, named Florence de Ia Hougue who, in 1172, followed Henry II. into Ireland, and laid the foundation of this building.

† *"The Banks of Banna"* have been celebrated in the sweetly pastoral ballad, so called, written by Mr. OgIe, a gentleman of this county. The green shores, spreading along the edge of the great ocean, are in themselves full of the wild and striking beauties of nature. They arerichly wooded, and produce a diversity of rich and beautiful scenery, which will scarcely sink in estimation when compared with river-views more celebrated, because situated in parts of the island more frequently visited.

service, in conjunction with the subjects of Dermot, the traitor-king of Leinster, who had invited them into Ireland. "Such," observes a modern historian, "was the original scheme of an invasion, which in the event proved of so great importance. An odious fugitive, driven from his province by faction and revenge, gains a few adventurers in Wales, whom youthful ardour or distress of fortune led into Ireland, in hopes of some advantageous settlement." It is not my intention to follow these brave soldiers through their arduous struggles before they obtained a partial footing in the country; but I may add, that the memorable arrival of Fitzstephen and his followers at this place, has given rise to the well-known proverb—

> "At the head of Bag-en-bon
> Ireland was lost and won."

The Saltees are a cluster of uninhabited islands, lying about three miles from the shore; they are of trifling extent and difficult access, scarcely worthy of special notice, had they not acquired a melancholy notoriety by having teen the place of concealment for the unfortunate Bagenal Harvey and John Colclough, two gentlemen of birth and fortune, in the county Wexford, who were unhappily seduced or intimidated to take part in the Rebellion of 1798. After the town of Wexford had been retaken by the king's forces, Harvey and Colclough escaped, and took refuge in one of these islands. Mrs. Harvey and a maid-servant accompanied these two fugitives to their retreat, which was a cavern, so ingeniously contrived by nature, that it was next to an impossibility to discover the entrance to it. They had provisions for six months, with all their plate and money, and so complete was their concealment, that, although government had information that they were hidden in the island, and had offered a reward of £3,000 for their apprehension, they continued to elude the vigilance of the crews of the king's cutters, who, day after day, traversed every nook and corner in the island without obtaining the slightest trace of them. At length the discovery of their retreat was made by accident, and through the incautiousness of the servant who had spilled suds at the mouth of the cave, the traces of which were detected by three officers, who had been sporting on the island. Their suspicions were naturally excited, and by drawing aside some tall heath, which appeared growing out of the face of the rock, they discovered the entrance to the cavern. They entered immediately, and called on those within to surrender, telling them that resistance was useless, as the cave was surrounded by armed men, and that they would be fired on if they gave any indications of resistance. On this they submitted; but on quitting the cave, they appeared extremely mortified at not seeing the force they were led to expect, as they were well supplied with arms and ammunition for their defence. They were led to a small boat, which was waiting for the officers, and lodged securely in Wexford. The remainder of this tragical tale is history.

In a statistic return, made by the incumbent of the parish to which these islands are attached, they are said to form a part of the inland county Tipperary; but the authority upon which this strange allocation is founded, is not stated.

The coast eastward from Bannow is low and flat, presenting few features of pictorial interest, until we reach the Tuskar light-house, built on a small island-rock, lying off Carnsore Point, which forms the south-eastern angle of Ireland. From this point the shore bends suddenly northward, and we soon enter the picturesque harbour of Wexford, through a narrow inlet. "It is formed," says Mr. Hay, "by two narrow necks of land bending towards each other, like two arms closing after an extension from the body, which appearance the river's mouth assumes by its banks, not very unlike the old Piræus of Athens. The extremities of these peninsulas, denominated the Raven on the north and Roslare on the south, form the entrance into the harbour, which is about a mile and a half broad, defended by a fort erected at the point of Roslare."

The bay, into which the river Slaney discharges itself, is spacious, and well defended from the sea; but the obstruction of a bar of shifting sand near the entrance, and the shallowness of the water in the harbour, which will not allow vessels of more than two hundred tons burthen to enter it, has considerably lessened the advantages which it would otherwise have derived from its excellent situation in a commercial point of view.* The town of Wexford is of great antiquity, and was possessed at an early period by the Danish settlers in Ireland; and that it was long the emporium of the south-eastern part of the country, and the principal port of passage between England and Ireland, there are abundant evidences to prove.† The town was anciently surrounded by walls, some traces of which are still discernible; but a large part of the modern town lies outside of the former mural lines of defence.

That portion of the county of Wexford which forms the line of coast between the harbours of Waterford and Wexford comprehends the baronies of Forth and Bargie, the inhabitants of which are so distinguished by some striking peculiarities from the natives of the other parts of the island, that I cannot pass it by unnoticed. These two baronies, called emphatically (the *English* settlement,) were granted by Dermott Mac Murrough to Harvey de Monte Maresco, who planted there the first English colony nearly seven hundred years ago. Since that time the inhabitants of this district have preserved themselves in a distinct community as regards habits and manners, until a very recent period; whereas, in other parts of the island, the customs and language of the new settlers gradually merged into those of the people with whom they had

---

* This shallowness of the harbour, according to Mr. Beaufort, was the origin of the present name of the town, *Wexford.* "It was founded," he asserts, "in the ninth century, by a colony of Ostmen, Danes or Frisians, on a bay denominated *Garman,* but by them Wæsfiord or Wash-ford; which imports a bay formed by the tide, but left nearly dry at low-water, and in this sense the same as the English washes of Cambridgeshire and Lincolnshire."

become identified. The reproach that they had become "more Irish than the Irish," made by Hollinshed and other writers against the English who had fallen into the Irish habits, leads us to conclude, that there must have been some strong attraction in the wild exciting mode of life of the natives, which could induce men to relapse from what has been called civilization into a state of comparative barbarism. It is not, however, difficult to conceive, from the graphic pictures which the master hand of Scott has drawn of the battles, forays, huntings, and feastings of a Highland chieftain and his faithful adherents, that the charms of such a life would very soon draw men from the trammels which society in a more advanced state imposes. We have every day instances in the back woods of America, of the facility with which people accommodate themselves to a semi-barbarous life, and the reluctance they feel at being obliged to relinquish it, and conform to the irksome conventionalities of the world.

Through some means or another, the descendants of the colonists of this little corner of the island retained the customs and dialect of their forefathers until the middle of the eighteenth century.‡ The description given in the subjoined note of the habits and manners of the inhabitants of these remote baronies would not apply to the present time, as the gradual interchanges of society, which have taken place within the last half-century, have caused the abandonment of many of the peculiarities of this primitive and industrious people. The late eccentric and unfortunate J. B. Trotter, in his Pedestrian Tour through Ireland, in the year 1817, has made some excellent observations upon this district, which he calls "the Flanders of Ireland." But even at the time he visited it, the ancient customs had begun to disappear, for he

† It was here that the slave-merchants assembled the serfs or slaves which they had purchased in England. "Here might be seen," says an old Monkish writer, "whole ranks of fine, young men and beautiful women, exposed to sale in the slave-market on the hill. They were sold in part to the Irish noblesse and herdsmen, while others fell to the share of foreign merchants, and were exhibited in the slave-marts of Rome and Italy."

‡ General Vallancey, in a paper contained in the second volume of the Transactions of the Royal Irish Academy, makes the following curious remarks on the state of this singular colony:

"When we were first acquainted with it, a few of both sexes wore the ancient dress; that of the men was a short coat, waistcoat, and trunk-breeches, with a round hat and narrow brim. That of the women, was a short jacket, a petticoat bordered at the bottom with one, two, or three rows of ribband or tape of a different colour; the dress of the head was a kireher. The people of these baronies live well, are industrious, cleanly, and of good morals; the poorest farmer eats meat twice a week, and the table of the wealthy farmer is daily covered with beef, mutton, or fowl. The beverage is a home-brewed ale; of an excellent flavour and colour. The houses of the poorest are well built and well thatched; all have out-offices for cattle, fowls, carts, or cars. The people, who are well-clothed, are strong and laborious. The women do all manner of rustic work, ploughing excepted, and receive equal wages with the men. The professed religion here is the Roman Catholic: there are about one hundred Catholics to one Protestant. Marriage is solemnized much in the same manner as with the Irish. The relations and friends bring a profusion of viands of all kinds, and feasting and dancing continue all the night; the bride sits veiled at the head of the table, unless called out to dance, when the chair is filled by one of the bride-maids. At every marriage an apple is cut into small pieces and thrown among the crowd. This custom they brought with them from England; the origin of it has not descended with it."

says, "It is observable that the English and Irish customs are happily blended here. Neither are conquered, but both harmoniously assimilated. There is all the valuable independence of character which has made England a great nation; and there is a great deal of the sweetness and pleasantness of the Irish mind and manner united to it. Their accent is very peculiar, but we heard nothing of the ancient dialect. It appeared to us very like the retired mountaineers of Wales speaking English; the tone and pronunciation was nearly the same." This peculiarity in the mode of speaking English is unlike anything heard in other parts of Ireland; neither have the people here ever adopted the Irish tongue. The language which anciently prevailed in this district is said to be a dialect of the Anglo-Saxon mingled with Welsh. General Vallancey has published a Vocabulary of the language of Forth and Bargie, which shows its close affinity to the Anglo-Saxon;* and the Count de Montmorency asserts that some traces of this ancient dialect are still to be found amongst the lower orders of the people in Somersetshire. The original settlers who followed Fitzstephen and Hervey de Montmorency, being composed of adventurers from Pembrokeshire and Somersetshire, the intermixture of the Welsh with the English language is clearly accounted for.

Amongst the minor peculiarities which distinguish the peasantry of this district, the custom of regularly going to bed for about two hours after dinner during the summer season, prevailed until a very recent period. In consequence of this indulgence, the farm-labourers were used to work until a late hour in the evening. Wherever this practice is retained, the doors' are closed, and a silence, like that of deep night, reigns at mid-day. Notwithstanding the amalgamation which is gradually taking place between those descendants of the first English settlers and the native Irish, there are still some striking traits which distinguish them from each other. The people of Forth, unlike the old Irish, are exceedingly temperate; they are shy and distant in their manner, as if unused to the world, and have none of the easy familiarity of their more volatile neighbours. In stature and personal appearance they are inferior to the Irish, and are generally fair-haired, with rather broad faces and ruddy complexions, forming a marked contrast to the dark hair and long visages of the descendants of the ancient Milesians. The villages of Forth closely resemble Welsh hamlets; the cottages are nearly all whitewashed, and their household utensils are bright and clean. The women employ much of their time in knitting and in field-labour, the men being for the most part engaged in fishing.

---

* The Rev. W. Eastwood, who wrote the Statistical Survey of some of the parishes in the barony of Forth, observes, that being in a field on his farm, reading Chaucer's Canterbury Tales, and near to the labourers, who were conversing in the ancient language of the south of Wexford; it chanced that he threw his eve towards some words that he fancied might resemble those they were repeating if sounded. He arrested their attention whilst he read the lines, and discovered "that they were fully competent to interpret, explain, and even to translate every line and passage." The same writer notices the simple form of salutation which prevails amongst these people. On meeting, one asks the other, *"Is it long since?"* meaning—Do you consider the time heavy since we parted?—the artless and courteous reply is, *"Yea joi."*

I must now request my readers to return with me to the entrance of Cork harbour, (from whence we have been coasting eastward,) and to accompany me in my progress along the wild shores and noble bays that lie westward of that point Oyster Haven and Roberts's Cove are the first inlets that we meet; the latter is known as a picturesque creek, visited during the summer by water-parties from Cork. Kinsale comes next in order,* and though its harbour is not so capacious as that of Cork, it is of sufficient depth for the reception of vessels of the largest size. It is protected by a strong fortification on the eastern side of the harbour, called Charles Fort, in honour of Charles II. during whose reign it was built. The south side of the harbour is defended by a bold promontory, which runs a considerable way into the sea, and is well known to mariners as the Old Head of Kinsale.† A fine light-house is erected on the extremity of the headland. On this promontory also stood the ancient residence of the Lords of Kinsale. Smith, the historian of Cork, says, that the castle was formerly called Duncearma, and that in old records it is described as having been "a royal seat of the kings of Ireland." From the situation of this fastness it is fearfully exposed to the assaults of the elements, and its rude and weatherbeaten appearance agrees well with the bleakness and desolation by which it is surrounded. The coast here begins to assume the stern features which characterize the western shores; among the cliffs are found eyries or hawks, and of that large species of the osprey, commonly called the sea-eagle. Court-macsherry is a mere fishing-hamlet, adjoining to the marine villa of the Earl of Shannon. Sailing round an irregularly-shaped peninsula, we enter Clonakilty Bay, a place of little consideration in a commercial

---

* Kinsale was, in times long past, the most celebrated port on the southern coast of Ireland, and in consequence of the superiority it then possessed as a place of debarkation, it was not unfrequently the scene of events important in the history of Ireland. In 1601 a large Spanish force, under the command of Don Juan D'Aquila, landed, and took possession of Kinsale, where they were besieged by the Lord Deputy Mountjoy, and the Lord President Sir George Carew. A victory obtained by the English forces over the insurgent army of Tyrone and O'Donnel, who had marched to the assistance of the invaders, caused the latter to surrender the town after they had kept possession of it for more than three months. In March 1689, James II. landed at Kinsale from Brest, with the vain hope of recovering in Ireland the crown he had lost in England. The town was held in his name by Sir Edward Scot, who maintained it for twenty-four days against the army of William III., commanded by the Earl of Marlborough and the Prince of Wirtemberg, and so gallantly was the defence conducted, that the gar-rison, consisting of one thousand two hundred men, was allowed to march out of the town with arms and baggage.

† Sir Henry Sidney, who made a progress through Ireland in the early part of Elizabeth's reign, speaking of Kinsale with regard to its natural capabilities of defence, says, "The Old Head, six miles distant beyond the town, is one of the *forticablest places* that I ever came in."

It may be appropriately remarked, that the gloomy and troubled spirit of Swift was soothed into repose by the sublime and awful grandeur of this region. It is related, that he passed several months of the year 1723, at the house of a clergyman in this neighbourhood, and was particularly gratified by making little voyages along the coast from Glandon harbour towards Baltimore. The mingled charms and terrors displayed to the voyager between those places, he has celebrated in an elegant Latin Poem, entitled *Carberiæ Rupes,* which has been translated into English by the Rev. Dr. Dunkin.

point of view, but possessed of rare attractions for the antiquarian and painter. The country along the shores of the bay is singularly varied, and broken into picturesquely shaped hills; the vales are watered by many nameless brooks and rivulets, and the coast presents a succession of bold cliffs, whose romantic beauty charm and astonish the spectator. Galley Head, a noble promontory jutting boldly into the sea, as if to impede our further progress, is doubled at length, and we enter a splendid bay, which contains within it the lesser harbours of Ross and Glandon. A line of coast more bold, various, and rich in marine scenery can scarcely be imagined than that which now opens on the sight; winding wooded inlets of the sea, which Mr. Inglis says, reminds him of the Norwegian fords, penetrate into the land, and form creeks and coves of unequalled beauty. To a mind prepared by its native energies, or by a cultivated taste for the sublime, the coast-scenery here will yield a feast of almost inexhaustible delight.

Leaving the Stags of Castlehaven behind us, we next pass Baltimore Bay, a safe asylum for inward and outward-bound American vessels. I shall not, however, delay to enumerate the endless bays and islands that are clustered along this coast, but hasten at once to the romantic island of Cape Clear, known since Ireland was first visited by mariners, and now more conspicuous by a bright revolving light, announcing to the mariner, long tossed on the "storm-vexed" Atlantic, the cheering tidings of his approach to home. This land was once thought to be the most southern point of Ireland; incorrectly though, as it is now generally known to be an island, and the honour of fixing the extreme southern termination of the beautiful "jern of the sea," has been generally transferred to Mizen Head. But this is also geographically incorrect, for the more accurate observations of modern days have ascertained that the neighbouring promontory of Brow Head, next to it eastward, is by a few seconds more south then Mizen Head, and therefore entitled to the distinction of being named the most southern point of Ireland. Cape Clear is, indeed, a curious place. It is scarcely three miles long, and not more than one and a half wide; high, rugged, and precipitous, accessible only by two coves on opposite sides of the island, which, trenching deep into the land, nearly divide it into two, giving it an appearance somewhat similar to that of an immense wasp. On the summit of its highest cliff is a lake, said to be endued with the singular and almost invaluable quality of purifying any vessel that is plunged into it. Train-oil casks, it is asserted, when suffered to lie in it for a few days, are fit, without further preparation, for the reception of new milk. The inhabitants, who do not amount to more than nine hundred, are a hardy and primitive people; they contrive to support themselves by fishing, and by cultivating the few patches of productive land that the island contains. The chief family anciently residing on it was that of O'Driscoll,* a race of gigantic size and strength, as is testified by the bones of one of their chieftains, still preserved. This dynasty ruled their limited dominion by laws peculiar to themselves; some of them appear singularly amusing: for instance, the punishment for offences of peculiar turpitude, was transportation to the main land. Life out of the island was deemed more insufferable than death within it :—a fine illustration of that attachment which nature has implanted in man's heart for the spot which he calls his *home.* Though to other eyes it may appear rude, barren, and unlovely; it possesses for him all the charms of Paradise— outside which there is no happiness to be found. The native of the frozen zone pants for the pleasure of guiding his fleet reindeer across trackless wastes of snow—the South Sea Islander delights to paddle his slight canoe through the flashing breakers—the Red Indian loves the deep forest solitudes—the Arab, the wide and sandy desert:

> "Thus every good his native wilds impart,
> Imprints the patriot passion in his heart;
> And e'en those ills that round his mansion rise,
> Enhance the bliss his scanty fund supplies."

During the wars of Elizabeth this little island had its stirring history, which wants only a pen like his who threw a charm over the cold and barren Orkneys, to immortalize persons, places, and circumstances, now known only to the curious inquirer into Ireland's romantic legends.

To proceed :—Dunmanus Bay is the first harbour of any note we meet after doubling Mizen Head; but though both large and safe, it is little frequented by vessels. So well is it sheltered by the surrounding mountains and the outstretching headlands, that it has all the appearance of an extensive lake when viewed from several points on the shore. On the eastern shore of the bay are the ruins of a fortress, called Dunmanus Castle. It was built by the O'Mahony sept, and was formerly a place of some strength. Dunmanus Bay is separated from that of Bantry by a narrow rugged peninsula, of which Sheep Head forms the extreme headland.

We have now reached Bantry Bay. I have already described this noble spreading bay as viewed from the land, but it presents so many new and magnificent features to the spectator, sailing up from the entrance of the harbour to the town of Bantry, who has leisure to behold the picturesque and varied shores of this great estuary, that I cannot pass them by without briefly noticing them. The length of the bay exceeds thirty miles, in breadth it varies from three to eight miles, and in some places it is forty fathoms in depth. The shores of this vast sheet of water are agreeably

---

* O'Driscoll's castle is well suited in situation to the daring character which tradition has assigned to the tribe to whom it belonged . The ruins are seated on a lofty rock, overhanging the sea at the south-western extremity of the island. It is approached in no other way than by a narrow path on a ledge of rock, about thirty feet in length. This passage is high and steep on both sides, whilst the waters roar beneath on either hand, Towards the ocean, the rock on which the castle stands is quite precipitous. Even when the wind is quiet, the Atlantic is subject to a prodigious swell, and in the calmest weather its waves break against this rock with a violence that resounds along the shore to a great distance.

diversified; on the north side, the mountain barriers which confine it seem to start up precipitously from the water's edge, and give a wild and impressive character to the scenery. At the north-eastern extremity, the junction of the mountain streams that rush from the romantic Glengariffe form a lesser bay of great beauty. The scenery in the vicinity of the town is softer and more graceful than on the opposite shore; the grounds and demesne of the Earl of Bantry, which adjoins the town, sweep in the fine wooded undulations and beautiful glades down to the margin of the bay. Around all, the blue lofty chain of Killarney and the Reeks, Glengariffe and Gougaun-Barra, with other mountains of the boldest and most fantastic outlines, gird, as it were, with a zone, this magnificent picture. The bay is studded with islands, of which Bere Island and Whiddy are the principal. The first, which is bold and rocky, lies close under the northern shore in an arm of the bay, called Berehaven: the second is of lesser extent, but greater fertility than Bere Island. It is situated opposite to Glengariffe at the head of the bay, and consists of three gently undulating hills, the centre one of them being crowned with the ruins of an old castle, erected by the O'Sullivans* in the reign of Henry VI.

In quitting Bantry Bay, I feel that I shall be quite unable to convey to my readers a perfect idea of the wild magnificence of the coast-scenery of this district. Filled with unspeakable awe and admiration at the majesty and vastness of the picture, the spectator at first cannot find language to express the impressions he has received, and it is only by repeated inspection that he becomes able to separate and analyse the multitude of images and emotions that crowd upon his mind. As we continue our course northward, we find the leading characteristics of wildness and grandeur still preserved in the aspect of the coast. The stupendous masses of rock which form headlands, and protect the numerous bays against the mighty waves of the Atlantic; the rocky mountains, which line the shores of the bays and harbours, and the wild mountain solitudes between the Bantry and the northern confines of Kerry, are as fertile in scenes of bold and striking grandeur as the most ardent admirer of pictorial sublimity could desire.

Along the coast of Kerry are the protecting harbours of Kenmare, a long and beautiful estuary, called a river: Kilmashallog, Sneem, Ballinskellig, Valentia, Dingle, Ventry, Castlemaine, Dunmore, Smerwick, Brandon, and Tralee. Of these Ballinskellig Bay is the first we meet of any importance. It is a spacious haven, almost entirely encompassed by lofty mountains. The shores, which stretch out into headlands, are bold and varied, and the islets with which the spacious basin is agreeably diversified, add much to the beauty of the scenery. On the green margin of

---

* The greater part of the south-western extremity of the county of Cork, comprehending an extensive line of sea-coast, was once the territory of the family of O'Sullivan. This powerful sept was divided into two branches, who were distinguished from the locality of their possessions, as O'Sullivan *Bear* or *Bere,* and O'Sullivan *Bantry.* They were persevering in their hostility to the English, but, failing in their attempts to overthrow the power of the invaders, only hastened their own downfall.

a sheltered creek, running in from this bay, in the most romantic situation imaginable, stands Derrynane Abbey, the seat of Daniel O'Connell, Esq. It is a singular looking patchwork edifice, having been enlarged by additions made at different periods and in various styles. The mountains which rise precipitously behind, and on either side of the house, completely hem it in, and give it an extremely solitary appearance. The only means of communicating with the country inland, is by a narrow road, or more properly a track, winding through the craggy defiles of the mountain, and altogether impassable for any vehicle; so that a more secluded and interesting spot than Derrynane it would be difficult to find. The ruins of the little abbey, from which the mansion takes its name, stand within view of the house on the extremity of a low tongue of land running into the sea. Some pretty islets lie in front of the house, and give an agreeable variety to the scenery of the bay.

The Skellig Islands, which lie outside the bay of Ballinskellig, have some of the romance of antiquity hanging round them. They are all three now uninteresting, and, except one, mere rocks of marble. Yet there was a time when religion selected them as a spot suited to secluded devotion. An abbey was founded on the largest by St. Finian, but the bleakness of the situation and the difficulty of access, induced the residents to remove in after times to the main land, where the monastery of Ballinskellig still marks the circumstance of their change of place; while the remains of the monastic structures on the island indicate the prior location of the brotherhood there. Though barren, these islands enjoy the blessings of springs of pure water. Old Geoffry Keating, in his account of them, tells us of "an attractive virtue in the soil, which draws down all the birds which attempt to fly over them, and obliges them to light upon the rock and rest there." Such is the antiquarian's tale. Ireland's Poet has picked up this rough relic of traditionary lore, and enchased it with his own refined imagery :—

> "Islets so freshly fair,
> That never hath bird come nigh them,
> But from his course through air,
> Rath been won downward by them."

So sings the Poet. What says the philosopher? How does *he* account for the magic attraction doubly immortalized by the precious *erugo* of antiquity, and the brilliant emblazonry of modern song? "The origin of this story,"—meaning worthy Geoffry's,—"may be accounted for by the fact, that the Gannet or Solon goose breeds on these rocks, and nowhere else on the coast of Munster. From the sublime to the ridiculous—from the wonderful to the absurd." Poor Geoffry's tale of wonder and Moore's flight of fancy end in the downfall of a wild goose!

The scenery along this coast is of a singularly wild and solitary character. "The mountains," says Mr. Inglis, "jut out into the sea on every side; the island of Valentia

341

lies opposite, separated from the main land by a narrow channel; and the small town, enclosed among the brown mountain slopes, seems like a place at the world's end." Valentia, so called by the Spaniards, who formerly had an extensive trade along the western coasts of Ireland, is the property of the Knight of Kerry, who derives a large sum annually from the fine slate and flag-quarries which the island contains. A handsome cottage in which the knight resides is pleasantly situated on the east side of the island. Public attention was drawn to Valentia a few years ago, in consequence of the proposition made by an eminent engineer for establishing there a station for the American and West Indian steam-packets. The plan proposed was, that the coal necessary for the steamers should be sent from Liverpool and other English ports to Valentia, and that these ships should return laden with Transatlantic cargoes brought thither by the steamers, whose regularity of passage to and fro was to be by these means secured. The contrivance was certainly ingenious, but whether practicable or not, I shall not attempt to determine. As a harbour, Valentia possesses great advantages; it has plenty of water, is well sheltered, and from its situation vessels can enter it or sail out of it with any wind. In the old wars between the English and French, the latter made great use of it as a privateering station. By keeping a good look out at each end, their vessels which lay concealed there, ready to pounce out upon the unwary coasters or straggling merchantmen from the westward, were prepared at the shortest notice to cut and run out of one end of the channel, on an intimation of the appearance of an English ship of war at the other.

The sail from Valentia to Dingle on a fine summer-day is exceedingly beautiful; the intelligent tourist whom I have quoted fully appreciates the magnificence of the coast scenery. He thus speaks of his voyage, which was undertaken in a heavy fishing-boat. "There was scarcely a breath of wind, and we were forced to row the whole way; sometimes, indeed, profiting by the brief course of a passing breeze to hoist our sail, but losing more than we gained by the suspension of rowing. This must, indeed, be a frightful navigation with a heavy rolling sea before an Atlantic north-wester; and being only desirous of reaching Dingle before nightfall, I did not regret the slowness of our progress and the tranquillity of the sea, which encouraged a more leisurely observation of the fine scenery that lay on every side. The tide did not permit us to steer directly for Dingle; and accordingly we made the opposite shore considerably to the west, and then rowed under the rocks eastward, passing in succession Ventry Harbour, numerous bold headlands, and singularly-formed rocks, and many curious sea-worn caves, never visited but by the sea-fowl, that are congregated in thousands along this coast—riding on the wave, covering the rocks, and wheeling on the sides of the cliffs. I noticed many varieties of sea-fowl; some were of the purest white, some were white all but the tips of the wings, and some were speckle-bodied, with red feet and bills."

The Bay of Dingle is excelled by few places on the coast in magnificent marine scenery. Ranges of mountains, whose fantastic summits pierce the clouds, rise boldly from the shores, and form a singularly picturesque screen to the noble haven which they overhang. At the northern entrance of this bay lie the BIasquets, a group of islets, twelve in number, but four of them are mere rocks. They formerly belonged to the great Earl of Desmond, who gave them to the family of Ferriter, whence they have derived a second name. They have also, a bird to boast of, as being peculiar to themselves, but of a nature somewhat more substantial than the airy creatures of Keating and Moore. A small bird, named Gouler, is said to be peculiar to these islands. It is somewhat larger than a sparrow; the feathers on the back are black, those on the tail white; the bill is straight, short, and thick: it is web-footed. The bird is almost one lump of fat, and when roasted is considered so delicious as to be preferred to the ortolan. In recording this fact, many persons will say that I have done more for Ireland than all the antiquarians, from the extravagant Keating to the envious Ledwich, and all the poets from Amergin, brother of Heber and Heremon, down to the modern bard of Erin. Greenwich and its white-bait will be despised when bait of such exquisite relish may be found by making a pilgrimage to the Blasquets. Killarney may fail in its attractions, but a bird superior in flavour to the ortolan is irresistible, particularly after a long coasting voyage, when the digestive organs are all in their happiest mood and ripe for action.

Doubling round Sybil Head we come upon a place of melancholy notoriety, Smerwick. Here it was that a garrison of Spaniards, which had landed and taken possession of the town for the Earl of Desmond, then in rebellion against Queen Elizabeth, was slaughtered in cold blood after its surrender by the commander of the English forces. This act was afterwards brought against Sir Walter Raleigh as one of the charges on his trial. He exculpated himself by pleading his subordinate station which obliged him to obey the commands of his superior officer, but he was unable fully to exculpate himself from a participation in this foul transaction, which must ever remain a dark blot and disgrace upon the character of this ill-fated man.

We next reach Brandon Bay, situated on the northern shoulder of that bold peninsula which runs westward from Tralee to the Atlantic. It is twenty-six miles in length, and not more than six miles in width near the mainland; and consists altogether of craggy mountains heaped together in the wildest confusion, rising, in some places, to a considerable height. The lofty Brandon and Connor Hill are conspicuous amongst their lofty brethren for their superior altitude and picturesque forms. The channel up to the town of Tralee, which lies at the head of the bay of that name, is fit only for small craft. The town itself is inconveniently situated for commercial purposes; but a ship canal, which was completed a few years ago, has done much to remedy the defective navigation of the channel, and will in time bring to Tralee the shipping business, which was hitherto carried on at Blennerville, a small port a mile below the town. The scenery around Tralee is remarkably fine; the view

Ballybunnian

Cove in Malbay

345

of the wide-spreading bay which faces the town, the wild and rugged mountains of Brandon peninsula, stretching away to the westward, and the softer beauties of the rich vale that extends on the other side towards Castle Island, form a panorama of surpassing and varied beauty. Ballyheigh Bay is only an inlet on the northern boundary of that great indenture in the coast which is known as Tralee Bay. It affords no shelter for ships, and has often proved fatal to homeward-bound West Indian and American vessels, from its having been mistaken for the mouth of the Shannon, in consequence of an error of latitude in many of the charts.

Between Cashin Bay, which forms the estuary of the little river Geale and Kinconly Point, are situated the CAVES OF BALLYBUNNIAN; but having been noticed at some length in the first volume of this work, I shall not now enter upon any further description of them, but strongly recommend all tourists in the, western parts of Ireland not to neglect visiting those singular natural labyrinths, an examination of which will amply repay the trouble of exploring them.

The neat little VILLAGE OF BALLYBUNNIAN, which is only a short distance from these celebrated caves, affords good accommodation for travellers :—in the summer months it is much frequented by bathers from Limerick and other inland places. We have now reached the northern limits of the County Kerry, which can boast of some of the wildest, most romantic, and diversified scenery to be met with in any part of Ireland. That portion of Kerry which lies in the neighbourhood of the Shannon is less elevated than the southern parts. The central district is an upland country, gradually rising towards the confines of Limerick and Cork. The valleys in this tract consist mostly of reclaimable bog, from which several streams and rivulets descend southward to Dingle Bay, and eastward by the Blackwater towards Cork. The southern district is composed of lofty mountain-ranges, of which I have spoken when describing Killarney, Glengariffe, and the coast-scenery northward from Kenmare River. The prevailing component of this mountain-chain is clay; slate-quarries, of which have been worked with considerable success at Valentia and other places along the coast. Coal, culm, and limestone, also abound throughout this county, and a valuable copper-mine is now in full work at Ross-Island, in the Lake of Killarney. Hard and beautiful crystals, known to lapidaries as Kerry stones and Irish diamonds, are found in the limestone caverns along the coast. Amethysts and pearls have also been discovered in some of the lakes and rivers :—in short, Kerry county may be said to possess all the ingredients for creating wealth; yet, strange to say, the progress of improvement has been hitherto slower here than in any other part of the island. Latterly, however, some attempts have been made to give a stimulus to industry, by opening roads through wild and remote districts—which, with the encouragement afforded by government to the fisheries* on the coast, will, it is hoped, tend materially to ameliorate the present wretched condition of the people. Sailing across the broad estuary of the Shannon, whose noble stream might be made

346

a source of infinite wealth to Ireland, we reach Loop Head in the county Clare, where there is a light-house, marked by a brilliant fixed light from fifteen lamps. The western coast of Clare is marked but by one bay of magnitude, and that a mark of evil omen. "The space between Loop Head and the Arran Islands is usually denominated Malbay, and justly so, for if a vessel happens to be embayed therein, the only places where there is the least chance of saving the ship are on the north sides of Dunbeg and Liscannor." A melancholy anticipation for an exhausted worn-out West Indian when nearing this part of the coast with an in-blowing gale. KILKEE is a beautiful watering-place, situated on a little creek, which runs in off Malbay. It has risen considerably in importance within the last few years, and is now the most fashionable resort for bathers on the whole line of this romantic coast.

Earlier in this work, the PUFFING HOLE, near Kilkee, will be found minutely described. There are numerous other caverns formed by the hand of nature in the cliffs on the shore, but none of them are of sufficient importance to require further notice. The artist who has illustrated this work made a drawing of a singular COVE IN MALBAY, which gives a very correct idea of the manner in which the ceaseless action of the Atlantic waves have worn away, and scooped the stratified cliffs into NATURAL BRIDGES, caverns, and chasms, so as to give the shores here the appearance of stupendous ruins, or the fragments of a half-formed world thrown into the wildest confusion by the hand of nature.

When Conn of the hundred battles, and Mowa Eoghan, two of the descendants of Milesius, undertook to divide Ireland between them, they drew a line from Dublin to Galway, calling the portion north of that line Leah Cuin, and that to the south Leah Mow, or Conn's and Eoghan's shares.

The Bay of Galway was in days of yore one of the most important of the entrances to Ireland. It ought to be so still. Its geographical position, and its great natural advantages entitle it to this distinction; political causes have counteracted the intentions of nature. The entrance to this magnificent basin is sheltered by the islands of Arran. They are three in number—Arranmore, Innismain, and Innishere. The two larger are separated from each other by a strait, called St. Gregory's Sound. The largest is nine miles long, and is a parish in itself; all taken together form one of the seventeen baronies into which Galway is divided. These islands are said by ancient annalists to be the remains of a high barrier of land, which the Atlantic broke through at an early period of the world. Kirwan, the mineralogist, in his Essay on the primitive state of the globe, says, that the Bay of Galway appears to have been originally a granite mountain, shattered and swallowed during a great convulsion, which he supposes to have taken place, and adds, that a vast mass of

* Besides the deep-sea fishing along the coast, the shores afford a large supply, particularly of shell-fish. The lobsters in many places are of large size and excellent flavour.

347

Natural Bridges near Kilkee

Kilkee

349

granite, called "the Gregory," stood on one side of the islands one hundred feet at least above the level of the sea, which was torn to pieces by lightning in 1774. Bare as they stand at present, and unsheltered from the fury of the western blasts, they were once overshadowed with woods, many vestiges of which are still distinctly visible. This circumstance, combined with their retired situation and wild appearance, rendered them peculiarly adapted to the celebration of the Pagan rites of the ancient Irish. The immense cairns, upright stones, circles, altars, and other Druidical remains yet to be seen in them, prove that they were formerly one of the favourite retreats of this mysterious order of the heathen priesthood. Giraldus Cambrensis, some of whose amusing, though not very veracious anecdotes I have already had occasion to quote, attributes a peculiar property to the air of these islands. They were too singular—too much savouring of the romance of legendary lore to be passed unnoticed by him. In the words of his translator, Stanihurst, he says, "There is in the west of Connaught an island placed in the sea, called Aren, to which St. Brendon had often recourse. The dead bodies neede not be graveled, for the ayre is so pure, that the contagion of any carrion may not infect it; there may the son see his father, his grandfather, and his great-grandfather," &c. Another peculiarity related by the same writer is, that, although Ireland abounds with rats and mice, this island is free from them, for if one of these vermin be brought there, "either it leapeth into the sea, or else being stayed it dyeth presently." I must confess that I have been unable to establish the truth of either of these marvellous relations, which appear to have had their origin in the fanciful imagination of the writer. During the civil wars the islands of Arran were deemed a position of great military importance, and were ultimately surrendered on terms to the Republican general Reynolds, and afterwards fell into the hands of Erasmus Smith, an English settler. The people of the islands are an extremely primitive race, supporting themselves chiefly by fishing and the making of kelp, by burning a particular species of sea-weed that grows upon the shore. A small breed of sheep, highly esteemed for their delicate flavour, are reared upon these islands and exported to Galway. Puffin catching is also much practised by the inhabitants. The manner of capturing these birds is similar to that pursued in the Hebrides and in Norway, where they lower a man by means of a rope down the face of a cliff, who seizes them while they sleep.

The bay contains a number of lesser creeks, inlets, and harbours, of which that of Galway itself is the most important, and from which a valuable and extensive trade by water might be carried on with the interior of the country, by merely forming a short canal from the town into Lough Corrib, which with its neighbouring lakes of Mask, Carra, and Conn, would form a navigable chain, extending through the nearly unknown districts of Connaught, that in a commercial and social point of view would be of incalculable benefit to the country. Sailing into Galway Bay, the shores present a great deal of diversity. On the right-hand the noble range of the Burrin mountains in the county Clare form a majestic boundary to the scene. On the Galway side, the country is delightfully varied, exhibiting the mingled beauties of rich cultivation and primeval wildness. The town of Galway is finely situated on a narrow neck of land between an arm of the great bay and Lough Corrib, a noble lake thirty miles long. The picturesque and ancient appearance of this old Spanish town, with its antique gateways and arched passages has been already described in this work. I shall not, therefore, dilate further upon the singularity of its narrow streets and gloomy-looking mansions, which, though highly interesting to the antiquarian and painter, convey to the mind of the utilitarian anything but ideas of comfort and cleanliness. Behind the town the land rises into a succession of bold and picturesque hills, which stretch along Lough Corrib as far as Killery harbour to the north-west, inclosing within their chain the wild and romantic tract, known as Connemara and Joyce's country. In the first volume of this work a description has been given of the most striking beauties which arrest the attention of a traveller journeying through this remote and interesting district; but no land-view can equal in sublimity and grandeur the coast-scenery that presents itself upon quitting the Bay of Galway through the northern passage. A succession of noble bays open to the view, protected from the fury of the Atlantic waves by the numerous islands which lie near their entrance. A glance at the map will he sufficient to show the singular formation of the coast, whose irregular indentations, running far into the land, form deep harbours, where the navies of Great Britain might lie at anchor; yet so completely unknown and unfrequented, that scarcely a sail, save those of the poor fishermen's boats, is ever to be seen on their undisturbed broad waters. Some idea may be formed of the extraordinary facilities which this sequestered district possesses for trade and commerce, when, according to a late eminent engineer's report, no part of it is more than four miles distant from existing navigation. "There are," says he, "upwards of twenty safe and capacious harbours fit for vessels of any burthen; about twenty-five navigable lakes in the interior of a mile or more in length, besides hundreds smaller: the sea-coast and all these lakes abound with fish. The district with its islands possesses no less than four hundred miles of sea-shore. On Lough Corrib it has about fifty miles of shore, so that with Lough Mask, &c. there are, perhaps, as many miles of the shore of the sea or navigable lakes as there are square miles of surface." Of the harbours on the sea-coast, the principal are Costello, Greatman's, Casheen, Kilkerran, Roundstone, Birterbuy, Benowen, Ardfert, Cleggan, Ballinakill, and Killery, which last separates the counties of Galway and Mayo. Kilkerran is the largest of these bays; it runs into the land upwards of ten miles, and contains within its spacious bosom the inhabited islands of Garomna, Letterman, and several of lesser note.

Scene from Clonacartin Hill

Ballynahinch

Birterbuy Bay is also of considerable extent; the beautiful little river of Ballinahinch falls into the bay at its upper extremity. This river has its rise in BALLINAHINCH LAKE, at about four miles distance from the sea-shore. On the banks of this lovely and secluded sheet of water stands Ballinahinch House, the residence of Thomas Martin, Esq., the proprietor of the greater part of this wild district. The mansion is a plain building, but the situation it occupies is surpassingly beautiful, overlooking the lake that sleeps in calm repose at the foot of the impending sides of Lettery and Bengower,* which here form the front of the magnificent group of conical mountains, called the Twelve Pins of Binabola. From the bridge which crosses the river near the house, a fine view may be obtained of the lake and the ruins of the old castle,* standing on a small island in the lake, and forming a picturesque object in the landscape. This castle, it is said, was built by the powerful sept of O'Flaherty, once the possessors of vast estates in the western parts of the county. Their frequent acts of oppression and lawless violence towards their weaker neighbours, obtained for them the appellation of "The bloody O'Flahertys," and so great was the terror with which their fierce aggressions inspired the peaceable inhabitants of Galway, that the west gate of the town, (that on the side nearest to their troublesome visitors) bore, until the gate was taken down, the following inscription:

"FROM THE FEROCIOUS O'FLAHERTYS—GOOD LORD DELIVER US!"

The peasantry, who here and in every part of Ireland shudder at the desecration of any person or place devoted to the service of their religion, ascribe the downfall of this turbulent family to the alleged fact, that the chief of the O'Flahertys, who built the Castle of Ballinahinch, pulled down the convent of Timbola on the mainland in order to obtain materials for his work, and that he compelled the friars to carry the stones on their backs to the shore of the lake, where they were placed in boats and Conveyed to the island. The spot where the fathers are said to have deposed their burthens, has from this circumstance obtained a name in Irish, of which the English signification is, *"The Friar's bend or stoop,"* referring to the attitude of a man carrying a heavy load.

The river of Ballinahinch affords salmon of superior flavour, and the surrounding country abundance of game of every description.* Mr. Martin's deer-park, situated somewhat singularly on the island of Cruanakeely, several miles out in the bay, is well stocked with the fallow-deer. The island which is of considerable size, is uninhabited except by the antlered community;—it is very rugged and thickly overgrown with tall

---

* The late eccentric Colonel Thomas Martin, for many year the representative in Parliament of the county Galway, resided at one period in this castle; more recently it was converted into a sporting-lodge for the accommodation of the owner's friends during the shooting season; latterly, however, it has been suffered to fall into decay, and is now a complete ruin.

354

ferns, innumerable wild flowers, and a great variety of beautiful heaths. It also commands a fine view of the mainland, with the stupendous Binabola group in the distance, and more nearly the triple-headed mountain of Urrisbeg : seaward the dark Atlantic's multitudinous waves are seen breaking upon the white sandy coves and frowning headlands which form the shores of the noble bay. The shooting of a deer upon the island is an interesting and animated scene. When one of these animals has been decreed to die, a boat with twelve or more athletic mountaineers, accompanied by a gamekeeper, proceed to the island. The men start the herd of deer, whom they hunt round the island with an activity only equalled by the creatures they are pursuing. They urge the chase with indefatigable ardour and wild shouts, until they succeed in separating the buck they have selected from the rest of the herd; then driving their panting and terrified victim to a favourable situation, the gamekeeper with little trouble brings him down with his rifle. It is generally supposed that the old Irish red deer is not now to be found anywhere in Ireland except at Killarney; but it is well known that this rare and noble animal still exists in the solitudes of the Connemara mountains. A lady, upon whose veracity I can rely, related to me, that, being one fine autumnal day boating on the romantic Lough Ina, which lies in the midst of the wild and gigantic scenery of the Binabola mountains, the men who rowed the boat got a glimpse of a red deer browsing on the tender grass amongst the copse-wood of a small island on the lake. The rowers, eager for sport, pulled to the island, jumped ashore, and by their shouts startled the deer, who, tossing his noble antlers into the air, bounded towards the shore, plunged into the water, and shaped his course towards his native fastnesses on the main land. The boatmen, however, were not long in regaining their boat, and rowing away lustily, succeeded in intercepting the creature's retreat, who, powerless in the water, suffered those in the boat to place his head upon the gunnel, and examine his enormous palmy antlers, a feat which would have been attended with considerable difficulty and danger had he been at large on terra firma. After having sufficiently satisfied their curiosity, the terrified animal was liberated and allowed to pursue its way to the shore; my narrator having first plucked a few hairs from the crest of her prisoner, which she still retains as a memorial of her exploit.

On Roundstone Bay stands the modern village of Roundstone, built by the late Alexander Nimmo, the celebrated engineer, whose scientific knowledge led him to the conviction that the best mode of raising the commercial prosperity of Ireland, was by means of her noble harbours on the western coast. Impressed with this opinion, he expended large sums of money in building a handsome pier and

---

* A singular species of trout, called the *Gillaroo*, peculiar to some of the lakes in the west of Ireland, is esteemed a great delicacy. It differs little in external appearance from the common trout, but internally it has a different organization, possessing a thick muscular stomach, somewhat resembling the gizzard of a fowl, to enable it to digest the small shell-fish on which it subsists; from which peculiarity it is frequently called the *Gizzard trout.*

Lough Ina

Clifden, Connemara

erecting houses at Roundstone; but his exertions were received with apathy or jealousy by those who should have aided his efforts, and he died in the prime of life, leaving his noble designs unaccomplished; but not until he had done enough to prove the soundness of his theory and the correctness of his expanded views. The Bay of Roundstone is backed by the lofty mountain of Urrisbeg, upon whose steep activities grow many rare and beautiful plants. Mr. Inglis enumerates several, and amongst them the Mediterranean heath, which I believe is not found elsewhere in Ireland.

The same writer, speaking of the view from the summit of Urrisbeg, describes it as "more singular than beautiful." "Here," says he, "Cunnemara is perceived to be truly that which its name denotes, *'Bays of the Sea.'* The whole western coast of Cunnemara is laid open with its innumerable bays and inlets: but the most striking and singular part of the view is that to the north, over the districts called Urrisbeg and Urrismore. These are wide level districts, spotted by an unaccountable number of lakes, and mostly entirely uncultivated and uninhabited. I endeavoured from my position to reckon the number of lakes, and succeeded in counting upwards of one hundred and sixty. Shoulders of the mountain, however, shut out from the view some of the nearer part of the plain, and other parts were too distant to allow any very accurate observation; so that I have no doubt there may be three hundred lakes, large and small, in this wild and very singular district. Several of the lakes have islands upon them, and by the aid of a good telescope which I carried with me, I perceived that many of these islands were wooded."

From Roundstone our seaward course lies round the far projecting promontory of Sline Head, upon whose rocky shores the wreck of many a stately argosy has been strewn. On the northern side of this peninsula lies the sequestered little Bay of Ardbear, on a navigable inlet of which stands the neat and thriving town of CLIFDEN. Two miles from the town, on the shores of the bay, CLIFDEN CASTLE, the seat of D'Arcy, Esq. attracts the traveller's attention, delightfully situated in the midst of a thickly and beautifully planted demesne. The natural charms of this paradise in the wilderness have been heightened by the tasteful improvements of the excellent proprietor. A grotto formed of the various beautiful marbles of Connemara, and a fanciful pavilion, constructed principally of stalactites, shells, and bits of ore, gathered from the caves, the shores, and hills of this rich but unregarded district, deserve the attention of every visitor of this truly picturesque scene. From Clifden and its lovely bay I sailed round Dog's Head, another of those bold peninsulas, which, jutting into the ocean, receive the first shock of the Atl antic billows. A little to the northward of Dog's Head, and about six miles distant from the mainland, the island of Ennisbofine may be seen, rearing its dark form above the waves. Though now little thought of in a political point of view, it was esteemed of sufficient importance during the stormy period of the civil war to be made a place of arms. A castle built there by Cromwell was besieged by King William's army, and surrendered upon honourable terms. Near the extremity of the narrow headland, which lies between the harbours of Ballinakill, stands the solitary mansion of Renvyle, which, with the surrounding improvements, forms an interesting feature in the coast scenery, and engaged my attention while our little cutter was gliding towards Killery Harbour. As we slowly sailed up this narrow inlet, I was forcibly struck by the novel character of the scenery, which, Mr. Inglis says, resembles a Norwegian fiord more than anything he had elsewhere seen nearer home. The harbour, which is deep enough to receive vessels of great burthen, is, in many places, not more than a quarter of a mile across; and the shores rising precipitously from the water's edge, impart an air of stern grandeur and majestic beauty to the picture, to which my pen cannot do the justice it deserves in description. But the shores, though picturesque in form, are unadorned with wood, without which no landscape can be perfect. This deficiency was noticed by the intelligent tourist just quoted, who observes, that, "if the mountain sides on the Killery were wooded, it would be almost unnecessary to travel into Norway in search of scenery:" The little mountain river Owen Erive, which has its source in the county Mayo, falls into the sea at the HEAD OF KILLERY HARBOUR, where, confined by the picturesque shores within its narrowest limits, it presents to the eye one of the most romantic and sequestered scenes, that this region of the sublime and beautiful can produce. At a short distance from this place stands the poor straggling village of LEENANE, remarkable for nothing but the natural beauty of its situation in the midst of the most magnificent scenery, and for being the *capital* where the renowned potentate of this district, height *Jack Joyce,* resided.*

We have now reached the northern confines of Galway, having, in my cruise from the Harbour of Wexford hither, taken a hasty view of the principal bays, havens, and objects of pictorial interest along this magnificent line of coast; so hasty, indeed, that I have been compelled to dismiss much that was curious and interesting, to give place to that which through its paramount importance forced itself upon my notice. Here, then, I terminate my pleasant voyage; too conscious that my pen has been unequal to the task of depicting truly the romantic scenery of this beautiful—

"Nurse of full streams, and lifter up of proud
Sky-mingling mountains, that o'erlook the cloud."

* For a description of this singular man, well known to every tourist through the wilds of Connemara, see Vol. i. p. 76. One trait of his character has, however, undergone a considerable change since that portion of this work passed the press. Jack has become a teetotaller, and has taken the "pledge" from Father Matthew, the Temperance Apostle in Ireland. A gentleman who visited him last summer, found him washing down his dinner with a jug of milk instead of a noggin of potteen. But though Jack was thus abstemious himself, he set before his guest wine and spirits in abundance, of which he hospitably pressed him to partake.

But I trust I have been able to excite in the mind of my readers a curiosity to visit the scenes I have endeavoured to describe. Let their own eyes be the judges, and I fear not they will agree with me in saying, that no island in the world presents such an outline of coast for beauty or for utility—for all that the eye of the painter or the soul of the poet could desire—all that the hand of power, or the grasp of mercantile avarice could court. Bays, where the proudest fleets could ride in safety; rivers, carrying wealth from the extremities to the centre; islands, creeks, and coves, with all the appliances and means that nature in her most bountiful mood could tender to vary the plenty with which the same all-liberal hand has spread over its surface in hills of waving crops, valleys of pasture, and mountains redolent of the sweetest herbage. Look at Australia, the largest island in the world, or more properly a fifth continent: it does not contain so many practicable harbours throughout the whole extent of its vast circumference, as that portion of the Irish coast between Wexford and Connemara. I might expatiate upon this point, but I find that I must hasten onward to the fruitful plains of Leinster, and bid farewell with a sigh to the romantic region of the west, to the giant hills—

> "Rock-ribbed and ancient as the sun; the vales,
> Stretching in pensive quietness between;
> The venerable woods;—rivers that move
> In majesty; and the complaining brooks,
> That make the meadows green, and poured round all
> Old ocean's grey and melancholy waste."

XXII.

THE principal road from Galway into Leinster, by way of Ballinasloe and Athlone, possesses few charms for the tourist. After passing the village of Oranmore pleasantly situated on an inlet at the head of the Bay of Gaiway, and commanding a fine view of the Burrin mountains, and the broad expanse of the bay, I entered upon a cheerless and desolate tract of country, where large sheep farms, inclosed by fences of loose stones, dreary-looking bogs, with patches of wretched tillage, and miserable dwellings of the peasantry, presented a painful picture of neglect and poverty. A few stunted thorns are the only approaches to wood to be met with, except in the neighbourhood of the thickly-scattered seats of the gentry, where the improvements in their immediate vicinity relieve, in some degree, the desert and monotonous character of the surrounding scenery. The same bleak and uninteresting aspect of the country continued until I had left behind me the straggling town of Loughrea, the property of the Marquis of Clanricarde, built upon the borders of a small lake, which, if the high grounds on the south side were planted, would make an exceedingly pleasing feature in the landscape. The mansion and plantations of Roxborough, the seat of Mr. Persse, embosomed amidst lofty hills, have a picturesque effect as seen from the high road near Loughrea. The suburbs of this town are amongst the poorest and dirtiest now to be found in Ireland, where, I am happy to say, that the reproach which attached to Irish towns and cities generally, from the miserable condition of their outlets, is wearing fast away, and that the wretchedness which made such an unfavourable and frequently an indelible impression upon a stranger entering a town, is giving place to an appearance of neatness and regularity, extremely gratifying to behold. The country to the eastward of Loughrea assumes a more cheerful appearance than that which lies between it and Galway. Good farms, respectable cultivation, and marks of distribution of property begin to exhibit themselves on every side, but still there is a want of wood, which gives a tameness to what would be otherwise a very pleasing prospect. The high road passes through the little village of Aughrim, within three miles of Ballinasloe, rendered remarkable from the battle which was fought by the armies of James and William, on the neighbouring heights of Kilcommadan in 1691, when the forces of the former were totally defeated, and General St. Ruth, the commander of James's army, was killed by a cannon shot.

Ballinasloe is a neat and thriving town, watered by the river Suck, one of the tributaries of that monarch of Irish rivers—the Shannon, which it joins about six miles eastward of this place. The plantations of the Earl of Clancarty, adjoining the town, have been laid out with great taste, but the general appearance of the country is bald and uninteresting; the great extent of bog and lowlands which lie on the Galway side of the town, and in the direction of the Shannon, being altogether opposed to the picturesque in landscape scenery. The trade, however,, of this town is considerable; in the streets and shops I was struck with the air of business and an appearance of prosperous industry which I had not observed since I left Cork. The extension of the Grand Canal to Ballinasloe has considerably increased its intercourse with the fertile counties through which the Shannon flows, and it may be now considered as the centre of the inland trade and commerce of Ireland. This town has been long celebrated for its two great fairs, held in May and October, the first for the sale of wool, the second and principal for horses, black cattle, and sheep; as many as ninety thousand of the latter animals being frequently brought to it from the surrounding districts. During the week which the fair lasts, the town is literally overflowed with people from every part of Ireland, and to a stranger, desirous of studying the characteristics of the inhabitants of the different provinces, no better or more favourable opportunity could possibly present itself. There he will see drawn together as to a common centre, the long-visaged and dark-eyed people of the west, slender in form, but agile and hardy as mountain-deer. In contrast with them, he may remark the stalwart men of Tipperary and of the eastern portion of Limerick, distinguishable by their great stature, by a certain reckless daring in their looks, and a freedom in their gait,—marking them as the finest and most turbulent peasantry in the kingdom. Let him next observe the groups of grey frieze-coated men, of middle height but well knit frames, from the adjoining counties in Leinster, whose broad faces, blue eyes, and light hair, show the admixture of the Danish and British blood with the primitive stock :—and, lastly, when he sees a stout-built, well-dressed peasant, quiet in his demeanour, and with a countenance indicative of more shrewdness than humour, and more cool resolution than eager courage, he may set him down as a dealer from Ulster, in whom the peculiarities of our Scottish neighbours are developed in a very remarkable degree.

In short, every class and description of people are to be met with at Ballinasloe fair. Obsequious shopkeepers from Dublin, with "a large assortment of the most fashionable articles," selected from their unsaleable stock; Mayo jockies, who offer to sell you, "the best bit of blood that ever crossed a country," leaving it to the buyer's judgment to discover that the animal is broken down, spavined, and blind of one eye. Sheep-farmers from Galway and Roscommon, cattle-graziers from the banks of the Shannon; horse-dealers from Kildare; gamblers, showmen, and quacks from every place; forming altogether as miscellaneous an assemblage as can be well imagined; all and each in pursuit of gain—that great object for which men toil and strive from the cradle to the grave.

The road from Ballinasloe to Athlone runs parallel to, but at four miles distance from the banks of the Shannon, which are here flat and boggy. In the winter season, or after heavy rains, these lowlands are overflowed by the river, and present a most dreary and unpicturesque appearance.

In this neighbourhood I once witnessed a scene of so painful a nature, that it made an indelible impression on my mind; and as it illustrates one of the ancient customs of the people, and exhibits a fearful picture of the results of those agrarian combinations which disturbed the country at that period, I shall make no apology for relating it.

It was about the middle of June, some twelve years since, I was returning to Athlone, after a long summer day's stroll through the country; the evening was delightfully fine, and even in those unromantic plains, the face of nature wore an attractive smile,—when I was struck by the superior air of comfort which distinguished a road-side cottage, around which a thick hedge of flowering thorn, and dark green elder bushes grew in wild luxuriance. A little garden filled with flowers, and laid out with considerable taste, lay between the cottage and the road. Outside the garden-gate, which was open, a girl, seemingly about fourteen years of age, was seated on a bank of turf weeping bitterly. I could not see her features, but I could hear her convulsive sobs and low moans, as with her elbows resting on her knees, and her face hidden between her hands, she rocked her body to and fro with an incessant and regular motion. I approached the young mourner, and endeavoured to draw from her the cause of her affliction. At the sound of my voice she looked up, and showed a countenance ghastly pale and bathed in tears. I repeated my question, but the poignancy of her sorrow seemed to have obliterated all her faculties, for she shook her head, and with a look of unutterable anguish resumed her position without replying to me. At that moment the mournful wail of the Caoine, or Song of Lamentation,* burst from the cottage. I then knew that the hand of the Angel of

---

* The Caoine, or Lamentation for the Dead, is one of the most ancient customs that has been preserved through ages of progressive civilization in any country. Its origin is of the utmost antiquity; that it was practised amongst the Greeks and Romans, there is not the slightest doubt, and that it was also practised by the Jews and other nations of the East, there is strong evidence to prove. Dr. Campbell observes, that the conclamatio amongst the Romans agrees with the Irish caoine or funeral cry; and that the mulieres preficæ exactly correspond with the women who precede funerals in Ireland, and who make an outcry too outrageous to be the effect of real grief:—

"Ut qui conducti plorant in funere, dicunt
At faciunt prope plura dolentibus ex animo.—"

The conclamatio over Dido as described by Virgil, shows that this custom prevailed amongst the Phœnicians—

"Lamentis gemituque et fæmineo ululatu
Tecta fremunt"

The Doctor further remarks on the Irish exclamation of sorrow, ullaloo—that it has a strong affinity to the Roman ululates, and the Greek word of the same import. Sir Walter Scott informs us, that the Highland coronach, which is identical with the Irish caoine, is precisely similar to these classical dirges for the dead. The author of the "Historical Memoirs of the Irish Bards," insists on the high antiquity of the Irish funeral cry, "from the circumstance of its obstinately refusing the accompaniment of a bass." The sacred writings are full of allusions to this custom of mourning for the dead—"Call for the mourning women that they may come," is an allusion to the practice too clear to be doubted. In former times it was the duty of the bard and the retainers of the family to raise the funeral lament, and sing the praises of the deceased when any member of it died; but since the decline of the Irish minstrelsy this office has been generally discharged by old women, who attend the wakes and funerals as professional mourners, and are remunerated for their services by the relations of the deceased. In the Transactions of the Royal Irish Academy, this singular custom is described in the following manner :— "The Irish have always been remarkable for their funeral lamentations, and this peculiarity has been noticed by almost every traveller who has visited them; and it seems derived from their Celtic ancestors, the primeval inhabitants of this isle. Cambrensis, in the twelfth century, says, the Irish then musically expressed their griefs; that is, they applied their musical art—in which they excelled all others—to the orderly celebration of funeral obsequies, by dividing the mourners into two bodies, each alternately singing their part, the whole at times joining in full chorus. The body of the deceased, dressed in grave-clothes, and ornamented with flowers, was placed on a bier or some elevated spot. The relations and keeners (singing mourners) then ranged themselves in two divisions; one at the head and the other at the feet of the corpse. The bards and croteries had before prepared the funeral caoinan. The chief bard of the head chorus began by singing the first stanza in a low, doleful tone, which was softly accompanied by the harp; at the conclusion, the foot semichorus began the lamentation, or ullaloo, from the final note of the preceding stanza, in which they were answered by the head semichorus; then both united in one general chorus. The chorus of the first stanza being ended, the chief bard of the foot semi-chorus began the second gol or lamentation, which was answered by the head, and, as before, both united in one common chorus. Thus, alternately, the song and the chorus were performed during the night." The genealogy, rank, professions, the virtues and vices of the dead were rehearsed, and a number of interrogations were addressed to the deceased—as Why did he die?— if married, whether his wife were faithful to him, his sons dutiful to him, or good hunters and warriors?—if a woman, whether her daughters were fair or chaste?—if a young man, whether he had been crossed in love? or if the blue-eyed maids of Erin had treated him with scorn?

Death had fallen upon that household, and without further inquiry I walked towards the cabin-door, which on these sad occasions is open to all corners. On entering I perceived a crowd of people, sitting on wooden forms, ranged a hong the walls, or grouped around small deal tables, disposed, without any regard to regularity, through the apartment, which was dimly lighted by a few small candles stuck into raw potatoes, that had been ingeniously contrived to supply the place of candle-sticks. At the further end of the room, on a platform constructed of a few loose boards supported on chairs,—the corpse, that of a middle-aged man of strongly marked features, was laid, decently covered with a snow-white linen sheet. Another similar cloth, hung like a curtain at the head of the corpse, to which were attached flowers and evergreens, which were also scattered over the bier, and a small crucifix with a little reservoir at its foot containing 'holy water, was suspended from the curtain directly over the head of the dead man. Twelve candles were burning on either side of the bier, and on the breast of the corpse was laid a plate containing salt.* Upon a table close by, a quantity of snuff and tobacco, and a formidable array of pipes were spread for the accommodation of the numerous visitors, who were regaling themselves with the potent contents of several large jugs, that, as often as they were emptied, which was pretty frequently, were replenished from a punch manufactory, carried on in an adjoining apartment under the superintendence of some elderly friend or relative of the family. The sounds of sorrow which I had heard, proceeded from an old woman, one of a group seated around the bier,—who poured out in the Irish tongue an eloquent recital of the good qualities of the deceased in a low, wailing chaunt, which as she proceeded increased in pathos and energy until the singer became exhausted, when another of the aged mourners took up the wild and mournful song. I instantly recognised in these aged crones the professional keeners, who have obtained a reputation for chaunting these funeral verses, and who wander about the country, subsisting partly on charity, and partly on the rewards they receive

---

* The custom of placing salt on the bosom of the dead before the corpse is laid in the coffin is of great antiquity, though the reason for doing so is lost to us. By some it is imagined that salt, from its anti-putrescent quality, is adopted as a symbol of immortality. Mingled salt and earth are placed on the breast of the deceased in some parts of Scotland.

Translations amid imitations of the Caoine, or Song of Sorrow, having been given by Mr. Crofton Croker, and other writers on the ancient customs of Ireland, I shall confine myself here to giving a single stanza of one of these deeply impassioned and figurative compositions—literally translated from the Irish.

"Cold and silent is thy repose! Thou wast to me as the nerve of my throbbing heart: for thy sake only was this world dear. Thou wast brave, thou wast generous, thou wast just, thou wast loved by all. But why look back on thy virtues? Why recal those scenes to memory that are no more to be beheld? for he whose they were has passed away; he is gone for ever to return no more—

Cold and silent is now thy repose!"

It should be observed, that the last line forms the chorus to the Lament, which is repeated at the beginning and end of every stanza.

on those occasions, where their melancholy services are required. Contrasted strongly with the noisy grief of the keeners, was the silent hut poignant sorrow of a woman who sat at the head of the bed, her hands clasped together, and her tearless eyes fixed intently on the face of the dead man. Her lips were half apart, as if she would have given utterance to the emotions that struggled in her bosom, but her tongue refused its office, and a convulsive motion in the muscles of her throat was the only sign of life she exhibited. This was the bereaved wife of the deceased, who, I learned, had been an industrious and honest peasant, renting a small but productive farm at an easy rent. He had married at an early age,—as most of the Irish peasantry do,—and had a family of six children, three of whom were now sitting weeping at their mother's feet, though too young to comprehend the full extent of the loss they had sustained. The girl whose lamentations had attracted my notice outside the cottage was the eldest daughter. Blessed in the love of an affectionate wife and children, Walter Kelly (the name of the deceased) led a life of perfect happiness, until in an evil hour he was induced to join one of those secret societies, which had for their object the redress of certain real or fancied social wrongs. The specious arguments of the leaders of these illegal associations overcame the scruples of Walter Kelly, and lie deluded himself with the belief that he was performing a meritorious duty in lending his aid to remove the oppression under which his country groaned. In pursuance of their wild system of disturbance, large parties scoured the country every night, issuing their arbitrary edicts to the terrified and peaceable inhabitants, demanding arms, and not unfrequently committing acts of personal outrage upon individuals who had dared to disobey the mandates of these secret legislators. It was in one of these nocturnal expeditions that Kelly met the awful fate that brought death and desolation beneath his roof. He had accompanied a body of his lawless associates to the house of a rich farmer, who, in consequence of taking some land from which the former tenant had been ejected, had drawn upon himself the hostility of the association. The object of their vengeance had, however, by some means become acquainted with the intentions of the gang, and upon application to a neighbouring magistrate procured a party of police, who were privately stationed in the farmer's house on the night of the expected attack. At midnight the party arrived outside the farmer's door, and with dreadful imprecations ordered him to open it. A volley from the police, concealed within, was the answer, which wounded two of the party, and killed Walter Kelly on the spot,—a ball having passed through his heart. The remainder of the band, confounded at this unexpected reception, fled hastily, pursued by the police, who succeeded in securing two more of them. On the following day an inquest was held on the body of the unfortunate Walter Kelly, and a verdict of "justifiable homicide" being returned, his remains were restored to his distracted widow and family.

This, alas! is no uncommon picture of the events, which, within a comparatively recent time, blotted with blood and tears the pages of Ireland's domestic history. Let us hope, however, that a brighter day is breaking on this distracted land and that the heart—burnings and discords which have for ages torn the bosom of the country may be soothed to rest, and the stormy elements of party strife "mingled in peace."

Athlone is the last town in Connaught through which the traveller passes on this road; in fact, only a portion of it lies in that province, as it is situated on both sides of the Shannon, which here divides the counties of Roscommon and Westmeath; the connecting link between them being the old narrow bridge., the approaches to which are through confined aud dirty lanes, in which all the numerous obstructions of an old Irish street appear to have been collected. Yet this old bridge—unprepossessing as it looks, with its clumsy buttresses and narrow arches frowning over the broad river—should not be overlooked by the tourist, for it was the scene of one of the most memorable events connected with the history of ireland in former days. Here it was, in the war of the Revolution, in 1691, that the concentrated forces of England, under the command of General de Ginkel, effected the passage of the Shannon in opposition to the Irish garrison commanded by Colonel Grace, and their French auxiliaries headed by General St. Ruth. Never was a place defended with more obstinate bravery than this important bridge, which formed at that time the key to the province of Connaught. One of the arches of this bridge was broken down, and though the heavy artillery of De Ginkel, posted on the Westmeath side of the river, had battered the old castle commanding the bridge on the western side, and reduced the walls and defences of the town to a heap of ruins, still lie was unable to effect passage over the broken arch. In the repeated attempts made by the British to force this resolutely maintained position, numerous instances of intrepidity and devoted heroism were exhibited on both sides: the following has, perhaps, been seldom equalled in the history of modern warfare. The English had, on their side of the broken arch, thrown up a regular breastwork, while the defence on the part of the Irish was constructed altogether of earth anti wattles, which was set fire to by the grenades and other burning missiles of the opposing force. "While it was fiercely burning," says a writer on Pie subject, "the English, concealed by the flame and smoke, succeeded in pushing a large beam across the chasm, and now it was only necessary to place boards over the beams, and the river was crossed; when an lrish sergeant and ten men in armour leaped across the burning breastwork, and proceeded to tear up the beams and planks. The British were astonished at such hardihood, arid actually paused in making any opposition, but the next instant a shower of grape-shot and grenades swept these brave men away, who, nevertheless, were instantly succeeded by another party, that, in spite of the iron hail-storm, tore up planks and beams, and foiled the enterprise of their foes. Of this second party, only two escaped: there is scarcely on record a nobler instance of heroism than this deliberate act of these Irish soldiers, who have died without *a name*." There is little doubt that the valour of the brave garrison would have foiled all the attempts of the besiegers to gain possession of the town, had not chance favoured. their designs in an extraordinary manner. The river, which had fallen lower than it had ever been known to do before, was discovered by two Danish soldiers to be fordable below the bridge; availing themselves of this fortunate circumstance, a party of sixty chosen soldiers crossed the river at day-break, and succeeded in placing planks across the chasm in tire bridge, over which the whole body of the British forces poured into the town. The Irish, who were taken by surprise, made no defence, but fled in the utmost disorder in every direction. The French general, St. Ruth, whose confidence in the strength of the town had betrayed him into culpable security, had been amusing himself with his officers, dancing and gambling in a house about a mile from the town, of which the ruins are still pointed out, and laughed to scorn the first account which was brought him of the English having taken the town. The disastrous intelligence was, however, soon fully confirmed, and this rash but brave man, was obliged to make a precipitate retreat into Connaught. where he shortly after ended his unfortunate career, being killed at the battle of Aughrim, as I have already mentioned.

This bridge was built in the early part of Elizabeth's reign, by an architect named Peter Levis, (who was also a dignitary of Christ Church, Dublin,) under the superintendence of Sir Henry Sidney. Ail this is recorded in a monument, which contains in one of its compartments the figure of a man in a clerical habit, grasping in his right hand a pistol, or something which has been conjectured to represent one. Upon thus weapon appears an animal resembling a rat in the act of biting the thumb of the man's hand.

There is a curious story related of this sculpture :—it is said, that the figure of the man represents Peter Levis, at one time a monk in an English monastery, who, having adopted the reformed mode of faith, came to Ireland and obtained preferment in the Protestant church. But the converted monk, though fortunate in his worldly ambition, could never enjoy his prosperity; he was tormented night and day by a good Catholic rat, who, indignant at his apostasy, haunted him at beth and board. For a length of time he bore patiently with this annoyance, until one day, descending from the pulpit where he had been preaching, he perceived the filthy animal hidden in the sleeve of his gown. Unable longer to master his rage, he drew a pistol from his breast, and thought to shoot his persecutor; but before he could execute his intention, the rat sprung at his hand and bit him in the thumb. The wound produced mortification, which terminated in the death of the unfortunate Peter Levis.

Athlone is still one of the principal. military stations in Ireland; its central situation, in a cheap and fertile country, rendering it desirable quarters for the army. The best view of the country around the town is to be obtained from the hill on which the battery is erected. The prospect from thence is certainly extensive, but

367

almost wholly destitute of pictorial interest. Looking eastward, I had close upon my left, Lough Ree, which in fact, is only an extension of the Shannon, that in its course expands into no fewer than five great river-lakes, besides several lesser sheets of water, forming an important feature in the diversified character of this magnificent river.* Behind me lay the unpicturesque tract through which I had been travelling; before me stretched the undulating hills, rich meadows, and broad pastures of Westmeath; while on the south, as far as the eye could reach, the Shannon, after issuing from Lough Ree, swept its heavy waters through a vast and naked plain.

On leaving Athlone I deviated from the direct road, for the purpose of making a little pilgrimage to the hamlet of Lissoy, (now called Auburn) immortalized in Goldsmith's charming poem of "The Deserted Village." It is distant about seven miles from Athlone, near the shores of Lough Ree, which are here more remarkable for quiet pastoral beauty than romantic grandeur—a characteristic that pervades all the writings of this delightful poet of nature. Goldsmith first saw the light at Pallice, near Ballymahon, a few miles from Lissoy, but he spent many of his youthful days at the latter place, where his brother Charles, the curate of a neighbouring parish, resided. His house is still pointed out, but, alas! time and neglect have reduced it to ruins, and a roofless shell is all that now remains to point out the place where

"The village preacher's modest mansion rose."†

But though the mouldering walls be crumbled into dust, and the hearth be cold around which "the long-remembered beggar," "the ruined spendthrift," and "the broken soldier" forgot their sorrows, the memory of that good man, whose picture has been drawn with the feeling of a poet and the affection of a brother, will live for ever on the purest page of English literature. It was to this brother, to whom he was tenderly attached, that Goldsmith dedicated his exquisite Poem of "The Traveller."

---

* In a pamphlet, published a few years since by C. W. Williams, Esq., the following summary of the advantages possessed by this unrivalled river may afford the reader a general idea of their extent and importance. "How," says he, "can we convey to English eyes the picture of the Shannon through its great course? Let us suppose a navigable river taking its risc in some distant county in England, as far from Liverpool as Essex or Middlesex. Suppose it occasionally spreading into noble and picturesque sheets of water of more than twenty miles in length, with numerous islands, receiving the waters of many rivers, and stretching its bays into the adjacent counties, as it were to increase the measure of its utility arid beauty. See it wind. ing its way through Hertfordshire and Bed fordshire, Northamptonshire, and Warwickshire, and the rich soil of Leicestershire, and after passing by Staffordshire, Derbyshire, and Cheshire, falling into the estuary of the Mersey in Lancashire. See it presenting to each of these counties the benefit of fifty miles of navigation, and we shall have a correct view of the extent and capabilities of this river."

†Although Goldsmith laid the scene of this beautiful poem in England, it canot be questioned that the principal features in the landscape, and, perhaps, many of the personages also, have been delineated from his recollections of scenes and personages associated with his boyish years.

"The hawthorn bush, with seats beneath the shade,"
stood until lately in the front of the house,
"Where nut-brown draughts inspired."

Remains of Kilcolman Castle

The scenery in the neighbourhood of Goldsmith's birth-place is delightfully rural; it was on the picturesque banks of the river Inny, with its green islets, and clear waters sparkling and foaming over their rocky bed, that the young poet received the first impressions which called forth the latent spirit of song in his breast. It was to these scenes of his boyish days that he turned in after years with a deeply cherished affection, which the attractions of the world could never eradicate. The fervent wish he entertained of ending his days amongst them, is thus beautifully expressed by himself :—

> "In all my wand'rings through this world of care,
> In all my griefs—and God has giv'n my share—
> I still had hopes, my latest hours to crown,
> Amidst these humble bow'rs to lay me down
> To husband out life's taper at the close,
> And keep the flame from wasting by repose."

While I am upon the subject of places rendered famous by the residence of celebrated poets, I must not pass by unnoticed, KICOLMAN CASTLE, where Spenser, the gifted child of song, composed his inimitable "Faery Queen," and other poems of great merit. The description of a castle in the county of Cork may appear to be unaptly introduced here; but my readers will, I trust, excuse the violation of the unity of place, for the sake of bringing into proximity two poets who have celebrated in sweetly descriptive verses the rural scenery of Ireland.

I confess that I could not view the ruins of this noble castle, within whose deserted walls the proud Desmonds once held sway, and which more recently had been the dwelling-place of one of England's most accomplished poets, without a feeling of deep sadness. The desolate pile, resting in lonely grandeur on the banks of the "Mulha fair and bright," seemed brooding over its vanished greatness, while the poet's favourite stream murmured sadly as it rolled along. It will be recollected by

---

The ale-house, a modern building, which has been erected on the site of the old one, is distinguished by the sign of "The Three Pigeons," which Goldsmith also introduces in his Comedy of "She stoops to Conquer."

"The decent church which tops the neighbouring hill,"

occupies a situation precisely as he describes it. Some of the minor objects, however, have dis-appeared in the lapse of years. The village schoolmaster's "noisy mansion," and "the busy mill" have been swept away by the effacing fingers of Time; but it is stated by the Rev. Mr. Graham, that, "A lady from the neighbourhood of Portglenone, in the county of Antrim, vi-sited Lissoy in the summer of 1817, and was fortunate enough to find in a cottage adjoining the ale-house the identical print of 'the twelve good rules' which ornamented that rural tavern, along with 'the royal game of goose, the wooden clock,'" &c.

I have myself no doubt that the village pedagogue was an actual portrait, and it is not much to suppose, that the original might have been Goldsmith's early instructor; at all events, it would be impossible for any one who has observed the character of the Irish schoolmaster, not to perceive that the picture was drawn from an individual of that singular class.

those who have read Spenser's biography, that he was one of those English settlers to whom Elizabeth granted the forfeited estates in Munster, on condition that no Irish should be permitted to live upon them. The result of this impolitic and impracticable design, as might be foreseen, was to increase the hatred with which the Irish naturally regarded these intruders, and to expose the latter more effectually to the vengeance of their enemies. Spenser had obtained, in 1586, a grant of three thousand acres of land, part of the forfeited estates of the Earl of Desmond :—the following year he took up his residence in his Castle of Kilcolman, and in the favourable retirement of its ancient walls, or wandering along the banks of his beloved Mulla, he composed his beautiful poem of "The Faery Queen," a work which for brilliancy of fancy and richness of thought, is unequalled by anything of a similar nature in the English language. Throughout his poems we find numerous allusions to the scenery in the neighbourhood of Kilcolman and of Castletown Roche, where he possessed another small estate. In the sixth Canto of "The Faery Queen" he particularly notices several remarkable features in the landscape around Kilcolman. In "Mutability" he celebrates the barony of Armoy, or Fermoy, under the name of Armilla; and in "Colin Clout's come home again," he bestows the tribute of his admiration upon the river Mulla, a poetical name substituted by him for the less musical one of the Awbeg, which it still retains. This poem is a beautiful memorial of the friendship which subsisted between Spenser and Sir Walter Raleigh. The poet describes his friend as a Shepherd of the Ocean, coming to visit him in his retirement, in the following exquisite lines :—

> "I sate, as was my trade,
> Under the foot of Mole, that mountain bore;
> Keeping my sheep amongst the cooly shade
> Of the green alders, by the Mulla's shore.
> There a strange shepherd chaunc'd to find me out;
> Whether allured with my pipe's delight,
> Whose pleasing sound yshrilled far about,
> Or thither led by chance, I know not right;
> And now ne might ? himself he did ycleep,
> The Shepierd of the Ocean by name,
> And said he came far from the main sea-deep."

Spenser, it should be observed, especially describes Ireland as a country formerly of such "wealth and goodness," that the gods used to resort thereto for "pleasure and for rest; "his muse expatiates upon tire beauty of her rivers and mountains, and of the delicious verdure of the

> "Woods and forests which therein abound;"

but with all his poetic admiration of the scenery of the country, he displays in his "View of the State of Ireland" a decided dislike and prejudice against the people, arid there can be no doubt that the antipathy was mutual. When the rebellion of Tyrone

371

broke out in 1598, Spenser was compelled to fly to England to escape the fearful retaliations which were everywhere being directed against the English settlers lie saved his life; but his castle was burned, and all his property plundered by the rebels. It is not therefore surprising that he should have written with acrimony against the Irish, whom he regarded as natural and implacable enemies—overlooking the fact, that he had himself been in the first instance a party to the indefensible policy of England in her barbarous design of crushing and exterminating the people of a whole province.

Mr. Trotter, an eccentric but benevolent man, who made a pedestrian tour of Ireland in the year 1814, remarks, that amongst the peasantry of this neighbourhood "the name and condition of Spenser is handed down traditionally, but they seem to entertain no sentiment of respect or affection for his memory;" and, again, in speaking of some engaging traits in the character of the Irish, he says, "It is somewhat surprising that Spenser appears not to have appreciated their good qualities as they merited; but he spoke not their language, and came to their country full of prejudice against them."

The situation of the castle is bleak and cheerless, the surrounding mountains being completely destitute of timber—although a tradition exists that the woods of Kilcolman extended to Buttevant, three miles distance. The estates have long since passed away from the poet's family, who are now supposed to be extinct. The chief portion of the property was forfeited by a grandson of Spenser's, through his attachment to the cause of the unfortunate James II.

This digression done, I return to Lissoy, and with a parting glance at its peaceful bowers,—

"Where smiling spring its earliest visit paid,
And parting summer's ling'ring blooms delay'd,"—

I resume my route towards Dublin.

At Ballymahon I took my passage to Mullingar in one of the iron fly-boats on the Royal Canal. These boats, which are constructed on an improved principle, are tracked by two horses, and travel with sufficient rapidity to compensate, in some measure, for the very limited accommodation they afford to passengers. Being built almost wholly with a view to swiftness, they are made extremely sharp and narrow, and are in this respect a vast improvement on the unwieldy old passage-boats, that literally have been unable to keep pace with the march of knowledge in travelling.

The vicinity of Mullingar is adorned with numerous villas and mansions of the gentry; and the face of the country, though not strikingly picturesque, is luxuriant in wood and water. Several beautiful lakes are scattered throughout this district, and two of the most beautiful of these sheets of water, Lough Ouel and Lough Ennel, are situated within a short distance of Mullingar. The first of these is a sweet little lake, about a mile in width, and not more than three in length, boasting—it is true—none of the sublime characteristics of Killarney, the wild magnificence of the mountain lakes of Connemara, or the solitary grandeur of Gougane Barra, or Glendalough; yet excelled by none mn the softer traits of pastoral beauty, and the many charms of richly cultivated hills and verdant lawns, sloping gently to the margin of the tranquil lake, which holds in its fond embrace—

> "The gay
> Young group of tufted islands born of him."

There is an old legend relating to this charming little lake, which struck me as being singularly romantic arid original. It is said that the lake originally was situated in some part of Connaught, and formed the principal ornament of a certain fairy's domains. Another fairy, who dwelt in Leinster, being on a visit to her Connaught sister, became so charmed with the beauty of this sweet little mountain lough, that she besought the Connaught fairy to lend it to her for a few days; to which the latter readily consented. The borrower instantly gathered the lake in the skirt of her gown, and hastening home to Westmeath, deposited her borrowed waters in the valley where Lough Ouel now reposes. The period for which the Connaught fairy had lent her lake having elapsed, sine civilly demanded it back; but the Leinster lady, acting upon the legal axiom, that "possession is nine points of the law," flatly refused to restore the property, and the other being unable to assert her right by force, was obliged to return to the lonely mountain glen which had once contained her beautiful lake, and mourn in silence for her lost treasure. An elderly gentleman of my acquaintance who knows a good deal of the world, concludes the legend differently, He says, that the Connaught fairy commenced a suit in chancery for the recovery of her right, and that the lake remains in statu quo until the case shall be decided.

Lough Ennel, or, as it is now called, Belvedere Lake, lies between two and three miles south of Mullingar: it is somewhat larger than Lough Ouel, and partakes of the same pastoral character in its scenery. Its eastern shore, adorned with gentlemen s residences, has a rich park-like appearance, and the numerous woody islands that are scattered over its surface add considerably to the beauty of the picture.

After leaving Mullingar, I proceeded by a cross-road to Trim, the assize-town of the county Meath. Though of considerable antiquity, the town is now of little importance, and, with the exception of a handsome Corinthian pillar, erected in commemoration of the victories of the Duke of Wellington, and surmounted by a statue of the hero of Waterloo, it contains nothing of modern date that merits attention. The principal object of curiosity in Trim is its ancient castle, whose venerable ruins, occupying a commanding situation on the banks of the memorable Boyne, bear evidence of its former strength arid importance. It was erected, according to the most authentic authorities, at an early period after the arrival of the English, by Hugh de Lacy, the favourite and confidant of Henry II, to whom lie made the grant of a vast extent of the surrounding country. It is not my intention to trace the history of this old fortress through the various fortunes it experienced during five centuries of strife and bloodshed. I am not about to recount all the sieges and assaults, the burnings and sackings it has suffered in that time, nor to tell how often it changed masters as the scale of war preponderated one way or the other; it will be sufficient for me to state, that it has been at various times the scene of action in the civil commotions of Ireland, until the year 1650, when the castle was dismantled, and permitted to fall into decay.* On the, opposite side of the river are the ruins of an extensive abbey, destroyed in the was of the seventeenth century :—it is said to have been founded by St. Patrick, and the church served as a cathedral to Trim, which was the see of a bishop until it became united with the diocese of Meath.

At a short distance from Trim on the south, is the parsonage of Laracor, occasionally the residence of the eccentric Dean Swift, and during his absences inhabited by the unfortunate and accomplished Esther Johnson, immortalized by his pen under the name of "Stella," whose generous attachment to a selfish man, through a life clouded by public reproach, merited a far better fate than she experienced.

Between Trim arid the pretty little town of Summerhill stand the ruins of DANGAN CASTLE, celebrated as being the birth-place of England's greatest general, ARTHUR DUKE OF WELLINGTON, who, on the 1st of May, 1769, came "into this breathing world," unheralded by any prodigy, undistinguished by any omen which might foreshadow the high and glorious destiny which awaited him. The remains of the ancient castle consist of the outer walls of the keep, to which a modern mansion, built in the Italian style, has been added by one of the modern possessors. The general effect of this once noble edifice must have been exceedingly beautiful when viewed in its perfect state, with its battlements and turrets emerging from the crowding woods. But unfortunately the demnesne and castle passed from their original possessor's into the hands of stranger's : they were sold by the Marquess of Wellesley to Colonel Burrows, and by him let to Mr. O'Connor. While in the possession of the latter gentleman it was destroyed by fire, and all that now remains of this once stately pile is a naked arid desolate shell.† The noble woods, too, which adorned the demesne have shared in the general destruction, and all the giants of the sylvan scene have been prostrated beneath the ruthless axe. How different was the appearance it presented when Mr. Trotter visited it in 1814. "From every part of the adjacent country," he writes, "the woods, and frequently the Castle of Dangan were visible. We continued to walk on magic ground :—the varied landscapes of a fine

---

* The castle of Trim enjoys the reputation of having been at one time a royal prison. Richard II. when in Ireland being alarmed at the success of his rival, the Duke of Lancaster, in England, imprisoned in Trim Castle the duke's son, Henry, who had accompanied him in his Irish expe-dition. It is scarcely necessary to add, that the illustrious captive was afterwards King Henry V.

† I believe that even these venerable relics of its former grandeur have now disappeared, and that "two small pillars which crown tine summits of two verdant hills," are the only vestiges which remain to mark the birth-place of the illustrious warrior.

corn-country, always terminated by the widely extended woods of Dangan, could not but please." Yet even at that time decay and neglect had begun to do their work upon the place, for he also remarks, that, "the improvements and lakes which once highly adorned the demesne are lost through neglect, and the fine gardens are uncultivated." This intelligent traveller learnt, while lingering in this neighbourhood, that a cottage, in which the Duke of Wellington had resided in great privacy for two or three years, when the Marquis of Wellesley was proposing to sell Dangan, was to be seen near Trim. If this retreat of the future victor of Waterloo be still in existence, I have not been fortunate enough to see it. Mr. Trotter thus describes his visit in a very animated mariner. "We proceeded," say's he, "with much eagerness to this little country-house : we soon saw it buried in trees, We reached the gate of its avenue, which is straight, of modest appearance, and lined with tall ash-trees. The house is perfectly rural, with a small lawn, and pretty shrubberies round it; but very simple, and just fit for a small domestic family. The apartments are commodious, and all the accommodations good, but on the most modest scale. The garden pleased us most; it is good and quite rural, suiting to the character' of the place." It is not improbable that thee duke was residing in this secluded habitation when his great rival, Bonaparte, was pursuing his splendid career in Italy.

I suppose it would be considered a grave offence were I to quit the county Meath without noticing the famous "Hill of Tara," celebrated by ancient bards and historians for its Teaghmor, or Great House, where, down to the middle of the sixth century, triennial parliaments of the kingdom were held;—for its sumptuous palace, the residence of a long and illustrious line of monarchs; and for its college of learned men, where the arts and sciences were cultivated and taught. Keating, O'Halloran, and O'Flaherty, whose poetic histories abound with florid descriptions of the grandeur and magnificence of the royal residence of Teaghmor, have dwelt with fond delight upon the solemnities of the periodical parliament, at which the kings of Leinster, Ulster, Munster, and Connaught are said to have assisted, in conjunction with the toparchs, dynasts, bards or sennachies, priests, and "men of learning, distinguished by their abilities in all arts and professions, "in framing laws, and

---

* There is preserved in the library of Trinity College, Dublin, an Irish manuscript containing a curious description of the Banqueting-Hall of Teaghmor. It states, that the palace was formerly the seat of Conn of the Hundred Battles, and of every king who ruled in Teaghmor to the time of Niall. In the reign of Cormac, the palace was nine hundred feet square; the surrounding rath, seven din, or casts of a dart : it contained one hundred and fifty apartments, one hundred and fifty dormitories for the guards, with sixty men in each. The height was twenty-seven cubits; it had twelve doors, twelve porches, and one thousand guests daily, besides princes, orators, men of science, engravers of gold and silver, carvers, modellers, and nobles. The eating-hall had twelve divisions in each wing, with tables and passages round them; sixteen attendants on each side; eight to tine astrologers, historians, and secretaries, in the rear of the hall, and two to each table at the door. Two oxen, two sheep, and two hogs were divided equally at each meal to each side. The quantity of meat and butter consumed is incredible. There were twenty-seven kitchens, one hundred and fifty common drinking-horns, and nine cisterns for washing the hands rind feet of the guests.

making wise ordinances for the government of the kingdom.* But, alas! for the past glory of Ireland, there remain no traces now of these stately palaces—not a vestige exists of the proud halls, where "chiefs and ladies bright." were wont to assemble; the voice of the bard is hushed—and "the harp," as Moore touchingly sings :—

> "The harp, that once through Tara's halls
> The soul of music shed,
> Now hangs as maute on Tara's walls
> As if that soul were fled."

Unfortunately, however, not even a wall has been left on which a bard's harp or antiquarian's conjecture might be huing. The remains of a few circular earthen entrenchments on the summit of a lofty green hill, rising from the centre of an extensive plain, are all that the most curious eye can now discover of the vanished splendour of the Hill of Tara. Notwithstanding that I differ with those writers, whose heated fancies would invest every object connected with Ireland's ancient history with a halo of gorgeous light, and in their eagerness to vindicate the fallen greatness of their native country, have suffered themselves to wander into the fairy regions of romance; I am far from coinciding with those cold sceptics who deny that civilization had considerably advanced in Ireland before Britain had emerged from the depths of barbarism.

When the incursions of the northern barbarians had extinguished almost every ray of knowledge in southern Europe, Ireland, remote and insulated, enjoyed a happy tranquillity. Her seminaries and colleges bestowed gratuitous instruction, not only upon her own children, but also upon literary foreigners, who were supplied with every accommodation free of expense. It was thus that while native genius was fostered, foreign talents received liberal encouragement, and Ireland became a great school in which learned strangers pursued their studies in tranquillity. We have incontrovertible evidence to prove that Ireland produced at a very early period men eminent in every department of literature. Of these none have been more celebrated than Johannes Erigena, the preceptor and counsellor of Alfred the Great, a profound theologian and philosopher, who opposed the doctrine of the Real Presence, and was the first who blended the scholastic theology with the mystic, and formed them into one system. Attempts have been made to rob Ireland of the honour of his birth, but Camden and Mosheim have completely established the fact of his Milesian nativity. The latter learned writer pays the following honourable tribute to the country and to the man. "The philosophy and logic," says he, "that were taught in the European schools in the ninth century scarcely deserved such honourable titles, and were little better than an empty jargon. There were, however, to be found in various places, *particularly among the Irish,* men of acute parts arid extensive knowledge, who were perfectly well entitled to the appellation of philosophers. The chief of them was Johannes Scotus Erigena, a native of Ireland, the friend and companion of Charles the Bald." Startling as it may seem to some persons, we are also indebted to this eminent man for tIre origin of the System of Phrenology, the rudiments of which will be found in his noble work "Margarita Philosophicæ" or "The Pearl of Philosophy," which contains an engraving of the human cranium, mapped, and divided into organs, in exactly tire same manner that modern phrenology teaches, differing only in the arrangement and nomenclature of the faculties. Feargil, or, as his name was latinized, Vergilius, afterwards bishop of Saltzburg, was the first who asserted the sphericity of the earth, and the doctrine of the antipodes, for which heretical opinions he was persecuted by Pope Boniface, who directed that he should be expelled the church. Both these illustrious men lived before Wickliffe, Luther, Galileo, and Copernicus, and were consequently the discoverers of the reformed systems of religion and astronomy, which produced such momentous results throughout Europe. The celebrity which the universities of Ireland obtained may be estimated by a Latin line which grew into a kind of proverb :—"Amandatus est ad disciplinam *in Hibernia,*" was the necessary character to constitute the gentleman and the scholar in the middle ages; it was what the "Doctus Athenis vivere" was to the Romans in the Augustan age. Scaliger the younger writes, "Du temps du Charlemagne, deux cents ans après *omnes ferè docti étoint d'Irelande.*" But it would be idle to accumulate evidence upon a point which appears so clearly established :—that Ireland eclipsed all competitors in the literature of those early ages, and freely imparted to less favoured countries the benefits she had acquired, few will be found to deny. The causes of the gradual decay of the arts of peace, and the decline of literature in the island, will be found in the ensangurned pages of its history; let those who read it wonder no longer that piety and wisdom fled affrighted from their desecrated retreats, when rapine and slaughter spread their terrors through the land. Yet under every disadvantage a deep passion for poetry and letters still exists amongst the Irish people. In the remote mountain districts of the west, it was no unusual thing, a few years since, to meet a half-clad peasant well acquainted with the classics, and until very lately Greek and Latin were commonly taught in all the hedge-schools of Cork and Kerry.

To return : it has been conjectured that the Hall of Tarn, though not built of stone, might have been constructed of less durable materials, with a considerable degree of elegance, which would account satisfactorily for the non-existence of any ruins; and when we recollect that King John, on his arrival in Dublin, lodged in a palace of wattles, or wickerwork, plastered with clay, there can be no reasonable grounds for rejecting the hypothesis with respect to the court of Teaghmor. Hollingshed, though he disputes the accuracy of the Irish historians in their description of the magnificence of this palace, admits that, "the place seemeth to bear the show of an ancient and famous monument," and thus infers that some memorial of its ancient grandeur existed in his time.*

Instead of proceeding from Trim to Dublin by the more direct Enniskillen road, I preferred making a little detour for the purpose of regaining the great western road, which passes through the pretty villages of Leixlip and Lucan, and the picturesque country bordering the Liffey. A little to the westward of the straggling town of Kilcock stands the hill of Cappagh, which, though not more than three hundred feet above the sea, is supposed to be one of the highest points between Dublin and Galway. From the summit of this hill the prospect extends over the rich pastures of Meath, the fertile plains of Kildare, and to the borders of the distant bog of Allen on the south. This immense bog, or rather series of bogs, stretches from the borders of the county Dublin, across the county Kildare and the King's county as far as the Shannon, and beyond it westward into the counties of Galway and Roscommon; spreading laterally through the counties of Meath and Westmeath to the north, and the Queen's county and the county Tipperary to the south. It has been computed that it formerly contained 1,000,000 of acres, but by means of cultivation and drainage it is now diminished to 300,000 acres, and it is extremely probable that in a few years these immense and dreary tracts will be entirely reclaimed. Travellers who have seen only the morasses of England and other countries must not form an idea of the Irish bogs from these low swampy wastes, which no art could render productive. The Irish bogs, on the contrary, are generally found in elevated situations,† and are capable of being reclaimed and brought into productive cultivation by means of drainage and manuring. Various ingenious conjectures have been made respecting their origin; but all being founded on uncertain data, I shall not hazard a positive opinion on the subject. It seems, however, to be generally admitted, that they are not of primary formation, but have been produced by accidental and gradual means. The most generally received theory is, that they owe their origin to stagnant water, collected by means of the immense forests which formerly overspread the island. It has been surmised that quantities of timber, overthrown by storms, earthquakes, or fire, and remaining intermingled upon the ground, retained the water of the floods and rains, and that the portion of vegetable

---

* Alfred, king of the Northumbrian Saxons, who, according to Bede, returned to Ireland to avoid the persecution of his brother, about the year 685, devoted himself while in exile to study, and composed a poem in the Irish language, describing what he had observed in various parts of Ireland. Speaking of the palace of Teaghmor, he says :—

> "I found in the great fortress of Meath,
> Valour, hospitality, and truth,
> Bravery, purity, and mirth—
> The protection of all Ireland."

† The Bog of Allen, for instance, at its highest elevation, is two hundred and seventy feet above the level of the sea; more than one river has its origin in this bog, and the water which supplies the highest level of the Grand Canal is drawn from the same source.

matter composing the leaves, bark, and lesser branches, decayed and formed the ground-work of a rank vegetation, which, in process of time, overspread the districts where those obstructions had occurred. This conjecture of the accidental and comparatively recent formation of bogs is borne out by the fact, that, under some bogs of considerable extent, there have been discovered indubitable proofs that the submerged surface had at one time afforded an abiding-place for man;—household utensils, farming implements, weapons of warfare, ancient leather shoes, ornaments of dress, and a variety of other articles of a like nature are constantly dug up from bogs at various depths. Trees, too, have been found in great abundance;—some of them appear to have been broken as by the wind, others retain the marks of the axe upon their trunks, and many exhibit the agency of fire, by which means Mr. Wakefield imagines they were levelled during the early wars of the inhabitants, when these dense forests formed places of refuge and defence. The strong antiseptic quality of the Irish hogs is a singular but well authenticated fact, which still further removes them from the characteristics of the common morass. It is impossible to penetrate any depth below the surface of any of them without discovering the miscellaneous debris of animal and vegetable substances, free from important marks of decay. But while the bog is a known preservative of some substances; it is a no less powerful agent in the decomposition of others; thus, while the timber of a tree is found perfectly sound, not a vestige of the bark remains, and while the most delicate plants are preserved uninjured, the mould from which they drew their support has entirely disappeared. It is remarkable, also, though these bogs usually contain a vast quantity of stagnant water, that the persons who dwell in their vicinity are not subject to any of those diseases to which people who inhabit low or swampy districts elsewhere are invariably subject.

Although the bogs of Ireland in their natural state are unprofitable to the agriculturist, they are not without their advantages to the poor peasantry, who derive from them all their fuel; and those dingy and barren wastes covered with patches of coarse grass and brown heath, which suggest to the mind only feelings of desolation, contain within their dark bosoms the cheerful peat that bestow's warmth and light to the cotter's humble hearth. Great quantities of this peat or turf are transported from the Bog of Allen to Dublin, by means of long flat-bottomed boats, which ply on the canal. The condition of the poor people, whose employment it is to cut and prepare this turf for sale, is miserable in the extreme. Their dwellings, which are mere hovels constructed of sods, are scattered along the banks of the canal, and present a melancholy picture to the eye of the traveller unaccustomed to the scenes of abject wretchedness, which are too frequently to be found amongst the poor of Ireland. The manner in which one of these turf-cutters commences operations is exceedingly primitive, and reminds us of the operations of an emigrant making a first settlement in the back-woods of America. His first care is to rent a small patch of bog in a favourable situation, near the canal; his next, to provide himself and his family with a dwelling : for this purpose he seeks a bank in a dry situation, where he excavates his future habitation to such a depth that little more is visible than the roof, which is composed of sods pared from the bog, the herbage of which being turned upwards, so perfectly assimilates with the surrounding scenery, that the eye would pass it over unnoticed, were it not attracted by a number of half-naked chubby children, grouped round the door, with the cat, the dog, and the pig, the joint inmates of the cabin; while a cloud of smoke, penetrating through, and curling over the crannied roof—presents more the appearance of a reeking turf-heap than a human habitation.

The phenomenon of a moving bog has frequently been seen in Ireland; large portions of the surface sliding or flowing from their original position, cover the adjacent country, and in many cases cause a great deal of damage, by destroying arable land and overwhelming houses, corn, and hay-stacks. In September, 1835, the inhabitants in the neighbourhood of the extensive bog of Sloggan, which lies near the coach-road between Randalstown and Ballymena, were alarmed by several loud reports, hike discharges of artillery or distinct claps of thunder, proceeding from the bog; an immense field of which, to their astonishment, they beheld slowly moving towards the road, which it completely covered to the extent of fifty perches, and continued its progress downwards to the river Main, into which it flowed and nearly choked up the channel. These singular disruptions are believed to be caused by the lodgment of a body of water between the porous bog and the substratum of hard clay or gravel upon which it usually rests; so that when the bog, as is frequently the case, lies higher than the land in its vicinity, and when the water has accumulated to a certain degree, it forces up the superincumbent mass, and carries it away to a less elevated situation.

Leaving Kilcock, the coach-road passes through the neat little town of Maynooth, chiefly remarkable for containing the modern college of St. Patrick, in which the Irish Roman Catholic clergy are now, with few exceptions, educated. The ruins of the ancient Castle of Maynooth—once a principal for-tress of the bold Geraldines, ancestors of the present Duke of Leincester, are an object of great interest to every visitor acquainted with the eventful history of their noble owners. What stirring tales might be recounted of the long race of warriors who kept their state within these princely towers, beloved by their friends and followers, and hated and feared by their enemies! Indeed, the peculiar characteristics of a Geraldine's mind were eminently suited to secure popular affection : easily displeased, sooner appeased— warm friends and bitter foes—turbulent subjects—mild governors—liberal, brave, pious, and merciful. The anecdote recorded of the fiery Gerald, the eighth earl of Kildare, would be equally characteristic of any other of the family.

"In a rage with one of his followers, an English horseman seeing the chafed earl in his fearful mood, offered Master Boice,* a gentleman of his household, an Irish hobby, (pony,) on condition that he would go up to his lord and pluck a hair out of his black beard. Boice, who knew his master, and felt how far he might venture on a Geraldine's nature, even while boiling in the heat of his choler, approached his lord, and said, 'Here, my master, is one who has promised me a choice horse, if I snip one hair out of your honour's chin.' 'One hair,' quoth the earl, 'I agree to; but mark me, Boice, thou malapert varlet, if thou pluckest more than one, I promise thee to bring my fist from thine ear.' "lt was said of this stout earl, that he was made by Henry VIII. ruler over all Ireland because Ireland could not rule him, and that he excused himself for burning the cathedral of Cashel, by assuring his majesty he would not have done so, were he not informed that the archbishop was therein. Where, in like manner, could the romancist find a subject of such singular interest as in the rash career of Lord Thomas Fitzgerald, or, as he was usually called, "Silken Thomas,"† whose chivalric courage, mad ambition, arid melancholy fate, form one of the most remarkable pieces of personal history anywhere recorded ?

Within a mile of the town of Maynooth is Carton, the spacious but irregularly built mansion of the Duke of Lerncester; it stands in the midst of a noble demesne, laid out with judicious taste, and offering to the eye a great variety of scenery, partaking, however, more of the graceful and tranquil than of the wild and magnificent in its character.

The little town of Leixlip is delightfully situated near the banks of the Liffey, in a

---

* A pithy saying has been recorded of this Boice; the occasion of which being *a-propos* to the subject I am upon, I shall relate. When Lord Thomas Fitzgerald, *(Silken Thomas)* was in rebellion against England, his castle of Maynooth was invested by Sir William Brereton, Lord Thomas being then absent in Munster. After a siege of fourteen days, little impression was made upon the castle, and in all probability the English commander would have been compelled to retire baffled in his design, were it riot for the perfidy of the governor, Christopher Parese, a faithless *foster-brother* to Lord Thomas, who bargained with the enemy to betray the fortress into their hands for a stipulated sum of money. Accordingly, the garrison having been encouraged to a deep carouse, and the soldiers overcome with wine and sleep, the traitorous governor gave the concerted signal, when the English entered, and took possession of the castle with little opposition. The double-dyed traitor, Parese, expecting great honour for the part Ire had played, presented himself with unblushing effrontery before the lord-deputy, who thus ad-dressed him—"Master Parese, thou hast certainly saved our lord the king much charge and many of his subjects' lives; but that I may better know how to advise his Highness how to reward three, I would ascertain what the Lord Thomas Fitzgerald hath done for thee." Parese, thinking to enhance his services, recounted minutely every favour that the Geraldine had conferred on him from his youth up. To which the deputy replied, "And how, Parese, couldst thou find in thy heart to betray the castle of so kind a lord ? Here, Mr. Treasurer, pay down the money that he has covenanted for, and here also, had I known of this, your lordship should not have had the castle so easily." Whereupon one Mr. Boice, a friend of Fitzgerald, who was standing by, cried out, *"Antraugh," (too late,)* which gave rise to a proverbial saying used long after in Ireland, *"Too late, quoth Boice."*

† This ill-fated young nobleman received the title of *"Silken Thomas"* from the magnificence of Iris attire, and that of his retainers, the housings of whose horses were gorgeously embroidered with silk. The history of his mad rebellion, his overthrow, and subsequent execution in England, would occupy more space than could be devoted to it in this work.

richly diversified country. From the bridge the view is beautiful beyond description; on either hand the river is seen foaming and fretting over its rugged bed, until it is lost between its picturesque banks, while on a commanding eminence the old castle of Leixlip lifts its embattled towers above the thick oak woods that surround it. At a short distance above the town is that romantic spot called THE SALMON LEAP, where the river, tumbling over a succession of rocky ledges, forms a beautiful cascade; the precipitous banks are thickly covered with wood, and the whole scene, though not on so extensive a scale as many of the celebrated falls in Scotland or Switzerland, is excelled by few in natural beauty. Indeed, but for the barbarous intrusion of a modern business-like, stone-built, and slated mill, which has been erected close to the falls by some plodding trader, it would be difficult to find a place in which so many picturesque beauties are combined. The Salmon Leap is a favourite place for picnic parties of the citizens of Dublin, who make excursions to it in the summer months—dining on the grassy shore—or on the broad tabular rocks, which in the dry season are left bare by the fallen waters, and afford convenient platforms for the accommodation of the gay groups assembled there, who,

> Forth from tIre crowded city's dust and noise,
> Wander abroad to taste pure Nature's joys;
> To laugh and sport, amid spend the hive-long day,
> In harmless merriment and jocund play.

XXIII.

FEW cities are more fortunate than Dublin in the beauty of their environs. On the east it has its noble bay, which by many travellers has been placed in rivalry with the far-famed Bay of Naples; on the north the villages of Glasnevin and Finglas, seated upon the banks of the meandering Tolka, in whose picturesque vicinity Addison, Swift, Steele, Tickell, Delaney, and Parnell, had their constant or occasional residence,—the rich meadows of Artane, and the green lanes and pleasant shores of Clontarf, terminated by the magnificent promontory of Howth; westward stretches the Ph Park with the beauteous vale, through which winds the Liffey's silver stream, its steep banks enriched with gardens, pleasure-houses, and charming villas, backed by the blue chain of Wicklow Mountains, extending towards the south; on which side lie the pleasant outlet of Rathmines, the bathing village of Blackrock, favourably

Salmon Leap at Laxlip

situated in a sheltered nook of the bay, Kingstown and its fine harbour, Killiney Bay and Hill, and the magnificent sweep of coast extending from thence to Bray Head, forming a succession of picturesque objects, which, for beauty and variety, is not approached by the suburbs of any capital in the world. After leaving Leixlip we enter the county Dublin, and passing through the richly wooded demesne of Colonel Vesey, bordering on the river, we reach the Spa House Hotel, near Lucan, erected for the accommodation of the numerous visitors who, some years since, resorted to a chalybeate spa, discovered here in 1758; the waters of which are said to possess singular virtues in cutaneous and some other diseases. Fashion, however, whose capricious taste merit cannot command, withdrew her favouring influence from the Lucan Spa, and it is now little frequented, except by those who, attracted by the romantic scenery, spend a few weeks of the summer season in its delightful neighbourhood. From Lucan the road runs nearly parallel to the course of the Liffey, whose banks, enriched by ancient woods, over-hanging the silent waters, or spreading into verdant slopes, never fail to elicit the admiration of every beholder. It would be impossible for a stranger to pass the demesne of Woodlands, the seat of Colonel White, without being struck by its eminently beautiful situation. The fine lawn in front of the house is girt by rich woods, in which are many romantic rides and walks, leading through sylvan glades or deep glens, where the sparkling of bright streams and the glad sound of waters murmuring over their pebbly beds, or leaping down the rocks, soothe the mind to kindred repose. But the chief point of attraction on this road—at least to the good people of Dublin is the range of steep banks that rise above the river near Castleknock,* which, from the extensive cultivation of, strawberries upon their southern side, have received the name of "The Strawberry Beds." Here, in the genial month of June, when the fruit is ripe, the citizens repair in great numbers, and here they may be seen on fine sunny evenings sauntering along

* On a green circular knoll in the demesne of Castleknock are the remarkable ruins of the ancient castle of that name, once of considerable strength and celebrity; it was founded in the reign of Henry II. by Hugh Tyrrell, in whose family it remained until taken by Edward Bruce, when he invaded Ireland, in 1316. It was also captured in 1642 by Colonel Monk, who inhumanly put its defenders to death. This is the matter-of-fact history of the castle; but there are two singular legends attached to it, which it would be unpardonable to omit. The first relates to an old window, still pointed out to the curious, in the shattered wall of the ruin, of which old Stanihurst, says, "Though it be neither glazed nor latticed, but open, yet let the weather he stormy, and the wind bluster boisterously on any side of the house, and place a candle there, and it will burn as quietly as if no puff of wind blew. This may be tried at this day, whoso shall be willing to put it in practice." The other legend is even more marvellous than that of the window, which rests on the accuracy of an oral tradition. It relates that St. Patrick once came to Castleknock to endeavour to convert to Christianity Morrishtac, a Danish king, who then possessed the castle. The old infidel, after listening patiently to the saint's harangue for a considerable time, at length began to nod, and, finally, came out with a most irreverent snore at the conclusion of one of the preacher's strongest arguments. The saint, enraged beyond bounds at the unchristian conduct of the king, prayed that he might sleep in the same place and posture till the last day. It is scarcely necessary to add, that his prayer was granted, and that the sleeping monarch remains to the present day inclosed in an underground chamber, to which a winding passage in the thickness of the walls is said to conduct.

the banks of the river, scrambling up the precipitous banks, or seated in social groups in the little summer-houses and tea-gardens that invitingly tempt the "passing traveller to stay," committing fearful destruction upon the delicious produce of "the Beds," which is sometimes eaten au naturel, but more frequently, as the old song says, "smothered in cream." Oh! the pleasures of a strawberry frolic—none but those who have enjoyed one can appreciate it as it deserves. The drive down to "the Beds" on an outside jaunting-car, on a fine summer's afternoon, is delightful beyond description, particularly if you remember to secure your seat on the left side of the vehicle, by which means you may, while riding along the picturesque road through the Park, survey at your leisure all the beauties of the Lower road, and trace the Liffey's silver stream meandering through verdant meadows, and watering the rich valley, where stands the romantic village of Chapel Izod, formerly the suburban residence of the viceroys of Ireland. Indeed, I know of no place from whence a more comprehensive and finer view of Dublin may be obtained than from the eminence near the magazine in the Phœnix Park. From this point the spectator sees before him the entire extent of the city, its magnificent bridges, the domes and spires of its public buildings and churches; the beautiful "Nelson Pillar," erected in honour of the hero of the Nile, rising from the broad mass of houses; and close upon his left, the "Wellington Testimonial," a lofty and massive, but not remarkably elegant obelisk, intended to commemorate the victories of the great captain of the age.* The Phœnix Park is situated on the north-west side of the city,† and whether we view it as a royal demesne, containing the summer residence of the viceroy, or an extensive place of resort, for the recreation and exercise of the citizens of Dublin, it is equally worthy the tourist's inspection. Though hitherto little indebted to the hand of art for improvement, except in the immediate vicinity of the vice-regal lodge, and that portion which adjoins the Zoological Gardens and the grand entrance-gate, this demesne contains many picturesque spots, romantic glens, and wild retreats—where nature displays her choicest charms to those who love to seek her in her sequestered haunts. Numerous hawthorn groves are scattered through the park, which in spring time are loaded with snow-white blossoms, and give a delicious fragrance to the air.

---

* This obelisk, erected on a rising ground, near the grand entrance of the Ph Park, forms a conspicuous object in almost every view of Dublin. On the summit of a flight of steps a simple square pedestal is placed, on the four sides of which are spaces designed to receive panels, on which are to be sculptured figures in relief, emblematical of the principal victories won by the duke. But this portion of time design, as well as the proposed equestrian statue of his grace, intended to surmount a smaller pedestal in front of the larger one, has been properly left unfinished during the lifetime of the renowned warrior. From the platform a massive obelisk rises, on the four sides of which are inscribed the names of all the victories gained by the Duke of Wellington. The whole structure is of plain mountain granite, without any other decoration whatever. The base, formed by the steps, is one hundred and twenty feet on each side, and twenty feet in perpendicular height. Sub-plinth of pedestal on the top of the steps sixty feet square by ten feet high. Pedestal, fifty-six feet square by twenty-four feet high. Obelisk, twenty-eight feet square at the base, and one hundred and fifty feet high, diminishing one inch in every foot. Total height of the monument, two hundred and five feet.

The open spaces between the woods and copses are for the most part irregular and uneven; the principal level plain, so to call it, is "the Fifteen Acres;" thotigh why so named, it would be difficult to determine, as its area is said to contain three hundred acres. This space is used for exercising the troops of the garrison : reviews and sham battles being frequently exhibited here during the summer season. But the Fifteen Acres has obtained its principal notoriety from its being the favourite ground on which affairs of honour, in the hair-trigger days of Ireland, were commonly settled at ten paces distance. I was much amused by the observations of an old man whom I met early one summer's morning, wandering near this celebrated spot. At first, I thought he might have been engaged gathering decayed brambles for firewood; but I was soon undeceived in my supposition, for I perceived that he kept gliding from place to place, apparently without any object. This singular conduct excited my curiosity. I determined, if possible, to learn what business he was upon, and intercepting the old man in one of his traverses, I commenced a conversation, in which, like most of his countrymen, he seemed perfectly willingly to take his part.

"A fine morning, my friend," said I.

"Beautiful, sir, praise be to God for it! The rain last night will bring up the late pyatees finely, though it has made the grass mighty damp, and my ould shoes an't in the best ordher for keeping out that same," replied the man, exhibiting a pair of tattered and crannied shoes, into which the wet had soaked and penetrated in every direction.

"Why then do you walk here?" said I, "the road and foot-paths of the park are dry and pleasant. But you may have business ?"

"Sorra hap'orth of business has myself here now, sir; but it wasnt always so— many's the guinea I airned before five o'clock in the morning on this very spot, when times was good;—and though my purfission ain't worth following of late, I can't break myself of my ould ways, and I come wandhering out to the ould spot every morning just as I used to do."

This speech of the old man's puzzled me exceedingly, and I inquired what his profession might be.

"Why then, sir," replied he, "I'll never deny it, I 'm by trade a tailor, but I gave up stitching long ago, and went into the *jewelling* line."

† Doctor Walsh in his History of Dublin, says, that this park derives its name from a corruption of the Irish term *"Fionn-uisge"* (clear or fair water)—pronounced *finniské,* and which articulated in the English manner, might be easily changed into the word Phœnix The spring, or well, believed to have given the name to this demesne, is a strong chalybeate, and is situated, according to the Doctor, "in a glen beside the lower lake, near the grand entrance into the vice-regal lodge, and has been frequented from time immemorial, for the supposed salubrity of its waters." Notwithstanding the celebrity of the spring, it remained neglected and exposed until the year 1800, when the Duke of Richmond, then lord lieutenant of Ireland, having derived great benefit from the use of its waters, had it inclosed and covered over with a small structure of Portland stone. Behind the spring is a rustic cottage, containing seats for the accommodation of those who visit the well to drink of the sanative but nauseous beverage it affords.

"The jewelling line?" I repeated, rather surprised.

"Yes, sir; I'm the boy that you might have heerd tell of;—Mick Delany, that attended on all the jintlemen who used to come out here to fight jewels before their breakfasts."

"Oh!" cried I, with some difficulty repressing my inclination to indulge in a hearty fit of laughter,—when I understood that the *jewels* my informant alluded to were those hostile meetings which so frequently took place on that ground. "And pray in what capacity did you act in these affairs of honour?"

"Why, sir," said he, with inimitable gravity, "I was the regulather. I could point out the exact spot every *jewel* had been fought for the last five-and-forty years, and be the same token I was prisent by at the most of them myself; and so, sir, by that manes, when jintlemin came here to settle their little differences quiet and asy; they were always glad to meet a knowledgable boy like myself who could put them up to the business in style, and keep a sharp look out for the murdhering villyans of polis, that was always spiling our sport."

"But how," I inquired, "did it happen that you were present at so many of these affairs?"

"Oh, asy enough, sir! I used to get up at cock-shout every morning regular, and walk out here to the Fifteen Acres, where I was as sure of falling in with two or three *jewelling* parties in the week, as I'd be of finding parthridges in stubbles. Most of the jintlemin ped me for my sarvices, and those that had no occasion for them ped me to get quit of me."

"So that in either way you were certain of being paid," said I.

"In coorse, sir; but that was in the good ould times when *jewelling* was in fashion, and when no jintleman could purshume to howld up his head amongst jintlemin till he had been *out* a couple of times at laste. Now, sir, they settle all their disputes in a mane and dirty way tipon paper; there's no sperrit among the quality of late, like as there was when bould Harry Grattan, and little counsellor Curran, Bully Egan, and the ould joker Lord Norbury, that by all accounts *shot* himself up to be a judge, used to take the shine in Dublin. Them was the right sort of jintlemin, sir; them was the chaps for making any fellow that 'ud say 'black is the white of your eye'—shiver upon daisy, in no time. But, Lord help us, sir, there's nothing hut changes in this world, and all of them for the worse too—the polis and the teetotallers have taken the *misnagh** out of the people; jintlemen don't now get into a quarrel over their wine or punch at night, and get out of it on the sod in the morning. They 're grown as paceable as mice, sir, and a man might walk the Fifteen Acres for a twelve-month of Sundays without seeing the laste bit of divarsion in regard of a *jewel*."

"I am glad to find that the barbarous custom which has been so long a disgrace to our country is wearing rapidly away," I replied.

* *Misnagh,* courage.

387

"Barbarous, sir! d 'ye call a fair jewel at eight or tin paces—barbarous?"

"Certainly: the idea of two men going out coolly and deliberately for the purpose of imbruing their hands in each other's blood is perfectly horrible."

"But consider the convaynience of the thing, sir; they come out here in the cool of the morning with their sickonds and hair-trigger pistols, and settle their difference at once; and if one of them ain't shot clane out, they'll go home together greater friends than ever. I'm sure that's a shorter and better way of making pace than by going to law, and keeping up all sorts of hathred and ill-will towards each other."

"But, my good friend, I do not advocate litigation, because I object to violence. 'Let the angry man,' as the eastern proverb has it, 'drink of the waters of reflection.'"

"I wish you a good morning, sir," said my new acquaintance, abruptly turning on his heel, "I must be going," and as he hurried away I could hear him muttering between his teeth, "'Drink of the wathers!' I might have asily kown he was a teetotaller."

The vice-regal lodge, an unostentatious but tasteful building is situated near the principal road through the park. At a short distance from the lodge, in the centre of a small area, stands a fluted Corinthian pillar, thirty feet in height, surmounted by a Phœnix forming a picturesque object when viewed through the leafy avenues which conduct to it. It was erected by the celebrated Earl of Chesterfield, who was governor of Ireland in 1745. The Royal Infirmary, or hospital for the soldiers of the garrison, which occupies a pleasant and healthful site near the grand entrance of the park, and the Hibernian School for the maintenance and education of soldiers' orphans, situated in the south-west angle of this spacious demesne, are both deserving the attention of strangers; nor should the Royal Hospital of Kilmainham be passed unnoticed, whose tall chimneys and formal spire may be seen on the opposite side of the Liffey, emerging from the thick foliage of the lofty elm trees which surround it.* This is the Military Asylum for invalid soldiers and officers, where about two hundred veterans selected from the out-pensioners of Ireland, are supplied with every necessary and convenience, similar to that afforded at Chelsea Hospital near London. The dining-hall of the hospital, where amongst other portraits, are those of Charles II., William and Mary, Queen Anne, and Prince George of Denmark, is an object of curiosity to visitors, as is the ceiling and altar-screen of the chapel, the former being enriched with elaborate and beautiful ornaments in stucco, and the latter an exquisite specimen of carving in oak, said to have been executed by the celebrated Gibbons. But, certainly, the most interesting and amusing spot within the limits of the Phœnix Park, is the Zoological Gardens,†

---

* The first stone of this excellent institution was laid by the Duke of Ormond, in 1680. It was erected from the designs of Sir Christopher Wren, and was completed in less than four years at a cost of £23,559, which was defrayed by a levy of sixpence in the pound out of the pay of every soldier and officer on the military establishment of Ireland.

charmingly situated on a plot of ground sloping to the margin of a small lake. The natural beauties of this place, heightened and embellished as it is by the hand of art, have rendered it a fashionable promenade for the inhabitants of Dublin during the summer season. The animals, though not so numerous as in the gardens of the London Society, have been selected with great care, and it has been asserted that "there is no collection in Europe in which the animals are generally in such fine condition, or in which the proportion of deaths is so small."

The only thoroughfare between Dublin and the Park was formerly through Barrack Street, a disreputable outlet in the immediate vicinity of the Royal Barracks. where scenes of debauchery and drunkenness too frequently met the eyes and shocked the feelings of the respectable portion of the community. This nuisance has, however, been obviated by the erection of the beautiful metal bridge which crosses the Liffey, near the entrance of the Park, and which has been named King's Bridge, to commemorate the visit of George IV. to Ireland, in 1821.*

Before entering upon a description of the city of Dublin, let us take a glance at its ancient history. The earliest authentic mention we have of Dublin is by Ptolemy, who flourished in the second century after Christ, and who notices it under the name of Eblana. By the ancient Irish it was called *Ath-cliath,* or the *Ford of the Hurdles,* and *Bally-ath-cliath,* or the *Town of the Ford of Hurdles.* Stanihurst, on the authority of Giraldus Cambrensis, asserts, that the present name of the city is derived from Avellanus, a Danish sea-king, who at an early period established himself on the spot where it now stands; and he draws his etymological conclusion thus—Avellana—Eblana—Dublana. "But this cannot be the derivation," observes a writer in the Dublin Penny Journal, "for Ptolemy, upwards of six hundred years before, gave it the title of Eblana Civitas." After all, perhaps, the most simple and obvious etymology of the name will be found the Irish *Dubh-linn,* signifying Black-water, by which designation the ford upon the Liffey at this place was known to the inhabitants. We have unquestionable historical evidence to show that it was the Ostmen or Danes who first fortified Dublin, and who, in the words of Harris, the historian, "rendered it fit for defence and security soon after they possessed it, which seems to have been about the year 838." It is certain that although these barbarous intruders were

---

† For the establishment of this intellectual and beautiful place of recreation the people of Dublin are mainly indebted to the exertions of Sir Philip Crampton the Surgeon General, and Doctor Stokes, the Professor of Natural History in the University. The Duke of Northumberland, under the sanction of Government, gave a site for the garden in the Phœnix Park, on the spot where formerly stood the residence of the Irish Secretary of War, and in the month of August, 1831, the Zoological Gardens were opened with a small collection of animals, principally presents from the Zoological Society of London.

* A sum of £13,000 was raised by public subscription for the purpose of erecting a national monument to perpetuate this event—but the good sense of the managers of the undertaking substituted a work not only ornamental but highly useful to the city. for an idle pillar-trophy, which it was the original intention to erect with the funds subscribed.

opposed by the Irish, they were enabled to maintain the settlement they had made in Dublin and the contiguous districts, until the year 1014, when a number of Irish chieftains united in a patriotic league under the renowned monarch, Brian Boroimh, for the purpose of extirpating these unwelcome intruders. The Danish king Sitrig, collected a large army to oppose him, and the ad-verse forces met at Clontarf, near the city, on the 23rd April, when was fought one of the most memorable battles in which the Irish were ever engaged with a foreign enemy upon their own shores. This sanguinary action terminated in the defeat of the Danes, but the brave Brian was slain in his tent by a straggling party of the enemy while in the act of returning thanks to heaven for his victory. But though the power of the Ostmen was much reduced in Ireland after their defeat at Clontarf, they still maintained possession of Dublin for many succeeding years. When the Anglo-Normans obtained a footing in the country, the lordship of Dublin was bestowed upon Earl Strongbow, who appointed Milo de Cogan as his deputy.

In 1171, Dublin was invested by a large army under the command of Asculph the Dane, but the brave Milo de Cogan succeeded in repulsing the enemy with great slaughter, and the fierce Asculph being taken prisoner, his head was struck off and placed upon a spike on the castle gate. Thus terminated the sway of the Sea Kings in Ireland, for this was the last attempt made by the Danes to regain pos-session of the city. "Many of them," writes Harris, "had before incorporated with the Irish, and now upon this great revolution, such as remained in the city or neighbourhood became quiet subjects of the English, and by degrees one people with them." The visit of Henry II. to Ireland, in 1172, was productive of the most important consequences. On his arrival in Dublin, he summoned all the Irish kings to attend and do him homage as their liege lord. He was obeyed by the greater number of these petty dynasts; and in a spacious pavilion, constructed of smooth wattles plastered with clay, Henry kept his Christmas with as muck pomp and ceremony as were — under the circumstances. Here, surrounded by mail-clad chivalry of England, he entertained the Irish princes, and confirmed them in the opinion of his wealth and power. Having established courts of justice, held a parliament, and exercised other prerogatives of the sovereign, he returned to England, distributing his new and easily acquired kingdom amongst those leaders who had first invaded the island. From this date a new era commences in the history of Dublin. To use the words of a writer on the subject, "We have hitherto viewed the city as the abode of a rude colony, whose territory was limited to the district immediately contiguous. We are now to consider Dublin ascending progressively in the scale of cities; first, as the capital of the English pale, and afterwards as the metropolis of the whole kingdom."

The history of Dublin for the five succeeding centuries, until the Revolution, which placed William III. on the throne of these kingdoms, though not deficient in interest, is principally occupied with the bloody struggles which were obstinately

St. Patricks, Dublin

maintained between the English and Irish interests. Subsequent to the Revolution, the annals of the metropolis are of a more peaceable character, and during that favourable period the city assumed a new aspect, and so rapidly did it improve in appearance, that at the commencement of the present century no European city of similar extent could vie with it, in the magnificence of its streets, squares, and public buildings.

The ancient ecclesiastical edifices of a city are generally the first objects to which strangers direct their attention. In Dublin, the venerable CATHEDRAL OF ST. PATRICK claims precedence on account of its extent, importance, and high antiquity. Its situation, however, is most objectionable, being built on the lowest ground in the city, and surrounded on every side with old narrow streets, of the meanest and filthiest description. The reason for selecting such an unfavourable site for the principal cathedral, was the peculiar sanctity of the place, for on this spot, according to the best authorities, stood a small church, which it is supposed, with every appearance of probability, was founded by native converts to Christianity long before the Danes acquired possession of the city, as it was dedicated to the apostle of Ireland, and was erected in the vicinity of a holy well, also (dedicated to St. Patrick. John Comyn, the first archbishop of Dublin, pulled down the ancient church, and erected on the same place a more extensive structure, in which he placed a collegiate establishment. Henry de Loundres, the successor of this prelate, made it a cathedral in 1225, uniting it with the priory of the Holy Trinity or Christ Church, and securing to the latter the prerogative of honour. The architectural character of the pile is of the early pointed style, with some occasional innovations in the additions which have been made at various periods. The most remarkable of these supplementary portions of the edifice are the square steeple and spire; the former owes its erection to Archbishop Minot, in 1370, and the latter to a legacy bequeathed by Dr. Sterne, in 1750. This spire has been compared, not unaptly, to a vast extinguisher. The height of the steeple or tower is one hundred and twenty feet, that of the spire by which it is surmounted, one hundred and one feet, making a total of two hundred and twenty-one feet. Notwithstanding this elevation is very considerable, the structure is far from possessing that grandeur of appearance one might expect; this is owing partly to the low situation in which it stands, and in a great degree to the clumsiness of its proportions, for it is only by comparing it with the buildings in its neighbourhood that we can form an idea of its great height. The interior of the cathedral is somewhat gloomy and monotonous, being built in the simple style which marks the first regular structures in this species of architecture.* The nave is separated from its aisles by unadorned arches and octangular pillars. The choir is the most interesting

* This cathedral, which had fallen into a lamentable state of decay has been recently rebuilt according to its original design, and is now likely to stand for many ages a fine specimen of the early architecture of Ireland.

portion of the interior; the arches, which divide the centre from the side aisles, spring from clustered columns, each component shaft of which terminates in a small capital composed of foliage. The archbishop's throne, which is of oak richly carved; the stalls of the knights of St. Patrick, over each of which are displayed the banner, helmet, and sword of the knight the tall lancet-shaped windows, the fine altar-piece, and the magnificent organ placed in the screen that divides the nave and the choir, form a combination of objects, which irresistibly recal the mind to the times when religion and chivalry mingled their solemn arid gorgeous pageants. The cathedral contains several monumental sculptures, more remarkable for the celebrity of the names they commemorate than for the excellence of their design or execution. Amongst them the stranger will pause with interest before the black marble slab, which bears the name of Jonathan Swift, dean of this cathedral, whose w it and public spirit need no encomium here. Near to time remains of the eccentric dean, lie the ashes of Mrs. Johnson, celebrated by his muse under the name of STELLA; the history of this lady, and nature of her connexion with Swift, are still involved in a mystery that there is no probability will be ever satisfactorily cleared up. The most conspicuous and elaborate, but at the same time the most tasteless monument in this part of the church, is that on the right of the altar, intended to perpetuate the memory of sixteen individuals of the family of Boyle Earl of Cork. It was erected by Richard "the Great Earl," in the reign of Charles I., and remains a huge memorial of the gaudy and tasteless style which prevailed at the period of its erection. On the opposite side of the choir is a mural tablet in black marble, to the memory of Frederick Duke of Schomberg, the celebrated general of William III., who was killed at the battle of the Boyne. The ashes of this brave man were suffered to remain without any monumental record, until Dean Swift erected the simple tablet above mentioned at his own cost. Mr. Brewer says that "Swift did not undertake his task until he had made repeated unsuccessful applications to the family, who derived the whole of its affluence and honours from the duke; and the indignant severity with which he composed the inscription on a tablet thus raised by alien hands, although it gave some offence at the time, redounds to the honour of his humanity and public spirit."

Christ Church Cathedral, though not so extensive as that of St. Patrick, is undoubtedly of greater antiquity; the site, say historians, was given by Sitrig, a Danish prince, to Donat, a bishop of Dublin, who about the year 1038 erected upon it a church in honour of the Blessed Trinity.* This edifice was afterwards enlarged by Earl Strongbow, whose supposed tomb near the southern wall of the nave, attracts the attention of every visitor. Upon an oblong block of stone is rudely sculptured the

---

* There was attached to the church a monastic establishment, which existed until the dissolution of these religious communities by Henry VIII., when the priory was changed into a dean and chapter, and the ancient name of Church of the Blessed Trinity was altered to that of Christ Church.

figure of a mail-clad warrior, with crossed legs and folded hands, bearing on his left arm a shield with armorial bearings. Inserted in the wall over the figure is an inscription, which states that the monument hand been broken by the fall of the roof of tIme church, in 1562, and had been "set up" again in 1570, by Sir Henry Sydney, then lord-deputy of Ireland. Some doubts have been entertained as to the propriety of attributing the effigy ot the knight on the monument to Strongbow, as the arms emblazoned on the shield are not those which belonged to that chieftain. This may reasonably raise a doubt as to the identity of the monument; but from the testimony of Giraldus Cambrensis, a contemporary historian, there can be no doubt that his mortal remains have their resting-place within these venerable walls. By the side of the figure ascribed to Earl Strong-bow, is a half-length statue, which was reputed to be that of his son. He was a youth of seventeen, who, as tradition records, deserted his father in a battle with the Danes, and fled to Dublin in the utmost consternation, declaring that his father and all his forces had perished. When convinced of his mistake, he appeared before the earl to congratulate him upon his victory; but the incensed warrior, after sharply upbraiding his degenerate offspring for his cowardice, caused him to be put to death, the executioner severing him in the middle with a sword. This story, though related by Stanihurst, has probably no other foundation than the fiction of some romancer, who invented it for a people delighting in the marvellous: the effigy in question appears to be that of a female, constructed, as was frequently the case, in half-length proportions, without any reference to the hand of the executioner. It is now generally said to represent the Lady Eva, wife of Earl Stronghow.

I cannot attempt to give even a cursory description of the numerous other churches of every denomination with which Dublin abounds. Those who delight in antiquarian research will examine the interesting ruin, called Lord Portlester's Chapel, which constitutes a portion of St. Audeon's Church, and contains amongst many interesting monumental remains, the tomb of Roland Fitz Eustace Baron Portlester, erected in the year 1455, which is still remarkably perfect. The lovers of scientific inquiry will not fail to visit the vaults of St. Michan's Church, which are remarkable for a strong antiseptic quality, by which bodies deposited there some centuries since have been kept in such a state of preservation, that the features are still discernible, and the bones, cartilages, and skin, astonishingly perfect. A minute description of these vaults was written by a professional gentleman of Dublin, about twenty years back, when their singular properties first attracted public attention. "The bodies," says he, "of those a long time deposited, appear in all their awful solitariness at full length, the coffins having mouldered to pieces; but from those, and even the more recently entombed, not the least cadaverous smell is discoverable; and all the bodies exhibit a similar appearance, dry, and of a dark colour. The floor, walls, and atmosphere of the vaults of St. Michan's are perfectly dry, the flooring is even covered with dust, and the walls are composed of a stone peculiarly calculated to resist moisture. This combination of circumstances contributes to aid nature in rendering the atmosphere of those gloomy regions more dry than the atmosphere we enjoy. In one vault are shown the remains of a nun who died at the advanced age of *one hundred and eleven;* the body has now been thirty years in this mansion of death, and although there is scarcely a remnant of the coffin, the body is as completely preserved as if it had been embalmed, with the exception of the hair. In the same vault are to be seen the bodies of two Roman Catholic clergymen, which have been fifty years deposited here, even more perfect than the nun. In general, it was observed that the old were much better preserved than the young. A convincing proof of this was afforded in the instance of a lady who died in childbirth, and was laid in those vaults with her infant in her arms. Not long after, the infant putrified and dropped away, while the mother became like the other melancholy partners of this gloomy habitation."The headless trunks of the two ill-fated brothers, named Shears, who during the rebellion of 1798 were executed on the same day for high-treason, are amongst the ghastly relics of mortality preserved in these vaults.

Of the modern religious edifices St. George's Church is decidedly the handsomest in Dublin, although the union of the Grecian with the Gothic style of architecture which it exhibits has been much censured. The Roman Catholic church of the Conception, in Marlborough Street, is a splendid pile built in the Grecian style, with a portico of six Doric columns in imitation of the façade of the temple of Theseus at Athens. The grand aisle is inclosed by a double range of columns, so massive that they completely obstruct the view, and injure the fine effect which the simple grandeur of the interior would otherwise produce.

Notwithstanding its antiquity, Dublin has few ancient edifices, either public or private; the massy labours of the early inhabitants having given place to the lighter works of their sons. Even the castle of Dublin, nominally ancient,* is in reality a modern building. It was formerly moated and flanked with towers; but the ditch has been long since filled up, and the old buildings rased; the Wardrobe or Record Tower excepted, which still remains.† The castle at present consists of two courts, called the upper and lower castle yards, the former of which is an oblong square formed by four manges of buildings, which contain the state and private apartments of the viceroy. The external appearance of this quadrangle is exceedingly plain; the grand entrance to it from the city is by a fine gate, surmounted by a statue of Justice. The lower castle yard contains several of the government offices, and the beautiful little

---

* The building of tine castle of Dublin was commenced about the ear 1205, by Meyler Fitzhenry, Lord Justice of Ireland, and was completed in 1220 by Henry de Loundres. Bishmop of Dublin. But it was not until the reign of Queen Elizabeth that it became the seat of govern ment. Time court was previously held, sometimes at the archbishop's at St. Sepulchre's, sometimes at Thomas Court, and sometimes at the Castle of Kilmainham

The Four Courts, Dublin

Gothic chapel, built by the Duke of Bedford in 1814. A late writer remarks of it, that "though of limited dimensions, it must be viewed as the most elaborate effort made in recent years to revive the ancient ecclesiastical style of building, and is beyond a question the richest modern casket of pointed architecture to be witnessed in the British empire." It must, however, be confessed though Dublin Castle is pretty, and even magnificent in some of its parts, it is deficient as a whole; it has no uniformity of plan, and as it is so scattered that the eye can take in little of it at once, it has no dignity of appearance—it bears too evident marks of the various repairs it has undergone, and, like Sir John Cutter's worsted stockings, so often darned with black silk, that they changed their original nature,— it has lost all traces of its venerable origin in the incongruous embellishments of modern art.

It is not my intention to speak of all the public buildings and valuable institutions with which this metropolis is embellished; they will be found accurately described in various Guide-books : but I cannot deny myself the pleasure of taking a stroll with my reader along the line of noble quays, which stretch east and west through the centre of the city from the Military Road to the North Wall Light House, a distance of three miles. Travellers who have only seen the busy wharfs, docks, and quays of other sea-port towns, black, dirty, and crowded with dingy-looking warehouses, can scarcely form an idea of the beauty and grandeur of appearance of the Liffey, confined by walls and parapets of hewn stone, and its numerous magnificent bridges, connecting the handsome quays that extend on either side of the river. Commencing then at the castellated entrance to the Military Road, which forms an agreeable promenade between the Royal Hospital and the city on the north side of the river, we proceed in an easterly direction along Ussher's Island and Ussher's Quay. Our attention is first attracted by the colonnade of Home's Hotel and General Mart, an extensive building, erected, by the enterprising individual whose name it bears. I regret to add that the speculation has been unfortunate as regards the Mart, which it was the projector's intention should become a general commercial bazaar for the convenience of country shopkeepers, who, if it were established, would be enabled to purchase every variety of goods in a building attached to their hotel. The idea was a good one : but the Irish people have a strange objection to innovation, and, after a vain attempt to bring buyers or sellers to his mart, Mr. Home was obliged to abandon his project.

As we proceed, Barrack Bridge, Queen's Bridge, Whitworth Bridge, and Richmond Bridge, successively attract our attention, and by their handsome

† In the Record Tower are now preserved the statute rolls, the parliamentary and other national records : the walls are of great thickness, and it is built upon a rock of black stone. It was originally called the Ward Tower, and was the prison of the castle, in which for five hundred years all state offenders were confined. The last who suffered incarceration there, were Arthur O'Connor and some of his revolutionary colleagues.

proportions give an air of picturesque grandeur to the river. Midway between the two last-named bridges on the north side of the Liffey, stands THE FOUR COURTS, a noble edifice, presenting a beautiful portico facing time river, consisting of six Corinthian columns, supporting a pediment ornamented with three statues, of Moses, Justice, and Mercy. At the two extremities of the front are corresponding statues of Wisdom and Authority. From the centre of the building rises a circular colonnade, surmounted by a handsome dome, whose massive proportions injure the effect of the light and elegant portico beneath. The arrangement of the interior is not liable to the same objection as the exterior; the great circular hall, around which are situated the law courts and offices, is conspicuous for the beauty and simplicity of its design. During Term time this hall is the grand nucleus where barristers, attorneys, and clients meet as in one common centre,

> "To talk of fees,
> Bonds, and horrible mortgagees,
> To say nothing of assignees, lessees,
> And an endless quantity more of these"
> Uneasy things that end in *ee s*."

But it is not law alone that fills the heads or busies the tongues of the wigged and gowned gentry of the hall; the news of the day, politics, castle gossip, steeple-chasing, and public characters are here freely discussed; and half the bon mots, epigrams, and witticisms which are scattered upon the stream of Dublin society emanate from the hall of the Four Courts. This freedom from professional solemnity is not confined to the lawyers; it is equally observable amongst the followers of Esculapius. "The physicians here," says an entertaining writer upon Dublin society, "do not forget that they are men and Irishmen :—they converse, laugh, and drink, and have thrown aside the formal airs and formal manners with the large wigs and gold-headed canes of their predecessors; they have a candour and openness of address, an ease and dignity of deportment, far superior to that of their London brethren. The truth is, a physician here is almost at the pinnacle of greatness; there are few resident nobility or gentry since the union, and the professors of law and medicine may be said to form the aristocracy of the place. They have therefore all the advantages of manner which a lofty sense of superiority, along with much association with mankind never fail to produce. A London practitioner is little better than a bon bourgeois, whom people of rank call in when they are sick, but have no intercourse with when they are well." It is an indisputable fact, that the medical men of Dublin combine a profound knowledge of their profession with refined taste and polished manners. That it is not an incongruous union we have the authority of the facetious George Coleman, who asks

> "And why should this be thought so odd;
> Can 't men have taste who cure a phthisic ?
> Of poetry through patron god.
> Apollo patronizes physic."

But I fear I have been digressing too far—let us resume our walk. We have now reached Essex Bridge, built upon a model of Westminster Bridge, but, of course, of much smaller dimensions. Looking up Parliament Street, which forms the avenue to the bridge on the north side, may be seen a portion of the Royal Exchange, an extensive and elegant building, situated on Cork Hill, which, it has been generally admitted, forms one of the principal ornaments of the city. The form of this superb edifice is nearly a square of one hundred feet, having three beautiful fronts of Portland stone in the Corinthian order. The building is surrounded at the top by a handsome balustrade—a low dome rising from the centre. Owing to the acclivity upon which the Exchange stands, the grand entrance on the west side is by a kind of terrace, protected by a light metal balustrade supported by rustic-work.* The interior of the edifice is even more remarkable for architectural beauty than the exterior, and the effect produced upon the spectator when he enters it is strikingly impressive. "Twelve fluted pillars of the composite order, thirty-two feet high, are circularly disposed in the centre of a square area, covered by a highly enriched entablature; above which is a beautiful cylindrical lantern, about ten feet high, perforated with twelve circular windows ornamented with festoons of laurel-leaves; the whole crowned with a handsome spherical dome, divided into hexagonal compartments, enriched and well proportioned, and lighted from the centre by a large circular skylight." The pillars, columns, floor, and staircase are all of Portland stone. Opposite to the north entrance is a statue, by Van Nost, of George III. in a Roman military costume. On the stairs in the north-western angle of the building, is one of Dr. Lucas, through whose exertions in Parliament a grant was obtained to aid in the building of the Exchange;† and in the centre of the circular hall stands a finely executed statue to the memory of Henry Grattan, Ireland's greatest patriot. It bears the following brief but touching inscription :— *"Filio optimo carissimo Henrico Grattan Patria non ingrata."*

Resuming our route along the quays, we pass Wellington Bridge, a light handsome metal structure, spanning the river by a single arch. It was built by two private individuals; and is intended for foot-passengers only, each person crossing it paving a toll of one halfpenny.

Carlisle Bridge, the most frequented passage between tIme northern and southern sides of the city, forms the limit of the navigation of the river,—vessels of considerable burthen being able to come close up to it at high-water. The panorama of the river, and the city which encircles the spectator on this bridge, is un-equalled

* On the 24th of April, 1814, a vast crowd having assembled to witness the whipping of a sweep, who had caused the death of his apprentice by cruelty, the balustrade gave way. and numbers were precipitated into the street; several persons were killed, on the spot and others seriously injured.

† The first stone of the Exchange was laid on the 2nd of August, 1709, by Lord Townsend. then Lord Lieutenant of Ireland. The entire expenditure, including the purchase of the ground amounted to about £40,000.

Sackville Street, Dublin

in grandeur and beauty, by the noblest prospects which could be obtained from any single point in any other European city. I remember, several years ago, having been so struck with tine splendid but solitary picture which presented itself to me while standing on Carlisle Bridge, soon after sunrise on a glorious summer morning, that I committed to paper at the time my impressions of the scene. I have the pages containing them now before me, from which I shall extract so much as may be relevant to my present purpose. "Philosophers and writers, have, according to their temperament or caprice, selected for themselves different places for meditation. Some have chosen to bury themselves in the deep recesses of an ancient wood, where 'day's garish eye' could scarcely penetrate the thick canopy of leaves which overshadowed them : some have delighted to fling their 'listless length' beside a babbling stream, lulled by the murmur of its gentle song : some have wandered, rapt in fancy's dream, in the delicious wilderness of a flower-garden; some have mused by the wave-beaten shore, and others in the deep seclusion of a cobwebbed library. But, for my part, I know of no situation more calculated to awaken feelings of deep awe, or to call up images of universal desolation, than the silent solitary streets of a great city viewed through the purplish haze of an early summer's morning. Almost every person living in Dublin has, at one time or another, experienced the solemn effect produced on the mind while standing on Carlisle Bridge at daybreak on a calm morning in June. How full of strange beauty is the scene!—all is hushed and still as death—not a sound disturbs nature's profound repose, save at intervals the shrill bark of a watch-dog from the decks of some of those numerous vessels lying below the bridge, whose taper masts shoot like a forest of leafless pines into the cloudless sky, which has already began to assume the lady Aurora's livery. Far as the eye can stretch on the other hand, the silent quays and bridges reflect their shadowy outlines in the still waters that sleep within their bosom; or if a dimpling circle should break the mirror-like surface of the tide, it is but caused by the rapid wing of some hungry swallow pursuing Iris insect prey.

"Behind us lies Westmorland Street, terminated by the ancient walls of Trinity College, and the noble Corinthian portico of tine Batik of Ireland; on the opposite side of the river, SACKVILLE STREET extends its full perspective of architectural beauty—uninterrupted, save by the memorial of the brave Nelson,* whose pillar seems to have been dropped there in defrance of all the laws of good taste. Let us walk up this beautiful street—we are now opposite the Post Office,† and who can say

---

* The Nelson pillar consists of a pedestal, fluted column, and capital of the Tuscan order, surmounted by a statue of the naval hero. The entire height of the pillar and statues is one hundred and thirty-four feet four inches. From the top an extensive view of the city, the bay, and the surrounding country will well repay time trouble of the ascent.

† This superb edifice, of which the foundation stone was Paid inn 1815, is two hundred and twenty-three feet in length, one hundred and fifty in depth, and fifty feet in height. The grand Ionic portico in front imparts a striking air of grandeur to the building, which adds considerably to the architectural beauty of Sackville Street.

that the republic of *letters* is declining, when they look upon that magnificent pile? But *allons!* for while we remain here we are preventing the poor pigeons, who are fluttering about the cornices and pillars of the portico, from seeking for their early meal in the silent streets. Before us lies the Rotunda, where revelry so often holds its court, while 'meek-eyed charity extends its hand to succour the children of misery'* Let us now turn round, and survey from this eminence the splendid scene which lies before us :—the deserted streets, like the exhumated cities of Pompei and Herculaneum, seem but as the monuments of departed splendour. Where is now the dark line of moving forms that a few hours since thronged these footpaths? where the waving plumes and the glittering equipages? where the merchant's busy face, and the proud beauty's conquering glance? All fled! there is no form of life—no vitality in the scene—and thus will the resistless scythe of time sweep these streets of palaces, and the antiquary of future ages will seek in vain for some relics of those noble works of art that we presumptuously hope may outlive the great destroyer himself."

Trinity College and the Bank of Ireland, when viewed from Carlisle Bridge, have a very noble and imposing appearance; but the combined effect of their magnificence is seen to the greatest advantage from the south side of College Green. The centre of this area is adorned with an equestrian statue of King William III., erected in 1701, by the citizens of Dublin to commemorate the Revolution of 1688. The Jacobites regarded this memorial of their defeat with no very amicable feelings, and from the time of its erection until very recently, the unoffending statue became a fruitful source of discord and ill-will between the Protestant and Roman Catholic inhabitants. The extensive and ornamental front of Trinity College forms the boundary of College Green on the east. This university, as is generally known, was founded in the reign of Queen Elizabeth, and richly endowed by that sovereign.† It is styled in the charter, "the College of the Holy and Undivided Trinity, near Dublin;" though it is now almost in the centre of the city, so rapidly has it increased in size in little more than two centuries. The college is governed by a provost, vice-provost, senior and junior fellows. When a vacancy occurs amongst the senior fellows, the

---

* The Rotunda, which stands at the extremity of Upper Sackville Street, is united with the Lying-in Hospital, and with it forms a very distinguishing feature in the city. The circular room of the Rotunda is eighty feet in diameter, without any central support. Balls, concerts, and public meetings for festive or serious purposes are occasionally held in this room, from which the funds of the hospital derive much support. Formerly, when the nobilty and gentry of Ireland had their town residences in Dublin, the subscription balls, card assemblies, and masquerades of the Rotunda were regularly and fashionably attended throughout the winter; and the public promenades on the terrace of the ornamental gardens, formed in summer unfailing attractions to the lovers of pleasure. The promenades alone have survived as a regular entertainment; on certain evenings in the week during the summer season, the gardens are still open to the public at the trifling admission-charge of sixpence. The terrace on these occasions is illuminated, and one or more military bands contribute to the gaiety of the scene.

† The first stone of Trinity College was laid on tine 13th of March, 1591, and students were admitted the 9th of January, 1593.

402

eldest of the juniors, if no objection lies against him, is elected by the provost and seniors to a senior fellowship within three days after the vacancy is reported; but the admission to a junior fellowship is obtained only by sustaining one of the severest trials of the human faculties of which we have any modern experience or even knowledge from history. The examination is in Latin, and the days appointed for it are the four days immediately preceding Trinity Sunday. None but young men of the highest abilities ever think of standing for a fellowship : they generally read from fourteen to eighteen hours a day for a period of five, often of seven years, before venturing to undergo an examination. Such intense study has materially injured the constitution of hundreds—many have become blind—many have lost their lives from the fatal effects of such continued mental exertion; nor is there, perhaps, a solitary instance of a fellow whose health has not been injured and talents impaired by it. The principal buildings of the college are comprehended in three spacious quadrangles : a description of them separately would considerably exceed our limits, but visitors will be much gratified by an inspection of the museum, the chapel, the dining-hall, the examination-hall, and the library. Of the latter interesting building, which strikes every stranger upon entering, with its superb and lofty magnificence, l cannot forbear saying a few words. It is built of hewn stone, with an elegant Corinthian entablature, crowned with a balustrade and ornamented windows, and consists of an extensive centre, and two advanced pavilions. In the western pavilion are the librarians' apartments, and the grand staircase, from which, by folding-doors, you enter the library, by far the finest room in Europe applied to a similar purpose, and of whose magnificent proportions George IV. expressed his admiration. The galleries, which are of Irish oak, varnished, are adorned with the busts of many illustrious writers and illustrious characters, executed in white marble by able masters; and on the shelves are to be found an admirable collection of the best writers on every subject, in number exceeding one haundred and thirty thousand volumes, which are daily increasing. At the extremity of the great room is a smaller apartment, called the Fagel Library, containing the vast collection of books of the Fagel family in Holland, which were removed from that country upon the invasion of the French, and purchased by the university of Dublin for £8,000. The manuscript room over the Fagel library contains a great number of Irish, Icelandic, and Oriental MSS. of inestimable value.

The Bank of Ireland, in College Green, is decidedly the noblest specimen of architecture which the metropolis can boast; indeed, it is scarcely saying too much to assert, that it is unequalled in grandeur of design, simplicity of arrangement, and majesty of effect by any public building in the empire. This magnificent pile was originally the Parliament House of Ireland, but in the year 1802, after the incorporation of the Irish senate with that of England, by the union of the two countries, the building was purchased by the governors of the Bank of Ireland for a sum of nearly £40,000. The central façade and projecting wings, which form a collonade of the Ionic order, are admitted to be a *chef d'œuvre* of modern art. This noble portico, which is without any of the usual architectural decorations, (withy the exception of three statues surmounting the centre pediment,) derives all its beauty from the harmony of its proportions, and is one of the few instances of simple form only expressing true symmetry. On the conversion of this building into a bank, several alterations internally and externally were found necessary, to adapt it for its present purposes, which, however, have been executed with judicious taste, and a strict regard to the preservation of the original design of the edifice.

Proceeding westward along the quays, at a short distance from Carlisle Bridge, we reach the CUSTOM-HOUSE, a magnificent structure, whose great defect is that it is placed so close to the water's edge that the spectator is unable to see to advantage the noble front which it presents on that side. When viewed, as Sir Richard Hoare observes, from the opposite bank of the river, it has a very striking effect, and combined with the numerous shipping immediately adjoining it, reminds one strongly of those subjects which the painter Canaletti selected for his pencil at Venice. The building, which is a quadrangle, is completely insulated, exhibiting four fronts to view, those to the north and south being the principal. Over the portico, on tire south side, is a handsome cupola covered with copper, on the top of which is a disproportionately large statue of Hope. The warehouses and wet-docks to the east of the building are spacious and commodious; but they have been constructed on far too extensive a scale for the decaying trade of Dublin, and the appearance of these magnificent, but deserted basins and wharfs, awaken sensations more nearly allied to sadness than pleasure, such as might be experienced while contemplating the ruins of some noble work of antiquity.* After passing the Custom-House, the Liffey is confined by a handsome and solid stone causeway one either side—called the North Wall and the South Wall —erected for the purpose of keeping the channel free from tire sands which accumulate on tire flat shores of the bay at the embouchure of the river. The SOUTH WALL runs on a straight line into the bay, a distance of nearly three and a half miles; at the extremity of it is a fine LIGHTHOUSE. The North Wall, which is not quite one mile in length, has also at its terminus a lighthouse, but of much smaller dimensions than the other. A few years ago the North Wall was a lonely and unfrequented place, but since the establishment of the "City of Dublin Steam Company's" packets between Dublin and Liverpool, and the building of their warehouses, it has become one of the busiest localities in the city, from whence immense quantities of horned cattle, sheep, and pigs are daily shipped for England by the company's Steamers. Those who have never witnessed the departure of one of these "cattle-boats," as they are called, can scarcely form an

---

* About ten years since these splendid warehouses were burned to the ground, and property to a great amount destroyed. The fire, it was imagined, was caused hey the spontaneous combustion of some goods deposited in the building.

The Custom House, Dublin

405

South Wall Light house

idea of the animated and extraordinary scene which the North Wall then presents. Fancy, good reader, a noble-looking steamer lying alongside the quay,

"Her streamers waving in the wind,"

the black smoke issuing in massive wreaths from her chimney, and blotting the fair face of heaven, while the tyrannous steam, impatient of constraint, disgorges its slender grey stream with a giant's roar into the clouds. The privileged quarter-deck is covered with a miscellaneous collection of trunks, boxes, baskets, travelling-bags, and packages of every size and figure. Persons of both sexes are seen in groups, either engaged in deep discourse or leaning idly over the rail which divides the after part of the vessel from the main deck, where the crew are busily lowering tine cargo into the hold. The last cask is in the slings—the mate's rough voice sings out, "Lower away," the chain runs off—the cask descends—and the work is done. Further forward in tine vessel another widely different scene is being enacted :there, a miscellaneous collection of pigs, sheep, oxen, and ragged but merry *spalpecns** are hurrying aboard in an undistinguished throng; the only marked difference between the brute and the man is, that the former seems reluctant to quit a land in which he had enjoyed a share of nature's common bounty, while the latter evidently parts with little regret from a country where starvation is tine lot of the poor. All is now nearly ready—on the shore the clamour of the gingerbread and apple-women, the porters, the car-boys, and the beggars exceeds all description. The friends and relatives of the frize-coated emigrants, having drowned their sorrow in a parting drop with "the poor boy that's going to seek his fortin in furrin parts;" have formed themselves into distinct groups, surveying with intense curiosity the manifold wonders of the "smoky devil;" all commenting, ejaculating, and arguing, in the varied guttural terms of their native dialect, on the novelty of every object that attracts their notice. The horned cattle are easily driven aboard, but the pigs, with the proverbial obstinacy of their race, are much more refractory, nor is it until after sundry grotesque pirouettes and demi-voltes, squeakings, and squallings, that the last grunter is got quietly on board. l should not have said quietly, for the creatures still express, by every modulation of grunt on the swinish gamut, their perfect disapprobation of their present situation. But, hist! the last bell rings, the captain takes his post on the paddle-box, trumpet in hand—the loungers all hurry to the gangway—tender adieus and hearty farewells are taken—

"A smile, or a grasp of the hand, hastening on,
Is all we can hope,"—

for the plank has been hauled away the last careless loiterer regains the shore with a bound—the paddles begin to revolve the stern-fast is cast off handkerchiefs are

---

* An Irish term of contempt for an ignorant country fellow.

waving amid the crowd, while murmured blessings burst from many a sorrowing heart for the weal of some dear friend, lover, or relative, whose fate is linked with the safety of the gallant vessel, that, apparently endowed with vital energy and conscious power, dashes through the blue waters, and shapes her course for the distant shores of merry England.

The antiquarian traveller who finds himself in Dublin should not omit visiting the little village of CLONDALKIN. It is picturesquely situated on the Naas road, about five miles from town, and exhibits a rare combination of hoary relics of ancient days, with the graceful productions of modern art. Adjoining the road may be seen one of those mysterious pillar-towers which appear to have been raised—

"For time to count his ages by,"

in close proximity with a cottage *ornée;* the ruins of an old castle hold pleasant neighbourhood with a neat school-house; and in the vicinity of the shapeless remains of the ancient abbey, the white walls of a modern church gleam through the foliage of the surrounding trees. Of the Round Towers of Ireland I have already spoken at some length. I shall therefore merely observe, that the pillar at Clondalkin, which is one of the plainest in the kingdom, is eighty-four feet in height, the diameter fifteen feet. The doorway is about twelve feet from the ground, and near the summit are four square openings or windows, from which the prospect of the surrounding country is extremely fine. There are no traces of a stairway in the tower, but ladders have been put up so as to enable the curious visitor to reach the uppermost story. Clondalkin was originally a Danish camp or fortress, and continued to be a favourite place of residence of these barbarous people while they maintained their sway in Ireland.

The Bay of Dublin spreads out into a noble expanse of water to the eastward of the city; its shores are agreeably diversified, and present all the various features, from the rugged and severe to the soft and smiling, in landscape-scenery. From the northern shore of the bay we obtain a most interesting view of its extensive surface, with the South Wall and light-house, and the mountains of Dublin and Wicklow forming an outline of enchanting beauty in the distance. Marino, the classical seat of the Earl of Charlemont, occupies a delightful situation on the margin of the bay, in the immediate vicinity of the city. The demesne, which the liberality of his lordship has thrown open for the recreation of the respectable citizens of Dublin, is laid out with great taste, and contains an exquisitely proportioned temple, built of white marble, from a design of the late earl, which cannot fail commanding the admiration of every visitor.

The villages of Clontarf* and Dollymount are pleasant little bathing-places, much frequented in the summer months. Behind Clontarf, the country, thickly planted, is intersected by sequestered roads, called "The Green Lanes:"—the appearance from

Clondalkin

the bay of the long, low, woody shore, studded by detached clusters of white cottages and handsome villas, is peculiarly beautiful. The views, both coastwise and inland, as we sweep round the north side of the bay, are singularly attractive; as we approach the promontory of Howth, the shores become bold and rugged, but picturesque. The peninsula, or, as it is usually called, the Hill of Howth, jutting into the sea, forms the northern headland of Dublin Bay, and the little town and harbour, with the CASTLE OF HOWTH, are pleasantly. situated under the shelter of the bill which rises precipitously behind them. The town, which is a mere fishing village consists of one straggling street; the inhabitants are a rude, hardy race, the greater number of them being fishermen, who hold their cabins rent-free on the ancient tenor of supplying the lord of the manor with the best fish taken in each boat. The first object which on entering the town arrests the attention of the tourist or traveller, particularly if he be infected with the antiquarian manna, is the ruined abbey, which occupies a romantic site on the cliff overhanging the sea. By the way, although generally called an abbey, the claims of the building to this distinction are dubious: we find no mention of it in the Monasticon, and in early days it was only known as a prebendal church, dedicated to the Virgin Mary. Surrounded by a strong embattled wall, it presents a striking evidence of the half-monk, half-soldier character of its founders, and a specimen of the general state of society at its erection, when it it was not unusual, or considered particularly unbecoming, for the professed minister of peace to join the ranks of war, and distinguish himself in the sanguinary *mélée*, or to find the prior or abbot of a monastery, the ostensible temple of religion, and the calm retreat of meditation and virtue, marshalling his vassals for the onset, or fortifying his sanctuary by fosse and battlement. Viewed from a favourable point on the commanding eminence of the hill, the white battlements of the venerable castle are seen emerging from the thick woods in which it is embosomed; lower down, the square tower of Howth church shows itself above the trees; and beyond these, the harbour and piers,† the sea-worn islands of Ireland's Eye and Lambay‡ and the vast expanse of sea, constantly enlivened by the appearance of ships and boats under sail, form a picture whose features are as varied as they are beautiful and extensive.

Howth Castle, the venerable mansion of the ancient family of St. Lawrence, enobled by the baronial title of Howth, is an object of considerable antiquarian and

* Clontarf, as I have elsewhere mentioned, is celebrated for the memorable battle fought there on Good Friday, 1014, between time Danes and the Irish, in which the latter, under their heroic monarch, Brian Boroihme, obtained an important victory over their enemies.

† This excellent harbour was constructed at an expense of nearly £700,000 as a station for the Holyhead mail-packets, when sailing-vessels were employed in that service; but since the introduction of steamers, and the completion of the harbour at Kingstown, the packet-station has been transferred to the latter place, and the magnificent harbour of Howth has been wholly abandoned.

Howth Castle

pictorial interest : the estate, over which it appears constructed to reign, includes the whole romantic peninsula of Howth, which, unlike most Irish estates, Lambay, another small island lying further out to sea than Ireland's Eye, forms a conspicuous object in the picture. It was granted by Edward VI. to John Chaloner, on the condition of his colonizing the island, and protecting it from the pirates who infested tine coast. This person built on it a small castle, which is kept in good repair, and occasionally occupied as a fishing-lodge by the Talbots of Malahide, to whom the island now belongs. The celebrated Archbishop Usher received a grant of Lambay from Queen Elizabeth, and is said to have written a considerable part of his works in its seclusion. The island is abundantly stocked with rabbits, and is the resort of immense quantities of sea-fowl. has continued in the family, without increase or diminutron, for upwards of six centuries. The name of thee great ancestor of the Howth family was Sir Amoricus or Amorey Tristram : he came over with the first adventurers from England, and obtained by conquest the lands and title of Howth. Several stories are recorded in his life which are more extraordinary than those of any hero of romance : amongst others it is related, that, after a variety of wild and perilous adventures in Ireland, he was surrounded by a superior force in Connaught, and being in imminent peril, some of his mounted followers were about to avail themselves of their horses arid save themselves by flight; but their leader, dismounting, drew his sword arid cried out, "Who will may preserve his life by flight on horseback, but assuredly my heart will not suffer me to leave these my poor friends, with whom l would sooner die, than live with you in dishonour." At the same time he thrust his sword into his horse's side, saying, he should never serve against them with whom he had so worthily and truly served before. His example was followed by all the horsemen, except two young gentlemen, whom he ordered to retire to a hill and watch the issue of the unequal conflict, and carry the news of it to his brother. This done, he engaged the enemy, (who were said to be twenty thousand strong,) so desperately that one thousand were slain; but being overpowered by numbers, he and his brave companions perished to a man. "Thus," say the old Chroniclers, "died Sir Amorey Tristram, who among a thousand knights might be chosen for beauty and heroic courage, for humility and courtesy to his inferiors, yielding to none but in the way of gentleness."

‡ Ireland's Eye, a rocky islet, lying about a mile from the north side of the Hill of Howth, is not more than a mile in circumference : a huge rock on its eastern extremity, which appears to have been riven asunder by some convulsion of nature, presents a very singular appearance. The ruins of a small abbey, said to have been built by St. Nessan, in the year 570, are still to be seen on the island. In this quiet sanctuary the saint passed his days in religious exercises, and in it was preserved the celebrated book of the four Gospels, called "The Garland of Howth," which, according to Archbishop Alan, was "held in so much esteem and veneration, that good men scarcely dare take an oath on it, for fear of the judgments of God being immediately shown on those who should forswear themselves." One of the ridiculous martello towers which are scattered around the Irish coast, stands on the western point of the island.

Dublin Bay

There is another well-known romantic tradition of this family, respecting the kidnapping of the young heir of Howth by the celebrated sea-roamer Grana Uille, or Grace O'Malley, from whence arose the singular custom still observed in Howth Castle, of having its gates thrown open during the time that the Lord of Howth is at dinner, which has been related in another part of this work. A painting in one of the apartments is said to represent the abduction of the young lord, but there is no authority beyond that of tradition for ascribing the subject of the picture to the supposed exploit of the piratical Grana Uille. History informs us, that the original family name of Tristram was changed to St. Lawrence on the following occasion; one of the lords of Howth being in command of an army against the Danes, made a vow to St. Lawrence, (on whose anniversary tine battle was fought,) that if he were victorious he would assume the name of the saint, and entail it upon his posterity After a very hot but successful engagement, he performed his vow by taking the name which has since continued the family sirname; and to perpetuate his victory, the two-handed sword with which he defeated the Danes is still hanging up in the spacious mall, amongst a curious collection of pieces of armour and weapons of former days.

On a steep cliff at the eastern extremity of the peninsula of Howth stands the old lighthouse, which has not been used since a new one was erected upon the southern side of the headland, on a small promontory nearly detached from the main hand by a deep ravine, which has obtained, from its constant bright verdure, the name of the Green Bailley, signifying the *green town*. Here, it is said, that the remnant of the Danes who escaped from the battle of Clontarf insulated themselves by digging a fosse across the neck of the promontory, and defended their little fortress until they were carried off in their vessels.

Twenty-five years ago the handsome and improving town of Kingstown, situated on the south side of the Bay of Dublin, was a poor village called Dunleary,* consisting almost entirely of fishermen's cabins. The construction there of a splendid artificial harbour,† where the post-office packets between Liverpool and Dublin deliver and

---

* It was from this place that George IV. embarked, when quitting Ireland after his memorable visit in 1821; to commemorate this event, a tasteless obelisk was erected on the pier, and the old Irish name of Dunleary changed to Kingstown.

† The first stone of this immense work was laid in 1817, by Lord Whitworth, then Lord-Lieutenant of Ireland. The pier extends two thousand eight hundred feet into the sea, and is at the base two hundred feet in breadth; it terminates in a nearly perpendicular face on the side of the harbour, and an inclined plane towards the sea. A quay, fifty feet wide, runs along the summit, protected by a parapet eight feet high on the outside, and a beacon marks the harbour on the extremity of the pier. There is a suffcent depth of water at the lowest springs to admit a frigate of thirty-six guns, or a merchantman of eight hundred tons to take refuge within the harbour, and at two hours flood there is sufficient water to admit a seventy-four.

"By tire big hill of Howth,
That's a lump of an oath."—IRISH SONG.

Killiney Hill

Killiney Bay

receive the mails, was the first and great step for the prosperity of the town, which has been further advanced by the recent formation of a railroad, which in less than half-an-hour conveys the citizens of Dublin from the middle of a crowded capital to one of the finest sea-bays in Ireland. The view of DUBLIN BAY from the hills adjoining Kingstown, from whence the stones used in the construction of the pier have been quarried, is exceedingly beautiful. Looking across the bay, which is here about six miles in breadth, we perceive the "big hill of Howth," with the flat sandy isthmus which unites it to the mainland. The remainder of the shore on the northern side is low, but all along studded with groups of white-walled houses—behind which the land swells into gentle eminences, clothed with wood, and sprinkled with the villas of the gentry. At the extremity of a long straight line of wall, and apparently in the centre of the bay, stands the South Wall lighthouse, already mentioned; while nearer to the spectator the cheerful-looking streets, houses, and gardens of Kingstown, with the basin of the magnificent harbour, circumscribed by its massive piers, lie distinctly mapped out beneath Iris feet. The stranger, on ascending KILLINEY HILL from Kingston finds that he has crossed the neck of a promontory, and looking either backward or forward has a noble view of the sea. Beneath him lies the silvery shore of KILLINEY BAY, bending its graceful crescent-line until it terminates in the noble promontory of Bray Head; land ward, his eye rests upon the quiet intervening vale, with the mountains, pile upon pile, above it, and the greater and lesser Sugar-loaf lifting their blue pinnacles over all.* When he has satiated his eyes with this glorious prospect, he has but to turn round, and a scene of inexpressible richness, variety, and grandeur meets his eye. Looking over Kingstown Harbour, he beholds, to use the language of an enthusiastic tourist, "the most splendid bay in Europe, spreading for miles its vast and lake-like level, adorned with all imaginable objects that can animate and diversify; the towns and shinning outlets, the piers, docks, batteries, and beacons, the sails of every form—the darkening curve of steam—the cloud-like canopy of Dublin and Howth,

'Like a leviathan afloat on the wave,'

shutting in the bay at a distance of a dozen miles."

* It must be humiliating to every lover of Ireland to perceive the almost general desire which prevails amongst what is termed the "better class of people" in this country, to change the ancient Irish names of places, often highly poetical, and always strikingly descriptive, into something singularly common-place or absurd. For instance, these remarkable hills, whose conical summits of white quartz, furnish with picturesque peaks the mountain-scenery of Wicklow, were (according to Mr. Monk Mason) called by the native Irish a name which signifies "The Gilt Spears," derived from their retaining the light of the sun after the rest of the surrounding landscape was involved in darkness. This name, than which nothing could be imagined more picturesque and significant, has been altered by the English into the vulgar grocery appellation of "The Sugar-loaves." In like manner, in America, the beautiful and expressive Indian designations of places have been changed into pompous classical names; and it is no uncommon timing to find yourself crossing the Scamander or Tibur in a canoe—shooting squirrels on Mount Hymettus—from whence you may possibly obtain a glimpse through the clearings of the forest, of the hog-edifices and thriving settlements of Athens or Troy.

One of the most striking features in the view from Killiney Hill is Dalkey Island, which lies off the promontory. It is divided from the mainland by a channel, Dalkey Sound, where ships may safely ride at anchor in eight fathoms water, sheltered by the island from the north-east wind, to which every other part of Dublin Bay lies exposed. This island is said to contain eighteen acres, and although covered with rocks, is esteemed an excellent pasturage for cattle of all kinds. The manner in which the people convey black cattle hither from the mountains is exceedingly curious and primitive. They fasten one end of a rope about the beast's horns, and tie the other end to the stern of a boat, which is pulled with oars in the direction of the island. By this means they drag the animal into the sea, and force it to swim after the boat across the sound, a distance of about a quarter of a mile. Besides good pasturage, Dalkey Island produces some medicinal plants; and there is a ruin on it, said to be that of a church dedicated to St. Benedict but, the belfry excepted, no trace survives that would induce a person to suppose it a place of worship. The aisle of the structure, where some trace of an altar might be expected, presents no such appearance; on the contrary, a fire-place and chimney are to be seen where the altar should stand, had the building been for ecclesiastical uses. There are also visible vestiges of its having been lofted. It is, therefore, probable that the fabric, which is small, was used for domestic or commercial purposes. Tradition says, that when Dublin was visited by the great plague of 1575, the corporation and some of the principal citizens, retired there to escape the nobility upon his most approved counsellors, the titles being always taken from the names of localities in the neighbourhood, as "The Earl of Bullick," from a small fishing village at no great distance; "Viscount Killiney," from the hill above Dalkey; or, "Baron Muglins," from a cluster of rocks close to the island. The last King of Dalkey was elected in 1797; the rebellion, which broke out the following year, interrupted this harmless festive custom, which has not since been revived. There is a battery crowned by a martello tour, which forms a conspicuous object upon the island. The village of Dalkey, which is situated on the mainland opposite the island, was once a place of considerable mercantile importance, and its harbour constituted one of the principal resorts of the shipping engaged in the trade carried on between Ireland and England. No less than seven castles were erected there for the protection of the goods of merchants and others, three of which are still in tolerable preservation; but of the former commercial greatness of Dalkey, not a vestige now remains.

XXIV.

THE county Wicklow has justly been termed "The Garden of Ireland," for in no other district of the island are to be found assembled such a variety of natural beauties, heightened and improved by the hand of art. There we may behold lakes of more than Alpine beauty; streams that wind through quiet dells, or roll their sparkling waters down rugged precipices; deep glens, and sombre ravines, where the dark mountain shadows make twilight of the summer noon; mountains whose bare and craggy peaks seem to pierce the clouds; romantic woods and picturesque glades—with fertile fields and warm and pleasant valleys, whose quiet pastoral features remind us of the pictures of the golden age—

> "Such as Arcadian song
> Transmits from ancient uncorrupted times."

The beauties of this terrestrial paradise have been lauded poets of every grade on Parnassus; they have more than once afforded a subject for the graceful pen of Ireland's sweetest lyrist. "The Meeting of the Waters," one of the first and most charming of the Irish Melodies, celebrates a delicious spot in the vale of Ovoca :— the tree is still pointed out under which, it is said, he composed the song.

Another of the Melodies, commencing,

> " By that lake whose gloomy shore"

commemorates a romantic legend of Glendalough. The charms of these romantic scenes are considerably enhanced by their proximity to the metropolis, the nearest point of the county Wicklow being not more than ten miles from the city. There are several routes by which the tourist may reach it, but that which passes through the villages of Dundrum and Enniskerry is most generally chosen, from the attractions its romantic scenery offers. Dundrum is an unpretending hamlet, seated at the base of the lofty mountains, around which the road winds; it is noted for the salubrity of its air, and is much frequented by invalids, who repair thither to recruit their broken health by inhaling the fresh breezes from the hills, and drinking the goat's milk, for which this place has long been celebrated, and whose peculiar sanative qualities have been attributed to the animals that yield the milk being in the habit of browsing upon the medicinal herbs and plants which grow upon these mountains. Ere reaching Enniskerry, the traveller beholds before him that immense natural cleft in the heart of the mountain, called "The Scalp," through which the road runs, and which, viewed at a little distance, presents the appearance of the letter V. The sides of this singular defile are covered with huge masses of disjointed granite, conveying to the mind of the passenger the not very agreeable idea, that they are momentarily in danger of toppling down on his head. Occasionally in the winter season, or after heavy rains,

Enniskerry

Powerscourt from the Dargle

some of these loosened crags are precipitated to the bottom of the ravine, and completely choke up the road, from whence they are removed with considerable difficulty and vast labour. With the popular tendency of the peasantry to connect the wild and wonderful in nature with superhuman agency—the formation of this singular chasm has been attributed to his satanic majesty, who on one occasion, driving a flock of sheep from Wicklow into Dublin, was impeded in his progress by a steep and rugged mountain; but caring little for such an insignificant obstacle, he kicked through the opposing granite, and made a smooth and level road for his flock, as it still remains.

The VILLAGE OF ENNISKERRY may be considered the threshold to the beauties of Wicklow; it is picturesquely situated in the lap of gently sloping hills, its white cottages contrasting cheerfully with the bright verdure of the foliage with which it is partially screened. At a short distance, on the rise of the hill above the village, is the entrance to the demesne of Powerscourt, the property of Viscount Powerscourt, which for beauty and variety of scenery can scarcely he equalled anywhere. It would be impossible to convey an adequate idea of the numerous points in this demesne from which prospects of unrivalled magnificence may be obtained; but, perhaps, none are excelled by that which is gained shortly after entering the grounds. "Here," says an observant tourist, "as we approach the house, the first break of scenery towards the south is inconceivably grand, soft, and various. Mountains, often cultivated high towards their summits, and sometimes rudely majestic in the unaided tints of nature, form the impressive background at a happy distance. The undulating tracts which lie between that range of mountains and the lofty ridge on which the spectator is placed, comprises the rich woods and plantations on the demesne of Charleville." Amidst this romantic scene, the river Dargle pursues its devious course, gliding, rippling, or foaming through a lovely glen towards the ocean.

The noble mansion of POWERSCOURT shows to most picturesque advantage from the eminence above the Dargle. Surrounded by magnificent woods, and gleaming with its fine granite façade above the deep and leafy valley which it dominates, it looks like the proper residence of a lord of the soil. There is something very Italian too, or rather I should say, something like the compositions of the Italian masters in the scenery of this valley. Tennehinch, the seat of Ireland's eloquent patriot,

Grattan, forms such a feature in the picture as a painter would introduce, lying lower down on the banks of one of those tributary streams, which mingle their waters with those of the romantic Dargle, that

> "Undisturbed, save by the harmless brawl
> Of mimic rapid or slight waterfall,
> Pursue their way
> By mossy bank and darkly waving wood,
> By rock, that since the deluge fixed has stood,
> Showing to sun and moon their crisping flood;
> By night and day."

The deer-park of Powerscourt is rich in natural beauties, but its principal attraction is the celebrated POWERSCOURT WATERFALL, which is seen at the extremity of a beautiful semicircular amphitheatre, (formed by mountains wooded to their summits) tumbling over an almost perpendicular wall of ferruginous basalt, nearly two hundred feet in height. This picturesque cascade is supplied from a very inconsiderable stream, and when unaugmented by heavy rains, the volume of descending water is so very small, that the face of the rock is seen through the thin veil of its delicate transparency. But in winter, or when the channels of the mountain have been charged by recent rain, the tumultuous fury with which the thundering cataract dashes at one wild hound down the frightful depth of its descent, fills the beholder's mind with wonder, and makes us

"Feel
A nameless grandeur swell the soul.
With joy that makes the senses reel,
Half wishing in the flood to roll."

The profound seclusion of the glen favours the peculiar awe with which this scene never fails to impress the spectator, when beheld under favourable circumstances; the dark masses of the contiguous woods, rising in sylvan beauty to the tops of the mountains, lend a delightful contrast in colouring to the white foam of the cataract and the dancing waters of the stream, sparkling in the gleams of rich sun— light, that break through the branches of the overarching trees.

On the opposite bank of the river is Charleville, the handsome mansion of the Earl of Rathdowne. The demesne, which participates in the attractive features displayed in the romantic scenery of Powerscourt, extends over twelve hundred acres, and is adorned with noble forest-trees. Pursuing the course of the river downwards from the Waterfall, the tourist arrives at the spot where its waters emerge. from a deep ravine, whose precipitous sides are clothed with luxuriant oak-wood, through whose thick foliage vast masses of rock occasionally protrude their rugged forms over the chasm beneath. This romantic glen, which is considerably more than a mile in length, takes its name of "THE DARGLE" from the river which flows through it. Entering the majestic woods by a path cut through them, and which overhangs the stream, we obtain at every opening in the trees views of unparalleled beauty and variety, the prevailing features of which partake in a great degree of the sublime. The opposite side of the glen appears one mass of thick foliage rising precipitously from the brink of the river, whose progress is heard, but whose bed is stink so far below the surface of the woods in which it is lost, that one might suppose, without any extraordinary stretch of the imagination, it was a river in some inner world, laid open by a Titanic throe, that had cracked asunder the rocky crust of this shallow earth; —the soil, and the deep—striking roots ot the trees terminating far above us, looking like a black rim on the enclosing precipices. When occasionally we catch a glimpse of the troubled waters through the gleam of the overhanging woods, they afford no silvery

Powerscourt Fall

The Dargle

relief to the solemn grandeur of their majestic channel, but taking a sombre tinge from the shadow of the impending precipices, "boil and bubble" darkly over their rocky bed. About midway down the glen, a huge mass of rock, projecting at a great height over the river, has received the name of "The Lover's Leap," though I confess I have not been able to discover that any heart-striken swains or damsels were ever silly enough to follow the example of Sappho, by precipitating themselves from the dizzy precipice. The prospect from this spot is magnificent, and the most vivid powers of imagination must fail adequately to describe a scene of such exquisite beauty as here spreads before the view. The eve from this elevated site comprehends every part of the deep glen below, catching, at intervals, the river breaking over fantastic fragments of rock detached from the cliffs above. To the left, the glen gradually expands into an open champaign country, bounded in the distance by the blue expanse of the sea; to the right, the vales and hills of Powerscourt, richly verdant and adorned with majestic timber, and hemmed in by lofty and rugged mountains, form an interesting and noble landscape. Another new and delicious view of THE DARGLE is obtained from a small patch of green sward at the bottom of the glen, close beside a broad pool, in which the waters of the river, dammed in by a ledge of rocks, sleep in unbroken tranquillity. Looking up the stream, the waters are seen tumbling through a rocky channel from the dark woods, which, rising to a vast height on either side, exclude every other object. Perched on the shoulder of a precipitous cliff, the thatched roof and rustic pillars of a charming little cottage, called the Moss-House, peep through the foliage of the trees that grow above and beneath it, and form a singularly pleasing object in the landscape. This delicious spot is a favourite haunt for picnic parties from Dublin :—on the smooth turf which spreads its inviting carpet beside the clear stream, many a happy group may be seen, in the pheasant summer-time, laughing, dancing, singing, or dining *al fresco,* with that perfect contempt of care or ceremony which so strikingly distinguishes the light-hearted people of this country. Following the course of the Dargle downwards, we reach, at a distance of four miles, the neat little TOWN OF BRAY, situated on the sea-shore, about a mile behind the promontory of Bray Head. From its vicinity to the sea and some of the finest scenery in the county Wicklow, it has become the head-quarters for numbers of pilgrims in search of the picturesque and beautiful. Bray is fortunate in the possession of one of the best inns in England or Ireland. Quin's Hotel is a place one regrets to leave; it is admirably arranged, and has the important adjunct of a private garden, extending a full mile from the hotel to the sea-beach. Few, indeed, who have tasted the repose, comfort, amid seclusion which they enjoyed while sojourning in this most excellent resting-place, will readily lose the pleasing impressions they received there. Naturally enough with the charms I have mentioned, Quin's Hotel is a favourite resort for bridal parties, and many happy couples repair thither to pass their honey-moon amid the picturesque scenery which

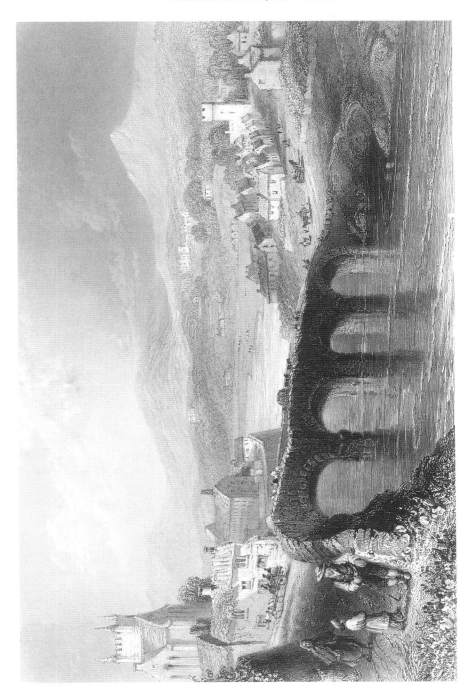

Glen of the Downs

environs it. From Bray the tourist generally proceeds to visit the GLEN OF THE DOWNS; a beautiful dell, resembling the Dargle, though (in a somewhat smaller scale, which lies a few miles south of Bray. This glen is walled in by mountains, clothed in many parts with oak, ash, and evergreen shrubs,) so precipitous as barely to leave room for the narrow road and the small bright stream that glides through the romantic vale, whose devious course produces at every step a constant succession of new charms. High upon the wooded hill, to the left going from Bray, stands a banquetting-house and a romantic cottage, so delightfully situated as to impart an air of poetry to the whole landscape. These tasteful accessories to the beauty of the scene have been constructed by Mrs. Latouche, through whose extensive and finely-wooded demesne of Belleview this enchanting glen runs. From an octangular room in the banquetting-house, the best view of the surrounding country may he obtained;—the glen far beneath, with the many-tinted sides of the rocky steeps by which it is overhung, rich in native woods and abundant plantations, and the sublime galaxy of neighbouring mountains, amongst which the dazzlingly white peaks of the two Sugar-loaf hills tower conspicuously, present a scene of luxurious softness, combined with grandeur and magnificence.

On clearing the glen we reach the pretty hamlet of Delgany with its Gothic church, picturesquely situated on the side of a romantic hill; and about three miles further south we arrive at the village of Newtown Mount Kennedy, which, from its position in the centre of a tract of beautiful country, is generally made a *point d'appui*, from whence the tourist may visit at his ease the several objects of interest in its neighbourhood. The most remarkable of these is the wild ravine, called *"The Devil's Glen,"* a combination of rock, wood, and water, so beautiful as to have conferred more properly the name of *"Glen of the God's"* upon this delicious spot. Inferior in majestic character to the Dargle, and destitute of the softness mingled with grandeur of the highly adorned Glen of the Downs, it is marked by some combinations of pictorial objects, blended in forms unknown to either of those districts. The river Vantrey forms at THE HEAD OF THE DEVIL'S GLEN a fine fall of one hundred feet in height, in an unbroken descent, which is not exceeded in beauty by any waterfall in Ireland. Indeed I know no spot better suited for the indulgence of deep meditation than this solitary and secluded glen. It has been the cradle of an accomplished poetess, for at a short distance is Rosanna, the home of Mrs. Tighie, the amiable and highly-gifted author of *"Psyche,"* one of the most graceful poems in the language. It was in the retirement of the romantic scenery of this residence that she improved her taste for natural beauty, and strengthened the power's of her imagination. Endowed by nature with a refined and susceptible mind, and surrounded by the incitements to social happiness, and a highly picturesque country, she devoted herself to the refined enjoyments of literature, and rendered herself not less beloved for the estimable qualities of her heart than admired for the brilliant effusions of her fancy.* The romantic pass of Dunran in this vicinity should not he unvisited by the tourist; it is one of the sumblime gems which enrich the eastern part of the county Wicklow, and though it assimilates with the general character of the magnificent scenery of the district, it possesses individual attractions to amply compensate the labour of ascending the eminence from whence t may be advantageously viewed.

From Newtown Mount Kennedy we diverge, in a westerly direction, to the village of Roundwood. The immediate neighbourhood of Roundwood is not particularly interesting, it is chiefly noted as a halting-place for visitors to Glendalough and Luggelaw. Of the latter place I shall speak first. After ascending a gentle elevation two or three miles to the northward, the traveller conies suddenly upon the beautiful sheet of water called Lugelaw.† It is encompassed on all sides, bowl-like, by mountains, some of them of the wildest, and others of the richest arid most pleasing character. In the outline of one of the precipitous rocks, is distinctly traced a gigantic resemblance of a human face, looking gloomily on the lake below. The eye-brows, broad and dilating, are marked by moss and heath, and the prominent cheeks and deep-sunk eyes perfectly formed by the clefts in the rock. The mouth appear's open, but when you remove to some distance it closes, but without producing any alteration in the features. Embosomed in a deep valley, which runs into the mountains at one end of the lake, stands a handsome mansion, belonging to the La Touches of Delgany, surrounded by rich meadows and luxuriant plantations. Higher up, the valley closes with a vast amphitheatre of rocks, down which pours a small but pretty waterfall, forming at the foot a little stream, which, winding through the meadows, mingles with the still waters of the lake. Such is the picturesque spot, which art, improving upon natural advantages, has formed in the midst of a wild country. I can imagine no more pleasurable surprise, than a stranger would experience on being led to this sequestered spot, without any previous preparation for a scene of such matchless beauty. It would be strange if the wild charms of Luggelaw had remained uncelebrated in the minstrelsy of Ireland; the bards of former days have devoted to it more than one "sweet wreath of song, and Erin's modern and immortal lyrist has commemorated its beauties by the adaptation of probably the choicest of his poetic strains in the "Irish Melodies," to the delicious old air of "Luggehaw."

* This amiable lady was snatched from the society of her friends and the literature of her country, which she enriched and adorned, in the thirty-seventh year of her age. Her surviving friends devised a mode congenial with her character, of commemorating her genius and her virtues, by having her poems collected and published, and the profits applied to tine endowment of an hospital ward in the "House of Refuge," a charitable institution founded by her mother.

† It has been conjectured that the true name is *Lough Hela,* or, *The Lake of Death,* derived from the *Hela* (death) of the Danish mythology. The title must have been peculiarly appropriate to this dark lake, before the hand of cultivation had softened tine wild horrors of the valley; and it is not improbable, that it was bestowed upon it by that people while they possessed this part of the island, and handed down from them; though the derivation is lost in the corrupted name by which it is now known.

Head of the Devils Glen

Luggelaw

We will now turn our steps to Glendalough, or, the *Valley of the Two Lakes,* a spot, which if it offer fewer natural beauties to the observer of nature than other portions of the county Wicklow, is possessed of more than common interest to the lover of Irish antiquities. It is about half-a-mile west of the bridge and village of Laragh, where the mountain-streams which pour from the various lakes and ravines in the district unite under the name of the Avonmore, and flow in a south-easterly direction through the beautiful vale of Clara, until they mingle with the waters of the Avonbeg in the vale of Ovoca, from whence they roll into the sea a few miles further down into Acklow.

The valley of *Glendalough,* or, as it is frequently called, *The Seven Churches,* is twenty eight miles distant from Dublin, and thirteen from Wicklow. It is about two miles and a half in extent, open in the eastern extremity, but enclosed on every other side by lofty and precipitous mountains. Ascending the valley, through which the road winds for nearly a mile and a half, we obtain the first view of the once celebrated GLENDALOUGH, the site of the "mountain city," where religion and literature flourished in former times, but which now presents to the curious traveller nought save a melancholy waste, whose sombre character is deepened by the mouldering relics of past greatness, that lie scattered through the glen. On an eminence that slopes gently down from the mountain towards the lake, the principal ruins of Glendalough form an exceedingly picturesque group; the first object that attracts our attention is the stately *Round Tower,* (one of the finest in the kingdom)—in the vicinity of which are seen the *Cathedral;—Our Lady's Church;—*a stone-roofed building, with its singular belfry-tower, called *Kevin's Kitchen;* at a little distance, in the bottom of the vale, the remains of the venerable *Abbey;* and beyond these the still waters of the lake, thrown into solemn shade by the precipitous and gloomy mountains which overhang them, and form here a world of their own, dark, silent, and motionless as the grave. "There is nothing in these buildings particularly interesting," says Mr. Otway, in his entertaining Sketches, "except their extraordinary position in the midst of the lonely mountains, placed at the entrance of a glen, singularly deep and secluded, with its two dark lakes lying in gloom and solitariness, and over which deep vale hang mountains of the most abrupt forms, in whose every fissure and gorge there is a wild and romantic clothing of oak, birch, and holly." It is, indeed, a region where the wild, solitary enthusiast might conjure up visions of things that mortal eye had ne'er beheld; a dim valley over which the angel of death seems to have spread the shadowy of his dark wings; a tomb where every human passion is buried, and within whose gloomy precincts the sombre goddess, Melancholy, walks in lonely meditation rapt. To this dreary solitude did St Coemgan or Kevin* (a holy man who flourished in the fifth century) retire after he had assumed the cowl : there

---

* The beauty of the saint, when an infant, was so remarkable, that it is said an angel descended from heaven, and, having kissed the babe, bestowed upon him the name of Coemgan or Kevin, which in the Irish language signifies "pretty boy."

he wrote many learned works, and founded the Abbey of Glendalough, over which he presided as abbot and bishop for many years, dying in the odour of sanctity on the 3rd of June, 618, at the great age of one hundred and twenty years. His extraordinary piety and virtue, no less than the numerous miracles wrought by him, drew, as the Monasticon Hibernicum informs us, "multitudes from towns and cities, from ease and affluence, from the cares and avocations of civil life, and from the comforts and joys of society, to be spectators of his pious acts and sharers in his merits, and with him to encounter every severity of climate and condition. This influence extended even to Britain, and induced St. Mochuorog to Convey himself hither; who fixed his residence in a cell on the east side of Glendalough, where a city soon sprang up, and a seminary was founded, from whence were sent forth many saints and exemplary men, whose sanctity and learning diffused around the western world that universal light of letters and religion, which, in the earlier ages, shone so resplendent throughout this remote, and at that time tranquil isle, and were almost exclusively confined to it."

Such is the brief history of the foundation of the ecclesiastical city that once adorned these mountain solitudes, but of which the decaying ruins are all that now remain. Even the identity of the Seven Churches, for which this valley has been for centuries celebrated, and which at the present time confer a second name upon time spot, cannot be exactly ascertained; and of the famous city of Glendalough, built by St. Mochuorog, not a vestige remains, except a small paved plot of ground, of a quadrangular form, which indicates the site of the market-place of the fallen city. No traces of domestic buildings have been discovered; but the remains of a way, extending from the ancient market-place to Hollywood, on the borders of the county Kildare, are still visible. This laborious work of art was about twelve feet in width, and was composed of blocks of roughly-hewn stone set edgewise, not unlike the Roman roads which are frequently met with in England.

Of the religious edifices of Glendalough, the *Cathedral,* which owes its origin to St. Kevin, claims precedence. It was of small dimensions, being no more than forty-eight feet in length and thirty in width; the architecture was of the rudest style, and almost destitute of ornament. This building is now little better than a heap of ruins. Adjoining the cathedral is a small dilapidated structure, called *"The Priests'-house,* which was probably the sacristy where the priests' vestments and the reliques were preserved. A miraculous property of preventing future headaches has been attributed to this building :—the individual wishing to obtain this immunity being required to turn himself three times round in the closet, with an entire faith in the power of the blessed St. Kevin. Of the many crosses scattered amongst these ruins, a remarkable one, which stands in the spacious cemetery, eleven feet in height, and formed of a single block of granite, has also some miraculous qualities attached to it. To obtain the benefit of these, it is necessary that tIme supplieant should so completely

Glendalough

Round Tower and Glendalough

embrace the cross, that his hands shall meet on the opposite side A stranger naturally approaches the front of the cross, and endeavours to perform the required ceremony, but from the great breadth of the stone he is unable to unite his hands on the other side. The guides, however, for a small fee undertake to remove this difficulty, by causing the person making the attempt to change his position, and by placing him chose to the narrow side of the shaft, enable him to accomplish his design without any trouble. Within the walls of the cemetery stands THE ROUND TOWER, one hundred and ten feet in height, uncommonly well built and in fine preservation, the roof alone having suffered by the hand of time. The contrast which this lofty monument of Pagan sepulture* offers

* Since the preceding portion of this work went through the press, some important discoveries have been made relative to the Round Towers, which will serve materially to elucidate the mystery in which their origin was involved. The reader, by referring in this volume, will perceive it stated, that an opinion had been recently entertained, (arising from the fact of human remains having been found within the foundation of the Round Tower at Ardmore,) that these pillars were monuments erected over tine graves of illustrious persons. Within the last month, (June 1842) "The Cork Southern Reporter," a respectable journal, contained the following interesting paragraph. After alluding to the investigation made in the early part of the preceding year, it continues : "We shall now proceed to state the discoveries made subsequently to that of Ardmore. In the month of September, 1841, several of our fellow citizens met by appointment at Cashel, the very Rev. Dr Cotton, of Lismore, and Mr. Odell, whose labours we before mentioned : the Round Tower was then examined : although human remains were found within that structure, yet because they were near the surface, mixed with earth and decayed timber, it was supposed they had been thrown in the adjacent cathedral. But it is now to be noted that there was evidence of a previous delving, and the discoveries since made show, at least a probability that the human bones there found had been disturbed from their original resting-place within the foundation-walls. It must however be admitted, that the Cashel researches cannot be adduced as a positive instance of the sepulchral character of these towers. Not so with Cloyne, there, at a depth from the doorway of about thirteen feet, being very near the same as at Ardmore, were found the bones of four human skeletons, lying in the direction from west to east. 'The space in which they lay was an irregular serrated oval, of about six feet and a half by four The Roscrea Tower was opened about three weeks since, at the request of our society by Mr. E. Wall of that town, who discovered human remains mull through, from the doorway downwards, in a depth of over ten feet. The correspondence with Sir W. Betham has shown the success of the discoveries to which that learned and zealous antiquary humus been instrumental. His noble friend. the Marquis of Downshire, caused to be opened the Round Tower of Drumbo. The Tower of Maghera has also been opened, in both of which has been found human remains. Similar results had previously attended the opening of the Tower on Rain Island. Two remarkable instances remain to be mentioned. We have the authority of Sir W. Betham, that in the Tower of Timahoe there were not only human bones, but the sepuchral urn was found; and by Mr. Black's History we learn, that in Abernethy Tower, (Scotland.) human skills and bones were found in great numbers, and there was also discovered an urn. These two facts prove that Timahoe and Abernethy Towers, at least, were Pagan structures, and leave a strong presumption in favour of the same inference with regard to the others." The conclusion at which we inevitably arrive, after reading the foregoing statement, is, first, that these tower's were of Pagan origin; imitated, perhaps, by the early Christian missionaries, but certainly converted by them in many instances to the purposes of their own religion, in accordance within their practice of changing the object of the people's worship, from a false to a true God, by maintaining the reverence they entertained for their ancient places of Pagan adoration. Secondly, that they were devoted to sepulchral uses, and very probably marked the burial-place

of the priests of the ancient fire and star worship, which there is reason to believe prevailed in Ireland before the introduction of Christianity. The confirmation of this supposition would reconcile the theory of their being devoted to the obscure forum of religion indicated by the element of fire, with the ascertained fact, that they were intended as monumental pillars.

to the humble head-stones which mark the resting—places of the Christian dead, must awaken a train of interesting ideas in every reflective mind. The poetic fancy of Mr. Otway dwelt with peculiar pleasure upon this scene. "I would rather ponder," says he, "on such a spot as this at Glendalough, surrounded as it us with mighty mountains, dark winding glens; all its lakes, streams, rocks, and water-falls, in keeping and accordant association with a place of ruins; ruins that testify of altars, and of a priesthood overthrown—a workshop made desolate—a people 'scattered and peeled,' where the long continuous shadow of the lofty and slender round tower moves slowly from morn to eve over wasted churches, scattered yew-trees, and the tombs, now undistinguishable, of bishops, abbots, and anchorites, walking its round as time-sentinel, and telling forth to the Ancient of Days bow many suns have run their diurnal and annual course since these holy men had descended to their graves."

The small building with the miniature of a Round Tower at one end, shown by the artist on the right-hand side of the accompanying engraving, popularly but incorrectly called *St. Kevin's Kitchen,* is now the most perfect of the Seven Churches : the roof, which is very curious, is composed of thin stones laid horizontally, and rising in the form of a wedge to an acute angle, the extreme height being about thirty feet. The remarkable round belfry, which rises from the west end of the church, is forty-five feet in height, the roof, like that of the church, is formed of thin stones, very neatly laid. A groove that has been discovered cut in the east end of the building, shows that this was not the original round tower, which there is reason to suppose was a distinct structure from the church, the latter being erected so as to incorporate with the edifice.

Our Lady's Church, a small ruinous structure, stands to the west of the cathedral, the architecture of which appears to have been less rude than that of the other churches. There are several recesses in the wall, in which women who desire to become matrons, are recommended to turn round three times. The effects of the pirouette, under the influence of the "blessed mother," are said to be truly miraculous. *The Rhefeart,* or *Sepulchre of Kings,* is situated between the two lakes, and is celebrated as the burial-place of the O'Tooles, the ancient dynasts of this country. On a tomb in this church is an inscription in the Irish character, defaced by age, which indicated it as "the resting-place" of a prince of that race, who died in the year 810. The *Priory of St. Saviour,* commonly called the *Eastern Church,* and the *Ivy Church,* which has obtained its name from the plant with which its ruins are overgrown, are not of sufficient importance to require more than a passing notice. *Teampull na Skellig,* or the *Temple of the Rock* or *Desert,* situated in a solitary nook beneath the impending mountain of Lugduff, is the last of what are commonly called the *"Seven Churches"* of this glen. To this small rude fabric, almost inaccessible except by water, St. Kevin was wont to retire during the season of Lent, devoting himself to prayer and devout exercises. Tradition relates, that on one occasion, when the holy man was praying at a window in this chapel, with one hand extended in a supplicating attitude, a blackbird descended and deposited her eggs in his open palm. The saint, moved with compassion for the bird, did not withdraw his hand, but remained in the same position until the creature had hatched her eggs. For which reason in all representations of St. Kevin he is shown with an out-stretched arm, and supporting in his hand a bird's nest. *The Abbey,* though now completely in ruins, is the most extensive and the most interesting of the architectural vestiges of Glendalough. It consisted originally of two buildings, lying parallel to each other, of rare and beautiful workmanship, adorned with curious sculptures; but of these only detached fragments are now visible : the earth rises in wavy hillocks over the fallen enrichments, and matted trees and brambles over-grow the decaying walls. Some of the specimens of ancient sculpture found in the vicinity of the abbey, though rude, are of great interest. On one stone is represented wolf gnawing a human head; on another, the head of a young man, whose long hair is entwined with the tail of the animal. A writer of great antiquarian knowledge observes, that "the hair thus thrown back from the fore-head was the genuine Irish Cooleen or Glibb." Wolves were not wholly extirpated until the year 1710, and in attaching the hair of the man to the tail of the animal, the sculptor intended, perhaps, to typify the fondness of the one for the pursuit of the other.

It may be necessary to explain here, that the ancient Irish shaved or clipped the hair close on the forepart of the head, and suffered it to grow long behind : these flowing locks were called a *Glibbe* or *Coolin.* The policy of the English government being ever to remove every national distinction from a people whom they had but partially subdued, a parliament was held in Dublin, in the year 1295, by which an act was passed, strictly enjoining all persons to wear, at least as to the head, the English habit and tonsure, and not to presume longer to turn their hair into a Coolin, under a severe penalty, and deprivation of the benefit of the law. A native bard, indignant at this arbitrary edict, composed a song, in which an Irish virgin declares her preference for her lover, who wears the dear Coolin above those who had assumed tine stranger fashion. The exquisitely plaintive and universally admired air, known as *"The Coolin,"* is all that has descended to us of this song, to which Mr. Moore has adapted very beautiful and appropriate words in his "Irish Melodies." The mention of this circumstance reminds me of the singular change in the politics of the hair, which has taken place in Ireland since the edict was passed against the Coolin. The hostility of the ancient Irish to the English sway, was shown by the long locks of the Coolin; the disaffection of the modern Irish, in the rebellion of 1798, was exhibited

439

in the close-cut hair of the rebels, from which they derived the contemptuous epithet of "Croppies." This close cropping of the hair was a mark of Republican sentiments, and first came into fashion in Ireland at the period of the French revolution.

The last object of interest in this wild glen to which I shall direct my readers' attention, is the celebrated *St. Kevin's Bed,* a small cave hollowed in the face of the perpendicular rock, and overhanging, at a considerable height, the dark waters of the lake. The path which conducts to the aerial couch of the solitary recluse is fearfully narrow, and the stranger must be endowed with more than ordinary nerve, who (though assured by the guides that there is not the least danger in the attempt) can muster courage enough to climb the perilous-looking track without an involuntary shudder, or a consciousness of

> "That sense of danger which sublimes
> The breathless moment, when his daring step
> Is on the verge of the cliff, and he can hear
> The low dash of the wave with startled ear,
> Like the death-music of his coming doom."

The romantic tradition attached to this cave, even more than its singular situation, has given it an extraordinary celebrity, and has formed the subject of Moore's Irish Melody—commencing,

> "By that lake whose gloomy shore
> Sky-lark never warbles o'er," &c.

It is related that St. Kevin, who in his youth was not less remarkable for his exemplary piety than for his personal beauty, captivated the heart of a beautiful and high-born maiden, named Kathleen. In the words of the song,—

> "She had loved him well and long,
> Wished him hers, nor thought it wrong :
> Wheresoe'er the saint would fly,
> Still he heard her light foot nigh;
> East or west, where'er he turned,
> Still her eyes before him burned."

But the warm glances from Kathleen's "eyes of most unholy blue," had no power to melt the young anchorite's frigid heart; and in order to be freed from the interruptions of her visits, he concealed himself in a cave, which he had formed in the face of Lugduff mountain. In this sequestered spot he fancied himself secure from the temptations of the sex; but the fond girl had tracked her lover's steps to Iris rocky couch, and—

> 'Even now, while calm hue sleeps,
> Kathleen o'r him leans and weeps."

Head of Glendmalure

Castle Howard, Vale of Ovoca

The catastrophe of the story is more creditable to the saint's purity than his humanity; for awakening from his slumbers, and perceiving a female beside his couch, he, in a moment of sudden anger, hurled her from the cliff into the lake below, No sooner had the gentle Kathleen sunk into the dark waters, than the saint reproached himself for his cruel conduct; and though he could not save the life of her who loved him so tenderly, he put up a prayer to heaven that no other mortal might find a watery grave in that lake; a prayer that the peasantry in the neighbourhood firmly believe was granted.

Quitting the solitary and awe-inspiring Glendalough, the tourist intending to visit the delightful vale of Ovoca, proceeds by the military road to GLENMALURE, a beautiful valley through which for several miles winds the Avonbeg, one of the rivers which lower down combine in the Meeting of the Waters. The character of this glen is altogether different from the picturesque beauty of the wooded Dargle, or the softer features of the Glen of the Downs; its aspect is wild and impressive, the rude and barren rocks which rise abruptly on either hand, giving a savage grandeur to the scene. THE HEAD OF GLENMALURE, where the waters of a small stream, flowing down the precipitous face of a steep mountain, forms the Ess Fall, is especially striking, and merits the praise of a modern tourist, who asserts, that it is by far the finest of the Wicklow Glens, and, with the exception of the Killeries in Connemara, is not to be equalled in the kingdom.

The outlet of Glenmalure, proceeding towards Rathdrum, is extremely pleasing : the valley expands, the hills slope gently away, and being wooded down to the banks of the river, the features of the landscape are not so wild and rugged as in the upper part of the glen. At the junction of Glenmalure with the Vale of Avoca, the most striking object is CASTLE HOWARD, the residence of Mrs. Howard, picturesquely perched on the brow of a lofty eminence, apparently upheld by the tops of the trees, for from the towers to the river side it is one mass of luxuriant foliage. Directly below this romantic structure, the Avonbeg and the Avonmore, stealing forth from their secluded glens, unite their streams; and here the Vale of Avoca, which stretches from hence to the sea at Arklow, may be said to commence. The confluence of these rivers is generally termed THE MEETING OF THE WATERS. Nature has here scattered her charms with a liberal hand : waving woods, clear waters, and verdant shores combine to render the scene one of delicious softness and beautiful tranquillity. "It is not a scene," says a late writer, "which a poet or painter would visit if he wished to elevate his imagination by sublime views of nature, or by images of terror; but if he desired to represent the calm repose of peace and love, he would chose this glen as their place of residence." No language could adequately convey to the reader a faithful picture of the serene beauty of this enchanting valley, but the emotions which the contemplation of them excites in the human breast, has been deliciously described by the graceful pen or Ireland's Bard. Who does not remember that warm effusion of his early muse, consecrated to "The Meeting of the Waters," commencing with the following stanza—

"There is not in the wide world a valley so sweet,
As tire vale in whose bosom the bright waters meet;
Oh, the last rays of feeling and life must depart,
Ere the bloom of that valley shall fade from my heart."

From "The Meeting of the Waters," the river pursues its devious course to the sea through a fertile valley, whose mountainous sides are thrown into an endless variety of lovely pictures, by the irregularity of their positions. These mountainous ridges are covered with the thick foliage of the oak,* and are richly pictorial in heaths, furze, and other upland vegetation. Further onward the vale gradually expands into broad and verdant slopes, dotted at intervals with white cottages, through which the river glides gently towards the sea, whose blue waters make a noble boundary to a combination of the grandest and softest scenery which nature has ever produced.

Although l have in the preceding pages noticed many of the most attractive scenes in this romantic district, it would he impossible within the limits of a work of this nature to enumerate all the beautiful spots that invite the attention of the tourist. I cannot, however, complete my desultory sketches without noticing a remarkable waterfall, at a place called POUL-A-PHOUCA,† on the north-eastern borders of this county. The cataract is formed by the descent of the river Liffey through a narrow opening in a craggy precipice, falling from a height of upwards of one hundred and eighty feet, over several progressive ledges of rocks, till it is precipitated into a dark abyss, where it forms a whirlpool of frightful appearance and immense depth. Owing to the manner m which the water is broken in its descent, Poul-a-Phouca is by many considered the most picturesque fall in the county Wicklow. A handsome bridge of a single Gothic arch has been thrown across the chasm through which the water rushes. The span of this arch is sixty-five feet, and its key-stone is one hundred and eighty feet above the level of the river. On one side, the glen for some distance, both above and below the fall, is overhung by abrupt and naked rocks; on the other, the banks being less precipitous are cut into walks, and otherwise tastefully embellished.

* Ireland was once celebrated for her oak woods, and, according to the authority of Spenser, the county Wicklow. so recently as the reign of Elizabeth, was greatly encumbered with a redundance of wood. The oak woods of Shillelah (a barony so called) conferred that universally-known appellation on the redoubtable cudgel of the Irish peasant, whose toughness can only he equalled by the heads to which it is so frequently applied in the little scrummages that occur at the fairs, patrons, and merry-makings through the country. It was these woods that supplied the architect of Westminster Hall with the oak-timber of which the roof of that noble and venerable edifice was constructed. But the glories of Shillelah are departed; a few straggling trees are all that now remain to perpetuate the wooded pride of that famous district.

† Poul-a-Phouca, i.e. The Phoucas Hole. In the Fairy Mythology of Ireland the Phouca or Pooka is described as a misshapen imp, haunting lonely glens and dark recesses; he resembles in his habits and disposition the Scotch Brownie and the Scandinavian Troll.

The Meeting of the Waters

This is a portion of the demesne of the Earl of Miltown, whose splendid mansion of Russborough, at a short distance from the fall, is the most conspicuous ornament of this part of the country.

As the united streams which form the Ovoca river approach the spot where their waters mingle with those of the sea, the vale expands, and the mountains subside into gentle undulations. Amidst this scenery Shelton Abbey, the seat of the Earl of Wicklow, is beautifully situated on the northern bank of the Ovoca. It stands at the base of a range of hills, which rise gently around it, and are luxuriantly clothed with oak and birch-wood. The mansion, which is of considerable antiquity, has received several important improvements from the present noble possessor, who has had it almost wholly reconstructed under his own inspection, and from a building of very moderate architectural pretensions, has converted it into an appropriate baronial residence—that of an abbey of the fourteenth century, with additions of a later date. The picturesque character of the edifice has a fine effect, and, with the surrounding scenery, forms one of the most charming landscapes of which this delightful county can boast. The demesne, stretches for a considerable distance along the bank of the river, and is thickly studded with beech and chestnut-trees, some of which have attained to an unusually noble growth. On the southern bank of the river, nearly opposite to Shelton, Kilcarra Castle, the seat of the Earl of Carysfort, stands girt by venerable woods, which extend almost to Arklow. This little town, when approached from the vale of Ovoca, presents, with the barracks and the ruins of the castle crowning the hill, and the bridge of nineteen arches spanning the waters, a very pleasing appearance. The town is divided into two parts; the upper town, in which the houses are neatly built, and the fishery, which consists of a number of mud cottages, irregularly huddled together, and wholly inhabited by fishermen and their families. Like the Chaddagh men of Galway, the fishermen of Arklow are a race distinct from the other inhabitants. They will allow no persons but those engaged in the fishery to live in the quarter of the town they have appropriated to themselves; and being wholly devoted to their own particular pursuits, they hold but little intercourse with their neighbours; neither will they, even when reduced to absolute distress, employ themselves in any occupations not connected with their favourite element. Their hives afford an incessant variety, which seems the zest of their existence. They endure all the hardships and privations of a seafaring life with astonishing patience and resolution; but as soon as the cause which urges them to exertion is removed, they relapse into indolence, and remain sitting at home by the fire-side for days together, in the full enjoyment of the pleasure of "doing nothing at all." Sometimes they have money in abundance, at others they are suffering under the bitterest effects of imprudence and poverty. But probably in these respects they differ little from the same class of men all over the world; and both their defects and good qualities, it is likely, may be traced in all cases to the same cause—a life of chance and adventure.

The herring-fishing on the coast between Wexford and Dublin, has of late years become an object of considerable importance, and consequently of increased attention; the fishing in the Bay of Arklow is considered, next to that of Galway, as the best on any of the Irish coasts.

The only relic of antiquity that Arklow boasts, is an old ivy-grown tower adjoining the barracks; the remains of the castle built by one of the Ormond family, who once held large possessions in this county. In 1331 it was taken from the English by the O'Tooles, the Irish princes of this district, who, however, were shortly after driven from it by Lord Bermingham. Subsequently the Irish became its masters, but were again expelled by the English. In 1641 the Irish surprised the castle, put the garrison to the sword, and kept possession of it till 1649, when it was captured by Oliver Cromwell, who dismantled it, and reduced it to a heap of ruins. The remains of a monastery, founded by Theobald Fitzwalter, Lord Butler of Ireland, in the reign of Henry II., were visible at the rear of the town at the close of the last century, but they have now wholly disappeared.

The county of Wicklow was the scene of several sanguinary conflicts during the rebellion of 1798. The town of Arklow, in particular, has acquired a melancholy celebrity on account of a battle fought there between the royal forces and the insurgent army, when the latter were defeated, after a desperate but ill-directed resistance. The following particular's of this action may not be uninteresting to my readers. After the defeat of Colonel Walpole's troops at Gorey on the 4th of June, the rebels, flushed with success, advanced to attack Arklow on the 9th. Their number probably amounted to twenty-seven thousand, of whom near five thousand were armed with grins, the rest with pikes; they were also furnished with three pieces of serviceable artillery. The troops posted for the defence of this, at that time, important station, consisted of sixteen hundred men, regulars and yeomanry. The rebels attacked the town on all sides, except that which is washed by the river, and the approach of the column which advanced by the sea-shore, was so rapid that the guard of yeoman-cavalry stationed in that quarter, with difficulty effected their escape through the flames of the thatched cabins, which had been fired by the rebels on entering the town. The further progress of the assailants was prevented by the charge of the regular cavalry, supported by the fire of the infantry.

As the rebels poured their fire from the shelter of ditches, so that the opposing fire of the soldiery had no effect, Colonel Skerritt, the second in command to General Needham, directed his men to stand with ordered arms, their left wing being covered by a breast-work, and the right by a natural rising of the ground, until the enemy, leaving their cover, should advance to an open attack. This open attack was made three times in most formidable force, the assailants charging within a few yards of the cannons' mouths; but they were received with so close and effective a fire, that they were repulsed with great slaughter in every attempt, and were at length obliged to retreat in confusion upon Gorey.

The valour displayed by the undisciplined and half-armed peasantry, in the various conflicts which took place during this deplorable struggle, would, under different circumstances, have redounded to their eternal honour; but, in the heat of party strife, the voice of the accuser alone was heard, and none had courage to publish the brave or generous deeds of the misguided men, whose virtues are interred in the grave—

"Where cold and unhonoured their relics are laid."

Few, however, will be found to deny, that there is no nation on earth upon whom the gift of natural courage is more largely bestowed than on the Irish. In the common people it too often displays itself in brawls and faction-fights—but in the disciplined soldier it rises to the loftiest pitch of intrepid gallantry. As far back as Spenser's time, the bravery of the Irish soldier was generally admitted. The poet, who was no friend of Ireland, writes : "I have heard some great warriors say, that in all the services which they had seen abroad in foreign countries, they never saw a more comely man than an Irishman, nor that cometh more bravely to his charge."

This disposition has gained for the Irish a character for pugnacity, and it has been humorously said, that while the Englishman fights for love of conquest, the Frenchman for love of glory, the German for love of discipline, and the Swiss for love of pay, the son of Erin fights for love of fun. A popular Irish song gives a very graphic description of this friendly hostile feeling in an Irish boy at Donny-brook fair, who—

"Goes into a tent, and he spends his half-crown,
Comes out, meets his friend—and for love knocks him down."

Carleton, in his admirable Stories of the Irish Peasantry, illustrates this disposition in a pugnacious little tailor, who exclaims, that he is "blue mowldy for the want of a bating." As a companion anecdote to that of Carleton's tailor, I once heard a story of an Irish labourer, who was in the employment of an English gentleman residing in Ireland. He was on one occasion about going to a fair, which was held annually at a neighbouring village, when his master endeavoured to dissuade him from his design. "You always," said he, "come back from the fair with a broken head; now, stay at home to-day, Darby, and I'll give you five shillings;" "I'm for ever and all obliged to your honour," replies Darby; "but does it stand to rason," added he, flourishing his shillelagh over his head, "does it stand to rason that I'd take five shillings for the bating I'm to get to-day ?"

This digression has caused me to wander from my subject;—to return then to the glens and mountains of Wicklow.—Bountifully has nature lavished her gifts upon this delicious garden of the west, for she has not only given beauty to its hills and valleys, but has enriched the bosom of the earth with her choicest treasures. Towards the close of the last century, a quantity of native gold, in lumps and grains, was picked up by the peasantry in a stream that descends from the mountain of Croghan, which excited the most extravagant hopes respecting the existence of a mine of the precious metal. Government in consequence established works on the mountain-streams, and sunk mines for the purpose of obtaining the gold, but with such little success, that they were induced, after some time, to abandon the enterprise. One might almost fancy that the protecting spirits of these mountain solitudes, indignant at having their quiet haunts profaned by the sordid hunters after mammon, had converted the golden stores of the mountain into slates and stones, as the gifts bestowed by the fairies upon mortals are said to be changed into something vile and worthless. It is a strange fact, that from the 24th of August to the 15th of October, 1795,—when government took possession of the prize,—the quantity of gold collected in this vicinity was no less than two thousand six hundred and sixty-six ounces, which was sold on the spot for £10,000 of the Irish currency of the time; but since then rarely any gold has been found, and, if any, only in very small grains indeed.

My tour through Wicklow is now drawn to a close :—but though I have been unable to pourtray in words all the charms that embellish this romantic region, I trust that the lovely scenes upon which the pencil of our artist has been employed may create a taste for the beautiful in nature in the minds of many of my readers :—or haply the glimpses we have given of the sweet haunts of this fairy land, may tempt some English tourists from the banks of "the lazy Scheldt or wandering Po," to enjoy, amid the scenery of a sister isle,—

> "The power, the beauty, and the majesty,
> That have their haunts in dale or piny mountain,
> Or forest by slow stream, or pebbly spring,
> Or chasms, or watery depths."

449

Dunbrody Abbey

APPENDIX

IN bringing this volume to a conclusion, I perceive that our artist has supplied three Engravings which have not been noticed in their proper places. As they will be found highly interesting, I deem it advisable to append a short description of them here.

The first of these illustrations is a view of DUNBRODY ABBEY, a venerable and extensive monument of antiquity in the county Wexford. It was founded, according to the best authorities, about the year 1182, by the celebrated Hervey the Montmorency, marshal to Henry II., who was amongst the first of the English adventurers that obtained a footing in Ireland. Hervey was related to Strongbow by marriage, being uncle to the lady Aliva de Montmaurisco, the earl's first wife. No less distinguished for his prudence than for his courage, he was made constable of Ireland by the English monarch, and obtained from Dermod Mac Morough, the traitorous king of Leinster,* extensive grants of land in this county. When Strongbow found it necessary to repair to England to remove the political jealousy of Henry, by surrendering formally all his Irish acquisitions to the royal disposal, he appointed Hervey de Montmorency senescnat of Leinster, and committed to him the command of the English forces. On Strongbow's return to his government, he made a pretext for quarrelling with Hervey, of whose increasing influence he began to grow jealous; in consequence of which the insulted chieftain quitted the army, and restored to Strongbow all the lands allotted to him, except a small portion in the barony of Shelburne. Here he erected and endowed a religions establishment, in which he settled monks of the Cistercian order, and, retiring from the stormy scenes in which he had been long engaged, assumed the cowl, and became the first abbot of the noble abbey he had founded. Dunbrody Abbey was originally dependent on that of Buildwas in Shropshire : an old poem with which I have met, after enumerating the several townships bestowed by the constable Hervey upon this religious house, concludes with the following couplet :—

> "These lands de Montmaurisco gave
> To Buildwas shrine,—his soul to save."

Subsequently Dunbrody became an independent abbacy, and its abbot sat in parliament as a spiritual lord, until the dissolution of the monasteries by Henry VIII. when it was granted to Sir Osborne Itchingham. The edifice, though considerably injured by the tooth of time and the hands of barbarous despoilers, is still one of the

---

* This was the monarch, who, being driven from his provincial throne for his cruelty and tyranny, adopted the base expedient of regaining his power by means of foreign arms, and procured the invasion of his native country by the English adventurers.

most perfect and interesting specimens of the ecclesiastical architecture of its age to be met with in the kingdom. It is situated upon the verge of an extensive bay or arm of the river, near the confluence of the Suir, with the Nore and Barrow, about five miles below the city of Waterford. This bay is so shallow, that at the recess of the tide a vast, unsightly mud-bank is left exposed; but at high-water, when the bank is overflown, the venerable ruins of the abbey, unsheltered by a single tree, and standing in naked and solitary grandeur beside the flood, present to the mind of the spectator a solemn image of fallen and deserted greatness. Visitors enter the building by an arched doorway at the western end; the workmanship of which, as well as that of the unique window above it, has been pronounced "magnificent" by every person who has seen them. The interior of the abbey, viewed from the entrance, is singularly striking :—before us lies the great aisle, divided from the cloisters by a double row of arches, supported by massive square pillars; the inside of these arches is adorned with a moulding, springing from beautiful consoles. In the centre of the edifice, sustained by noble arches, fifty feet in height, rises the great tower, whose grey battlements afford shelter to a community of daws, whose sable plumage and mournful cawings, might suggest to the mind of a Brahmin the idea, that the souls of the old monks who once paced these dim cloisters inhabited the bodies of these birds, and still lingered around the haunts they loved so well. Some curious tombs of the early benefactors of the abbey existed formerly within its walls, but they have long since been overturned and destroyed by the country people, in digging for hidden treasures, which popular tradition says are concealed amongst the ruins.

The remains of the venerable abbeys and the ancient castle of the Fitzgeralds in the neighbourhood of the little village of Adare, about eight miles from Limerick, form the subject of the second engraving.

The early history of Adare is involved in considerable obscurity; the ancient town, which derived its name from *Aith-dhar,* or *"The Ford of the Oaks,"* lay upon the eastern bank of the Maige, (a tributary stream to the Shannon,) about half-a-mile from the modern town, which is situated on the western side of the river, over which is a fine level bridge of fourteen arches, built by the fifth Earl of Kildare, still in a state of excellent preservation. There is not, perhaps, in the whole province of Munster a more beautifully situated village than Adare; the ruins of its magnificent castle, where the proud Desmonds held sway—the meadows, sloping gently to the margin of the stream—the ivy-mantled walls of the stately abbeys that once flourished here—the lonely shades—the venerable trees, and the quiet walks,

"Where heavenly meditation musing dwelt"

awaken in the contemplative mind emotions of the most exquisite nature The remains of three important religious houses are still to be seen here, viz. THE FRANCISCAN ABBEY, THE AUGUSTINIAN ABBEY, and the Abbey of the Holy Trinity.

Augustinian Abbey, Adare

Carrigogunnell Castle

The first of these was founded by Thomas Fitz-Maurice, seventh Earl of Kildare and his wife Joan; the second, an exceedingly picturesque ruin, was built in the year 1315 by John Fitz-Thomas, first Earl of Kildare, and forms a beautiful and striking object in the landscape. "A great part of this friary," says a writer who visited it in 1781 "still remains in good preservation; the steeple, similar to that of the Trinitarians. is supported by an arch; the choir is large, with stalls, and the nave answerable thereto, with a lateral aisle on the south side; to the north of the steeple are some beautiful cloisters with Gothic windows, within which, on three of the sides, are corridors, and on most of these windows are escutcheons with the English and saltire crosses, generally ranged alternately; the workmanship is simply elegant, the principal parts being of hewn limestone, which appears so fresh as to give it a modern yet venerable appearance."The monastery of the Holy Trinity was founded. and amply endowed, by the first Earl of Kildare, for the pious purpose of redeeming Christian captives from slavery. The entrance to it was by a low gate, on the west side, which, as well as the other remaining portions of this are of an extremely massive and gloomy character. The castle, built by the Earls of Desmond to command the bridge over the river, is now reduced to a pile of ruins; but the portions of the structure which remain show that it must have been a place of great strength, and that its position was admirably chosen to protect the pass it was intended to defend. It was finally destroyed in the rebellion of 1641. Adare gives the titles of baron and viscount to the ancient Irish family of Quin, Earls of Dunraven and Mountearl. Adare Castle, the family seat, is situated on the western bank or the river, in a very extensive and highly-ornamented demesne, and commands a fine view of the ancient castle and the venerable abbeys in its neighbourhood. The building of this noble mansion is not yet completed, but when finished, it will be one of the firmest edifices in the country.

The interesting ruins of Carrigogunnell Castle, of which our last engraving is a representation, are srtuated on the summit of a lofty rock, rising abruptly from an extensive plain on the banks of the Shannon, about six miles west from Limerick and presenting a noble and striking object to the surrounding country.

Archdall's *Monasticon Hibernicum* informs us, that there was a house for knights templars here, which, in the year 1530, was the seat of Donough O'Brien, Lord of Poble O'Brien. In 1691, when the Irish forces, after the disastrous battle of Aughrim, retreated to Limerick, Carrigogunnell Castle was held for King James. General Scravemore marching against it, forced the garrison to surrender, and the following month, (August,) the castle was dismantled and blown up. It is worthy of notice, that Dr. Story, who was Dean of Limerick at the time, and who afterwards wrote the History of the War in Ireland, received one hundred and sixty pounds to reimburse him for his expenses, buying powder, &c. to blow up Castle Connell and Carrigogunnell Castle, of which nothing now remain but piles of venerable ruins.